CONTENTS

Welcome to the Video Fringe
An Exceedingly Long (But Necessary) Introduction 9

Organization: Sections and Festivals 11
Defining the Territory: What's Included and What's Not 13
How to Use This Book 15
The Reviews 17
Critical Perspectives 18
Critical Terminology 20
A Few Words about Splatter 21
Further Reading 23

SECTION I: CREATURE FEATURES
An Unnatural History of Aliens, Monsters, and Mutations 25

1. *She's Got Slime All Over Her!*
   A Galaxy of Aliens, Plain and Fancy 28
2. *Big Guys, Big Foot, and Big Bores*
   A Miscellany of Monsters 46
3. *Changes for the Worse*
   A Mustering of Mutations 55
4. *Messing around with Mother Nature*
   A Symposium of Scientists, Mostly Mad 70
5. *Tooth and Claw*
   Nature Doesn't Just Get Mad — She Gets Even 79
6. *The Inner Brute*
   Werewolves and Other Shape-Shifters 87
7. *The Living Dead Will Never Die*
   A Zombie Homage to George Romero 96

SECTION II: OCCULT OCCASIONS
An Invocation of Supernatural Evils 109

8. *Ancient Enemies*
   A Demonstration of Demons and Devils 112
9. *Hostile Take-Overs*
   An Inventory of Possessions 125
10. *Troubled Spots*
    A Refrain of Hauntings 133
11. *Sorcerors, Witches, and Magic*
    An Exhibition of the Black Arts 150
12. *Down for the Count*
    A Coagulation of Vampiric Variations 162
13. *Mindless Over Matter*
    A Medium of Visions, Psychic Phenomena,
    and Dream Sequences 172
14. *More Is Usually Less*
    A Compendium of Anthologies 187

SECTION III: SLICE AND DICE
An Asylum of Psycho Killers 193

15. *Killers by the Calendar*
    A Psycho for Every Occasion 201
16. *A Very Little Learning*
    A Curriculum of Campus Killers 212
17. *The Kill of the Wild*
    Psychos in the Great Outdoors 221
18. *Home Sweet Homicide*
    A suburb of Psychos in Residence 230
19. *A Place for Murder, Every Murder in Its Place*
    The Omnipresent Psycho 238
20. *The Killer Next Door*
    Friendly Neighborhood Madmen 251

Ghastly Horror!

VIDEO

Outrageous Fantasy!

TRASH & TREASURES

And the Schlockiest Sci-Fi in the Galaxy!

by **L.A. Morse**

A Field Guide to the Video Unknown

HarperCollins*Publishers*Ltd

VIDEO TRASH & TREASURES. Copyright © 1989 by L. A. Morse. All rights reserved. No part of this book may be used or reproduced in any manner whatsoever without prior written permission except in the case of brief quotations embodied in reviews. For information address HarperCollins Publishers Ltd, Suite 2900, Hazelton Lanes, 55 Avenue Road, Toronto, Canada M5R 3L2.

First published by HarperCollins Publishers Ltd: 1989

Canadian Cataloguing in Publication Data

Morse, L. A.
  Video trash & treasures

ISBN 0-00-215439-0

1. Motion pictures – Reviews. 2. Video recordings – Reviews.
I. Title.

PN1995.M67 1989   719.4375   C89-094855-0

---

93 94 95 96 97 98 99 OFF 10 9 8 7 6 5 4 3

SECTION IV: GREAT QUESTS AND DANGEROUS JOURNEYS
Fantasy Adventures in Strange New Worlds 263

21. *Pecs and Flex*
    Sagas of Sword and Sorcery 267
22. *The Clones of Indiana Jones*
    Old-Fashioned Adventures in the Land of the Lost Golden
    Raiders of the Sun 287
23. *Future Schlock*
    A Program of Post-Apocalyptic Adventures 296
24. *Far, Far Away...*
    Space Adventures in Distant Galaxies 314
25. *Speculations*
    Time Warps, Future Visions, and Techno-Fantasies 324
26. *Untamed Worlds*
    Primitive Men, Cave Bimbos, and Jungle Honeys 338

Bonus Festival
Fool's Gold
Class Projects of the Edward D. Wood
Academy of Cinema Arts 348

Index of Directors and Their Films 353

Index of Titles 364

ACKNOWLEDGEMENTS

Besides the two obvious groups of people who made this book possible — the filmmakers whose dreams of big grosses (and bigger gross-outs) went directly to the video fringe, and the video store owners who can't resist an outrageously trashy title any more than I can — two people should be mentioned.

Beverley Beetham Endersby edited what turned out to be a rather daunting pile of paper, along the way catching numerous errors, switching my leisurely rambles into double speed mode, and not only leaving most of my jokes, but adding some of her own.

And, of course, there's Sheila, who was spared most of the really heavy-duty stuff, but who sat through more dreary dramas, unfunny comedies, and pretentious puffs of artsy flatulence than anyone should have to suffer who wasn't actually being paid to do so.

(I suppose I should also mention our two elderly cats, who were happy to keep me company for the heavy-duty stuff, but who would, periodically, offer their critical assessments by retching up a hairball or two.)

WELCOME TO THE VIDEO FRINGE

An Exceedingly Long (But Necessary) Introduction

"I want to see more — more than any man has ever seen."
— *From Beyond*

As you've probably already noticed, the book you're holding is not quite like any other guide to movies on video that you've seen. For one thing, the reviews are longer than the one or two lines that are most usually the case, and there are no stars or other ratings with the reviews. For another, the movies included here, with a very few exceptions, are all from the 1980s. Then there's the fact that the movies are not arranged alphabetically, and seem to be scattered all over the place. (They're not really, but we'll get to that in a bit.) Finally, and maybe most importantly, there are none of the movies or actors that are most familiar — no big hits such as *E.T.* or *Crocodile Dundee*, no brand-name stars such as Schwarzenegger, Stallone, or Eastwood.

This is a book dedicated to the other stuff, what I've called, for want of a better term, *the video fringe*. These are the movies that maybe played in theaters for a couple of weeks and then disappeared; or maybe never played at all in your city or town; or maybe never even had a theatrical release anywhere. These are the movies that perhaps you vaguely remember reading something about or that, even if you're an avid film buff, you've never heard of. These are the movies that fill a lot of shelf space in virtually every video store, and that are often the only ones left after the hot new releases, big hits, and brand names have all been rented.

Even if you're only an infrequent video consumer, you've undoubtedly been faced with the choice of either leaving the store empty-handed and accepting whatever the TV networks are dishing up that night (a "Moonlighting" rerun, a special that's anything but, a PBS report on toxic waste, or yet one more heart-warming Movie-of-the-Week about the heart-warming Affliction-of-the-Week) or else making a foray into the video unknown. Whether you're in the mood for high-quality filmmaking or high-energy schlock, you're reasonably sure that there are some decent efforts among all the unknown quantities, but you've been burned before — by dreary dramas, unfunny comedies, inert action flicks, thrillers that fizzle instead of sizzle, and purported horror gorefests that wouldn't even get a rise out of your sheltered maiden aunt. The question is: How do you find the ones that deliver the goods?

This book came about because I couldn't get an answer to that question. Certainly, you can't trust the video boxes, most of which have slickly lurid artwork and copy that hyperventilates with promises of unimaginable horror, tingling suspense, graphic gore, or lots of young honeys running around in less than their underwear, and I've yet to come across one that identified its contents as the soggy, dreary, amateurish, boring piece of shit that it actually is. Other comprehensive guides to movies either didn't deal with a lot of these titles — what Halliwell, rather stuffily missing the point, called a "nauseous flood of celluloid" — or else dismissed them as "mindless trash." (Of course it's mindless trash, but is it good trash or bad trash? Energetic trash or tedious trash? Trash with some style, or any reason at all to make it worth checking out?) And while there are some interesting and entertaining guides to specific types of trash (see "Further Reading" below), their focus was too narrow, and covered only a small part of the vast expanse of the video fringe.

No, as someone who loves all kinds of movies, good bad and absolutely terrible — as a video omnivore with broad tastes and a need to know what lies behind each wonderfully hyperbolic title — I could find no guide to provide the information that I wanted. The only solution seemed to be to see everything — *everything* — and hope that I came across enough good stuff along the way to make it worthwhile. While I was obsessive, compulsive, and curious enough to do this, I realized that this approach was not likely to be adopted by too many of my fellow video consumers, and I further knew from considerable experience that there are few things more annoying than wasting Prime Viewing Time (not to mention the rental cost) on an absolute stiff. Therefore, since I'd be doing it anyway, I decided, like the intrepid adventurers of earlier ages, to make a full report of my journey into the *terra incognita* of the video fringe so that those explorers who followed me would be more easily able to locate the splendid peaks and hidden treasures, while skipping over the boring bogs and scummy sloughs.

Now, because I was suckered by a snazzy illustration on a box, you won't have to be. Now, because I slogged through dozens of exercises in earnest tedium or artsy flatulence, you'll be able to zero in on the genuine charmers. Now, because I forked over my video dollars, you'll be able to get the goods on such titles as **OASIS OF THE ZOMBIES, BLOODSUCKERS FROM OUTER SPACE, SORORITY BABES IN THE SLIME-BALL BOWL-O-RAMA**, and **VIRGIN AMONG THE LIVING DEAD**. And now, because of the way the material has been arranged, you'll be able to locate and identify lots of other movies similar to ones you've already enjoyed.

Organization: Sections and Festivals

"The whole place is crawling with the beastly things."
— *Rats*

When you walk down the aisles of a supermarket, you see brand-name products, and right next to them, what are called "generics." These are similar products, supposedly just as good as the brand names, only considerably cheaper.

When you look at the shelves of your video store, you see much the same thing, especially in the sections that might be labeled "Horror," "Science Fiction," and "Action." Here you find your brand names — *Rambo, Star Wars, Alien* — surrounded by lots of similar movies (often *very* similar movies) that were made with the hope of grabbing even a small piece of the action that went to the big hits (the technical term for this "ripoff"). In the supermarket, the ratio is usually one generic product to several brand names, but in the video store it is exactly the opposite: the originals are far out-numbered by their imitators.

This phenomenon is certainly nothing new. In Hollywood's Golden Age, the big studios produced huge quantities of virtually identical films. These were the B-movies, and each neatly fit into one of several clearly defined genres — Westerns, war movies, gangster movies, private-eye movies, and so on. They were churned out, very quickly and cheaply, according to well-established formulas, on almost a weekly basis, to fill the bottom half of double bills in neighborhood theaters.

Today, most of these theaters have been torn down. Instead, we have neighborhood video stores with an even more ravenous appetite for new material and, as in the old days, a good part of that demand continues to be met with genre movies. Most of these are no longer produced by the big studios, and some of the genres have changed, but very little else has.

You all know what these movies are. These are your action-adventure-alien-demon-psycho-mutant-vigilante-zombie-ninja-monster-exploding post-apocalyptic revenge extravaganzas. These are your ultra-violent gross-outs, your cheapo, sicko, exploitative, sexploitative, oozing, dripping, slavering sleazebag epics. In other words, to use another technical term, this is your basic video trash. (Note: if it's not already clear, I should mention that "trash" is a reverential term, not a negative one.)

As you've probably noticed, there are staggering quantities of these movies in your video store. Indeed, there are so many that I don't find broad categories such as Horror or Action to be very interesting or useful, since each category contains many different kinds of movies. Instead, I have adopted the "Field Guide" approach, much like those used for identifying birds or wildflowers. Very specific types of movies — for instance, zombie flicks, or old-fashioned adventures modeled on those of Indiana Jones, or the contemporary versions of the *film noir* — have been collected together to form a *festival*, each of which constitutes a fairly precise and well-defined genre or subgenre. Each festival has an introduction that discusses and analyzes why and how these movies came to be and looks at the history and influences of the particular genre/subgenre, its elements, conventions, and identifying characteristics, its strengths and weaknesses, and/or whatever else seems most relevant. Related festivals have, in turn, been grouped into *sections*, each of which has its own introduction concerned with broader issues that apply to all the festivals in that grouping.

This volume of *Video Trash and Treasures* focuses on **HORROR**, **FANTASY**, and what video stores often categorize as **SCIENCE FICTION**. **Section I, Creature Features**, concerns those beings — aliens, mutants, werewolves, zombies, etc. — that, however weird or grotesque, are clearly part of the material world; they have form and substance, and although their shapes may shift from time to time, they always occupy three dimensions. By contrast, **Section II, Occult Ocassions**, invokes less-substantial entities — devils, demons, ghosts, and other supernatural manifestations — that generally make their appearance from some other plane of existence. **Section III** presents the **Slice-and-Dice Psycho**, the homicidal stalking slasher that, numerically at least, has been the dominant "monster" in the 1980s. And finally, in **Section IV** there are the **Fantasy Adventures** — the *Conan* clones, the *Road Warrior* ripoffs, the *Star Wars* spawn — that represent one side of the spectrum of action movies, and that make up some of the most distinctive genre efforts of the 1980s.

Section V; which opens the second volume of *Video Trash and Treasures*, contains the more traditional and down-to-earth **ACTION** flicks that make up one of the largest groups in most video stores, and that, because they are built around fights, chases, shoot-'em-ups and explosions, I have collected under the heading **Big Bangs**. For those with a sweet tooth for **SLEAZE** and prurience, **Section VI** offers up, in this age of hardcore XXX, some good old-fashioned softcore sexploitation. The **CHILLER THRILLERS** of **Section VII** serve up spies and suspense, mystery and machinations, and abundant twists and turns for those with a devious bent of their own. And **Section VIII** contains what I've called **SIGNIFICANT OTHERS** — the nongenre comedies and dramas, the odd, the off-beat, the original; although not all "great" movies, these are also not just more of the same old thing, and are the kind of pleasant surprises and happy discoveries that can reward the video explorer willing to venture off the beaten track.

Defining the Territory: What's Included and What's Not

"They're being born faster 'n we can kill 'em."
— *It's Alive III*

The video fringe, like the universe, is constantly expanding, and the reviews in this book cover movies released through the end of 1988. At the other end, with a few exceptions, movies made before 1980 have not been included. This date roughly marks the beginning of the "video revolution," which created not only a new form of home entertainment, but also a brand-new way for movies to make money for their producers. This important new source of financing and revenue has in turn led to greatly increased production, especially in the area of low-budget, independently made films — precisely the sort of movies that form a large part of the video fringe.

The determination of which movies are obscure and which are too well known to require inclusion can be quite subjective, influenced by how closely one follows film reviews and where one lives (some movies can be very popular in certain cities, but never play anywhere else). In order to apply an objective standard, I've been guided by *Variety*'s annual list of top money-makers that is published each January and shows all the movies released the previous year that earned at least $1 million in rentals. I arbitrarily decided that any movie with rentals over $5 million (which means a box office of roughly double that) was sufficiently familiar that it was not part of the fringe. Again, there are some exceptions here (33 in this volume), included either for completeness within a particular category or because I had the sense that the theatrical audience had been significantly different than the audience for home video. (According to industry surveys, over half of theatrical admissions are patrons under age 24, whereas I suspect that the main market for video rentals is considerably older.)

The "Significant Others" in Section VIII are, by definition, selective, and in order to come up with the 100-plus entries, I watched several times that number of fringe movies from North America and abroad. With the movies in the first seven sections, however, the principle was to be as comprehensive as possible. Put another way, lack of quality was hardly sufficient reason to exclude a piece of trash. Of course, the territory is too huge, and I don't pretend that I managed to cover all of it, even within my selected categories. (I'm particularly chagrined by my failure to locate *Hollywood Chainsaw Hookers*.) But I do believe that the more than 850 trash titles presented in the two volumes include a very good portion of what you're likely to find on the shelves of your own neighborhood video store.

Notable omissions: I have not included what might be termed the Tits-and-Laffs genre, the sophomoronic, sex-obsessed teen comedies descended from *Porky's*; after watching a couple of dozen of these exercises in breasts and braying, and growing progressively grimmer and more sullen with each one, I simply couldn't face the 100 or more that it would have taken to cover the field properly (if a horror or action movie fails badly enough, there's always the possibility of inadvertent humor, but a comedy that misses is only a leaden lump). Still, I may yet tackle these at a later date, along with such subgenres as sports movies, body-switch movies, gotta-dream movies, and baby movies.

With the exception of ninja movies (Festival 36 in the second volume), which form a well-defined and amusing subgenre, I have not included martial-arts flicks; there are just too damn many of the things to contend with, and they should probably have a book of their own. Nor are there any porno tapes, which are an entirely different breed of trash, and that do already have guides of their own.

More and more movies made for TV are being released on cassette, but have been omitted since I don't believe in paying for something that was originally free; however, the occasional movie made for Pay TV does turn up, along with a few movies originally broadcast on British or European television. With one exception, tapes of performances and concerts have not been included since the determining factor is usually how much one likes the particular comic or band, rather than the quality of the movie itself.

And finally, while you will find a lot of well-known actors in the pages that follow, you will not find (with just a couple of exceptions) genre movies that feature the really big brand names (Arnold, Burt, Charles, Chuck, Clint, Sly, etc.); these actors command phenomenal salaries precisely because of the recognition value they bring to their movies, and thus even their less well-known titles are not properly part of the video fringe.

How To Use This Book

"Pandora, open the niche hidden in the belly of Jove."
— *The Seven Magnificent Gladiators*

Although this guide is not as straightforward in its organization as those with alphabetical arrangements, I have tried to make it easy and fun to use, and I hope that once you have a little familiarity with it (and its logic), you will not find it needlessly cumbersome or confusing.

To locate a specific movie, there is an index of titles at the very end of the book, and the page references will quickly direct you to what you want to read about.

If you're interested in a particular type of movie, a quick glance over the table of contents will tell you which section or festival has what you want. Then you can look over the reviews in that festival to see if there are movies that sound interesting enough to seek out. It's never necessary to read the introductory material to a festival or section to utilize the reviews, but if you're curious about the origins or lineage of a particular kind of movie, or why there are so damn many of them around, I hope the introductions will answer your questions and perhaps give you something to think about. Also, seeing these movies *en masse* rather than as isolated entities can change the way you approach them, perhaps even adding an element of interest to something that would otherwise have very little.

There's an index of directors at the back of the book, showing the movies by each that are included in this guide. Since directors are frequently fairly consistent in the type and quality of their work, this could give you other titles to seek out (or avoid), both within and outside this book.

Where a movie could have been included in more than one festival, it has been presented in what seemed the most appropriate place and cross-referenced in the other(s). Similarly, movies with misleading titles have been cross-referenced in the festival where they sound like they belong, directing you to the festival where their subject and focus actually places them.

Finally, just as I enjoy browsing through the display shelves of video stores, seeing what interesting, peculiar or intriguing things there are, I hope you will browse through this book, opening it at random and reading a few pages, or picking a festival and reading it through. If you have a serious interest in movies, I think it can be worthwhile to read about different sorts, even if you're not especially keen to actually watch all of them. Besides, who knows — maybe you'll find something that catches your attention or that strikes a responsive chord, and you'll discover a whole new type of movie to explore.

The Reviews

"Horrible things are going to happen here."
— *Monster Dog*

Since this is a consumer guide rather than an encyclopedic reference book, I have not provided a complete list of credits, but limited it to what are usually regarded as the main perpetrators — the writers and directors — with noteworthy cast and other significant personalities mentioned where appropriate in the text of the reviews. I have also provided the copyright date given on the movie (which is not necessarily the year of its release), alternate titles when I've been aware of them, and, if other than the United States, the country or countries (in the case of co-productions) of origin. Sometimes I was unable to determine this data, or else had to guess at it, which I indicated by using a question mark. If the movie was made for Pay TV or television abroad, that, too, has been indicated, as has a release direct to videocassette. (Note: A great many of the movies in this book probably did not have a theatrical release in North America, but I have only shown "direct to cassette" where either the video box or *Variety* so indicated that.) If a movie is subtitled or dubbed, two factors that can greatly affect the viewing experience, this has also been indicated. Since I would estimate that 95 percent of the movies in this book run between 85 and 100 minutes, I did not see the purpose of giving the length, unless a particular movie happened to be unusually long or short. In the text, titles given in **CAPITAL LETTERS** refer to movies reviewed in this book, while *italicized titles* are not.

With regard to some of this information — alternate or previous titles, date, origin, and especially if the movie has been dubbed — I strongly believe that it's high time that video packagers or distributors be required to provide it on the boxes. The big, reputable distributors are usually pretty good about putting at least some information on the boxes, but beware of those that don't tell you very much. I don't know about you, but I'm pretty tired of discovering that what sounded like a brand-new piece of entertaining rubbish turns out to be an ancient, badly dubbed bit of Euro-sludge that I had already seen once before under another title. The home-video market is now a multibillion-dollar-a-year business, and truth-in-packaging regulations are long overdue.

All the reviews are based on video viewing, even if I happened to have seen the movie in theatrical release. Some movies — especially those with big effects or big action sequences — are considerably diminished on the home screen, but since this is a video guide, I have reported on what that experience is like. (Conversely, I've found that some movies — usually smaller, more intimate efforts that don't have enough to fill a big screen — play much better on the small one.)

For each review, I have tried to give some sense of the subject and what the movies are like, briefly highlighting what — if anything — distinguishes them and makes them worth taking a look at. Instead of a rating system, which I usually find more annoying than useful, I have attempted to convey enough information so that you can decide if a given movie sounds like something you'd be interested in. Please note that the judgments tend to be fairly relative: good movies are good movies, but saying that a genre movie is above average for its type may only mean that it's better than a lot of not very distinguished companions in that festival. In any case, a review can't help but be subjective — just one guy's opinion — so I should probably say a few words about the factors that have contributed to *this* guy's opinions.

Critical Perspectives

"Not many people have a code to live by these days."
— *Repo Man*

As already stated, I love movies, all kinds of movies, and I approach every movie wanting to like it, wanting to be entertained for 90 or so minutes. Furthermore, when you're talking about renting a movie for two or three dollars, I don't believe you should be as demanding as you are of something that you fork over six bucks or more to see in a theater. If it delivers a few laughs or a couple of good jolts, it might well be worth its modest rental cost, especially if the alternative is watching network tedium.

That said, I do require something more than the fact that images are moving in front of my glazed eyes. For instance: Are the characters/actors at all interesting and believable, or are they dumb, wooden, and/or annoying stereotypes? Does the script contain a few twists and surprises, or does it plod mechanically along from stupidity to implausibility to inanity? Did someone try to make it interesting to look at, give it a little style, disguise the fact that it had a low budget? Are the special effects at all special? Does it have any humor, intentional or otherwise? Does it have any originality or cleverness? And above all, does it have any energy and vitality? (If a movie has some genuine energy, I'm willing to overlook all sorts of shortcomings, but if it doesn't have energy, it hardly matters how good everything else is.)

Whether a movie's about a serious social issue or is nothing but a piece of genre junk out after a quick buck, the one thing it cannot be is boring. It's the filmmaker's job to grab our attention, if not through a dynamite story or fascinating characters, then with *something* — a really creepy monster, or a splash of great gore, or a spectacular pair of hooters. What this means is that I've tried to take the trash on its own terms, letting you know if it delivers the goods, or even if there's anything at all that stands out. Put another way, if you approach it with the right attitude, there are much worse things than honest and aggressive exploitation; you may find it unsavory or offensive, but it can frequently possess considerable vitality.

Besides, once you've seen all the good stuff, there's only trash left, so I figure you might as well sit back and try to enjoy it. Personally, I'm a firm believer in the premise that any movie with a little gratuitous violence and a little gratuitous sex can't be all bad. But of course, given the right talent (or lack thereof), even sleaze can be dull, and I've tried to alert you when it is.

> "You know — I've been here a long time and never seen anyone as wacko as you."
> — *The Invisible Strangler*

However, just because a movie is bad doesn't mean that there's not a reason to watch it. If you're seriously interested in movies, you can often learn much more from the bad ones than from the good ones. In a really good movie, everything works, the parts fit together seamlessly, and you're carried along; but in a bad movie, nothing works, and you become very aware of the whole creaking, sagging structure. These stiffs are clearly not any good *as movies* but, if you step back a little bit, they can be quite fascinating in other ways.

And, if they are deeply, truly, seriously terrible, they can manage to come full circle. This is Golden Turkey territory in which, as the Brothers Medved demonstrated in their wonderful pioneering research, a movie can be so mind-numbingly godawful that it becomes completely hilarious — far, far funnier than all but the greatest comedies. Since the bottom line is entertainment, these movies, in their own tacky, clunky, loopy way, can be regarded as another form of buried treasure. Fortunately for video explorers, the fringe is filled with more than a few of these frisky gobblers, and I hope you have as much fun discovering them for yourself as I have had in bringing them to your attention.

Critical Terminology

"That bastard's playing games with us."
— *My Bloody Valentine*

Trash-movie reviewing, like other highly specialized disciplines, has its own technical vocabulary, and thus it seems appropriate to define some of the terms that turn up in the reviews with a fair degree of frequency.

Asshole: In *reel* life, as in real life, an appallingly loutish and offensive character, usually male, and usually intended by the script to be amusing or appealing; he ain't; you'd avoid this type in a bar, so why would you want to pay money to watch him at home?

Backyard: A style of filmmaking distinguished by the paucity of the budget and an utter lack of professionalism in all departments; the resulting efforts are nothing that you and your friends couldn't do just as well.

Bimbo: A decorative young female character whom the script gives an I.Q. smaller than her chest measurement, and to whom nasty things often occur, usually with much screaming; does not refer to the actress herself, who frequently reveals considerable dramatic talents.

Bozo: The male equivalent to the preceding, usually with a less impressive chest; not as actively obnoxious as the Asshole, but pretty tiresome nonetheless.

Paint-by-numbers: A singularly mindless approach to structure and characterization that makes predictable, derivative and merely mechanical efforts seem positively brisk, lively and original.

Piece-o-shit: Bears the same relationship to an entertaining movie that "filet-o-fish" does to a lobster dinner; you wouldn't want to step in it, and you certainly don't want to rent it.

Sophomoronic: Most frequently applied to movies that display the wit and sensibility of Tits-and-Laffs teen comedies; combines the sophistication of degenerate pre-adolescents with the intelligence of vegetable matter, and assumes we will be amused by the antics of Assholes, Bimbos, and Bozos (see above).

Time-passer: Applied to movies that, while certainly nothing at all special, are sufficiently brisk and professional to fill 90 minutes in an innocuous fashion, and then to vanish completely from memory.

Time-waster: A step down from the preceding, but still competent enough not to be absolutely leaden or actively offensive; no reason to seek out, but okay for desperate situations.

A Few Words about Splatter

"It's the bloodiest mess I've ever seen."
— *Bloodsuckers from Outer Space*

With three sections devoted to horror films looming just a few pages away, this seems to be as good a place as any to say a few words about splatter.

According to John McCarty in *Splatter Movies*, the term "splatter" was coined by George Romero in describing his *Dawn of the Dead*. It means just what it says — the very explicit presentation of gory violence in which blood, brains and/or other bits and pieces ooze, seep, splash, spurt or otherwise go flying against actors, walls, and the camera lens. More generally, splatter is taken to mean the graphic depiction of the wide range of deliciously gruesome and loathsome material that is at the heart of many contemporary horror films.

In splatter cinema, the aim is not so much to frighten as to shock with the realism of the effect. The desired response to a tasty bit of splatter is

"Did you see that?" or, ideally, "Holy shit! Did you see that?" In other words, splatter elicits a visceral response, and in some of the more enthusiastic efforts — especially those by the Italian goremeisters — it does so with actual viscera.

In **RETURN TO HORROR HIGH**, the sleazeball producer of the movie-within-the-movie remarks that "everybody loves a good grossout," but that's not entirely true — one either likes this kind of thing or one doesn't. Those who don't — a stuffy, squeamish, weak-kneed lot as a rule — tend to get huffy and complain about gratuitous violence. Splatter is far from gratuitous, though; frequently it's the point of the exercise, the *raison d'être* of the movie.

One of the great appeals of the motion picture is its ability to show us things we've never seen before; in contemporary horror movies that can range from dismemberment, decapitation, and impaling; through slimy, tentacled, nightmarish monstrosities; to a young woman vomiting up her intestinal tract (**THE GATES OF HELL**, if you're curious). Even if the movie is generally a total stiff, special effects like these, if done well, really do make you sit up and take notice, and what you'll see is not likely to appear on, say, "The Cosby Show."

The wizards who conjure this stuff — current special-effects stars such as Tom Savini, Rick Baker, and Rob Bottin — are not only illusionists of the first order, but true artists. Their art may not appeal to everyone, but it most definitely has that quality that all real art has — the capacity to make some deeply buried nerves twitch and tingle. (For a behind-the-scenes look at the artistry involved, the first installment of the video series *Scream Greats* provides a fascinating study of Tom Savini's particular form of art and magic, which has figured so prominently in George Romero's films.)

Not all of the movies in the three horror sections are splatter movies, nor are all splatter movies devoid of such qualities as wit, humor, characterization, plot, and suspense. However, if you're among the millions who do love a good gross-out, you'll find in the following pages a fair number of exercises in messy excess that really do deliver the goods.

Further Reading

"You will need more than the power of the sword."
— *Krull*

The following are the books that I found invaluable in researching the festival introductions, and inspiring in terms of my own video explorations. All are recommended for those who wish to delve more deeply into the video fringe.

Balun, Chas. *Horror Holocaust*. New York: Fantaco Enterprises, Inc., 1986. A dementedly enthusiastic celebration of splatter filmmaking.

Briggs, Joe Bob (John Bloom). *Joe Bob Goes to the Drive-In*. New York: Delacorte Press, 1987. The definitive work of drive-in movie criticism, complete with breast counts and Joe Bob's escapades with Wanda Bodine.

Hardy, Phil, ed. *Horror (The Aurum Film Encyclopedia, Volume 3)*. London: Aurum Press, 1985. Huge, expensive, and not distributed in North America; for those interested in the history of the horror film from the earliest days to the early 1980s, this is the ultimate reference book, and well worth finding a bookseller who will special order it for you.

Maltin, Leonard, ed. *Leonard Maltin's TV Movies & Video Guide*. New York: New American Library, 1988. Len hardly needs a plug from me, but, although a little too squeamish and stuffy for hardcore fringe explorers, this is an otherwise remarkably reliable and useful guide to movies not included in this one.

McCarty, John. *PSYCHOS — Eighty Years of Mad Movies, Maniacs, and Murderous Deeds*. New York: St. Martin's Press, 1986. An interesting and informative survey of this most enduring villain.

McCarty, John. *SPLATTER MOVIES — Breaking the Last Taboo of the Screen*. New York: St. Martin's Press, 1984. Deliciously illustrated; the title tells all.

Medved, Harry and Michael. *The Golden Turkey Awards*. New York: Perigee Books, 1980. *Son of Golden Turkey Awards*. New York: Villard Books, 1986. The books that defined the form; hilarious even if you've never seen the movies.

Nicholls, Peter. *Fantastic Cinema*. London: Ebury Press, 1984. A survey of science fiction, horror, and fantasy films, with the emphasis on those after 1968; a fine analysis; beautifully produced and lavishly illustrated.

Peary, Danny. *Guide for the Film Fanatic*. New York: Simon & Schuster, Inc., 1986. Long, thoughtful and perceptive reviews of 1,600 movies of every type and period; a must for every serious explorer, with suggestions that will keep you busy for a long time.

Peary, Danny, ed. *Omni's Screen Flights/Screen Fantasies*. Garden City: Doubleday & Company, Inc., 1984. An excellent collection of essays on "the future according to science fiction cinema."

Stanley, John. *Revenge of the Creature Features Movie Guide*. Pacifica: Creatures at Large Press, 1988. Although I frequently disagree with the opinions, this is still a large, useful and entertaining guide to "fantastic cinema."

Vale, V. and Juno, Andrea, eds. *Re/Search #10: Incredibly Strange Films*. San Francisco: Re/Search, 1986. A beautifully designed and produced book celebrating cinematic oddities, complete with genre surveys and lengthy interviews with practitioners such as Larry Cohen, Frank Henenlotter, and Herschell Gordon Lewis; an absolute must for those with a taste for deviant cinema.

Weldon, Michael. *The Psychotronic Encyclopedia of Film*. New York: Ballantine Books, 1983. Informative, comprehensive, and frequently very funny, this is the last word on "Late Show" movies, an essential guide for anyone with a sweet tooth for tacky trash.

Bon Voyage

"You have to go to the foothills of Kilimanjaro,
where no one has ever gone before."
— *The Mines of Kilimanjaro*

Thanks for reading all of this. Now, it's over to you. As one of the bimbos (see "Critical Terminology" above) put it in **ROLLER BLADE**, a post-apoc Amazon rollerskating adventure: "Go forth and skate the path of righteousness."

I

CREATURE FEATURES

An Unnatural History of Aliens, Monsters, and Mutations

The seven festivals in this section offer a cinematic bestiary that runs from aliens to zombies, with non-alphabetical stops along the way for some monumental monsters and mutants, a convention of crazed scientists, and, less alliteratively, a pack of werewolves and some extremely pissed-off members of the animal kingdom.

The antecedents and influences for these movies are similarly diverse. Some go back to the 1930s, the first golden age of the monster movie; others back to the '50s, the second golden age; still others are more recent and include such films as *Night of the Living Dead, Jaws,* and *The Howling.* However, the one movie that was most influential in ushering in the current age of creature features (maybe the best era yet) is *Alien* (1979).

Before *Alien,* what kind of horrors did we have? In the 1970s we had zombies — basically guys in grisly makeup. We had sharks and other large carnivores. We had a few animals and insects that had grown to giant size but were otherwise unchanged. We had some sicko psychos. And we had demonic possessions, and other supernatural annoyances.

While a lot of these horrors certainly did the trick, they were not *creatures* — made-up monsters, hideous new lifeforms, imaginary organisms from the depths of the sea or beyond the stars. Indeed, with very few exceptions — mostly from Japan, mostly very tacky — scarcely a creature had walked among us for nearly two decades.

The cause of this lengthy absence is not hard to isolate, and can be inferred from the 1950s Slime People, Mole People, Things, Its, and Saucer Men that we all know and love from the "Late Show." These creations took a lot of different forms, but mostly the form was that of a guy dressed in a rubber suit, wearing a really cheesy-looking mask. Even when the director managed to build a little tension and suspense around them, the creatures were never as scary as the illustrations on the posters promised, and eventually audiences grew tired of being suckered and disappointed.

On the cargo ship *Nostromo*, however, 28 years after the ambulatory carrot known as "The Thing" first appeared, moviemaking technology caught up with the imagination, and the creature we had all been waiting for burst out of John Hurt's stomach. Interestingly enough, *Alien* was in fact a reworking of the 1958 "classic" *It! The Terror from Beyond Space*, only done the way we'd always wanted it. The movie had a great cast and a compelling look and, for the first time, the creature not only lived up to our expectations but exceeded them. And, boy, did it scare the shit out of us!

Even more to the point, *Alien* packed us in, becoming a multimillion-dollar megahit. The lesson was clear: creatures were back in fashion. So what if you don't have the budget for good sets or a good cast? So what if you don't have the talent to generate real suspense? Ooze is cheap, right? And if you can't afford a whole disgusting creature, you can always manage a tentacle or two.

While *Alien* figures prominently as a seminal influence for some of the creature features in this section, only a few of them are the direct spawn of it; however, by showing what *could* be done, *Alien* revived this species of movie, and special-effects wizards, using modern materials and techniques, have given us both a new menagerie of monsters and greatly enhanced versions of some of the old ones.

The movies themselves, though, while now frequently slicker and sexier, changed very little from what they had been in earlier eras. Barring the odd variation on the form, the narrative structure of the basic monster movie generally boils down to Us versus It, with Us racing against time to discover Its vulnerability. *Alien* certainly had this story line but, unlike most of its predecessors, dispensed with a great deal of the extraneous stuff — the tedious subplots, the boring romantic interest — that essentially served as padding to bulk thin material out to feature length. Besides the brilliant creature, *Alien*'s great achievement was to make *everything* either suspenseful or interesting to look at. Of course, it's much harder to do that than to come up with a decent monster or a few moments of splendid splatter, and thus what we see most frequently in the movies that follow is a few minutes of good stuff surrounded by lots of dull characters and piles of plot excreta.

If the good stuff is good enough, I figure one should be somewhat tolerant of the deficiencies. After all, few creature features ever reach the level of *Alien* or its incredible sequel, and if you hold out for unqualified successes, you'll be waiting quite a while between monsters. At the same time, I subscribe to the belief that if you have a creature worth making a movie about, you should show the damn thing. All too often what we get is nothing but tease — and crummy tease at that: if you didn't have the pause button, you'd never figure out what the hell the brute looks like.

In terms of quality, the creature features here are the typically mixed bag you find when you poke around the video fringe. Sometimes the special effects are splendidly horrific, sometimes there's nothing special about them, and sometimes the filmmakers, as though unaware of twenty years' worth of technical developments, give us yet more guys in lousy rubber suits. Likewise, the movies themselves range from the ludicrous to the dull, from the derivative to the mildly clever, with a few of them displaying considerable wit, energy, and inventiveness.

One thing that is certain, though, is that this age of creature features shows no signs of ending. Judging from the more than 100 titles that follow, it seems clear that our appetite for monsters of all sorts is at least as voracious as is theirs for us.

FESTIVAL 1

* * *

SHE'S GOT SLIME ALL OVER HER!
A Galaxy of Aliens, Plain and Fancy

> "Whatever it was, it wasn't a virus."
> — *Alien Contamination*

In *Star Wars* (1977) a lot of strange beings appeared in the famous space cantina scene, but they were sociable and were kept strictly in the background; the visitors from *Close Encounters* (also 1977) were friendly and scarcely seen. But *Alien* gave us a creature that took center stage . . . with a vengeance.

And, since it pulled in something around $100 million at the box office, it's not surprising that a number of its oozing, dripping, toothy, bellybursting close relatives followed, hot on its tentacles, in movies with remarkably similar looks, styles, settings, and characters.

However, most of the subsequent aliens were encountered on earth — with no elaborate sets to build, things become a lot cheaper and easier. Similarly, more than a few of these visitors either take over human bodies or already are basically humanoid in appearance, thus saving the price of complicated mechanical constructions. Still, even a bargain alien can avoid losing sight of the really important values, such as being hungry, hostile, and slimy.

Of course, not all aliens are nasty, and in 1983 Steven Spielberg gave us a very different kind of extraterrestrial. This one earned more money than any movie ever, but it has been less often imitated. Even hacks can recognize that *E.T.*'s success was based, not so much on the quality of the effects, as on the quality of the movie, and that sort of thing is hard to rip off. *E.T.* has, however, had some influence and, along with nice visitors such as *Starman* (1984) and the *Cocoon* (1985) people, its followers make up the other end of the alien spectrum.

Today, a full range of intergalactic lifeforms can be found on the shelves of your video store. If they're not all what you'd call wildly original, that probably just goes to demonstrate that certain fundamental equations apply throughout the universe — such as: a bucket of slime is equivalent to an ounce of creativity.

(*Note*: It's assumed that xenophiles are already familiar with the exceptional nasties from *Predator* [one of the more fascinating recent creations, though seen too briefly] and with those from John Carpenter's remake of *The Thing* [perhaps the most repulsive alien yet], and thus these are not included below.)

Aliens in Space

HORROR PLANET *(1980, British)*
wr Nick and Gloria Maley; dir Norman J. Warren

An archaeological expedition to a distant world discovers an ancient underground tomb, and pretty soon realizes that something nasty is going on. This one is nearly creatureless: some sort of vague shape appears for about two seconds — just long enough to rape Judy Geeson, who then kills people and eats their intestines as she grows rapidly more pregnant. Eventually, she gives birth to a pair of carnivorous alien half-breeds that look — during their seconds-long cameo — a little like the babies in *It's Alive*. The absence of a creature, though, is probably less significant than the absence of something to make up for it. There's a lot of slow walking through dimly lit tunnels, screaming and shrieking, some off-camera mayhem, and buckets of on-camera blood, but the couple of good moments and decent effects aren't enough to disguise the scarcity of tension and suspense. Originally titled *Inseminoid*, this is strictly a misconception.

GALAXY OF TERROR *(1981)*
wr Marc Siegler and B.D. Clark; dir B.D. Clark

Originally released as *Mindwarp* and *Planet of Horrors*. This Roger Corman production borrows its ultimate twist from *Forbidden Planet* (1956), but until then is less an *Alien* ripoff than an extremely faithful reproduction, even down to casting actors that resemble in appearance their *Nostromo* crew counterparts. Certainly, this approach simplifies things since the audience's familiarity with the original can be used to fill in any gaps in the story. Still, there are some moments of inspired grossness — a guy cuts off his own arm, which then kills him; a giant worm rapes one of the crew members (slimes her up real good); and we get to see Erin (Joanie from "Happy Days") Moran's head explode. And, if all that's not enough for you, this movie offers the rare opportunity to see Robert Englund *(Nightmare on Elm Street)* without his Freddie face. It's interesting to note that James Cameron, who went on to make *Terminator* and *Aliens*, served as a second unit director and production designer on this, and managed to give things a pretty good look despite what seems to have been a very limited budget.

CREATURE *(1985)*
wr William Malone and Alan Reed; dir William Malone

Yet another *Alien* clone in which a small research team is trapped on one of Saturn's moons, menaced by a creature that's been waiting 200,000 years for his next meal. This movie has a pretty good look and decent production values, but the characters are so undeveloped as to be nearly indistinguishable from one another, and the pace is very sluggish. There are a few decent effects — a face ripped off, and exploding head — but they're late arriving, and the creature itself appears briefly and indistinctly only at the end. This effort isn't really bad; it's just another damn tease that never puts out. From the director of **SCARED TO DEATH**. With Klaus Kinski, and Marie Laurin as Susan, the astrobimbo who sheds her spacesuit.

STAR CRYSTAL *(1985)*
wr and dir Lance Lindsay

This attempt to marry *Alien* with *E.T.* gives us five people on an isolated spacecraft with a lifeform that's been buried on Mars for 300,000 years. As though they don't have problems enough (a shortage of food and insufficient power to get home), the space travelers soon discover that *something* is sucking them dry. In a very short time, we're down to two (cheaper and easier that way), and then . . . but I don't want to spoil the plot twist that is at the heart of the story. This cheapie manages a pretty good look and has some ingenuity to compensate for the small budget. What nothing could compensate for is the dialog, which would have been

> *"You should never hitch a ride with a hearse."*
> NAIL GUN MASSACRE

more appropriate on "Love Boat," and some truly awful acting (most notably by early victims, thus sparing us having to endure it). The best moment is a chase shown as dots on a video screen *à la* Pacman, which, in terms of drama and tension, far surpasses anything the actors are capable of. Still, how can you not have a certain affection for a movie that contains the lines "All that emptiness makes you crazy after a while" and "She's got slime all over her!"

DEEP SPACE
Earth-spawned slimeball; see Festival 3
FORBIDDEN WORLD
Man-made metamorphic mutation; see Festival 3.

Dining Out on Earth

ALIEN CONTAMINATION *(1980, Italian, dubbed)*
wr and dir Lewis Coates (Luigi Cozzi)

This badly dubbed *Alien* ripoff was very quick off the mark . . . and it shows. A ghost ship, deserted except for a weird smell, cruises into New York harbor. The investigators find the ghastly pulp that is all that remains of the captain and, in a flash of brilliant insight, decide that "Whatever it was, it wasn't a virus." In the ship's hold, hidden in a shipment of coffee beans, they find big green eggs, which burst, causing any people around them to do likewise. Eventually, at the South American coffee plantation where the eggs are being raised, our heroes find a large latex monster called "Cyclops" with one lightbulb-eye. When the eye glows, the creature takes over its victim's mind, then inhales the rest through a green trunk. Dumb, dumb, dumb, but there is a lot of raw meat in the form of flayed and torn-apart bodies.

THE DEADLY SPAWN *(1983)*
wr and dir Douglas McKeown
Also released as *The Return of the Aliens: The Deadly Spawn*.

A meteor crashes to earth, bringing with it some very nasty extraterrestrial worms who move into a suburban cellar where they grow, reproduce, and devour a lot of people. Sure, this backyard exercise in messy excess is cheap and amateurish, with terrible sound, bad lighting, home-movie acting, and tedious dialog, but its mayhem is enthusiastic. Blood splatters by the drumload, heads are bitten off, hands are chewed up, skin is ripped off, and its creatures are not the least bit camera shy. Giant carnivorous tadpoles in their early stages, these admirably creepy things grow into arm-sized worms, then finally into a multi-headed eating machine that is nothing but a bouquet of toothy mouths. Clearly influenced by *Night of the Living Dead*, while not as uniformly relentless, this movie has enough energy at least to partially realize the same kind of nightmare quality, and turns out to be much more entertaining than a lot of more expensive efforts.

ALIEN PREY *(1984, British)*
wr Max Cuff; dir Norman J. Warren

An alien arrives on earth and assumes a male form, then hangs out in an isolated country house occupied by two rather highly strung young lesbians. The visitor occasionally reverts to his own shape — the snout is squarer; the teeth, sharper — to sample the local fauna, but the movie's primary concern is the relationship between the two women, at least one of whom is seriously loony. The two plots don't quite mesh, nor are they all that interesting, but there's a little sex and weirdness along the way to spice them up. Given the title, the twist ending is fairly easily predicted, but it too is better than nothing. For a low-budget backyard effort — a cast of three, no special effects — this movie isn't bad, even though it is really only a half-hour TV story dressed up with some skin and blood and dragged out to ninety minutes. From the director of **HORROR PLANET** and **BLOODY NEW YEAR**.

ALIEN PREDATOR *(1985)*
wr and dir Deran Sarafian

Three young American jerks (played by Dennis Christopher, Martin Hewitt, and Lynn-Holly Johnson) are traveling around Spain when their RV breaks down near a little town in which weird things are going on. Seems a chunk of an orbiting space lab fell to earth five years earlier, bringing with it a rather nasty alien microbe. According to The Scientist

> "What was left, you could put in a plastic bag."
> MONSTER DOG

(Luis Prinde), once it enters a body, "it uses the DNA of the host like a supermarket, picking and choosing the traits it needs." First it renders its victims psychotic, then it bursts out of their heads, making this kind of a cross between *The Andromeda Strain* (1970) and John Carpenter's remake of *The Thing* (1982). Annoyingly, we *hear* about what the creature does, and we get some quick looks at the pulped heads it leaves behind, but we don't ever get to *see* much. Only at the very end is there an actual head-bursting, with the creature — all crab legs and pointy, little teeth — putting in a ten-second appearance, which may be close to the record for the least screen time by an alien in a title role. Fast-forward to the end and catch the last five minutes; all you will have missed is a lot of lame dailog and a totally nonsenical plot.

LIFEFORCE *(1985)*
wr Dan O'Bannon and Don Jakoby; dir Tobe Hooper

This one gives new meaning to overlapping subgenres: we've got an alien spacecraft discovered in the head of Haley's Comet; we've got possessions and telepathic communication; we've got vampires; and there's London destroyed by hordes of lifeforce-sucking zombies. With a huge budget (over $22 million), the look and the effects are spectacular — light shows comparable to that at the end of *Raiders of the Lost Ark*, exploding zombies, dessicated corpses, geysers of blood, and an array of other neat stuff. Also spectacular is Mathilda May as the vampire queen; she's naked for most of her appearances and clearly possessed of impressive dramatic assets. There are, unfortunately, no interesting characters, and the story is less than attention-grabbing, which explains why this was a megaflop in theatrical release, but, considering some of the other movies in this section, those are hardly good reasons not to watch it. Based on Colin Wilson's novel *Space Vampires*.

DEMONWARP *(1987, direct to cassette)*
wr Jim Bertges and Bruce Akiyama; dir Emmett Alston

No demon here, but plenty of warp. Jack and four of his collegiate friends go into Demon Wood to see if they can find out what happened to Jack's uncle who mysteriously disappeared several weeks earlier. Before you can say "shag rug," they're attacked by a big-footed guy in an apesuit who likes to rip heads off. Next, they run into some zombies in varying states of decomposition. Finally, they run into the being responsible for all the weirdness, an alien with a taste for hearts, preferably those of bare-breasted bimbos. This one obviously doesn't have a brain in its tiny head, but the silliness moves along briskly enough to keep it from being boring, the effects are passable (if neither spectacular or original), and the ampleness of Pamela Gilbert and Mo-elle Baker is amply displayed. Not nearly as ludicrous as the director's *Nine Deaths of the Ninja*, but not for lack of trying. With George Kennedy along to raise the question: When was the last time this man was in even a semi-decent movie?

Alien Fugitives

THE BROTHER FROM ANOTHER PLANET *(1984)*
wr, dir and ed John Sayles

A black, mute, six-toed (three per foot) fugitive arrives in New York from somewhere in space and takes refuge in Harlem, where he fits right in as just another slightly off-center "brother." Although he is pursued by two sinister intergalactic policemen (hilariously played by Sayles and David Strathairn), the film is not about the chase, but about the brother's reactions to the strange new world he's in and his interactions with the people he meets there. Luminously played by Joe Morton, the brother is a marvelously empathetic being, and even though he doesn't speak, people like to talk to him. What they say is humorous, revealing, very real, and a delight to listen to. Indeed, on the whole the movie, aside from a few plot elements that don't quite work, is a complete delight — funny, touching and very, very engaging. Made on a minuscule budget, with no hardware or special effects to speak of, it is generously endowed with wit, intelligence, and heart. Those who haven't yet seen this one have a real treat in store.

CRITTERS *(1986)*
wr Stephen Herek and Dominic Muir; dir Stephen Herek

Gremlins eat Kansas. Intergalactic criminals called "Crites" escape across the galaxy to earth, pursued by two leather-clad bounty hunters with the

> *"I can't understand why you won't let anyone show any mercy on worldwide TV."*
> THE NEW GLADIATORS

capacity to transform themselves into whatever they want. Small critters with very large appetites who roll along the ground like omnivorous tumbleweeds, and can shoot little poison darts from their skin like porcupines, the Crites land in Grover's Bend, Kansas, and lay siege to a family farmhouse. Good production values, decent acting (Dee Wallace Stone, Scott Grimes, M. Emmet Walsh), some humor, and some good effects make this much more entertaining than *Gremlins* or **GHOULIES** — the two movies it most resembles.

CRITTERS 2 *(1988)*
wr D.T. Twohy and Mick Garris; dir Mick Garris

Tumblin' tumbleweeds! They're back! Seems a bunch of Crite eggs were overlooked, and they decide to get crackin' just in time for the big Easter Egg hunt in Grover's Bend. Fortunately, Scott Grimes, Don Opper, and bounty hunter Terrence Mann are back as well, and their expertise is the only thing that can keep the town from becoming an ambulatory buffet. This is very slow until the Crites turn up, but then delivers a few mildly amusing moments, the best being when one of the bounty hunters takes the spectacular shape of a Playboy centerfold (staple and all). The PG rating pre-empts seriously disgusting gobbling, and there's not enough else (including gags) to fill in the spaces. As sequels go, this one's okay, but certainly not a must.

THE HIDDEN *(1987)*
wr Bob Hunt; dir Jack Sholder

Kyle MacLachlin (*Blue Velvet*) plays an intergalactic policeman who comes to Los Angeles in pursuit of the nasty, foot-long, tentacled snail that killed his family. A kind of parasite that enters its victims through their mouths, then takes them over, causing them to go on virtually unstoppable psychotic rampages of pillage and slaughter, the killer alien hops from body to body, chased by Kyle, posing as an FBI agent teamed up with L.A. cop Michael Nouri (*Flashdance*). This is a very well-made and quite entertaining movie — slick, fast-paced, with some nice humorous bits, several impressive car chases, and enough bullets pumping into bodies for a half-dozen action flicks. MacLachlin is not one of my favorite actors, but he's perfectly cast here as the expressionless visitor to a world whose subtleties he doesn't yet understand. My only real quibble is that we only get a few seconds of the creature, which is so thoroughly creepy it would've been nice to spend a little more time with.

STRANDED *(1987)*
wr Alan Castle; dir Tex Fuller

Five humanoid aliens, apparently fugitives from an oppressive regime, arrive on earth, at a house occupied by a young woman (Ione Skye, *River's Edge*) and her spunky grandmother (Maureen O'Sullivan). An inadvertent shooting results in a hostage/siege situation, with the local police trying to cope with something far beyond what's covered in the manual. This is a modest movie, but a pleasant, effective, and engaging one. Its strength is not the effects — the alien makeup is good, the opticals not very impressive — but the characters and the way they interact. Without speaking, the aliens are nonetheless very expressive, and we can't help but be interested in their predicament and root for them. Although a different sort of movie, this clearly owes a bit to **THE BROTHER FROM ANOTHER PLANET**, a debt interestingly acknowledged in the casting of Joe Morton as the sheriff. The plot might have benefited from a few more twists and turns, but the movie is well-made, well-acted, and fast-paced, and it holds your attention for a generally entertaining 80 minutes.

Alien Tourists

WAVELENGTH *(1982)*
wr and dir Mike Gray

This one concerns four humanoid aliens — galactic tourists — who were inadvertently shot down during a weapons test, and are being dissected in an abandoned air force base in the Hollywood Hills. Are they alive or dead? Friendly or hostile? Innocuous or deadly? Obviously somewhat influenced by *Close Encounters*, this movie is not absolutely original, but it does have some energy and imagination, as well as enough plot twists to keep you alert and guessing at how things are going to turn out. The

> *"They ate George right in front of our eyes."*
> DR. BUTCHER M.D.

secondary characters are especially well drawn; they're not ghoulish scientists or robotic generals, but simply professionals trying to cope with a situation far beyond their experience or ability. The title, which is not really all that apt, alludes to the fact that the aliens are able to communicate telepathically, but only one person (Cherie Curie) is tuned in to their "wavelength." With Robert Carradine, Keenan Wynn, and music by Tangerine Dream.

ZONE TROOPERS *(1985)*
wr Danny Bilson and Paul DeMeo; dir Danny Bilson

In the closing days of the Second World War, a few American GIs get cut off behind German lines, where they discover the crash site of an alien spacecraft. Naturally, the SS is keen to get their hands on the advanced technology, and the good guys are out to stop them. The premise — "E.T. Goes to War" — is not a bad one, but the script doesn't use it to advantage. Indeed, it seems to go to extremes to avoid using anything that might be interesting, settling for lots of cheap, dull "action" sequences with machine guns ripping through countless German soldiers. If the aliens — sort of a cross between a warthog and a giant insect — had been given more attention, this could have been a passable movie. With Tim Thomerson (**TRANCERS**) as "The Iron Sarge."

MORONS FROM OUTER SPACE *(1985, British)*
wr Griff Rhys Jones and Mel Smith; dir Mike Hodges

As the advertising slogan for this one puts it: "They came, they saw, they did a little shopping." While out cruising in the intergalactic equivalent of an RV, three very dim humanoid aliens — Des, Sandra, and Julian — crash-land on the M1 motorway in England, and quickly become big media stars. Bernard, the fourth member of the party and the only one with any brains, comes down in Arizona and is immediately tossed into the loony bin. Smith and Jones, who wrote and star in this, have previously been involved in several very funny British TV programs ("Not the Nine O'Clock News", "Alias Smith and Jones"), and the movie displays the same sort of eccentric humor, along with numerous parodic references to other movies, most notably **Close Encounters**. Although it loses a little steam in the second half, it has more than enough effective silliness to provoke a number of smiles and a few laughs. Probably not for all tastes, but fans of British comedy will definitely want to check this one out.

Alien Dads

XTRO *(1982, British)*
wr Iain Cassie and Robert Smith; dir Harry Bromley Davenport

It's tough being an absentee father, especially when you've been abducted by aliens and turned into a rather nasty reptilian creature. Dad (Philip Sayer), who disappeared three years earlier, returns to earth to convert his son to the saurian persuasion and take him up to his new home. There are some good, gross effects — some nice tentacles, no skimping on blood and slime, a rape by reptileman, and his subsequent rebirth (literally a birth) into human form — and there's also a lot of cheap dull stuff (low-rent telekinesis, toys coming to life, etc.). A good premise homogenized into mundane domestic drama, badly directed and terribly lit. Still, if you're willing to overlook — or fast-forward through — the junk, this does deliver a few effective moments. Featuring the debut of Maryam D'Abo in the demanding role of an *au pair* girl who takes her clothes off twice.

BREEDERS *(1986, made for video)*
wr and dir Tim Kincaid

Alien wants virgins. The slimy black creature — a testament to the potential of latex and goo — living beneath the streets of New York, and seen mostly in shadow or in small pieces, needs virgins to reproduce, and thus the movie consists primarily of a series of rapes of the last six N.Y. virgins. A not-very-bright detective and an even dimmer doctor finally catch on that there might be a connection between the raped, mutilated ex-virgins turning up at Manhattan General. Miraculously, the victims recover and set off — stark naked — for the monster's lair, where they will deliver its offspring. The cop and Doc find the nest, a sort of hot tub filled with some creamy, viscous substance and, as often happens in this kind of movie, things wrap up in about two minutes, with little action or suspense. There are some moderately good effects, even though the budget precluded adequate creature footage, and we do get to see a great deal of the putative virgins. From the video schlockmeister who gave us **ROBOT HOLOCAUST** and *Bad Girls Dormitory*.

Entombed Aliens

TIME WALKER *(1982)*
wr Tom Friedman and Karen Levitt; dir Tom Kennedy

A mummy found in a previously undiscovered chamber in King Tut's tomb turns out to be an ailing alien that the Egyptians buried 3,000 years ago. Revived by a dose of X-ray radiation, it wanders around the campus of the Science Institute looking for the crystals stolen from the sarcophagus that it needs to return home. As an added bonus, an alien fungus has inhabited the mummy's bandages and consumes the flesh of anyone who touches it. A combination of *Chariots of the Gods* and *The Andromeda Strain* with the living-mummy motif from various classic horror films, this has a concept that, treated with some playfulness and energy, could have been a lot of fun. Done straight, as it is here, the result is earnest, dull, and old-fashioned. Matters are not helped by the fact that the mummy and the alien inside it are, you might say, kept under wraps. Alternate title: *Time Waster*.

MUNCHIES *(1987)*
wr Lance Smith; dir Bettina Hirsch

A very cheap *Gremlins* clone produced by Roger Corman. A small alien creature, discovered in an Incan ruin, is taken home and soon starts to cause havoc. It gets chopped into four pieces, each regenerating into a new creature, and the four little monsters really go on a tear. The Munchies, as they are dubbed, have lots of teeth and the instincts of sociopathic 12-years-olds: they like to go joy-riding, eat junk food, and look up girls' dresses. Actually, they're kind of amusing, but most of the footage ignores them, focusing instead on the kind of cartoon characters, dumb routines, and cheap gags commonly found in "comedy" skits on TV variety shows. Young kids might like this one, but there's not much to chew on here for the more demanding.

Aliens — '50s Style

STRANGE INVADERS *(1983)*
wr William Condon and Michael Laughlin; dir Michael Laughlin

The premise here is that all those ridiculous tabloid stories about aliens in our midst are actually true. In fact, the visitors have been here for 25 years, doing field-work, with the reluctant cooperation of the government. A nifty little idea — kind of an '80s version of '50s sci-fi — and it is enhanced by a really fine look and style. There's a good cast (Paul LeMat, Diana Scarwid, Nancy Allen, Louise Fletcher, Michael Lerner, Fiona Lewis), impressive alien-makeup effects, and a few nice bits of humor. Regrettably, the script barely limps along, failing to generate any suspense or sustain forward motion, and doesn't take much advantage of the premise's comic possibilities. The result, then, is more than a little disappointing — a movie more interesting for what it might have been.

INVADERS FROM MARS *(1986)*
wr Dan O'Bannon and Don Jakoby; dir Tobe Hooper

I don't understand why anyone would want to remake a modest piece of sci-fi from 1953 with limited nostalgic value, and spend megabucks to do it. Apparently, since this movie returned less than $2 million in North American rentals, no one else saw the point of it either. The story is generally faithful to the original, in which a young boy (Hunter Carson) sees a spaceship set down behind his house and its occupants take over his parents and the other townspeople to do their bidding. The glossy look of this film doesn't make up for the lack of real tension or suspense; the effects are big, but not really impressive; the creatures seem more peculiar than scary or amusing; and there is scarcely any humor or irony in the script to liven things up. Indeed, about the only reason to watch this one is to see Louise Fletcher, in what is surely one of the most

> *"The endless stairway will lead us to the center of the earth. Follow me."*
> HERCULES

embarrassing roles ever undertaken by a former Oscar-winner, devour a large live frog and then get eaten herself by a giant walking head. Really.

MONSTER IN THE CLOSET *(1986)*
wr and dir Bob Dahlen

This is from the folks at Troma Team, who specialize in lousy movies with irresistible titles (*Fat Guy Goes Nutzoid*, **SURF NAZIS MUST DIE**). The surprise here is that this one is pretty good, an '80s update of those great, classically bad sci-fi films of the '50s: a large and terrible creature appears from outer space to threaten life-as-we-know-it; no one knows what's happening at first; the monster does its destruction-panic-chaos thing; the authorities realize there is a problem and call out the army (lots of ineffectual tanks and jeeps); the monster seems unstoppable, and civilization doomed; one man figures out the way to defeat the creature and save the planet. Part parody and part tribute to the genre, this movie has all of the clichés and conventions down perfectly, and generally manages to walk an exceedingly narrow line, making the deliberately clunky and stupid amusing rather than annoying. Lots of familiar faces turn up in cameo parts (Claude Aikens, Howard Duff, John Carradine, Henry Gibson, Jesse White, and a briefly bare-breasted Stella Stevens). They have no trouble giving appropriately clichéd, overdrawn performances, and the result is a professional sheen not usually found in Troma Team offerings. Similar in style and intent to *Crimewave*, this movie is not quite as energetic or wildly clever, but it does provide a pleasantly silly 90 minutes.

NOT OF THIS EARTH *(1988)*
wr R.J. Robertson and Jim Wynorski; dir Jim Wynorski

Devoted recycler Roger Corman produced this remake of his own 1956 trash classic that many regard as his most entertaining sci-fi film. The writers of the original version (Charles Griffith and Mark Hanna) are cited in both the opening and the closing credit rolls, and this makes scarcely any changes in the story of an alien vampire (Arthur Roberts) who comes to earth to test the quality of human blood to determine if the planet should be subjugated and "pastured" as a food supply. About all that's missing is the charm, humor, and pace of the original, and about all that's been added are some unfunny jokes and a few large-breasted bimbos to flash what they've got — ex-porn star Traci Lords has the lead as the nurse. Besides the tits, the best part of this one is the opening-credit montage of monsters from earlier Corman films of the '80s, including **FORBIDDEN WORLD** and **HUMANOIDS FROM THE DEEP**, but, in retrospect it serves to point out what was omitted here. Another disappointing lump from the director who did the same to swords and sleazery in **DEATHSTALKER II**.

Unseen Aliens

THE TRIPODS *(1986, British, made for TV)*
wr Alick Rowe; dir Graham Theakston and Christopher Barry

Based upon a trilogy of novels by John Christopher, this movie is set 2089, about 100 years after the earth was taken over by Tripods — giant, three-legged ambulatory tanks whose origins are never explained and whose occupants are never shown. All we're told is that they have destroyed earth's cities and civilization, reducing life to what looks to be the technological level of the 18th Century. The aliens maintain their rule by "capping" all adults — installing a comb-like object in the skull that causes passivity and obedience. The story centers on two British farmboys who refuse to be capped and run away to find the last stronghold of free men in the mountains of France. Along the way, they are joined by a young Frenchman, and the trio has all sorts of adventures on the way to join the rebel forces. I don't know what the books are like, but this adaptation is a bore. It looks cheap, the characters are dull, the special effects are sparse and shabby, the dialog dreary, the adventures uninspired, and, at 2½ hours, there is at least an hour of padding. Proof that even the exalted BBC can produce tedious and mediocre televison.

REMOTE CONTROL *(1987, direct to cassette)*
wr and dir Jeff Lieberman

The hot item at the local video stores is a piece of '50s sci-fi trash called *Remote Control* about aliens taking over earth through the use of

> "It's only got two states — dangerous and dead."
> RAZORBACK

mind-control devices implanted in movies for home entertainment. Sure enough, anyone who watches the tape goes into a psychotic rage and slaughters everyone in the vicinity. Only Kevin Dillon and Deborah Goodrich realize what's going on, and it's up to them to try to destroy the tapes before the tapes erase humanity. A nice premise and the movie-within-a-movie in-a-movie is fun, but the material is thin and would have been more effective condensed to half an hour instead of expanded to an hour and a half. The first third is not bad, with a good low-budget look, decent performances, a few jokes, and some suspense. But it soon grows repetitious — yet another psychotic rage, another tape destroyed — and there aren't enough twists to keep up interest. Still, there is a little cleverness, energy, and creativity on display, which means that this cassette's probably not all that destructive to *your* mind.

ALIEN DEAD
BLOODSUCKERS FROM OUTER SPACE
NIGHT OF THE CREEPS
Alien-induced zoms; see Festival 7.

Alien Sludge

EVILS OF THE NIGHT *(1984)*
wr Mardi Rustam and Phillip D. Connors; dir Mardi Rustam

If you're in the mood for some seriously cheap and stupid sci-fi, just like they made in the 1950s, you'll have a hard time finding anything dimmer or dippier than this one. Three aliens — John Carradine, Tina Louise, and Julie Newmar (can you believe it?) — land on earth in order to extract blood platelets from the bodies of sex-obsessed young people to extend their own lives. They hire two lamebrained garage mechanics (Neville Brand! Aldo Ray!), cleverly disguised in ski masks, to grab the kid-victims while they're making out at the local lake. In practice, then, this is your basic psycho-in-the-woods: a few kids have sex, scream, then get grabbed and drained. This movie lurches from stupidity to inanity, to incoherence, and is propelled by a group of characters whose combined wattage wouldn't illuminate a refrigerator. A few unintended laughs, but not enough for serious turkey consideration.

BIOHAZARD *(1984)*
wr, prod, dir Fred Olen Ray

An homage to *Alien* by the '80s champ of cheapshit trash. A very large-breasted mindreader (Angelique Pettyjohn) brings in a package from another dimension containing a small guy in a rubber suit (Christopher Ray, presumably a family member), who proceeds to tear up the usual bunch of semi-pro overactors, bursting several oral blood capsules. As usual Fred O. keeps us guessing as to whether the stupidity and ineptitude were deliberate or the natural consequence of a what-the-hell, let-'er-fly, let's-get-this-sucker-in-the-can attitude. Not much here in terms of creatures, effects, splatter, suspense, or coherence, but there is a somewhat more sprightly form of dullness than Fred usually manages (perhaps he dropped into EDWACA [*see Bonus Festival*] for a refresher course). With Aldo Ray (any relation?) giving his usual subtle performance as an asshole general, Loren Crabtree as the bimbo with big tits who takes a gratuitous bath, and the director and Donald Jackson (**ROLLER BLADE**) as two medics. (Note: For another look at Angelique's major attributes, be sure to stick around for the out-takes during the closing credits.)

TERRORVISION *(1986)*
wr and dir Ted Nicolaou

Basically a yuppie **CRITTERS**. In some distant and bizarre galaxy mutants are disposed of by being converted into radio waves and beamed out into space. Naturally, something goes wrong; one of them is picked up by a suburban satellite dish, emerges through the television set, and begins to eat everything in sight. While this is supposed to be a comedy, the characters are all so unappealing that they are much more annoying than amusing. The production values and effects are fairly good but, in terms of horrible things that come out of a TV, the monster is much less off-putting than, say, commercials for various hygiene products. Mary Woronov, Bert Remsen, and Gerrit Graham all embarrass themselves.

PINK CHIQUITAS *(1986, Canadian)*
wr and dir Anthony Currie

More proof — as if more were needed — that there is nothing less funny than a comedy that doesn't make it. A meteor arrives from Uranus and

> *"There are no crazy people — we're all just on vacation."*
> ALONE IN THE DARK

turns the women of Beamsville into sex-starved Amazons, imbued with supernatural powers, who want to take over the world, and only Sly Stallone's brother, Frank, stands in their way. Eartha Kitt's voice, prominently featured in the credits as that of "Betty the Meteor," gurgles for about 45 seconds. Certainly not the worst movie ever made, but this one has a good shot at the short list. In 20 years or so, it could conceivably take on a patina of camp charm. Wait until then.

FESTIVAL 2

* * *

BIG GUYS, BIGFOOT, and BIG BORES
A Miscellany of Monsters

"Nature has a way of reminding man just how small he is."
— *Godzilla 1985*

The "monsters" featured in this festival are earth-spawned creatures who have long remained hidden from view. That they exist is generally unknown and unexpected until they make their presence felt, usually in some dramatic and emphatic fashion. These monsters may be freaks of nature, but, unlike the creatures in Festival 3, they are not recent mutations, but often have been immortalized in legends and folk tales — or at least so we're told. The movies these monsters appear in generally make little attempt to account for or to explain the monsters' origins. However, it is not uncommon for these monsters to be holdovers from some earlier period of earth's history ... or at least of moviemaking history.

King Kong (1933) put this kind of monster on the map, and they've been lumbering across it ever since. Willis O'Brien, the effects wizard responsible for the marvelous stop-motion animation in *Kong*, had already perfected the technique in a silent version of Arthur Conan Doyle's *The Lost World* (1925). This was the first dinosaur movie, a genre that has shown remarkable resilience over the decades with such titles as *When Dinosaurs Ruled the Earth* (1946), *The Beast from 20,000 Fathoms* (1953), *Journey to the Center of the Earth* (1959), *Dinosaurus* (1960), *Gorgo* (1961), *Reptilicus* (1962), *Valley of Gwangi* (1968), and *The Crater Lake Monster* (1977), not to mention numerous caveman epics in which dinosaurs have played supporting roles.

The Japanese, of course, have long been partial to large prehistoric creatures who live beneath the sea or on uncharted islands, though their monsters have more in common with fairy-tale dragons than with actual dinosaurs. Starting with Godzilla in 1954, they've treated us to a long list of low-rent behemoths — "Late Show" favorites with

> *'You guys ever see a baby like this?*
> IT'S ALIVE III

names like Gammera, Gargantuas, Gigan, Gigantis, Megalon, Mothra, and Rodan.

Although monsters are usually large, they don't have to be. Those of more diminutive stature have included the utterly hilarious Slime People (1962), Trog (befriended by Joan Crawford, in her last film appearance, in 1970), and one of the more popular creatures of the 1950s, the gilled denizen of the Black Lagoon (a close relative of whom can be found in this festival). From the filmmaker's point of view, there are certain advantages to monsters of modest size, the most obvious ones being that you don't need to trouble yourself with trick photography, large constructions, or miniature cities to be trampled, thus making for a creature that, if less than spectacular, is certainly cost effective.

In the 1980s, only one such monster — hairy Harry, run down by the Hendersons in 1987 — achieved any significant success, and he owed much more to E.T. than to any of his rampaging predecessors. From the evidence of this festival, it has not been a good decade for these blasts from the past. Perhaps we all agree with the Japanese prime minister who, upon learning that Godzilla was again among us, remarked, "I was hoping I'd never hear that name again."

However, there are few monsters — and their movies — that display a bit of vitality, so maybe the breed is not as moribund as it currently appears to be. Besides, as any cine-biologist knows, you can kill a rubber suit, but there will always be more latex.

The Brand Names

GODZILLA 1985 *(1985, Japanese, mostly dubbed)*
wr Shuichi Nagahara and Lisa Tomei; dir Koji Hasimoto and R.J. Kizer

Now, thirty years after he entrenched himself in our pop culture, the big guy is back and as pissed as ever at Tokyo. The budget is much bigger this time, but the monster and the effects are no less cheesy. Indeed, about all the glossier production accomplishes is the elimination of whatever camp charm the original possessed. This is basically a straight remake, and even includes inserts of Raymond Burr, looking almost as large as Godzilla himself, in which he intones such sentiments as "Nature has a way of reminding man just how small he is." Movies like this one have a way of reminding us just how gullible producers think we are. About the only reason to get this one is for Marv Newman's 90-second cartoon classic, *Bambi Meets Godzilla*, which New World thoughtfully provided before the opening credits.

KING KONG LIVES *(1986)*
wr Ronald Shusett and Steven Pressfield; dir John Guillermin

This is the sequel to the 1976 De Laurentiis remake which should never have been made — and things haven't improved. The world's most misunderstood giant primate still looks like a guy in an ape suit, and now we've added a second, modified, ape suit — this one with tits — for Mrs. Kong. This inert lump is not just stupid and dull, but maudlin enough to make you queasy. Absolutely the only reason to watch this one is to find out how KK could come back after dropping — with what seemed to be a certain finality — from the top of the World Trade Center. Let me do you a favor: the fall put him in a 10-year coma, from which he is revived by Linda Hamilton (*The Terminator*), who gives him an artificial heart the size of Toledo.

Legends Come to Life

GHOSTKEEPER *(1980, Canadian)*
wr James Makichuk and Douglas MacLeod; dir James Makichuk

Three very dull snowmobilers take shelter in an abandoned inn occupied by a strange old woman, her slasher son, and . . . something else. The something else is not the titular ghost, but a creature out of Indian legend called a windigo. A book conveniently left lying around identifies this creature as a "flesh-eating giant," which I guess makes it a kind of carnivorous bigfoot. I have to speculate because it's kept locked up and we never get to see it. *Never*. But the creature is not the only thing missing in this one. There is, likewise, no suspense, no tension and, from the murky look of things, no light source brighter than 25 watts.

Q *(1982)*
wr, prod, dir Larry Cohen

This is Larry Cohen's version of *King Kong*, with Quetzlcoatl, the flying feathered serpent of Aztec mythology, nesting at the top of the Chrysler Building. It, known as "Q" to its friends, flies over the city, biting the head off anyone unlucky enough to be on top of a skyscraper. Down on the ground, a true believer is performing human sacrifices in honor of the great flying god and, while police detective David Carradine tries to figure out what's going on, another "Q", Jimmy Quinn (Michael Moriarty), a small-time crook and full-time loser, sees this exploitable situation as his one chance to hit the big time. This typical Larry Cohen offering is at once very clever, quirky, and amusing and occasionally cheap and sloppy. Forget the ho-hum monster — from the glimpses we get of it, it looks like a flying brontosaurus — and watch the actors: Carradine gives a very funny deadpan performance, and Moriarty, who is usually either really good or really bad, is right on the mark here with his stunning portrayal of a two-bit hustler. The nice bits of humor and gore and the brisk pace make this quite an entertaining, above-average piece of trash. With Bobbi Burns as the topless sunbather snatched by Q.

JUNGLE HEAT *(1983)*
wr Gregory Weston King, Larry Johnson, and Michael Viner; dir Gus Trikonis

A stuffy but competent anthropologist (Deborah Raffin) hires a seedy, drunken, dissolute helicopter pilot (Peter Fonda) to take her to a research station deep in the Philippine jungle to look for a fabled lost tribe that turns out to be a bunch of anthropoid reptiles. Based on a Geoffrey Household novel, *Dance of the Dwarfs*, this doesn't know what kind of movie it wants to be. The first half, focusing on the misadventures of the mismatched pair, is a surprisingly amusing version of *The African Queen*; unfortunately, after they split up, the movie lurches into a very lame monster flick, lacking suspense, explanations, and lighting. It's too dim to make out what the creatures look like, and, in fact, the movie might have been better without them. As it is, this heatless effort ends up lost in the jungle.

NIGHT OF THE DEMON *(1983)*
wr Mike Williams; dir James C. Wasson

No demon here, but there is Bigfoot — and this one is a large anthropoid, covered in long fur that looks a little like the cheap nylon shag of which toilet-seat covers are made. The group of lamebrains from the university who go into the woods to track him down discover that the guy most emphatically does not like company. He does, however, like to cause severe bodily harm — yanking out intestines, pulling off arms, and tearing open throats. Although this is a very cheap, amateurish effort — badly plotted, with dreadful dialog and comparable acting — it is certainly enthusiastic in its mayhem and, with about a dozen victims, it makes the most of oozing, smearing, and spurting blood. Shoddy and mindless, perhaps, but you can't be too hard on any movie that hacks up a pair of Girl Scouts and rips off a guy's testicles while he's taking a piss. With Sally Swift as the naked girl who apparently screams herself to death.

BABY — SECRET OF THE LOST LEGEND *(1985)*
wr Clifford and Ellen Green; dir B.W.L. Norton

While doing research in West Africa, a junior paleontologist (Sean Young) and her sportswriter husband (William Katt) discover that the native legends surrounding a brontosaurus family living in the jungle are true. An evil paleontologist (Patrick McGoohan), also on their trail, kills the male and captures the female, leaving Sean and Bill to look after the baby, which they name, cleverly enough, "Baby." What ensues is a chase through the bush to protect Baby and rescue Mom. This might have raised some interesting ethical/ecological issues, but what we get is your basic old-fashioned jungle adventure with friendly natives, nasty soldiers, and lots of shoot-'em-up and explosions. The dinosaurs look pretty good in long shot, but strictly plastic-phony in the numerous close-ups. Even worse, the cold-blooded reptiles with brains the size of walnuts are anthropomorphized into Shirley Temple cutesiness. While not quite as maudlin as **KING KONG LIVES**, this registers pretty high on the soppy-and-sappy index. Maybe young kids won't mind, but for everyone else, this is one legend better left unfounded.

> *"Golly! If the girls back home could see me now."*
> BO DEREK IN TARZAN, THE APE MAN

THE STRANGENESS *(1985)*
wr David Michael Hillman and Chris Huntley; dir David Michael Hillman

Five young amateur actors and two older amateur actors go into an abandoned goldmine that, according to Indian legend, is inhabited by an evil spirit. About halfway through — the movie, not the mine — they start to get bumped off, and it becomes clear that something nasty lives in there. Since we're underground, a good part of the movie consists of spots of light moving across an otherwise black screen. The creature, which has an on-screen presence of maybe 30 seconds, looks like a mound of intestines (or maybe white sausages), with a few loose tentacles flapping in stop-motion (more stop than motion). This is strictly a cheap backyard movie — nothing that you and your friends couldn't easily do just as well with access to a mine shaft and 20 pounds of weisswurst. Early on, someone says, "How did we get stuck in this mess?" Unless you want to ask the same question, pass on this one.

(Note: There is another monster-in-a-mine movie called *The Boogens* [1981] that probably served as the model for the preceding piece-o-shit. I saw it when it first came out, but have failed to locate it in over a dozen video stores. My recollection is that there were some briefly seen tentacles, but nothing worth making a quest to find it.)

THE QUEST *(1986, Australian)*
wr Everett DeRoche; dir Brian Trenchard-Smith

Henry Thomas, fresh from his encounter with E.T., heads to Australia where he runs into a monster out of aboriginal legend called the "donkegin." The creature lives in a lake in an abandoned quarry, and a good part of the movie documents Henry's attempts to see it. Almost nothing else happens in this one, and the few things that do aren't all that interesting. Henry does a decent job as the adventurous, resourceful kid, and the movie's not badly made, but there's really nothing here to catch and hold your interest. Hell, even the monster gets explained away in the end. From the director of **DEAD-END DRIVE IN**, who should know better.

RAWHEAD REX *(1986, British)*
wr Clive Barker; dir George Pavlou

Adapted by Clive Barker from one of the stories in his *Books of Blood*, the movie features a title creature about eight feet tall, with a muscular body out of a Frazetta drawing, glowing red eyes, and a fang-filled snout like a slavering baboon's. It seems he was worshiped as some kind of god in neolithic times, but has been imprisoned underground ever since. Needless to say, he gets out at the top of the movie and — boy! — is he pissed off. The action largely consists of Rawhead roaming around the Irish countryside, breathing heavily and ripping off people's heads while all the humans wonder what the hell's going on. There's barely any plot — and what there is is pretty dumb — but the creature has enough energy and charisma (much more than any of the other characters) to make for some good, gory, mindless fun.

DEMON OF PARADISE *(1987)*
wr Frederick Bailey; dir Cirio H. Santiago

A herpetologist (Kathryn Witt) looking for a new species of lizard in an isolated part of Hawaii finds more than she bargained for when Akua, a mythological superstition, rears its seaweed-covered head. As our lady scientist explains, Akua seems to be the long-sought-for missing link between reptiles and apes (in practice, yet another guy in a really crummy rubber suit). Talk about your throwbacks! With the exception of 30 seconds of bimbo toplessness, there's absolutely nothing in this one that couldn't have been (and probably was) lifted intact from the creature features of the '50s. Only for viewers similarly time-warped.

An Amorphous Monster

THE STUFF *(1985)*
wr and dir Larry Cohen

"The Stuff" is a living, yogurt-like substance that is discovered seeping up from the ground and quickly becomes the latest dessert sensation, so addictively delicious that those who get hooked can never get enough. But as people are eating it, it's eating them (from the inside out), first taking over their minds, then consuming their bodies. Part spoof of, part homage to '50s sci-fi films, this is kind of a cross between *Invasion of the Body Snatchers* and the original *Blob*, with a satirical edge turned to big business, corporate cynicism, advertising, and the public's craze mentality. As in most of Cohen's films, there are enough twists that your're never entirely sure where things are headed as they move along, briskly, if not always logically. There are some intriguingly odd characters (especially Michael Moriarty as an industrial saboteur), a number of good lines, and some nice off-center humor. A few of the effects are good, but most are not very impressive, and were probably never meant to be. All in all, this one's a little too sloppy to really work, but it is frequently amusing and it does keep you interested.

Little Monsters

THE PIT *(1981)*
wr Ian A. Stuart; dir Lew Lehman

Twelve-year-old Jamie's got more than the usual range of problems: he's a loner; he's socially maladjusted; he's a junior voyeur; and when he talks to his teddy bear, it answers. And if all that weren't enough, Jamie is the only one who knows about the little hole in the ground in the woods inhabited by four strange little creatures that he calls Trogs, but that most resemble anthropoid badgers. Discovering that the creatures are voraciously carnivorous, he realizes that they are the perfect way to get rid of all the townspeople he dislikes. So what we have is kind of a cross between *The Bad Seed* and **CRITTERS** — a combo silly enough to provide inadvertent amusement, but so badly done as to be, to take the easy shot, the pits.

BRAIN DAMAGE *(1987)*
wr and dir Frank Henenlotter

The long awaited followup to **BASKET CASE** demonstrates that this writer/director has no peer when it come to movies about symbiotic relationships with mutant parasitic lifeforms. Here, it's a young man named Brian (Rick Herbst) who wakes up to discover that a foot-long talking worm-like creature has attached itself to him. We eventually learn, in one of the loopiest homages ever to *The Maltese Falcon*, that the creature is called the "Aylmer," and has been travelling from host to host for at least 700 years. In exchange for injecting a marvelous hallucinogen into its host's brain, the Aylmer incites its host to find it victims, from whom it sucks brains. Although Brian is repelled by what he's doing, he is hooked on the Aylmer's "juice," and thus has no choice but to comply with the worm's wishes. Either a subtly symbolic parable about crack or an excuse for 90 minutes of brainsuckings, juice-injections, and high-spirited weirdness, this is slicker and not quite as wildly demented as **BASKET CASE**, but delivers a fair amount of good gory fun and lots of little jokes (including an appearance by Kevin VanHentenryck with his basket, and a credit thanking the "J. Franco House of Pain"). Whatever this is, it's not quite like anything else, and we can only hope that it will not take another five years for Henenlotter to produce his next exercise in enthusiastic excess. (Not to be confused with the Al Adamson piece-o-shit with the same title in Festival 4.)

An Absentee Monster

BLOOD BEACH *(1980)*
wr and dir Jeffrey Bloom

Something is living under the Santa Monica pier, sucking the sun-'n-surf set into the sand in this dull, fraudulent excuse for a monster flick. This one is all chat and no creature, as Burt Young, John Saxon, David Huffman, and Mariana Hill desperately try to fill the spaces between infrequent sand-suckings while disguising the fact that *nothing* is happening. When the creature finally appears — for all of 10 seconds — it looks a little like an animate artichoke. At one point, a newscaster describes the situation on the beach as "a seemingly endless nightmare" and you're bound to agree if you let yourself get sucked into this one. With Stefan Gierasch as the world's slowest-talking coroner.

FESTIVAL 3

* * *

CHANGES FOR THE WORSE
A Mustering of Mutations

> "Oh shit! It's one of them!"
> — *It's Alive III*

Movie mutations are creatures, originally animal or human, that have physically altered from their customary form. Sometimes the mutants are born that way, but more commonly normal organisms undergo change. The mutations can spontaneously occur as a result of environmental factors; they can be the deliberate aim of scientific experiment; or they can be the inadvertent outcome of a lab accident or an experiment turned sour. Whatever the cause, the result is never an improvement.

As movie creatures go, mutations are definitely a post-Second World War phenomenon. The only exceptions, as far as I can determine, are the humans shrunk to tiny size in *The Devil-Doll* (1936) and *Dr. Cyclops* (1940), the animals turned into manimals in *The Island of Lost Souls* (1932), and the hybrid Chula the Ape/Pauline the Woman from three movies made in the mid-'40s.

In the 1950s, though, mutations reared their generally oversized heads and quickly became the dominant type of creature in a decade that suffered from no shortage of strange monsters. Some of the notable transformations include the modified humans in *The Creeping Unknown* (1956), *The Alligator People* (1959), the *Monster on the Campus* (1958), *The Sun Demon* (1959), *The She Creature* (1956), *She Demons* (1958), *The Wasp Woman* (1959), and of course *The Fly* (1958).

Impressive (?) though these specimens were, the era was definitely one in which bigger was better — in automobile tail fins and in monsters. Starting with the giant ants of *Them!* (1954), there was a seemingly endless procession of megamutations — scorpions, crabs, praying mantises, gila monsters, grasshoppers, octopi, shrews, tarantulas, a colossal man, a 50-foot woman, and a micro-variant — the shrinking man to whom the whole world came in the large economy size.

These bountiful beasts disappeared during the '60s, but a few hesitantly reemerged in the '70s with giant rabbits (*Night of the Lepus*, 1972), a *Giant Spider Invasion* (1975), big chickens and other barnyard inhabitants (*Food of the Gods*, 1976), Joan Collins and the *Empire of the Ants* (1977), and one even sidled into this festival with **ISLAND CLAWS**. All of which, I guess, goes to show that you can never underestimate the low-budget appeal of trick photography and rear-screen projection.

Thus far, the mutation with the biggest box-office appeal has been David Cronenberg's astonishing 1986 remake of *The Fly*. In terms of gruesome effects, this may well be one of the most profoundly disgusting movies ever made. It may also be one of the most truly creepy, but not significantly more so than many of Cronenberg's other films. With *Shivers* (1975), *Rabid* (1977), *The Brood* (1979), and *Videodrome* (1983), he has specialized in unflinchingly presenting the "horrors of the body" and has won wide recognition as one of the contemporary masters of horror fantasy. If you're not familiar with Cronenberg's work, considered too well-known for inclusion in this book, there are some rather nasty treats waiting for you in the video store. He has an absolutely unique and distinctive vision, and while the quality of his movies is somewhat uneven, they are all interesting, powerful, and definitely not for the squeamish.

Considering the kind of horror stories that appear in today's daily newspapers — pollution, toxic waste, chemical/biological warfare, the destruction of the environment, killer viruses, and the creation of new lifeforms through genesplicing — the movies that follow can almost be regarded as comic relief. Certainly they seem to represent ways of coping with what are very real fears and concerns. And, since there is no indication that we're eliminating the cause of these concerns, it seems likely that mutations will become an even more prevalent form of movie creature. As someone remarks in **IT'S ALIVE III**, "They're being born faster than we can kill 'em."

Killer Creations

SCARED TO DEATH *(1980)*
wr and dir William Malone

An experiment in genetic engineering goes out of control and dumps a new lifeform into the sewers of Los Angeles. It's called Syngenor (Synthetic Genetic Organism), and it's about eight feet of humanoid armored iguana that feeds on human spinal fluid, which it obtains by French kissing its victims with a needle-sharp tongue. The creature was obviously influenced, positively, by *Alien*, and the scenes involving Syngenor are fairly effective. Unfortunately, as is too often the case, the rest of the movie is little more than filler to separate the appearances of the monster. Still, with what must have been an extremely low budget, this is not bad at all, and if you zip through all the boring chat, it will deliver a few good moments.

PARASITE *(1982)*
wr Alan J. Adler, Michael Shoob, and Frank Levering; dir Charles Band

Set in the California desert in a post-apocalyptic near future, a scientist (Robert Glaudini) is on the run from the "Merchants," who want the pair of deadly parasites he's developed, one of which is in a canister, and the other, in his abdomen, growing in and feeding on him. The parasites are giant, toothy, flesh-eating worms, and the scientist has to find a way to kill them before they reproduce and destroy humanity. Since this was originally released in 3-D, the worms like to leap at the camera, and we are treated not just to an *Alien*-like belly-bursting, but to a head-burster as well. The effects are passable and occasionally fairly messy, but there aren't very many of them. Glaudini and Demi Moore (in an early appearance as the spunky young woman who helps him) give acceptable performances, but the pace is slow and the movie never generates the necessary tension and momentum. Not without a few good moments, but nothing special.

FORBIDDEN WORLD *(1982)*
wr Tim Curnen; dir Allan Holzman

On the distant planet of Xarbia, scientists doing genetic manipulations in an attempt to create an alternative food supply discover that they're on the menu when one of their experiments gets a little out of hand. This Roger Corman production borrows its set-up and metamorphosing monster from *Alien*, its sets from **GALAXY OF TERROR**, and its dogfight in space from **BATTLE BEYOND THE STARS**; what it lacks in originality, it compensates for with goo and gore. The creature is typical Corman low-budget — nothing very special — but there are some extraordinarily messy decomposing corpses, an unanesthetized liver removal, and a vomiting monster, all of which will probably catch your attention. To fill in the spaces in the nonexistent plot, Dawn Dunlop and June Chadwick each twice gratuitously removes her clothes. Dumb, suspenseless, derivative, exploitative, and disgusting — in short, a pretty good time.

DEEP SPACE *(1987, direct to cassette)*
wr Fred Olen Ray and T.L. Lankford; dir Fred Olen Ray

The satellite being used to store deadly creatures developed by the military tumbles to earth, and they get loose near Los Angeles, shredding, draining, and sliming anyone who gets close. The young of the species resemble lizard-headed scorpions, while Mama could be Alien's younger cousin; both look pretty good, if not very original, and clearly no expense was spared when it came to tentacles and bodily fluids. Once again, though, the problem is not the creature, but everything else. The plot is mindless and mechanical, with the police, the military, and the scientists vying for top honors in stupidity. Although slightly livelier and not as cheap as some of this director's other efforts (**SCALPS, ALIEN DEAD**), this production isn't exactly what you'd call fast-moving or glossy. Still, if you fast-forward, you'll find some vigorous splatter, especially the final battle in which Charles Napier takes a chainsaw to the critter and gets gored up nicely in return. With Julie Newmar as the psychic, without whose advice the movie never would have ended.

THE BLOB *(1988)*
wr Chuck Russel and Frank Darabont; dir Chuck Russel

This big budget, hi-tech remake of the 1958 trash classic stiffed at the box office, returning less than a quarter of its $15 million cost, but it's certainly worth checking out at home. In structure and style, it's a faithful reproduction of the good old-fashioned creature feature, with the addition

> "It's your fault, doctor — you and your lousy experiments."
> ALIEN PREDATOR

of a little contemporary humor and irony and a lot of contemporary gross-out effects — including an abundance of pink, tentacled slime; a number of folks digested and dissolved inside the title amorphoid; and, maybe the highlight, a guy sucked down a sink drain, head first. For the rest, there are some nice little jokes, a great many references to other films, from *The Birds* to *E.T.*, slick production values, and a brisk pace. Not as disgusting as John Carpenter's version of *The Thing* or as creepy as Cronenberg's remake of *The Fly*, but this delivers a fair amount of good gooey fun. From the director of *Nightmare on Elm Street III*, with Kevin Dillon (in the Steve McQueen role) and Shawnee Smith as the teens who save Arborville.

BIOHAZARD
No toxicity, cheapshit other-world rubber suit; see Festival 1.

Subterranean Terrors

C.H.U.D. *(1985)*
wr Parnell Hall; dir Douglas Cheek

An acronym for "Cannibalistic Humanoid Underground Dwellers"; in other words, a bunch of horribly mutated monsters are living in the tunnels and drains far below the streets of New York. While the concept certainly is appealing, the execution is too feeble to carry it. The production values are decent, the look is pretty good, and there is one good actor (John Heard). The script, though, is at best run of the mill, and the other performances barely that. While definitely above average, this should/could have been a lot better, and thus disappoints slightly. The creatures — melting flesh, sharp teeth, and glowing eyes — are effectively gruesome, but we don't see enough of them. Probably worth renting as long as expectations are not too high.

TRANSMUTATIONS *(1985, British)*
wr Clive Barker and James Caplin; dir George Pavlou

A strange drug developed by an even stranger scientist (Denholm Elliott) causes euphoric hallucinations, greatly increased strength, and an insensitivity to pain. So appealing is the high that those hooked on the drug continue to use it even though it also causes their faces to break out in horrible lumps and pustules. When the mutants kidnap a beautiful young prostitute (Nicola Cowper) — the only addict not deformed — her former lover (Larry Lamb), an ex-enforcer for a big-time gangster, goes looking for her. Although well acted and very slickly and stylishly shot, this one lacks the necessary zip. The next Barker-Pavlou collaboration, **RAWHEAD REX**, was much less ambitious but a lot more fun.

BLUE MONKEY *(1987)*
wr George Goldsmith; dir William Fruet

There are no simians in this one, blue or otherwise, but there is a seven-foot-tall insect — kind of a slime-dripping praying mantis — running around the basement of a hospital. Upstairs, a deadly bacteria has placed the hospital under quarantine. Two doctors (Susan Anspach, Gwynyth Walsh) are at work on the problems, and a police detective (Steve Railsback) is visiting his wounded partner. There are also various subplots, involving the hospital administrator (John Vernon), some annoying old ladies, some even more annoying kids, and a comic-relief couple (Joe Flaherty, Robin Duke) in the maternity ward. Outside, of course, the army is ready to blow up the place to keep the infection from spreading. What all this adds up to is about 20 minutes of fairly good stuff starring the insect buried beneath heaps of clichés mined from old monster movies. Presumably meant to be a humourous pastiche, much like **MONSTER IN THE CLOSET**, it's been played so straight that it becomes as clunky as the movies it's parodying. Still, the monster, clearly an offspring of Alien, is not bad, and you can fast-forward through the bullshit between the few effectively gross moments.

Small Packages

BASKET CASE *(1982)*
wr and dir Frank Henenlotter

This tender story of a young man named Duane (Kevin VanHentenryck) and his mutant Siamese twin, Belial, who he carries around in a basket

> *"I want the beasts of the forest. That's the only home for me."*
> LIONMAN II

like a cat, has earned a fairly vigorous cult following. When the twins were separated some years earlier by a skilled surgical team made up of veterinarians (James Herriot take note), Belial did not die as expected, and now wants revenge on the vets. The mutant is small but very strong, and before chewing up his victims, likes to tear out their tongues; he communicates with Duane telepathically, and is also jealous of him, feeling more than a little sibling sexual rivalry. So when Duane is attracted to one vet's bimbo receptionist and the feeling is returned ("Take me, Duane," she says, at a moment of high passion), Belial gives Duane a long-distance headache, and the poor kid remains horny and virginal. Very cheap, with some appallingly bad acting, this movie possesses a ton of energy, and enough effective moments, enthusiastic gore, and humor to give it a loopy sort of tasteless appeal. Joe Bob Briggs, the preeminent drive-in-movie critic, moved this right to the top of his Best of '82 List, and I'm not going to argue with J.B.

IT'S ALIVE III: ISLAND OF THE ALIVE *(1986)*
wr and dir Larry Cohen

A nervous cop says early on, "Oh Shit! It's one of them!", and indeed it is. Nearly a decade after we last saw them in *It Lives Again* (1978), the famous monster babies are back, and none too soon. At the time of Alive III's video release, *Three Men and a Baby* and *She's Having a Baby* were still in the theaters on the saccharine trail of *Baby Boom*. Talk about your welcome antidotes. One thing about Larry Cohen, while his movies may be silly and dumb — and this one is often both — he knows how to keep your interest and how to keep you from predicting where the story's going. I don't want to spoil the fun, so I'll just say the kids are growing up, and they are mightily annoyed. There's lots of blood, but the violence is largely left to our imaginations, as are the frisky little mutants themselves, who only appear long enough to give us a sense of their toothy charm. A little sluggish and sloppy in places, but there's humor, satire, and the kind of subversive quirkiness that distinguishes almost all of Cohen's movies. With Cohen's favorite actor, Michael Moriarty, as one of the proud parents.

A Meteoric Mutagen

THE CURSE *(1987)*
wr David Chasin; dir David Keith

A strange meteorite-like object crashes at an isolated farm in Tennessee. Only it's not a meteorite, and it soon dissolves, its disgusting green-brown interior fluid seeping into the ground, then into the farm's water supply. First the water tastes funny. Then the fruit and vegetables become weirdly decayed or filled with revolting-looking worms. Then the animals start to act strange, and become violent. Finally, the people on the farm develop ugly sores on their faces, and they too become deranged and violent. The local doctor eventually has the water tested, and some unknown mutagen is discovered in it — too late. There are a few problems with structure and pacing in this one, and things fall apart — literally — at the end, but the movie displays a degree of professional competence, and the creepiness is genuine, somewhat reminiscent of David Cronenberg's biological horrors. (And speaking of reminiscent, those familiar with the works of H.P. Lovecraft will notice a striking similarity to his terrific story "The Colour Out of Space," which for whatever reason is neither credited nor acknowledged.) With Claude Akins and Wil Wheaton.

Coastal Creatures

HUMANOIDS FROM THE DEEP *(1980)*
wr Frederick James; dir Barbara Peeters

Reminiscent, in title and structure, of the tacky creature features from the '50s, there's nothing old-fashioned about this tale of aquatic mutants with a penchant for ripping people apart and a yen for bouncing, bikinied young honeys. The creatures, the result of a little genetic tampering that got out of control, were designed by Rob Bottin (*The Howling*) as a kind of amphibious sasquatch (Big Webfoot?) — a nifty assemblage of long arms, dorsal fins, and a mouth crammed with sharp teeth. They turn up at a fishing village in the northwest, where they try to eliminate their human competition and reproduce themselves by raping the town's young

> *"I guess a career in the police didn't really prepare you for this, did it?"*
> THE HIDDEN

women. With a reasonably good script, fast pacing, decent acting, slick production values, gobs of gore, and a goodly number of young women carefully cast for their abundant talents, this one works hard to deliver the goods and generally succeeds. With Vic Morrow as the town jerk and Linda Shayne as the winner of the "Miss Salmon" contest who loses her bikini top.

ISLAND CLAWS *(1980)*
wr Jack Cowden and Ricou Browning; dir Hernan Cardenas

On an island off the coast of Florida, an accident at the local nuclear power plant affects a research project involving crab growth to produce a critter the size of a ranch house. This one's something of a curiosity — a faithful replication of all those giant-animal movies from the mid-'50s, without the essential wit, humor, irony, or acknowledgement of its roots. This has all the faults of its predecessors — the monster crab doesn't appear until the final ten minutes, after endless boring and pointless subplots and dull, dull, dull conversation — and none of their redeeming camp virtues. Students of stupid, mechanical, unoriginal filmmaking might find this of marginal interest, but anyone with a taste for King Krab would do better to wait for Roger Corman's *Attack of the Crab Monsters* to turn up on the "Late Show."

THE KINDRED *(1986)*
wr Stephen Carpenter, Jeffrey Obrow, John Penney, Earl Ghaffari and Joseph Stefano; dir Jeffrey Obrow and Stephen Carpenter

When his mother, a brilliant scientist, dies, John (David Allen Brooks), a researcher himself, is surprised to learn that he has a brother named Anthony and even more surprised that Anthony is large, tentacled, and very hostile. The result of a gene-splicing experiment gone awry, bro is some kind of human-octopodan hybrid that lives in the basement of Mom's isolated country house, and he's not exactly pleased when John and his grad-student assistants arrive to terminate the experiment. Forget the plot. With five writers credited, this splice of what seems to be three different stories was performed somewhat less successfully than Anthony's. It's cliché-ridden and doesn't make much sense, but it does at least move along briskly and eventually takes us to one of the more impressive — and messier — of Alien's descendants. This slimespurter really lets 'er fly, and whoever had the goo concession on this one has probably comfortably retired. The acting and the production values are pretty decent, and, as a bonus, we have Rod Steiger as a ridiculously hammy Mad Scientist. All in all, what with Rod and Anthony, the chuckles and energetic excess net good value for your rental.

Marsh Mutants

THE SWAMP THING *(1982)*
wr and dir Wes Craven

With a credit acknowledging that the movie is based upon characters from DC Comics, it's not surprising that this has a real comicbook feel to it. What is puzzling is that no self-irony or -awareness was used in the process, so what we end up with is a faithful, humorless rendition of a '50s creature feature. The story concerns a scientist who's "developing a plant with the instincts of an animal" — meaning, I guess, if you don't eat your broccoli, it might eat you. After a lab accident, the scientist turns into the Vegetableman of the title, and roams the watery wastes, performing good deeds. Since the creature is another guy in a lousy rubber suit, most of the movie's attention is wisely devoted to government agent Adrienne Barbeau's impressive chest, which moves much more vigorously than the story. There's even a brief (and distant) topless sequence, but as far as ambulatory vegetation goes, the walking tree in *From Hell It Came* (1957) is much more entertaining.

TERROR IN THE SWAMP *(1984)*
wr Billy Holliday; dir Joseph J. Catalanotto

The original title for this one was *Nutriaman, the Copasaw Creature*, which I trust gives you some idea of what we're dealing with here. A nutria, in case you don't know, is an aquatic rodent, also called a coypu, that is trapped for its fur. Researchers, using grown hormones to create a super-nutria for the bigger pelt, produce a guy in a ten-buck-a-day nylon-shag ape suit. It was thus not without reason that the filmmakers decided to give only a two-second glimpse on the creature. The rest of the time is devoted to a lot of swamp travel and good ol' boys hunting, fishing, drinking beer, and shooting their guns off. Dull and dumb, this backyard Louisiana cheapie is strictly swamp gas.

Tromaville Transformations

THE TOXIC AVENGER *(1984)*
wr Joe Ritter; dir Michael Herz and Samuel Weil (Lloyd Kaufman)

The setting here is Tromaville, proudly known as "the toxic-waste capital of the world." When Melvin, a 98-pound nerd, falls into a barrel of particularly noxious stuff, he mutates into the title character, a monster superhero dedicated to destroying evil wherever he finds it. This is a typical offering from the schlockmeisters at Troma Team — a high-level concept deflated by a low-budget and a very haphazard execution. Clearly a cartoonish parody, there's a lot of action and violence and some fairly impressive gore effects that are not meant to be taken very seriously. Unfortunately, although there are few funny bits, too much of the "humor" and the acting are on the level of the sophomoronic teen comedies descended from *Porky's*. Sure, this has something of a cult following, and sure, it's tough to resist a title like this, but I was disappointed, and found it too sloppy and heavy-handy to be genuinely amusing. With Cindy Manion as the bimbo who takes her top off once and Jennifer Baptist as the bimbo who takes her top off twice.

CLASS OF NUKE 'EM HIGH *(1986)*
wr Richard W. Haines, Mark Rudnitsky, Lloyd Kaufman, Stuart Strutin; dir Richard W. Haines and Samuel Weil (Lloyd Kaufman)

Further adventures in the town of Tromaville — this time a high school located next to a leaking nuclear power plant and some marijuana grown in radioactive waste. The killer weed delivers an "atomic high" and briefly turns clean-cut Warren (Gilbert Brenton) into another hulking avenger. It also causes virginal Chrissie (Janelle Brady) to reveal the measure of her talents, and later to vomit up a rather large, nasty tadpole. Said critter gets flushed down the toilet, munches on a nuclear spill in the school basement, and quickly grows into a toothy, slime-dripping tentacled monster that bears more than a passing resemblance to Alien. Some faces are familiar from **THE TOXIC AVENGER**, as are some of the meager strengths: a few good gross-out effects and a few funny bits — the highlight being a rendering of "The Star-Spangled Banner" by a band of nightmarish punks who call themselves The Cretins. Mostly, though, there's just a lot of relentlessly low-brow humor and very shabby production values. With more energy and wit, this could have been a nifty black comedy, but as it is, this class barely earns passing marks.

Other Toxic Towns

MUTANT *(1983)*
wr Peter Z. Orton, Michael Jones and John C. Kruze; dir John "Bud" Cardos

This is your basic toxic-waste-pollution-causing-a-town-to-get-very-weird movie, familiar territory for the director who earlier gave us mutated tarantulas in *Kingdom of the Spiders* (1977). Not really awful, but, at 100 minutes, it's too long, and since we know at the outset where we're headed, it's way too slow in getting there. Still, the production values are pretty good, the actors (including Wings Hauser and Bo Hopkins) don't embarrass themselves, and none of the characters seems positively brain dead. The mutants have more than a passing resemblance to George Romero's zombies, only they crave blood not flesh. In other words, there's absolutely nothing here that we haven't seen before, but if you want to see it again, I guess you could do worse than this one.

IMPULSE *(1984)*
wr Bart Davis and Don Carlos Dunaway; dir Graham Baker

The premise here is similar to that of **MUTANT**, but the warp is psychological rather than physical. When Jenny (Meg Tilly) and her doctor boyfriend (Tim Matheson) return to her home town after her mother's attempted suicide, they discover that Mom is not the only one in the farming community to be acting strange. It seems that something is suppressing the brain's "censoring device," causing those affected to act upon whatever impulse happens to seize them, no matter how violent or anti-social. Until the two-thirds mark, this is really quite intriguing, and it could have been a pretty good little thriller if it weren't for some very serious structural problems with the script. As it is, though, the big discovery turns out to be no big surprise — it's toxic waste — and the last third of the movie kind of disintegrates. Also, it seems like there was some darkly comic potential in the situation that should have been exploited. Too bad. There are lots of nice bits in this one, but it remains strictly a might-have-been.

NIGHTMARE AT NOON *(1987)*
wr Nico Mastorakis and Kirk Ellis; dir Nico Mastorakis

After their experience in **MUTANT**, you'd think Wings Hauser and Bo Hopkins would have learned to keep away from small towns, but here they are, passing through Canyonland just when an albino government agent (played by Brion James) decides to run an experiment in chemical warfare by contaminating the town's water supply. The formula has been improved since **WARNING SIGN**; this version not only induces psychopathic rages but turns the victim's blood into green acid. Although Sheriff George Kennedy says "We've got to act fast," almost no one does, and this rambles rather aimlessly around the Utah countryside. As clichéd and pointless as the meaningless title, this one delivers what you'd expect from the creator of *The Zero Boys* and **THE WIND**. The box claims the effects won an award at some European sci-fi film festival, but I have no idea why, since mostly what we have is just a lot of flames, shoot-'em-ups and explosions, none of which is the least bit special. Brion James is fun in his brief appearances and there are decent production values, but that's it — far more snooze than nightmare.

Radioactive Wastes

THE CHILDREN *(1980)*
wr Carlton J. Albright and Edward Terry; dir Max Kalmanowicz

After passing through a cloud of gas from the local nuclear power plant, six young kids develop black fingernails and the ability to barbecue whomever they touch. They produce a number of messy-looking corpses for the sheriff to muse over and he finally decides that the only way to stop the killers is to cut off their hands. It's hard to know what they thought they were doing with this one. There is no suspense or excitement; the effects are strictly cheap and backyard; and, as terrifying creatures go, kids with black fingernails are right up there with stuffed animals. Vacuous enough to provide a couple of laughs, but that's about it. With Rita Montone as the egocentric actress who bares more than her soul.

THE BEING *(1981)*
wr and dir Jackie Kong

A nuclear-waste dump near Pottsville, Idaho, contaminates the water supply and produces yet another of *Alien*'s numerous spawn. The title entity is not a bad clone — a one-eyed, toothy, flayed-skin slimeball — but dips only a clawed tentacle into frame until the end; by that time, it's far too late to save this tired and tiresome exercise. Stupid, sluggish, and all but creatureless, this is short on being and very long on nothingness. With Martin Landau, Jose Ferrar, Dorothy Malone, and Ruth Buzzi in small roles that did nothing to enliven their careers or this lump of toxic sludge.

PLUTONIUM BABY *(1987)*
wr Wayne Behar; dir Ray Hirschman

This touching tale of a nuclear family involves Danny, who's radioactive, and his mother, whose face has melted and who likes to run through the woods, ripping the intestines out of hunters and hikers. At least, that's the first half of the movie. The second half takes place in New York ten years later and concerns a grown-up Danny (who's starting to develop oozing sores on his leg) and a bad guy left over from the first half, who has spent

> *"I used to kill for science. Now I kill because I am addicted."*
> CRAWLSPACE

the intervening decade in a drum of nuclear waste; when he finally gets released, his face is kind of flaking off, and he wants to rip out some intestines for himself. That just about covers it, I think, except for the killer mutant gopher, and the fact that young Danny likes to swallow live trout whole. Unfortunately, this sounds much livelier than it actually is, and it turns out to be just another piece of amateurish toxic bilge. At one point, a guy who was bitten by the mutant gopher says, "I feel like I'm trapped in some B movie." He should be so lucky.

FESTIVAL 4

* * *

MESSING AROUND WITH MOTHER NATURE
A Symposium of Scientists, Mostly Mad

"The faculty makes this serum from the students' brains and
keeps it in a wine cellar."
— *Zombie High*

As Robert C. Cumbow points out in "Prometheus: The Scientist and His Creations," his analysis of the way scientists are presented in films *(Screen Flights/Screen Fantasies)*, the movies have long been ambivalent about science and its practitioners. Science is at once the solution and the cause of many menacing problems and, while we respect the dedication of the selfless researcher working to improve our lot, since we don't really understand what he's doing or why or how, it all makes us a little nervous. While the desire to unravel the mysteries of the universe is certainly admirable, there are, perhaps, as it was put in *The Invisible Ray* (1936), "some things man is not meant to know."

These conflicting views and feelings have found their focus in one of the most popular and enduring figures of horror fantasy, the Mad Scientist. As the character we love to hate, he goes back to the earliest days of the cinema and is far too familiar to require much of an introduction here.

It is worth noting, however, that the two members of the breed who have turned up most often in the movies, doctors Frankenstein and Jekyll, have their origins in 19th-Century literary works (1818 and 1886, respectively), and it is remarkable how little their cinematic descendants have changed over the years. The technology and the jargon are different, but the scientists themselves are just as obsessed, just as likely to assume a god-like stance, just as willing to sacrifice others for knowledge, and/or just as keen to experiment on themselves.

These dedicated men of science, and the findings of their less salubrious research efforts, are prominently featured in Festival 3. The movies in this festival have no shortage of creatures, but the real monsters are often

> *"The more I'm out here, the more I'm convinced there's nothing to see."*
> THE ALIEN DEAD

the scientists themselves. While you probably wouldn't want any of them as your family physician, you might very well benefit from a house call or two.

DEAD KIDS *(1981)*
wr Bill Condon and Michael Laughlin; dir Michael Laughlin
Also released as *Strange Behavior*

From the writer/director team who later made **STRANGE INVADERS**, this movie certainly is peculiar. Students who think they are taking part in a psych experiment are actually being programmed to kill by a deranged behaviouralist who wants to punish the town for harassing him and trying to stop his work. Part Mad Scientist, part Mad Slasher, part Mystery Thriller, some of the parts are effective — particularly Fiona Lewis as the equally deranged research assistant — but they don't really cohere. The pace and the narrative structure seem all wrong: things that should be suspenseful are merely tedious, and the big revelations are only surprising because the script has never prepared us for them. What could have been funny just seems flat and the kids aren't the only things that are dead. With Michael Murphy and Louise Fletcher, who did nothing in this one to enhance their careers.

SPARE PARTS *(1984, German, dubbed)*
wr and dir Rainer Erler

A very low-budget German version of *Coma*, set, for no apparent reason, in New Mexico and New York. While on her honeymoon, a German exchange student (Jutta Speidel) sees her husband abducted and carted off in a mysterious ambulance. After lots and lots of traveling around with a friendly trucker, our heroine turns up a network involved in the sale of human organs for transplant from decidedly unwilling donors. This premise, while scarcely original, could yield an effective thriller, but this one is far too lethargic and rambling to hold our attention. There's nothing vital about these organs.

WARNING SIGN *(1985)*
wr Hal Barwood and Matthew Robbins; dir Hal Barwood

In the Utah countryside, a government laboratory that everyone believes is doing agricultural research is, in fact, secretly working on biological warfare. Their big success — a virus that attacks the rage center of the brain, turning the victims into violent psychotics — is accidentally released in the lab. The building is sealed immediately and the government pros arrive to contain and cover up the situation. With elements from *The China Syndrome*, *Silkwood*, and *Night of the Living Dead*; really good production values and a great high-tech look; decent performances (Sam Waterston, Kathleen Quinlan, Yaphet Kotto, and a lot of familiar faces from TV); this should work, but doesn't. It's not really bad, not really much of anything. From the team who made the more successful **DRAGONSLAYER**.

THE BRIDE *(1985)*
wr Lloyd Fonvielle; dir Franc Roddam

This one must've looked good on paper: a lavish reworking of *The Bride of Frankenstein* (1935), complete with Sting as the good doctor, Jennifer Beals as his creation, and lots of feminist philosophical chat about freedom, independence, and the "New Woman." Presumably, the intention was to make Art out of Trash, and although often quite striking visually — especially the opening creation sequence — the ingredients add up to a recipe for tired, Earnest Hash. Sting is intense and tedious, and Jennifer Beals is pretty and vacuous, a complete blank even after she's been educated. Clancy Brown (**HIGHLANDER**) is not bad as the creature, but the script makes him queasily pathetic, as maudlin a monster ever let loose this side of King Kong. No thrills, no chills, no laughs: too solemn for Trash, too stupid for Art, this creation is more misbegotten than anything whipped up in the doc's gothic laboratory. Writer Fonvielle went on to make the much more effective **GOTHAM**.

DEADLY FRIEND *(1986)*
wr Bruce Joel Rubin; dir Wes Craven

A real mess from Wes. This starts off looking like a *Short Circuit* variant with a cutesily aggressive robot developed by Paul (Matthew Laborteaux) a teenage prodigy in the field of artificial intelligence. Then, after the 'bot is blown away by Anne Ramsey (*Throw Mama from the Train*), the movie segues into a "Frankenstein Jr." as Paul steals the corpse of the girl next door (Kristy Swanson) and performs brain surgery on her, implanting some computer chips. Re-animated, she goes out to take revenge on anyone who had been nasty to her before she died. Not a good movie and, what's worse, not even a fun movie, it seems to have been assembled from miscellaneous bits Wes had left over from other projects, including a couple of dream sequences from *Elm Street*. Wes should be ashamed of himself.

CRAWLSPACE (1986)
wr and dir David Schmoeller

Dr. Gunther (Klaus Kinski), the son of a Nazi war criminal, is obviously a graduate of the same med school as Dr. Butcher (see below). As he says, "I used to kill in the name of science. Now I kill because I'm addicted. It's the only way I can feel alive." He owns a small apartment house tenanted only by attractive young women ("Dr. Gunther always rents to the pretty ones") whom he spies on from the crawlspace in the heating duct. When he's not crawling and peeping, he's out killing their boyfriends, a ritual prefaced by a friendly round of Russian roulette: when he doesn't blow his brains out, he says "So be it," and slaughters somebody else, frequently via various deadly booby traps. He keeps a woman in a cage in the attic; he keeps her tongue in a glass jar, along with the eyes and fingers of other victims. Klaus has even more kinks, but you probably get the idea. Although there is no nudity or explicit violence, this one tries very hard to be sleazo and sicko, and generally succeeds. Indeed, it is so vigorous and single-minded in its desire to be crass and nasty in serving up a textbook of perversity that one can't help but admire the dedication. Fairly slickly made, and Klaus, right at home in a role he's had more than a little experience with, gives a performance that ranges from being high camp to genuinely creepy. Obviously not for all tastes but, whatever else this might be, it's not dull.

Lovecraftian Lunatics

RE-ANIMATOR (1985)
wr Dennis Paoli and William J. Norris; dir Stuart Gordon

What a pisser! The theatrical release of this ran 86 minutes and was praised for its humor and playfulness, on the one hand, and the enthusiastic excess of its effects, on the other. The 9 minutes added to the video release slow things down, and the gore has been diluted to the point that it's barely there except for some bloody make-up. Certainly, none of the spectacular moments I'd read about were in the version I saw, which kind of defeats the purpose of a movie whose *raison d'être* is its outrageous bad taste. So, what we have is a badly paced teaser that never delivers. It's well-enough done, I guess — slick, occasionally funny, with entertaining performances by David Gale and Jeffrey Combs as the competing mad scientists, but, unless you come across the original 86-minute version, prepare to be disappointed. With the luscious Barbara Crampton as the dean's daughter who gets stripped and fondled by the re-animated dead.

FROM BEYOND
wr Dennis Paoli; dir Stuart Gordon

From the folks who gave us **RE-ANIMATOR**, this is yet another modern adaptation of a H.P. Lovecraft story, but this one made it to video without any unfortunate lapses of good taste and restraint. A brilliant but deranged scientist (Ted Sorel) develops a machine known as the Sonic Resonator that stimulates the pineal gland, a dormant sensory organ sometimes referred to as the third eye. "I want to see more, more than any man has ever seen," he says, and gets his wish. What he sees and we are shown is a variety of nasty and hideous creatures that live all around us but are ordinarily invisible. This one's got it all: grotesque monsters, spectacular transformations, brain-suckings, head-eatings, a guy devoured by killer bees, and slime by the bucket, among other attractions. It's also got a very entertaining performance by Jeffrey Combs, a touch of kinky sex, and Barbara Crampton is again stripped and fondled by a nightmarish creature. What more could you ask for? Slick, fast and high-spirited; when it comes to gross good fun, this one delivers the goods.

> *"The first girl I ever kissed, and you destroyed her."*
> BASKET CASE

Secrets of Eternal Youth

EVIL TOWN *(1985)*
wr Larry Spiegel and Richard Benson; dir Edward Collins, Peter S. Traynor, and Larry Spiegel

Smalltown (pop. 666) is a nice place to live, but you sure wouldn't want to visit there. Seems there's a resident mad scientist who's discovered a way to stop the aging process through the use of human pituitary fluid. Of course, a constant supply of the stuff is required, which means that anyone who enters the town is unlikely to exit. While hardly original, this could have been an effective little thriller but, from the look of it, and since three directors are credited, it seems to have been assembled from bits and pieces shot over quite a long period of time. Whatever the case, the result isn't exactly what you'd call a driving narrative. Nonetheless, Dean Jagger, as the loony scientist, gives a seriously bizarre performance, and Lynda Weismeier shows a lot bounce in the part of the girl with the large exposed breasts. For amusement value only, and even that may be somewhat limited.

EVILS OF THE NIGHT
Alien youth-seekers; see Festival 1.

ZOMBIE HIGH *(1987)*
wr Tim Doyle, Aziz Ghazal, and Elizabeth Passarelli; dir Ron Link

Something strange is going at the Ettinger Academy — an exclusive prep school that has only just gone co-ed — but it seems to take new girl Virginia Madsen almost forever to find out what it is. Finally, after a very long, uneventful, unsuspenseful hour, it becomes clear that the faculty has discovered a way to prevent aging through a serum made from the blood and brain tissue of the students, which they harvest, then store in bottles in the wine cellar. In compensation they replace gray matter with a crystal that turns the students into emotionless automatons who go out into the world and become successful politicians and businessmen. Presumably, this was meant to be both funny and scary, but little is made of the satiric possibilities, and neither the director nor the writers has a clue how to generate tension, suspense, or even mild curiosity. About the best they manage is a sense of vague menace, but that soon runs thin when *nothing* happens. From the credits, it looks like this grew out of a student project at the USC film school but, while technically competent, it doesn't earn more than a C-minus.

THE REJUVENATOR *(1988)*
wr Simon Nuchtern and Brian Thomas Jones; dir Brian Thomas Jones

A long-since-faded movie star, desperate to be young again, takes the anti-aging serum developed by Dr. Ashton (John MacKay) and turns into Vivian Lanko. Of course, the serum, derived from human brains, is still in the experimental stage, and naturally there are what the doctor terms "some complications." These include growing extra talons on her hands, having her own cerebrum pulsate and expand outside her skull, and ripping off heads in order to munch on the cranial contents. This is a fairly low-budget number, but competently made. Although a bit sluggish in places, it generally manages to be cheerfully silly and serves up a fair amount of enthusiastic splatter. Not likely to make you forget the Lovecraftian excesses of Stuart Gordon, but these folks did make an effort, and do serve up a pretty respectable brain-eating sequence. It would certainly be interesting to see what this director would do with some more money to spend. Meanwhile, worth checking out, if you don't expect too much.

Two Brainless Brain Movies

(Note: These elderly losers are here because the distributors didn't put the dates on the boxes. I got taken in, but at least now you know what you'll be getting — not a whole helluva lot.)

BRAIN DAMAGE *(1971)*
wr Joe Van Rodgers; dir Al Adamson

Imagine my surprise when this one turned out to be the 1971 classic originally titled *Brain of Blood*. If you've got a sweet tooth for brain transplant movies made without budget or talent, in which the only brain involved is the one in the glass bowl, then this lame little gobbler might

> "They're always in season when you're hungry."
> THE FOREST

provide a couple of laughs. Despite the fact that the mad scientist has a psychopathic dwarf assistant who keeps a couple of bimbos chained in the basement, this is a disappointingly flat effort from the director of such cinematic high points as *Five Bloody Graves*, *Hell's Bloody Devils*, *Blood of Ghastly Horror*, *Horror of the Blood Monsters*, and *Blood of Dracula's Castle*.

GRAY MATTER (1972)
wr Thomas Hal Philips, Christian Garrison, and Joy N. Houck, Jr.; *dir* Joy N. Houck, Jr.

Two days after watching **BRAIN DAMAGE**, I fell for this one, another lamebrain plucked from well-deserved obscurity and deposited on the shelves of video stores in the hope of separating gullible customers from a few bucks. Here we have something called a "Brain Machine" that can see into the subject's mind, and a deranged army colonel who wants to test it on four unsuspecting volunteers. For what it's worth, this is much more amusing than the preceding effort, largely because of some astoundingly overwrought performances, and some of the most ridiculous "science" and "scientists" ever put onto celluloid. Although it's probably a little too slow and dull to be considered a true classic, those who collect moments of high cinematic ineptitude will not be disappointed with this one. Certified to be 100 percent free of the title stuff.

A Brain Movie with Guts

DOCTOR BUTCHER, M.D. (1982, Italian, dubbed)
wr and dir Frank Martin (Francesco Martino)
Originally titled *Queen of the Cannibals*

Made the same year as **ZOMBIE** (though not released until later), this is essentially the same movie — with a similar tropical setting and Ian McCulloch in the lead role — but with fewer zombies and even more innards. A series of ritual mutilations of corpses in Manhattan sends four investigators off to a remote Southeast Asian island where they encounter cannibals, zombies, and the title physician (Donald O'Brian), a dedicated man of science whose dream is to prolong human life through brain transplants. (His M.D., the box informs us, stands for "Medical Deviate.") Of course, as the good doctor says, progress "requires certain sacrifices" — a partial inventory of which includes a few mutilated corpses, a dissection, a scalping, a skull-removal, an eyeball-gouging, several disembowelings and slit throats, some blood-drinking and organ-munching, and a head chewed up in the blades of an outboard motor, all shown in enthusiastically explicit detail. As a bonus, Alexandra Cole gets stripped, body-painted, and worshiped, thus providing the rationale for the original title. In tradition of spaghetti splatter, this is cheap, shoddy, stupid, and gleefully disgusting. Would you have it any other way?

FESTIVAL 5

* * *

TOOTH AND CLAW
Nature Doesn't Just Get Mad — She Gets Even

> "Do you have any idea how many baboons are out there looking for dinner?"
> — *In the Shadow of Kilimanjaro*

The giant animals discussed in Festival 3 had pretty well disappeared by the end of the 1950s, but in 1963 Alfred Hitchcock gave us a new menace from Mother Nature. In *The Birds* (based on a story by Daphne du Maurier) there were no hideous mutations, just perfectly ordinary creatures, no longer timid and subservient to Man, but openly hostile and aggressive.

This sort of reversal in the natural order could easily be applied to more than just our feathered friends, and we have since seen similar revolts from other members of the animal kingdom. A partial list of the rebels includes *The Deadly Bees* (1967) and *The Swarm* (1978), *Frogs* (1972), *Piranha* (1978), rats in *Willard* (1971) and *Ben* (1972), ants in *Phase IV* (1974), worms in *Squirm* (1976), spiders in *The Kingdom of the ...* (1977), bats in *Nightwing* (1979) — to name a few.

In 1975, Steven Spielberg gave us yet another type of natural monster, which quickly became the biggest-grossing movie ever made, and today *Jaws* still occupies the fifth spot on *Variety*'s list of box-office champions. Other sharks soon followed in Bruce's sizeable wake, as did other brutes: *Grizzly* (1976), *Orca* (1977), and Stephen King's *Cujo* (1983).

These various animals were set in motion for differing reasons — environmental factors, disease, hunger, revenge — but the end result is always the same: Man is reminded that he's just another link in the food chain, and not necessarily the uppermost one.

In the movies that follow, both forms of natural monsters can be found. Sometimes they are, like the giant Great White, of unusually large size, but still generally within the realm of plausibility. Sometimes the battle for survival or supremacy involves the humans in a battle for

Preying Primates

IN THE SHADOW OF KILIMANJARO *(1986)*
wr Jeffrey Sneller and Michael Harry; dir Raju Patel

There is a drought in an isolated district in Kenya, and the baboons are starting to snack on the human population. Although supposedly based on an incident that occurred in 1984, there's nothing here that's not completely clichéd movie hokum, and badly executed, at that. We're told that there are 90,000 baboons out there but, except for some dull stock footage, we only get to see about 30 of them. Nor do we see Kilimanjaro or even its shadow. The closing credits proudly announce that no animals were harmed in the making of this movie, but say nothing about the reputations of the humans involved, including Timothy Bottoms and John Rhys-Davies. Go to the zoo instead.

LINK *(1986)*
wr Edward De Roche; dir Richard Franklin

This is your basic young-woman-trapped-in-an-isolated-country-house-and-menaced-by-a-smiling-psychopath movie, with a twist that the psycho killer is an ape wearing a butler's suit. Unfortunately, the execution fails to live up to the wonderfully loopy premise. The movie starts and ends with modest little jokes, but everything in between reproduces rather than bends the conventions of the genre. As is often the case, the ape is not only stronger than the humans, but smarter as well. In fact, the orangutan (for some reason identified as a chimp) gives the best, most appealing performance in the film, skewing our sympathies radically. With Terence Stamp and Elisabeth Shue; scripted by the author of **THE QUEST** and **RAZORBACK**.

BLUE MONKEY
No simians; a mutant mantis; see Festival 3.

> "I could easily kill you now, but I'm determined to have your brain."
> DR. BUTCHER M.D.

A Mad Menagerie

WILD BEASTS *(1983, Italian, dubbed)*
wr, prod, dir Franco E. Prosperi

PCP gets into the water supply of an appallingly bad German zoo, sending the animals into a violent frenzy, then into the streets of a panicking city. There's not much plot, suspense, or excitement here, but there's lots of badly dubbed screams and lots of stuff crashing and exploding. Naturally, there's some animal mayhem — rat-munchings, tiger-chewings, polar bear-rendings, elephant head-crushings — but although the blood flows freely, it's all pretty restrained, especially for the Italians who are not generally so reticent when it comes to graphic chowing-down. If you're not going to indulge in good old-fashioned explicit feeding frenzies, what's the point of letting all those carnivores loose? Tame and toothless, this is horror for quiche-eaters and the salad-bar set.

Cranky Canines

DOGS OF HELL *(1982)*
wr Tom McIntyre; dir Worth Keeter

Just for the record, Cerberus was the three-headed dog that guarded the entrance to Hades and was rarely in the mood to wag his serpent's tail. Unfortunately, the budget here isn't up to anything that spectacular, giving us instead a few slavering Rottweilers trained by the army to kill, who escape and terrorize a town. This is a seriously cheap movie with the gimmick that it was originally released in 3-D. Actually, it looks more like an old, unreleased movie tarted up with a few 3-D effects — sort of the old SCTV routine, "Dr. Tongue's 3-D House of Stewardesses," only longer and not as funny.

MONSTER DOG
Werehound; see Festival 6.
MONGREL
Humanoid werehound; see Festival 6.

PLAY DEAD
Black Magic mutt; see Festival 11.

Porcine Problems

PIGS *(1972)*
wr F.A. Foss; dir Marc Lawrence

I got suckered by this one — it had no date on the box and a blurb suggesting rampaging carnivorous porkers — but at least you won't be fooled. What I got was 1972 barnyard cinema about an escaped psycho (Toni Lawrence) who likes to carve up men and a loony farmer (Marc Lawrence) who has gotten into the habit of feeding corpses to his pigs. Too dull to be funny, it would be too easy a shot to call this one an utter bore, so I won't do it.

RAZORBACK *(1983, Australian)*
wr Everett De Roche; dir Russell Mulcahey

An outback *Jaws* — or, more properly, "Tusks". The title brute is a rampaging rhino-sized wild boar with a serious disposition problem. When his reporter wife disappears while on assignment in Australia, Gregory Harrison heads to the outback, where he discovers she was eaten by the monster hog. The creature is impressive though fleetingly seen, but he's a poor second in meanness to the loutish kangaroo-hunters Harrison also discovers. This movie is slickly made, takes full advantage of the spectacular scenery, and is filled with enough style and atmosphere for three or four movies. However, since the story rambles and never really grabs the way it should, style is about all there is to hold your interest and by the thirtieth dramatic haze-filtered backlit shot, even that starts to wear thin. Not uninteresting, but the parts are much better than the whole, a problem the director also had with **HIGHLANDER**.

> "Godzilla — I was hoping I'd never hear that name again."
> GODZILLA 1985

Ravenous Rodents

DEADLY EYES *(1982)*
wr Charles Eglee; dir Robert Clouse

After eating corn soaked in steroids, rats grow to the size of dachshunds and chew up a lot of people in the storm drains and subways of Toronto. In fact, the "rats" actually are dachshunds (about two dozen of them), stylishly outfitted in rat suits, with results that are not exactly what you'd call strikingly realistic. The dachsrats have a certain tacky charm, but not enough to compensate for the tedious romance subplots that fill in the long spaces between rat attacks. Based loosely on Frank Herbert's *The Rats* but paced like a '50s creature feature, this effort makes the pulp novel seem like high art. Silly enough to provide a few smiles. With Scatman Crothers as one of the first victims to get chewed.

RATS *(1983, Italian/French co-production, dubbed)*
wr Claudio Fragasso and Herve Piccini; dir Vincent Dawn (Bruno Mattei) and Clyde Anderson

Supposedly set 250 years into a post-apocalyptic future, where everyone wears mid-1980s clothes and hairstyles, this one features a band of motorcycle jerks besieged by about four dozen sluggish rats in an abandoned building. Listless though they are, the rats are more animated than the narrative and far more intelligent than the humans. The effects extend to a few rat-chewed corpses, and no farther, but if you're looking for laughable performances, ludicrous dialog, and absolutely wretched dubbing, there's a great deal in this one to be savored. With Ann Gisel Glass as the bimbo with hysterics, and Moune Duvivier as the naked bimbo who gets chewed up in her sleeping bag. Co-directed by the creators of **MONSTER DOG** and **NIGHT OF THE ZOMBIES**, each a low point in its festival.

OF UNKNOWN ORIGIN *(1983, Canadian)*
wr Brian Taggart; dir George P. Cosmatos

The second, made-in-Canada, giant-rat movie depicts the ultimate confrontation between Man and Rodent. Successful yuppie Peter Weller

(*Robocop*) discovers that his beautifully renovated townhouse has an unwanted — and unparalleled — inhabitant: SuperRat, a cat-sized package of meanness that does not take kindly to the human intruder in its domain. This rat is a better tactician than the combined Joint Chiefs of Staff, and Peter Weller quickly finds himself at a real disadvantage in the ensuing battle of wits. As one remedy after another — traps, bigger traps, poison, and so on — fails to do the trick, Weller becomes more and more obsessed with ridding himself of his adversary, to the point that he's willing to wreck his house in order to get the sucker. What we get then is a verminous version of *The Conversation* (1974), that manages to be both quietly funny and fairly creepy. The escalating battle and Weller's obsession with it are so absurd as to be comical, and clever visual references to *Moby Dick* and *The Old Man and the Sea* serve to put things into perspective. Of course, this is a very silly movie, but it's also a lot of fun and is perhaps the best Oversized Vermin film ever made.

Feathered Fiends

BEAKS *(1987, Spanish/ Puerto Rican, mostly dubbed)*
wr, prod, dir Rene Cardona, Jr.

Either unfamiliar with *The Birds* or convinced that no one else was after twenty-four years, the director of *Guyana, Cult of the Damned* (and son of the director of *The Wrestling Women Vs. the Aztec Mummy*) gives us avian avengers suddenly and inexplicably attacking anyone who ever ate a drumstick. Actually, it's mostly killer pigeons, and they're finicky eaters, pecking at only a few people in an unsatisfying, unconvincing, and unexciting fashion. This is packaged as a parody, but the only laughs will be on you if you take a flier on this exceedingly dull and shoddy bottom-of-the-birdcage exercise.

Rampaging Reptiles

ALLIGATOR *(1980)*
wr John Sayles; dir Lewis Teague

A baby alligator named Ramon is flushed down the toilet in an unnamed midwestern city. Twelve years later, after feeding on growth hormones dumped into the sewage system by a sleazy pharmaceutical company, Ramon is longer than an El Dorado and has an appetite to match. Talk about urban jaws! Actually, the story follows *Jaws* pretty closely, with a cop (Robert Forster) knowing that they have a *big* problem, while everyone else either denies it or tries to cover up. John Sayles's script is well plotted, with a few nice humorous touches (one of the first victims is a sewer worker named Edward Norton); the performances are at least adequate, and occasionally fairly amusing; and Ramon looks pretty good, generally a good deal less phony than Bruce, the mechanical shark. Throw in a few legs being chewed off and a limo being trashed, and you have a mildly entertaining version of one of the more widely spread urban myths.

COPPERHEAD *(1983)*
wr and dir Leland Payton

A family of deranged survivalists hides out in the Ozark Mountains with a valuable stolen necklace and blast away at the title serpents, of which they are rather hysterically phobic. Care to guess who gets fanged to death before this pathetic Missouri backyard piece-o-shit grinds to its foregone conclusion? Shot on video, with a budget apparently made up from spare change, this is utterly amateurish in every respect — so painfully bad it almost defies you to watch it. Get yourself a camcorder and a 1000-watt floodlight, and make your own version.

Flighty Fish

PIRANHA II — THE SPAWNING *(1981)*
wr H.A. Milton; dir James Cameron

A disappointing followup to the energetically silly 1978 original in which a special strain of the title fish developed by the army gets loose in a summer camp. The hungry little fellows are back, only this time at a Caribbean resort, and now they've got wings, so they flap around, looking a lot like giant carnivorous moths. (Yes, these probably *should* be with the mutants in Festival 3.) There are a good number of chewed-up faces and throats, but the plotting is mechanical, the pace slow, and there's no humor to buoy up the loopy premise. In fact, the most interesting thing about this one is that absolutely none of the abundant talent director Cameron displayed in *The Terminator* or *Aliens* is in evidence here. Only for those who are interested in the lousy early efforts of people who went on to become really fine directors.

Irascible Insects

CREEPERS *(1984, Italian, partly dubbed)*
wr Dario Argento and Franco Ferrini; dir Dario Argento

This jumble by one of the acknowledged masters of Italian splatter has so much plot stuff that it's eligible for at least three festivals (I chose to classify it by title). A young somnambulist (Jennifer Connelly), who communicates telepathically with insects to get them to do her bidding, is trapped in a walking nightmare. There's a slice-and-dice psycho murdering the girls at her exclusive Swiss boarding school. There's a cannibalistic mutated little boy with a pig snout and a mouth full of fangs. And there's even a trained chimpanzee wielding a straight razor. If you're wondering how all this fits together, it doesn't. Still, this one does try to make up for what lacks in sense and suspense by being deeply, truly nauseating. Various insects make appearances, but the best of breed goes to the maggots, who put in almost as much screen time as Donald Pleasence (on hand to deliver a gratuitous entomological exposition in an equally gratuitous bad Scottish accent). We see the little charmers on decomposing skulls and severed hands and under a microscope — up close and personal — perhaps the ultimate Italian maggot experience (see Festival 7). We also get to see our put-upon young heroine dumped into a tank filled with rotting bodies that is so queasy-making you can almost smell it. Sounds like your kind of flick, you're saying? It probably is. Often laughably nonsensical, occasionally enthusiastically revolting, this one is rarely dull.

FESTIVAL 6

* * *

THE INNER BRUTE
Werewolves and Other Shape-Shifters

"It doesn't sound like any coyotes I've ever heard."
— *Howling II*

Man-beasts and men who turn into beasts roam myths, folktales, and legends around the world. It doesn't require a degree in psychology to see the symbolism — the dual nature of man the "rational animal," with the emphasis on the emergence of the more lustful, beastly side.

In 1886, Robert Louis Stevenson made a new classic, *The Strange Case of Dr. Jekyll and Mr. Hyde*, from the old tale, and thirty-four years later, the two-faced doctor became the screen's original shape-shifter in a silent version of the story. He has continued to turn up with a fair degree of regularity ever since in both straight remakes and, as in this festival, rather labored spoofs. The best and most successful contemporary variation on the Jekyll/Hyde story was *Altered States* (1980), with a big budget, good effects, a literate script by Paddy Chayefsky, and Ken Russell's usual frenzied direction.

Of course, the movie shape-shifter that is best known is the werewolf. He first appeared in *The Werewolf of London* (1935), but the movie that really established him was *The Wolf Man* (1941). Lon Chaney, Jr., in the title role, was not one of the all-time scary creatures; as Peter Nicholls remarks in his excellent survey, *Fantastic Cinema*, Chaney's "spaniel-eyed portrayal nearly reduced the status of Gothic Monster to Household Pet." The movie, though, was popular, generating a number of progressively shabby sequels and establishing the pattern for most of the werewolf movies that followed. Indeed, most of what we know (or think we know) about the legend of the werewolf can probably be traced back to what we were told in *The Wolf Man*.

Cat People (1942) expanded the possibilities of shape-shifting, although the "beast inside" was clearly the libido this time. A film far superior to *The Wolf Man* — today it is considered a minor classic — it does not seem to have had any direct descendants until Paul Schrader's 1982 remake, which was much more explicitly sexy, but otherwise murky, muddled, and far less entertaining.

The 1940s also saw Chula the Ape turned into Pauline the Woman (*Captive Wild Woman*, 1943, with sequels in '44 and '45), but that's not quite the same thing. Among shape-shifters, only the werewolf became firmly established in the Monster Pantheon. In 1981 in *Wolfen*, based on Whitley Streiber's best-seller, we were given a different interpretation of the werewolf legend — a superwolf but not a shape-shifter. In the same year, though, we did finally get the werewolf movie we had been waiting for. In fact, we got two of them.

The first out was *The Howling* (directed by Joe Dante, with a script co-written by John Sayles), and for many, it remains the ultimate werewolf experience. The movie offered a great sense of fun and irony, a lot of sex and gore, and superior production values, but most important, gave us *transformations*. Before *The Howling*, man-into-wolf, when shown at all, tended to be done through time-lapse photography — at best as gripping as watching a flower open. Here, though, technology caught up with the imagination, and effects wizard Rob Bottin gave us transformations unlike anything we had ever seen. Indeed, they were so eye-popping (as well as muscle-, hair-, and snout-popping) that they became the dominant element in the movie and, in themselves, were worth the price of admission.

Seven months later saw the release of John Landis's *An American Werewolf in London*, which many others hold to be the ultimate werewolf experience. It too was a very good movie — maybe even better and funnier — and as its centerpiece, it had, courtesy of Rick Baker, transformations that were every bit as spectacular as those in *The Howling* (as well as Griffin Dunne as what is probably the cinema's funniest decomposing corpse).

In both movies, the effects were so strong that they viritually became the subject of the films. Since then we've been treated to a series of peeling, pulsating, bursting metamorphoses across the horror spectrum. Some have been messier and more disgusting, but when it comes to turning a man into a beast, the two 1981 movies set the standard against which all transformations must be judged.

Unfortunately few movies in this festival exhibit more than a nodding acquaintance with this standard. That's not to say that there's no good stuff here or no fun. But, if you're looking for movies with the quality and the impact of the two from 1981, you'll be disappointed. However, if you've got a taste for loopy lycanthropes or you figure that even a so-so transformation is better than nothing, there are a couple of items here that will serve you well enough.

As Christopher Lee remarked in **HOWLING II**, "The process of evolution is reversed." And it's about time, too.

Growlers and Howlers

THE COMPANY OF WOLVES *(1984, British)*
wr Angela Carter and Neil Jordan; dir Neil Jordan

Rosaleen (Sarah Patterson) is having what is apparently a very difficult puberty. As she tries to reconcile her awakening sexuality with her fears of the same, she has the dream that makes up this movie. Rosaleen's dream is "Little Red Ridinghood" with werewolves — the beast in man — and dripping with Freudian significance. Let me tell you — this one has atmosphere, symbolism, and artistic pretensions up the wazoo. But while this stuff is interesting to a point, it does not compensate for the absence of engaging characters and the static narrative. This one has a good production values, a couple of so-so transformations, and an interesting look — a little like the watercolor illustrations in old books of fairy tales — but I found it slow, repetitive, heavy-handed, and ultimately uninvolving. (In fairness, other reviewers have praised it, finding it far more intriguing than I did.) Angela Lansbury gets her head knocked off, so I guess it's not a total loss.

STEPHEN KING'S SILVER BULLET *(1985)*
wr Stephen King; dir Daniel Attias

Stephen King's name precedes the title, either because he insisted on it in his contract or because the producers were hoping to pull in a bigger audience than this rather pedestrian effort was likely to earn on its merits. The story is very traditional: a small town is plagued by a series of savage murders that are eventually revealed to be work of the resident werewolf. Competently made, but unfortunately no fun is poked at the genre and nothing new is added to it. Even the creature is a has-been: seen only fleetingly, it most resembles a standard-issue wolf, rampant (on its hind legs), and there is only the briefest of transformation scenes. More proof that, with a few exceptions, Stephen King's stories don't seem to translate all that well to the screen, even when King himself does the script. With Corey Haim as the kid who discovers the werewolf, and Gary Busey, seeming even larger and growlier than the beast, as Uncle Red.

HOWLING II *(1984; released 1986)*
wr Gary Bradner and Robert Sarno; dir Philippe Mora

Although this purports to follow on from the murder of Dee Wallace's character at the end of *The Howling*, about the only thing the two movies share is the book by Gary Bradner on which the original was based (he obviously retained the rights to the title). With none of the style, wit, humor, energy, or effects of the first one, what we have here is Christopher Lee as an "occult investigator" who's out to kill the Queen of the Werewolves (Sybil Danning) before she can celebrate her 10,000th birthday — an occasion on which werewolves around the world will rise up and we'll really be in deep shit. So Chris, accompanied by Annie McEnroe and Reb Brown (**YOR, HUNTER FROM THE FUTURE**), heads for Transylvania with a bandolier or two of silver bullets. (Sybil is immune to silver but — thank goodness for technology! — she is allergic to titanium.) This is a very cheap and stupid effort, badly plotted and acted, with lots of supernatural mumbo-jumbo, shoddy optical effects, and only briefly glimpsed fragments of transformations. On the plus side, it's got some S&M fantasy werewolves, a little werewolf sex, a werewolf orgy — and Sybil Danning. As in several other of her movies, Sybil's outrageous costumes are the best part of this one (including a blonde fur bodysuit) with one number in particular that has to be seen to be believed. The highlight of the film is arguably the scene in which Sybil rips open her dress to reveal why she has long been one of the most prominent figures in trash cinema.

> "Could you juice me again — the colors are starting to fade."
> BRAIN DAMAGE

HOWLING III *(1987, Australian)*
wr and dir Philippe Mora

This Australian effort is less a sequel than a variation on the theme, and while it's a big improvement over **II**, it won't do anything to make you forget the original. Despite one so-so transformation, some unconvincing wolf heads, no blood, and no sex worth mentioning, this is silly enough to be fairly entertaining. How can you resist a movie about marsupial werewolves Down Under? And Imogen Annesley does a good job as the werewolf heroine, complete with furred breasts and a cute little pouch. Vigorously cheap and stupid, this one does hold your interest, if only to see what the next bit of loopiness will be, and there's no shortage of possibles — werewolf nuns, a werewolf ballerina, a barbecued werewolf, and a marsupial-werewolf birth sequence. Kind of makes you wonder what they'll come up with for the next one. Amphibian werewolves? Ovine werewolves? Ninja werewolves? Unfortunately, what they came up with was . . .

HOWLING IV: THE ORIGINAL NIGHTMARE *(1988, Australian?) wr Clive Turner and Freddie Rowe; dir John Hough*

Unless leaden, unrelenting tedium gives you bad dreams, there's nothing nightmarish about this one, and there's certainly nothing original. Marie (Romy Windsor), a best-selling writer, is seeing things, so she and her husband head for a cottage in the woods for peace and quiet. As luck would have it, though, the nearby town is full of howlers, so Marie doesn't get much rest but you might nod off once or twice. Until extremely late in the proceedings, it looks like this one will be not only brainless, but werewolfless. During the last ten minutes, we get a couple of grudging transformations and a not bad melting-man stunt, but it's too little, too late. With Lamya Derval as the she-wolf who briefly bares her breasts, and a lot of folks behind the camera who need a refresher course in the fundamentals of lycanthropic exploitation.

The Cuddlies

TEEN WOLF TOO *(1987)*
wr R. Timothy King; dir Christopher Leitch

The third big werewolf movie of the '80s, *Teen Wolf*, gave us a domesticated comic version of the beast, where wolfism is just another part of adolescence. With Michael J. Fox as the teen with the hyperactive hormones, it was a pleasant enough — or at least an inoffensive — piece of fluff... that happened to pull in over $20 million at the box office. Naturally it led to this one (or, more precisely, this TOO). Less a sequel than a replica, this has cousin Todd (Jason Bateman) going to university to become a veterinarian and discovering that he himself might need one. Too's sport is boxing, not basketball, but everything else about it is exactly the same. Celebrity goes to Todd's head, he becomes a were-asshole, then he learns some important lessons about the things that really matter. In fact, the only aspects of *Teen Wolf* missing here are the originality and fun. Why bother?

MY DEMON LOVER *(1987)*
wr Leslie Ray; dir Charlie Loventhal

As the result of a gypsy curse, Kaz (Scott Valentine) has a small problem: whenever he gets sexually aroused, he is transformed into weird and hideous creatures. This understandably puts a crimp in his love life, and the problem becomes really serious when he falls for Denny (Michelle Little), a sweet little thing who's a sucker for every stray and lost cause in New York City. The situation clearly contains some potential for comedy, but the movie never delivers much more than what is immediately obvious on the surface, and the PG-13 rating means that there's no chance to do anything with the inherent erotic tension. Some of the creatures that Kaz turns into are amusing, but the makeup effects seem rather familiar and lackluster. While not badly done, this has neither the thrills nor the inventiveness that could have given it real punch, and thus it never rises above being an innocuous little comedy.

> *"He came here looking for the unknown, and the unknown found him."*
> JUNGLE HEAT

Euro-Were Sleaze

SHE WOLF *(1977, origin unknown, dubbed)*
wr Howard Ross; dir R.D. Silver

Golly! If it weren't for the video revolution we'd never have the chance to get suckered by this badly shot, dreadfully dubbed, ultra-cheap European lycanthropic lump that purports to be the true story of a large-breasted blonde who apparently inherited the ancestral curse that makes her dance naked in the moonlight and rip open the throats of the men she has sex with. Is she lupine or just loopy? Could we give a shit? Lots of nudity and sex, so there is a reason to occasionally focus your glazed-over eyes, but that's not enough to justify the effort of fast-forwarding through this one.

Were-Curs

MONGREL *(1982)*
wr and dir Robert A. Burns

When his only friend is accidentally electrocuted during a stupid roominghouse prank, Jerry the nerd (Terry Evans) starts to growl, prowl, and rip out the throats of the other people in the house. Is he possessed? Is he a werewolf who doesn't bother to transform? Is he a canine variant on the psycho? This Texas cheapie doesn't tell us, and by the time Jerry does his thing — at the very end of this misbegotten defanged mess — we're too bored to care. Bloodless, brainless, and utterly amateurish, don't let this one follow you home.

MONSTER DOG *(1985, Spanish?, partly dubbed)*
wr and dir Clyde Anderson

If you enjoy watching over-the-hill rock stars shamble through cheap, stupid, badly dubbed monster movies that are goreless and virtually creatureless, then this one's for you. Rocker Victor Raven (Alice Cooper) returns to the family home after an absence of 20 years in order to shoot a video and discovers that, like his father before him, he's really a werewolf. Well, not exactly a wolf. From the micro-glimpses we get of a shoddy *papier-mâché* head, he's more Great Dane. Among other non-effects, we're treated to one of the more pathetically shabby transformation scenes on record. If this one had any vigor at all, it might have provided some inadvertent humor, but virtually nothing happens. The title is an accurate and concise assessment of its merits — don't even be curious.

A Were-Cicada

THE BEAST WITHIN *(1982)*
wr Tom Holland; dir Philippe Mora

The whole point of this one is for the beast within to get out, and it takes over an hour for it to do so. That hour is filled with lots of Southern Gothic dark secrets that must stay hidden. Finally we get to the notorious transformation scene in which our young hero (Paul Clemens) sheds his skin "just like a cicada," revealing the inner beast. Is it worth the wait? Probably not, but if you keep a heavy thumb on the fast-forward button through all the plot stuff, you'll get to see some of the fairly impressive things you can do with inflatable heads. And don't worry about missing anything important while you're zipping along: beyond some vague nods at heredity, no explanations are given for the kid's mutation. The box dares us to watch the last thirty minutes. I dare you to watch the first sixty. An early transformation from the director of **HOWLING II** and **III**.

THE REJUVENATOR
Movie star into giant-brain beast; see Festival 4.

The Asshole Within

DR. HECKYL AND MR. HYPE *(1980)*
wr and dir Charles B. Griffith

As you've probably already deduced, this is a (supposedly) comic variation on the Jeckyll and Hyde story. As Dr. Heckyl, the world's ugliest

> *"It's my theory those creatures are driven to mate with man now."*
> HUMANOIDS FROM THE DEEP

podiatrist, Oliver Reed looks a little like a decomposing zombie, but he has a beautiful soul. Thanks to a potion created by one of the other quacks at the clinic where he works, his blue-green makeup vanishes and he's transformed into Mr. Hype, a debonair ladies' man whose suave exterior conceals the heart of a psycho killer. The premise certainly contains the potential for some good comic horror, but the movie falls seriously short in delivery. Aside from a couple of wonderfully bizarre bits involving feet, the attempts at humor are labored and clichéd. Likewise, what looks to be a microbudget clearly didn't permit any decent horror effects. In the hands of someone like John Landis, this might have been funny, sleazy, and gory. As it is, there's barely enough energy here to make it of interest to those who collect embarrassing performances by Oliver Reed.

JEKYLL AND HYDE ... TOGETHER AGAIN *(1982)*
wr Monica Johnson, Harvey Miller, Jerry Belson, and Michael Leeson; dir Jerry Belson

When brilliant scientist/sexless wimp Dr. Jekyll (Mark Blankfield) inadvertently snorts some white powder he was experimenting with in the lab, he sprouts gold jewelry and a Don King hairdo and turns into Mr. Hyde, disco party animal. This is nothing more that a mediocre late-night-TV routine dragged out endlessly with lots of mugging, sitcom gags, and cocaine jokes. I suppose there are a couple of smiles here... if you can stop gritting your teeth. A bit slicker than it's lame sidekick (above), it does at least have the decency to show Robert Louis Stevenson's skeleton turning over in its grave.

FESTIVAL 7

* * *

THE LIVING DEAD WILL NEVER DIE
A Zombie Homage to George Romero

"What do you mean I have no pulse? No blood pressure?"
— *Return of the Living Dead*

Zombies in the movies go back to the first golden age of horror, the tw[o] best-known titles being *White Zombie* (1932) with Bela Lugosi, and th[e] minor classic *I Walked With A Zombie* (1943). Early zombies were th[e] products of voodoo or other supernatural mumbo-jumbo and wer[e] raised from the grave by the villain, generally to be used as obedien[t] "walking dead" slave labor.

All that changed in Pittsburgh in 1968 when George Romero not onl[y] brought the dead to life, but gave them teeth. Made for $114,000 (an[d] only $60,000 of that up front), *Night of the Living Dead* started out as a[n] obscure regional film by a first-time director, but its horror vision wa[s] too potent to disappear after a few showings at local drive-ins. It quickl[y] became a cult favorite across North America, and one of the mos[t] successful of all the "midnight movies." Today, it is one of the undispute[d] classics of the contemporary horror film (a print is in the permaner[t] collection of New York's Museum of Modern Art) and it is often regarde[d] as the movie that ushered in the current era.

Night has been analyzed and written about at length in too man[y] places to require much comment here but, in terms of the movies in th[is] festival, there are a few points worth noting. First off, on a practical leve[l] it was *cheap*. As creatures go, the living dead are a bargain, requiring onl[y] a little makeup and a cast that can move slowly and stiffly (even your leas[t] histrionic friends and neighbors can probably manage that). The fact tha[t] Romero was able to make an asset of a low-budget liability has served a[s] both a lesson and an inspiration for subsequent backyard filmmaker[s]. (The ranks of those influenced include, among others, directors Joh[n] Carpenter, Wes Craven, and Tobe Hooper, who have themselves becom[e] inspirations for still more lower budget filmmakers.)

> *"Don't worry about me. I'm going right home."*
> NIGHTMARE

More specifically, in terms of story, structure, and style, *Night of the Living Dead* set the patterns from which few of its descendants have significantly deviated. Unlike almost every horror movie that had preceded it, *Night* skipped the long, gradual building of suspense and set the dead moving, right at the top, and never stopped. The reason for the re-animation of the dead was suggested (radiation), but the *why* was ignored; all that mattered was that the dead were living, and the living would soon be dead as a result. As plots and structures go, it's hard to find anything simpler and more stripped down than your basic zombie siege... or anything easier to duplicate.

Where the voodoo zombies were little more than mindless automatons, Romero's living dead were much more independent and goal-oriented. Far from being obedient slaves, the living dead were aggressive and hostile. And — they were hungry. And — they wanted to eat *us*. The unacknowledged source for *Night* was a Richard Matheson novel, *I Am Legend*, and Romero understood very well what he was borrowing. By combining a fundamental phobia — fear of the dead — with a fundamental taboo — cannibalism — in one package, there was a pretty good chance of getting a rise out of the viewer. Some of the zoms that have followed may be more discriminating in their tastes than the original flesh-eaters — brains only or maybe just blood — but all rigorously adhere to Dr. Romero's High Human Diet.

Another significant feature of *Night of the Living Dead* was that we actually saw the zoms feeding (real intestines were thoughtfully provided by a backer who was a butcher, by day). There had been a few earlier gore films — most notably those of Herschell Gordon Lewis — but none that reached the audiences that *Night* did. By today's standards, its excesses seem rather tame, but few viewers in 1968 had ever seen such nastiness presented so explicitly.

While *Night* laid out all of the essentials of today's zombie movie, it was not the direct progenitor of the efforts in this festival. That distinction belongs to Romero's sequel, *Dawn of the Dead* (1979). After the eleven-year hiatus, Romero had a lot more money to spend and a wealth of advances in special effects to draw upon. With the makeup artistry of Tom Savini, *Dawn* raised enthusiastic excess to such unprecedented heights that Romero had to coin a new expression to describe what he was doing — "splatter cinema."

The effects in *Dawn* were astonishingly graphic, but at the same time they were so spectacular and outrageous that you couldn't take them seriously. Indeed, the rhythm of the movie was structured around the big effects, with each new bit of hyperbolic full-color gore functioning as the punchline to the setup that preceded it. In essence, then, this was less a movie about zoms than about delivering big payoffs. (If you remove the graphic splatter from a movie like this — as was done with the heavily censored version of *Day of the Dead*, which was all that the brain police in Ontario, Canada, would let us have — the rhythm of the movie is destroyed, and the effect is like watching a stand-up comedian start a lot of jokes but never finish one.)

Dawn was a considerable success, not just in North America but in Europe as well. Before you could say "gross-out ripoff," low-budget hacks around the world were reaching for the green greasepaint and visiting their local abattoirs. The zom '80s had arrived.

In *Dawn*, George Romero mixed his abundant horror in equal parts with humor, and that's a combo most of the American zoms have tried to copy, with varying degrees of success. In Europe, however, and most especially in Italy, *Dawn* was seen (and copied) as a movie about gross-outs. Humor could be dispensed with, as could plot and character; all that mattered was effects sufficiently gruesome and graphic that they would, as Peter Nicholls put it in *Fantastic Cinema*, "bring an average audience to the brink of nausea."

In Italy, there was a tradition for this kind of movie that went back to the early 1960s. Called *giallo* cinema, it featured graphic violence that was not necessarily supposed to frighten, but was intended to sicken. Interestingly enough, Dario Argento, one of the founding fathers of *giallo* cinema, was co-producer of *Dawn of the Dead*, and given the gut-munching potential of cannibal zoms, its not too surprising that more Italians were soon up to their elbows in sheep's intestines.

Also from the *giallo* tradition, the Italians added an element of new realism to their living dead. I'm referring, of course, to the classic maggot shot that is now almost *de rigeur* among the Euro-zoms. What this means, for those who haven't yet had the pleasure, is that the zoms are not just hideous, hungry, and relentless, they're also rotting. And what do you find on rotting meat? Right. You find maggots crawling. The maggot shot is a loving close-up of a maggot-infested zombie head or a maggoty zombie

> "I will not be intimidated by a car."
> DARK OF THE NIGHT

hand or, if you're really stuck, a maggot-lively lump of unidentifiable putrescence. As I said, we're talking high realism here.

Now, I must confess I find the desire to nauseate and appal a curious approach to filmmaking. It does, however, show you things in quite considerable detail that you would not otherwise ever see, and that's not something to be dismissed out of hand. My biggest complaint with spaghetti splatter is not with the grossness of the images, but the mind-numbing awfulness of the movies that surround them — movies in which the maggots frequently deliver the most animated performances. But of course, that's why they invented fast-forward. While obviously not for all tastes, the *giallo* zoms are unquestionably unique, and for those wishing to test their machismo against that of the Italians, there are a couple of little numbers below that should do the trick quite nicely. (For those interested, a more complete discussion of *giallo* films and filmmakers is to be found in Chas. Balun's *Horror Holocaust*.)

For a group of movies that, in most respects, has worked very few changes on the original *Night of the Living Dead*, the entries in this festival range considerably in quality. There are some that are among the worst, most unwatchable movies in this book. There are some that are among the most spectacularly disgusting. There are some that nicely mix splatter and laughs for some solid entertainment. And there is one that I think is not just one of the best movies in this book, but also one of the decade's best examples of genre filmmaking.

* * *

ALIEN DEAD (1980)
wr Fred Olen Ray and Martin Alan Nicholas; dir Fred Olen Ray

Swamp zombies. After a meteor (or something) blows up a houseboat, the occupants don strange makeup and become blood-sucking underwater zoms. "Dead" is sure the operative word with this backyard Florida cheapie. No thrills, chills, or gore (a couple of oral blood capsules was as far as the effects budget would stretch), and too dull for more than a couple of unintended laughs, this is strictly "Night of the Living Bore." An early exercise in cheap, shoddy tedium from a director (see Directors' Index) who has proven himself a master of the form. With Buster Crabbe as the stupid sheriff.

BLOODSUCKERS FROM OUTER SPACE *(1984)*
wr and dir Glen Coburn

Another piece of enthusiastic backyard Texas splatter. An invisible, airborne alien organism takes over the bodies of its victims, turning their faces a nasty green and giving them an unquenchable thirst for human blood. Part parody and part faithful rendering of cheap, clunky sci-fi flicks, surprisingly, this one works quite nicely. Although a good deal of the acting is dreadfully stiff and amateurish, it is rather endearingly and entertainingly so, and perfectly appropriate to the cheerful, off-the-wall sense of humor that characterizes this one. And, of course, the geysers of blood, ripped-off arms, and bloodsucking kids help a lot. Although this ends up being too amateurish and low-budget to be really good, you could do a whole lot worse. With Samantha Walker as the top-heavy briefly topless bimbo.

RETURN OF THE LIVING DEAD *(1985)*
wr and dir Dan O'Bannon

Based on a story by John Russo, co-author of *Night of the Living Dead*, this is an "official" sequel of sorts, working from the premise that the events in *Night* actually occurred. Barrels containing specimens of the living dead stored in the basement of the Uneeda Medical Supply Company get opened, and before too long the inhabitants of the neighboring Resurrection Cemetery are climbing out of the ground as the punk hit "Do You Wanna Party?" blasts. (These particular living dead are definitely the gourmets of zomdom in that they only have eyes for brains.) I think this one is absolutely terrific. It combines zoms, punks, rock 'n' roll, black humor, and some great effects, and does so with enough energy for half a dozen movies. Even the zoms are vigorous, resourceful, and articulate. This is the first directing effort by Dan O'Bannon (who scripted *Alien*), and he manages to mix comedy and horror just about as well as anyone has ever done it. Slick, fast, wild, and gruesome, this is everything a B-movie should be, and exactly what you hope to find when you venture into the video fringe.

> *"Marines have no qualms about killing Martians."*
> INVADERS FROM MARS

NIGHT OF THE CREEPS *(1986)*
wr and dir Fred Dekker

As *two* prologues establish, a nasty alien life form has lain dormant for 27 years inside a frozen cadaver in a university lab. A fraternity initiation prank thaws the corpse, thereby releasing the creatures, who look like giant slugs and have an amusing tendency to leap into people's mouths. Once there, they take over, turning their hosts into homicidal zombies. And, wouldn't you know it, on prom night! Obviously, a movie thus titled is not meant to be taken utterly seriously, and the intent here was clearly to be both funny and scary (kind of "Nerds Meet the Living Dead"). Unfortunately, it doesn't really manage either, leaving us with a lame script, annoying characters, effects that we've seen before, and actors that we might not see again. This has decent production values and it's not seriously bad — just another disappointing example of a movie that fails to fulfill the promise of its title.

RETURN OF THE LIVING DEAD PART II *(1987)*
wr and dir Ken Wiederhorn

Conveniently close to a cemetery, the Army loses another barrel of the stuff that re-animates corpses, and once again a herd of those fun-loving brain-eaters shambles into our midst. True to the sequel form, this is basically a repeat of the original, even down to having James Karen and Thom Matthews reprise their roles as the two guys who don't realize they're dead. More importantly, it's got the same slick look, some more great makeup, and another large helping of gore. It also has the attitude that no matter how revolting things get — and they get pretty putrescent — none of it is meant to be taken very seriously. This is not as good as the original, but that's the only zombie comparison it suffers by. For a sequel, this delivers a fair amount of energy of its own, and it does hold your attention for 90 minutes of good-natured gruesome fun.

THE VIDEO DEAD *(1987)*
wr, prod, dir Robert Scott

A mysterious TV set provides the gateway through which five fairly lackluster zoms leave their video world and enter ours to kill a half-dozen folks in a woodsy suburb of San Francisco. This otherwise very routine backyard effort is enlivened with some enthusiastic splatter, including a zom getting his hand cut off, another getting an iron embedded in its head, and a third being cut in half. The highlight, though, is a zombie bride in a wedding dress running through the woods, wielding a chainsaw. For the rest, it's just the usual amateurish acting, dreadful dialog, lethargic direction, and missed comic potential. As far as cheap home movies go, it's better than average, but also nothing very special. With Jennifer Miro as the nude woman who steps out of the TV set.

MUTANT
Toxic waste bloodsuckers; see Festival 3.
ZOMBIE NIGHTMARE
Heavy Metal zom bodybuilder's revenge; see Bonus Festival.
NIGHTMARE WEEKEND
Techno-voodoo zoms; see Bonus Festival.
ZOMBIE HIGH
No zoms; brain stuff; see Festival 4.

The Euro-Zoms

ZOMBIE *(1980, Italian, partly dubbed)*
wr Elisa Briganti; dir Lucio Fulci

After an unmanned boat sails into New York harbor, some intrepid investigators (Ian McCullough, Tisa Farrow) head to an isolated Caribbean island on which a virus (or something) is causing the dead to get up and munch on the living. The zom '80s opened with this one and, setting the pattern for the Euro-zoms that followed, it consists of great lumps of slow, dull, cheap stupidity enlivened by a few moments of gross-out excess. We have the usual maggots, worms, and slime, a neck-ripping, and an innards-eating, but the highlights are the now-famous giant-splinter-in-the-eyeball gag and the aquatic zom who takes a bite out of a shark. A warmup exercise in zombie quease-inducement from the director of **THE GATES OF HELL**.

> *"Since when does a Kunyat give gifts to a Hungat?"*
> THE INVINCIBLE BARBARIAN

BURIAL GROUND *(1980, Italian, dubbed)*
wr Piero Regnoli; dir Andrea Bianchi

The box for this one makes reference to "unspeakable explicit horrors" and "gruesome realism," but unless I saw a greatly subdued version, it lied. There are herds of ponderously moving zombies, each of whom sports a nifty *papier-maché* head that might have come from the junior edition of the "Living Dead Home Makeup Kit." A few lethargic maggots crawl around, presumably realistically, but the only thing that's explicit about the rest of the effects is their cheap phoniness. Besides being murky and turgid, this one also boasts one of the all-time worst dubbing jobs — so bad it seems left over from some other movie. In its favor, it does have a couple of scenes of inspired zombie nuttiness — a monastery of zombie monks and a mother who's so pleased her son has risen from the dead that she lets him suck on her breast (needless to say, a big mistake). But even these bits are more entertaining to think about than to witness. Unless you're collecting a complete set of Italian maggot shots, there's no particular reason to exhume this one.

THE GATES OF HELL *(1981, Italian, partly dubbed)*
wr Lucio Fulci and Dardano Sacchetti; dir Lucio Fulci

A priest's suicide opens the title portals, and if they're not shut quickly, all the dead in the world will rise up and destroy the living. The plot, such as it is, is slow, muddled, and filled with mumblings about witchcraft and something called the "Book of Enoch." Of course, the story is merely the flimsiest excuse for effects that, even for *giallo*, are some of the messiest ever oozed across the screen. There are gobs of putrescence crawling with worms and a storm of maggots. (Fulci claims to have used 20 pounds of them.) Skulls are torn open and brains run out; eyeballs bleed; there's a pitchfork in the stomach, a drill through a head, and, in the now-classic highlight, a girl vomits up her entire intestinal tract. Far less frightening than disgusting, this dispenses with tension, suspense, and excitement and heads straight for quease. With Christopher George as the boring reporter who gets his brains ripped out.

OASIS OF THE ZOMBIES *(1982, French, dubbed)*
wr A.L. Mariaux; dir A.M. Frank
Also released as *Bloodsucking Nazi Zombies*.

Various groups of amateurish, badly dubbed actors seek Nazi gold in the middle of the North African desert, only to discover that the treasure is guarded by dead members of the Afrika Korps. The zombies, with bulging eyes and serious complexion problems, are completely lackluster, the gore is minimal, and the movie itself is as barren and lifeless as the dunes surrounding the oasis. All of which goes to show that the French are as capable as anyone else when it comes to making cheap, boring, lousy zombie pix.

NIGHT OF THE ZOMBIES *(1983, Spanish/Italian, dubbed)*
wr Claudio Fragasso and J.M. Cunilles; dir Vincent Dawn (Bruno Mattei)

An accident at a secret research facility in a remote part of New Guinea releases a gas that brings the dead back to life, but it's not nearly enough to animate this cheap, shoddy terminal stiff. Oh, there is the usual abattoir of Italian messiness — blood, innards, maggots, flayed skin, vomiting (twice) — but none of it is well-enough done even to be disgusting. There's lots of ancient, all-purpose jungle stock footage — thus giving us a glimpse of the rare New Guinea elephant — but no shocks, no suspense, no coherence, and no reason not to fast-forward through what may be one of the least-watchable movies in this book.

CITY OF THE WALKING DEAD *(1984, Spanish/Italian, dubbed)* *wr Piero Regnoli, Tony Corti, José Luis Delgado; dir Umberto Lenzi*

A mysterious plane lands and a bunch of knife-wielding guys with brown stuff (day-old guacamole?) caked on their faces rush out, slit throats, and then suck up the blood of their victims. Whatever's ailing them is apparently infectious, because the city's soon filled with people covered with brown stuff, the military is unable to cope, civilization is doomed. This dubbed effort is not able to maintain its own feeble logic and even the effects — a lot of blood, an eye gouged out, a nipple cut off, and number of zombie heads blown apart — are so badly done that there's no impact. Walk on by this one.

ZOMBIES' LAKE *(1984, French, dubbed)*
wr A.L. Mariaux; dir J.A. Laser (Jean Rollin)

The author of **OASIS OF THE ZOMBIES** obviously felt there was more to say about zombie German soldiers, and gives us half a dozen amphibious ones who live beneath the title body of water and periodically emerge to suck blood. Like its desert predecessor, this one is as cheap as you get, featuring some of the worst dubbing you'll ever hear and some of most laughably pitiful zoms ever to get their faces smeared with bright green greasepaint. While submarine Nazi zoms appeared earlier in *Shock Waves* (1975), there is some originality here: a touching subplot involving a zombie dad and his living daughter; a zombie fist fight; and the first-ever instance of a nude girls' volleyball team being attacked by aquatic zoms.

VIRGIN AMONG THE LIVING DEAD
No zoms; bad dreams; see Festival 13.
DOCTOR BUTCHER M.D.
A few zoms; lots of innards; see Festival 4.
CREEPERS
No zoms; the ultimate maggot experience; see Festival 5.
DAWN OF THE MUMMY
Ancient Egypto-Zoms; see Festival 11.

The Deadly Living

INVASION OF THE FLESH HUNTERS *(1982, Italian, partly dubbed)* *wr Jimmy Gould and Anthony M. Dawson (Antonio Margheriti); dir Anthony M. Dawson*

Through what is described as a "biological mutation due to psychic alteration" (whatever that means), three Vietnam vets bring back a disease that gives them an irresistible urge to eat human flesh. And since this is "contagious cannibalism," anyone they chomp on acquires similar tastes. Talk about post-Vietnam Syndrome! Although an Italian production, this was largely shot in Atlanta with mostly an English-speaking cast, and thus has a somewhat better, slicker look than is usual in Euro-zoms. However, the movie doesn't fully exploit the weird potential of its premise, overlooking opportunities for creepiness and suspense and settling for a lot of routine chases and shoot-outs as the cops go after the cannibals. Still, it's not badly done, and there are a number of fairly good cannibal effects (the gross-out highlight occurs when an infected lady doctor bites her boyfriend's tongue out during a kiss). Nothing really special, but as a change from decomposing zoms, you could do a lot worse than this toothsome morsel.

Underage Zoms

ZOMBIE CHILD (1977)
wr Ralph Lucas; dir Robert Voskanian

Watch out for crummy-looking video boxes that don't give the date of the movie. For the longest time, it looked like this might be a zombie-less zombie movie, then five guys with really shabby makeup showed up and removed even that distinction from this backyard bummer. For the record, there is no pre-pubescent living dead in this one, only a tedious little girl who apparently communicates with the zoms. Brief glimpses of a couple of pretty good chewed-up faces, but nothing to make it worth the effort.

I WAS A TEENAGE ZOMBIE (1986)
wr James Martin; dir John Elias Michalakis

Through circumstances too thoroughly dumb to relate, an improbable group of high-school buddies kills a sleazy dope dealer, then dumps his body in the river. Only there's been a problem at the nuclear plant upstream, and the water is contaminated in a way that revives the corpse, now more than a little ticked off and intent on revenge. He kills three of the group (pulls out a tongue, tears off a face, breaks a neck) and rape-murders the girlfriend of a fourth. The remaining guys decide the

> *"There's something about blasting the shit out of a razorback that brightens my whole day."*
> RAZORBACK

only way to fight a zombie is with a zombie, so they dump the one with a broken neck into the river (hence, the attention-grabbing title). Unfortunately, the title — conjuring up memories of classic drive-in movies from the late '50s — is the best thing about this shoddy exercise. Neither funny nor scary, this one doesn't even manage to have any significant camp appeal.

A Zombie Variant

SOLE SURVIVOR (1982)
wr and dir Thom Eberhardt

Anita Skinner is the miraculous sole survivor of a terrible plane crash, but her troubles are just beginning. Strange people start to watch her, then follow her, then break into her house. It eventually turns out that these visitors are recently deceased corpses, animated for the purpose of claiming Anita because she isn't supposed to be alive. Not a bad premise for a neat little supernatural thriller, but *this* movie doesn't seem to know what it's about. It mixes psychology, parapsychology, and the living dead, but fails to develop the mystery aspect, without which there isn't much tension or suspense. No significant effects to keep things lively; in fact, there isn't much of anything in this one, and whatever mild curiosity it initially generates is dissipated fairly quickly by the lethargic pace and unfocused narrative. With Brinke Stevens as the girl who loses her bra during strip poker.

II

OCCULT OCCASIONS

An Invocation of Supernatural Evils

Strange and horrible creatures appear in the festivals that follow, but unlike their creature-feature cousins these ones don't necessarily occupy the standard three dimensions with which we are familiar, but rather, like Shirley MacLaine, hail from another plane of existence. These entities — with their even-less-substantial spirit confrères, the products and practitioners of the Black Arts, and the powerful parapsychological forces of the human mind — constitute the cinematic realm of the supernatural.

Descended from the gothic novel — tales of creepy castles filled with dark mysteries and tormented souls, which first appeared in the late 18th Century — the supernatural-horror film dates back to the very earliest days of the movies. Indeed, in 1896 George Méliès, one of the great film pioneers and the first special-effects wizard, made a two-minute movie, *Le Manoir du Diable* (*The Devil's Manor*, also known as *The Haunted Castle*), in which a bat that turned into Mephistopheles raised assorted phantoms and witches and was dispatched by a crucifix. More than 90 years later, filmmakers are still conjuring up those same entities in an attempt to shock and amaze us. Whereas the aliens, mutants, and zombies we met earlier are clearly of more recent cinematic origin, the majority of the supernatural horrors that follow belong to a tradition that was already well established by the time the sound era arrived.

Naturally, the style and emphasis of these movies have changed over the years. In Europe, in the silent era, the supernatural was frequently given Expressionist treatment and was used to explore serious psychological issues and dark states of mind, an approach that was later picked up in the famous series of horror films Val Lewton produced in the early 1940s (including *Cat People* and *I Walked with a Zombie*). In contrast, American movies of the 1920s gave what seemed supernatural a rational and natural explanation.

In the early '50s, with the influx of aliens and the growth of mutants, the supernatural all but disappeared from the screen. By the end of the decade the appeal of these tacky creatures had waned and supernatural horrors were back. At first, thanks largely to Britain's Hammer Films and the Poe-inspired series cranked out by Roger Corman, they crept back to their original gothic settings. Then, as these costumed period pieces grew stale and repetitious, the supernatural came increasingly to intrude upon the modern world.

Starting in the 1960s, growing permissiveness gave new blood (and flesh) to some very erotic vampires. The great success of *Rosemary's Baby* (1968) and *The Exorcist* (1973) brought the Devil back with a vengeance, and *Carrie* (1976) showed that big psychic phenomena could bring in big audiences. And, in an era of rapidly escalating real estate prices, few things were more frightening to yuppies than the financial ruin that a house-haunting could bring about, as was shown in *The Amityville Horror* (1979). As the festivals that follow indicate, these types of supernatural horrors have continued unabated into the 1980s and, with them, two variations — the Demon Movie and the Bad Dream Movie — that, while not new forms, show up more often in this decade than previously.

While the movies that follow owe debts to a variety of sources, the single most influential one is *The Exorcist*. Although it is currently the thirteenth-biggest money-maker of all time, *The Exorcist* shot to the top of the list when it was released and was so successful that it became a phenomenon. Much media time and space was devoted to speculating on its social and religious implications and the normally skeptical, materialistic public's apparent acceptance of the idea of Evil. As would be true of the hand-wringing over the rash of slasher flicks seven years later, such theorizing missed the point entirely.

The Exorcist did not break box-office records because of its "religious implications" (which, if anything, were that the forces of Good are dull and ineffectual). No, the lines stretched around the block because stories circulated that people were throwing up in theater lavotories over the gruesomeness of it all. In other words, *The Exorcist* was the first big-budget, big-studio, big-scale splatter spectacle, and all of us wanted to see if we were tough enough to watch it without tossing our cookies. The real achievement, though, was not in *The Exorcist*'s excess, but in its packaging: by serving up its sensationalism with solemnity and "significance," it gained an aura of respectability. Thus, millions of folks who would never have gone to see an average schlocky gore-fest were able to get their cheap thrills with a clear conscience.

Too cynical? Perhaps. But what, then, is *The Exorcist*, which lacks both a real beginning and a real end, actually about? What is the point? Underneath its superficial seriousness, it's about levitations, rotating heads, projectile vomiting, and little Linda Blair getting really creepy. And the point, hardly a new one, is that this sort of thing sells tickets.

The hundred-plus supernatural horrors in this section are not about religious beliefs or the reality of paranormal experiences. While a couple of the movies that follow may pretend otherwise, the supernatural is really only a vehicle or a convention that allows for provision of shocks, scares, and special effects. Neither our beliefs nor those of the filmmakers are at issue; we accept the premise of the supernatural as easily as that of the alien, the zombie, and the psycho killer. What matters is not whether Magic exists, but whether movie magic can sucessfully depict it.

That success varies in the supernatural horrors that follow. There are a few examples of exceptional filmmaking here that rank among the highlights of the 1980s, and there is the usual assortment of backyard bullshit and semi-pro spookery that sparks a few laughs or is just plain numbingly awful. Mostly, there's a lot of mediocrity — decently made movies that miss the big charge, potential that's never quite realized — that might serve the purpose if there's nothing better around.

FESTIVAL 8

* * *

ANCIENT ENEMIES
A Demonstration of Demons and Devils

"Invoked or not, Evil will come."
— *Specters*

The demon has had a long cinematic career, primarily in witchcraft movies, and Satan himself put in some notable personal appearances in the 1970s. In the 1980s, the Devil has been much less prominent, but demons have materialized in record numbers and, thanks to advances in special-effects technology, in more graphic detail than ever before.

With a few exceptions, the movies in this festival are creature features with a supernatural twist. Instead of arriving from outer space or the depths of the sea, the creatures here — demons or their equivalents — appear from Hell or some equally dark region. They are just as ugly as their terrestrial/extraterrestrial relatives, though usually not as slimy, and they are as nasty, hostile and/or hungry. Because these transdimensional tourists often have little regard for the prevailing laws of nature, their ability to create messy mischief may even be slightly greater.

In terms of the narrative, the movies in this festival generally follow the standard Us vs. It/Them formula. However, since evil is often more difficult to get rid of than those annoying monsters, there is frequently the sense in these movies that our victory over It/Them is a temporary one.

Just as some aliens have or take human form, Satan appears in the shape of a man in a few of the movies below, following on from *The Omen* (1976). Fortunately, however, most of these movies owe more to *Alien* than to the Antichrist, and endeavor to show the beasts in all their taloned, toothy, glowing-eyed, scabrous splendor.

As a group, the movies that follow don't fare too badly. There are some total stiffs and a few annoying teases, but these are offset by a few fairly entertaining efforts and a couple of near-misses. And the two **EVIL DEAD**s, between them, have enough demonic panache to raise the level of the entire genre.

The Devil in the Flesh

THE NIGHTMARE NEVER ENDS *(1980)*
wr Philip Yordan; dir Tom McGowan, Philip Marshak, and Greg Tallos

Two too many directors is never a good sign, and the script, which seems to consist of scraps from the first two *Omen* installments, didn't help. Cheap, slow and murky, you often can't tell what's going on, and you're given no reason to care. This may be the only movie in which open-heart surgery is performed on Satan, but even this dubious distinction doesn't save it. With "Charles Moll" who, unless he's a twin, is an earlier, haired incarnation of the actor now calling himself Richard. Seemingly never-ending, this nightmare never gets started.

FEAR NO EVIL *(1981)*
wr and dir Frank LaLoggia

Lucifer is alive and well and living in the Thousand Islands of upstate New York, incarnated as skinny high-school nerd Andrew (Stefan Arngrim). He's quite a kidder, all right, dropping an iron on his mother's head, causing one of his male classmates to grow tits, crushing another with a basketball, and crucifying for real the lead during a production of the Passion Play. Fortunately for the fate of the world, one of Andrew's classmates (Kathleen Rowe McAllen) happens to be the incarnation of a good angel on a mission from God to defeat Evil. Unfortunately, for the viewer, the low-budget effects, weak script, and amateur acting are made worse by the pervasive fervid religiosity. A debut effort by an inexperienced filmmaker, it's way too ambitious for its own good, a problem similarly in evidence in the director's more recent **LADY IN WHITE**.

Last Judgments

BORN OF FIRE *(1986, Turkish)*
wr Ralicq Abdulla; dir Jamil Dehlavi

This is probably the strangest movie in this festival — and one of the oddest in this book. Basically, an Islamic version of the struggle between

Good and Evil, the latter being a djinn called the Master Musician who threatens to destroy the fabric of the world unless the former, British flutist Peter Firth, can discover the melody that will defeat him. Much more complex than this brief statement suggests — and not nearly as silly — this one manages, through mystery and mysticism rather than horror or shocks (though there are ample weird and creepy occurrences), to generate considerable suspense. Filmed in the almost unbelievably other-worldly Turkish region of Cappadocia, this is an extraordinarily beautiful movie, one of those rare efforts whose visuals are strong enough to hold your interest even if you're not always sure what's going on. In the end, I think it does cohere — although not entirely on the literal level — and the result is one of the most poetic and ethereal treatments of the supernatural ever made.

THE SEVENTH SIGN *(1988)*
wr W.W. Wicket and George Kaplan; dir Carl Schultz

There's no devil in this one, but God is so pissed off that He's decided to close down the shop, bringing about the end of the world according to signs given in the Book of Revelations. Pregnant Abby Quinn (Demi Moore) catches on to what's happening and realizes that the birth of her baby will be the title omen, the one that initiates the final apocalypse, unless she can head it off. This feels quite familiar — *The Omen* and *Rosemary's Baby* are obvious influences — but "dreadful prophecies coming true" is an effective type of story, and this is a perfectly respectable version, well-acted and nicely shot, and the script and direction are more concerned with serving up low-key suspense than with going for the big supernatural shocks. In fact, the biggest problem is that this one is too respectable and low key for its own good — jabbing away but never delivering any real big punches. Still, there are some quite good moments and performances, and it does keep you interested if not completely enthralled. And for those curious about what you can do with body molds, a pregnant Demi Moore taking a bath is most instructive.

"I'm going to take a bath."
BO DEREK IN TARZAN, THE APE MAN

Demonic Hordes

THE EVIL DEAD *(1982)*
wr and dir Sam Raimi

Identified in the closing credits as "the ultimate experience in grueling horror," this outrageous low-budget debut film attracted, and warrants, a cult following. Five collegiate types on an outing to an isolated cabin in the woods inadvertently invoke a bunch of extraordinarily nasty Sumerian demons, who promptly start to take possession of the young folks. Basically a demonic version of *Night of the Living Dead*, this wastes almost no time in getting down to business, and then relentlessly heaps hideousness upon gore, upon weirdness. Obviously not meant to be taken seriously, this one dispenses entirely with plot and characterization in its cheerfully single-minded determination to deliver the goods in a way few movies ever have. And, calling on nearly every effect in the book, it very nearly succeeds. Cheap and unpolished and amateurish in many respects, it displays considerable wit, intelligence, and energy; a real love of movie magic; and a great deal of talent and inventiveness. Only a lack of money kept this from being as good (and as disgusting) as it wanted to be, a problem that was remedied in . . .

EVIL DEAD II *(1987)*
wr Sam Raimi and Scott Spiegel; dir Sam Raimi

The Sumerian demons are back, and they have not exactly mellowed in the intervening years. Not as much a sequel as a deluxe remake of the original, this one starts with excess and then gets really gross. Mayhem and mutilation abound, and blood gushes as though spewed out of a firehose. The excess is both nonstop and the source of much of the humor; we sit back as gruesomeness follows bizarreness, and we never have to wait long for the next outrageous occurrence, carried along by the flamboyant camera work that is becoming Raimi's trademark. Definitely not for the squeamish — or those who insist on logic in their movies — but a hell of a lot of fun. As much an exercise in surrealism as in horror, this is one of the most spectacular pieces of filmmaking in the 1980s, and one of my personal favorites. (Note: I recommend that you watch both versions, in order.)

DEMONS *(1985, Italian, dubbed)*
wr Dario Argento, Lamberto Bava, Dardano Sacchetti, and Franco Ferrini; dir Lamberto Bava

A mysterious theater is showing a horror film, "Coming of the Demons," and — you guessed it — before too long they come in person. So, what we have is a film-within-a-film, and neither is very good, but they sure are gooey. The demons have more than a passing resemblance to Italian zombies, with a fondness for flesh-tearing and the delightful habit of belching up foamy green slime. The plot, such as it is, is essentially *Night of the Living Dead* in reverse, with the patrons trying to get out of the theater as more and more of their number are converted to the demon persuasion. Along the way, throats are ripped, eyes are gouged, a scalp is pulled off, and a hand is shot apart. The effects are abundant and, while not really all that convincing, do frequently manage to be fairly disgusting. For the rest, it's mostly dubbed hysteria, murky red lighting, and a pounding mid-'80s rock-and-roll soundtrack. Although a little slicker and quicker-paced than most of the oozing Italian numbers, this one's still probably only for those with a real taste for spaghetti splatter.

DEMONS 2 *(1987, Italian, dubbed)*
wr Dario Argento, Lamberto Bava, Franco Ferrini, and Dardano Sacchetti; dir Lamberto Bava

The filmmakers here obviously subscribe to the theory that the only proper sequel is a faithful remake of the original. Substitute a highrise apartment building for a movie theater and a television set for a movie screen, add a kid-demon and a demon terrier, and you've got the same film. These demons look even more like zombies than their predecessors, but other than some moderately flashy makeup, the effects are pretty scarce and generally subdued. Score this one Demons 2, Viewers 0.

NEON MANIACS *(1985)*
wr Mark Patrick Carducci; dir Joseph Mangine

There is no neon. The maniacs are a bunch of demonoid beings — apeman, surgeon, soldier, samurai, Indian: mutant Village People, in short — who live underneath San Francisco's Golden Gate Bridge and come out at night to slaughter a lot of brainless teens. The fact that the maniacs melt down when exposed to water is never, like most things here, explained, but you won't be interested enough to care. Another great title bites the dust.

THE GATE *(1987, Canadian)*
wr Michael Nankin; dir Tibor Takacs

Call this one "Goonies Go to Hell." A gate to the nether region opens up in a suburban backyard, and the ensuing demon infestation lowers property values. Mom and Dad are away for the weekend, so it's up to the kids to deal with the problem. Nothing much happens for the first half, then the special effects start. There are a few good ones — especially the litter of of Lilliputian carnivorous demons — but mostly it's the standard shakings, blowings, smoke, and light shows. Decently done, given the budget constraints, but too predictable to appeal to anyone older than the pre-teen protagonists. Keep this gate closed.

Horny Devils

INCUBUS *(1981)*
wr George Franklin; dir John Hough

According to my dictionary, the title entity has sexual intercourse with women while they are sleeping. The fella here (who appears for about 10 seconds at the end) is a little more direct: he rapes his victims while they're awake — at the beach, in a museum, in the shower, in a movie-theater lavatory — then kills them. He also puts a spike through a guy's forehead, pitchforks a German shepherd, and buries a shovel in the neck of another guy who then blows off his own feet with a shotgun. All of this takes maybe 5 minutes, leaving us with 95 minutes of "the Story." Since this is based on a novel by Ray Russell, there presumably was a story here at one time, but it seems to have been edited out. There are a few good effects, some unintentional humor (lots of chat about the quantity and quality of the rapist's sperm), and a bunch of memorably bad performances, most notably by John Cassavetes, looking intense to the point of psychopathy, and John Ireland, who keeps saying such things as "I've never seen such a brutal rape."

THE ENTITY *(1981)*
wr Frank DeFelitta; dir Sidney J. Furie

Supposedly based upon an actual incident in which Carla Moran, a young single mother, was sexually assualted in her bedroom by a large and powerful invisible presence. A good part of the movie is devoted to Carla's efforts to make people believe the presence is real, while her shrink patronizes her. Although about demon rape — fairly high up on the exploitation scale — this takes its parapsychological subject very seriously and, in so doing, tends to be painfully earnest and rather slow-moving. Among the usual shakings, slammings, and electrical discharges, there's a breast manipulated by invisible fingers, something that you probably haven't seen before, but what really distinguishes this movie — and gives it whatever energy and dignity it possesses — is Barbara Hershey's performance as Carla. She's in almost every frame and she's terrific, rising so high above the level of the material that she almost manages to take the movie up with her. In the end, it turns out to be a little too heavy for her, but she makes a hell of an effort nonetheless.

POSSESSION *(1983, German/French)*
wr and dir Andrezej Zulawski

Sam Neill goes around the bend when he discovers that his wife (Isabelle Adjani) is having an affair, then gets even more agitated when he finds out the lover is a slimy tentacled creature that she apparently conjured up. Part art film, part supernatural thriller, and part splatter horror, this one's an incomprehensible mess. The fact that the video version runs some 40 minutes shorter than the original probably doesn't help, but given the extraordinarily overwrought performances, it can't hurt either. The highlight is Isabelle having sex with the creature — a unique cinematic experience, but not sufficient reason to wallow through this one.

MY DEMON LOVER
Gypsy-cursed shape-shifter; see Festival 6.

Bottled Spirits

THE OUTING *(1986)*
wr Warren Chaney; dir Tom Daley

A bunch of Houston high-school lamebrains spend the night in a museum with a magic lamp from 3500 B.C. and the lamp's occupant, a genie who's kind of ticked off at being cooped up so long. This is slightly slicker and more professional than a lot of Texas cheapies, but that doesn't compensate for a lack of suspense, energy, and decent effects. The mayhem is always off-camera, and the genie is a low-rent version of the entity in **THE KEEP**. Slow, mechanical, and stupid, this one does have the distinction of being perhaps the first movie in which a Flintstone cartoon provides an important plot point. With Michelle Watkins as the topless bimbo who is djinned to death.

PRINCE OF DARKNESS *(1987)*
wr Martin Quatermass; dir John Carpenter

At the request of a priest (Donald Pleasence), a physicist (Victor Wong) and some graduate students (including Jameson Parker and Lisa Blount) go to an abandoned church to investigate the contents of a mysterious large glass jar that has been hidden there for almost 500 years. The stuff turns out to be essence of Satan that's getting ready to release itself in order to bring his father back into the world. The first half of this one is really good as science confronts the supernatural and Carpenter tightens the tension to create an unrelenting sense of impending menace. Unfortunately, he's unable to sustain it, and the second half is something of a disappointment. Still, this is very slickly made, with some good effects and performances (especially Wong's), and characters worth watching and listening to. (I believe it's Carpenter himself behind the writing credit, which is, of course, the name of the hero of a well-known trilogy of British sci-fi films.) While this didn't do very much business at the box office, it's certainly worth the rental cost.

SORORITY BABES IN THE SLIMEBALL BOWL-O-RAMA *(1987) wr Sergei Hasenecz; dir David DeCoteau*

As part of an initiation hazing, the title babes and three collegiate nerdos break into an bowling alley, where they accidentally release an imp from the bowling trophy in which he's been imprisoned for thirty years. A fun-loving little fiend, he turns three of the sisters into homicidal demons — one with a beehive hairdo, another with a serious complexion problem, and the third, a leather-clad dominatrix. The gals deep-fry one of the nerds, throw a gutter ball with the head of another, and rip a pledge in half. The mayhem is largely off-camera and the effects are nothing special, but this aims much more for laughs, and it delivers a few, maintaining a likably cheerful silliness. Not quite as dynamically tacky as its title — how could it be? — it has decent production values and performances (especially Linnea Quigley as a punkette burglar), a brisk pace, and the good sense to keep Michelle McClellan out of her clothes for a large part of the proceedings. A lot more fun than most of the offerings of Troma Team, which also feature outrageous titles, but rarely deliver the goods. (The tape also includes previews for *Galactic Gigolo* and *Assault of the Killer Bimbos*, which I regret I've not yet been able to locate.)

THE KEEP
Bricked-up demonoid vamp; see Festival 12.

Necronomiconia

FOREVER EVIL *(1987)*
dir Roger Evans

A vague borrowing from the mythology of H.P. Lovecraft, this one gives us a follower of Yog Kothag, one of the ancient evil gods who was exiled to a distant star, who is going around performing the necessary human sacrifices that will bring Yog back to earth and end the reign of man. This backyard Texas effort opens, in a sequence borrowed from **THE EVIL DEAD**, with the slaughter of five people in an isolated cottage by an unseen power. Then it segues into a supernatural thriller *à la The Night Stalker* (1971), as two survivors try to figure out what's going on. Along the way, there's also an unkillable decomposing zombie and a killer baby, like those from *It's Alive!* There is some good makeup and a bit of enthusiastic gore, but not enough to offset the endless chat (presumably improvised since no writer is credited). Use the fast-forward, and you could probably do worse than this one. One big effect — the graphic birth of a monster baby by self-administered Caesarian section — should catch your attention. With Diane Johnson as the naked bloody bimbo. (Not to be confused with **ETERNAL EVIL**.)

THE UNNAMABLE *(1988, direct to cassette)*
wr and dir Jean-Paul Ouellette

Based upon an H.P. Lovecraft story, this concerns some "indescribable horror," apparently conjured up through the *Necronomicon*, that's been locked in a haunted house for 300 years. Naturally, it's gotten kind of hungry over the centuries, so it's more than ready when dinner is delivered in the form of a bunch of bozos from the local college. This owes much more to *Friday the 13th* than to Lovecraft, and its not exactly a welcome deviation. The plotting is slow and mechanical and the characters are barely clichés. For a long time, it seems as though the creature will be unseen as well as unnamed, but it finally puts in an appearance and turns out to be a clawed albino hermaphrodite satyr that minces around on goat hooves. It's not bad, but the tedium of sex-obsessed frat boys outweighs the few good effects — a heart torn out, a throat-ripping. Mark Kinsey Stephenson gives an interesting performance as Randolph Carter, and Laura Albert shows to effect why she was cast as Wendy, the buxom bimbo who gets her head torn off.

Little Devils

GHOULIES *(1985)*
wr Luca Bercovici and Jeffrey Levy; dir Luca Bercovici

Faster than you can say bandwagon, this one jumped on it. The model, very obviously, was *Gremlins*, which demonstrated that small nasty creatures could be big box office. The title creatures here are even nastier than their Spielbergian predecessors — all sharp teeth and serious complexion problems — but that's to be expected, since they're actually some kind of minor demon, unfortunately in a minor role. They don't do much, except provide the title and the three minutes of snarling used in the TV commercial. Jonathan (Peter Liapis) inherits the house where his dead father had practiced the dark arts, and before you know it, he's down in the basement conjuring up the ghoulies, then a pair of rather bizarre dwarfs. When he and some friends raise his magician father from the grave, all hell breaks loose, so to speak. Amid the Black Magic hokum are lots of ho-hum effects (Dad's four-foot-long prehensile tongue isn't bad, though), but this one's basically a total stiff.

GHOULIES II *(1987 direct to cassette)*
wr Dennis Paoli; dir Albert Band

They're back, this time hanging out in the cheesy Chamber of Horrors of a fifth-rate traveling carnival, where they slime up some people with epoxy mucous, chew up a few more, and wreak the usual havoc. This is a much better movie than the original (though that may be like saying that serious facial warts are to be preferred to leprosy). The production values are good, the pace is fairly brisk, the Black Magic bullshit is kept to a minimum, and while the plot and the characters are nothing but clichés, at least the execution is competent. Some decent, if unspectacular effects, but the PG rating means no graphic munching or sleaze. Still you could do a lot worse. Like the following . . .

HOBGOBLINS *(1988)*
wr, prod, dir Rick Sloane

Five submoronic escapees from a Grade-Z teen comedy spend a very long night pursuing the title critters, mutated koala-bear handpuppets who appear to make dreams come true before destroying the dreamers. Makes **GHOULIES** look like an art film.

> *"You're much too beautiful a girl to be let yourself be broken into food for the royal dogs."*
> BARBARIAN QUEEN

Diverse Demons

DEADLY BLESSING *(1981)*
wr Glenn M. Benest, Matthew Barr, and Wes Craven; dir Wes Craven

Religious mania and repressed sexuality run rampant in the isolated farming community of the Hittites, a sect that makes "the Amish look like swingers." Folks are getting bumped off. Who or what is responsible? Is it virginal Melissa (Coleen Riley) who roams the countryside in her nightgown, brandishing a knife? Is it Lois Nettleton, who's phobic about men? Is it her peculiar daughter, Faith, who eventually turns out to be a boy? Or is it, as Hittite patriarch Ernest Borgnine keeps ranting, an incubus connected to the outsiders in their midst. All of the above, is my guess, but I was utterly confused. This is beautifully photographed, there are a couple of good shocks — a spider drops in Sharon Stone's mouth, a snake joins Maren Jensen in the bathtub — and the last 10 minutes or so are not bad, but it's probably not worth the wait. The incubus, by the way, is barely seen, appears for only a couple of seconds at the very end, seems completely gratuitous, and only serves to make matters even more muddled and pointless.

SPECTERS *(1987, Italian, mostly dubbed)*
wr Marcello Avallone, Andrea Purgatori, Dardano Sacchetti, and Maurizo Tedesco; dir Marcello Avallone

While excavating some of the catacombs beneath Rome, archaeologist Donald Pleasence comes upon a secret 2000-year-old tomb that houses a demon left over from pagan times. This has a good slick look, lots of atmosphere, and a sense of menace, but virtually nothing is done with it. The tomb's inscription reads "Invoked or not, Evil will come," but, for the longest time, doesn't. Finally, the demon — or at least his scaly, taloned hand — puts in an appearance to rip off a couple of faces and tear out a heart. The rest of the demon is shown so briefly and indistinctly that it's hard to be sure just what it is. While not actively bad, this one goes off on so many tangents it never gets anywhere.

THE UNHOLY *(1987)*
wr Philip Yordan and Fernando Fonseca; dir Camilo Vila

In New Orleans, Father Michael (Ben Cross, the Jewish runner in *Chariots of Fire*), a priest who's skeptical about the actual existence of the Devil and demons, eventually changes his mind when he reopens a church where the previous two priests had their throats slit, and he confronts the title entity, a super-demon who specializes in the temptation and murder of priests. It appears to him, first as a naked Nicole Fortier, who is indeed luscious enough to tempt a saint, then in its true form, which is considerably less appealing. This is a touch slow in the middle, but dripping with atmosphere and very stylishly made. It's also well-enough plotted to maintain tension and keep you guessing. There are a number of impressive effects, including a guy vomiting about 50 gallons of blood and a long concluding battle that doesn't stint on the demon (that has the most obscene tongue this side of Prince). With old pros such as Ned Beatty, Hal Holbrook, and Trevor Howard along to give the nonsense some credibility and some nudity for sizzle, this one manages to be consistently quite watchable and good for some mindless demonic fun.

MAUSOLEUM
Toothed-titted demonic possession; see Festival 9.
THE DEMON
No demon; clawed psycho killer; see Festival 19.
DEMONOID
No demon; sinister manual possession; see Festival 9.
NIGHT OF THE DEMON
No demon; bigfoot; see Festival 2.
DEMON OF PARADISE
No demon; webfoot; see Festival 2.
DEMONWARP
No demon; aliens, zombies, and bigfoot; see Festival 1.
FIEND
Ultra-lousy demonic optical effect; see Bonus Festival.

FESTIVAL 9

* * *

HOSTILE TAKEOVERS
An Inventory of Possessions

> "I don't feel like me anymore."
> — *The Awakening*

Movies about possessions — individuals being taken over by hostile spirits or demonic forces — go back to the silent era. It seems the earliest such effort was a 1924 Austrian version of *The Hands of Orlac*, a French novel by Maurice Renard. Here, after an accident, a pianist is given a new set of hands, only they turn out to have belonged to a murderer and have a homicidal will of their own. This story was remade several times, the best-known version being *Mad Love* (1935) with Peter Lorre. As well, movies have been made about the spirits of dead witches inhabiting the living in order to exact revenge, and about soul transfers (*The Mephisto Waltz,* 1971); and 1972 saw the release of *The Possession of Joel Delaney* in which the title character is taken over by a Puerto Rican sex-murderer.

Of course, the possession that made *everyone* aware of the phenomenon was little Linda Blair's in *The Exorcist* (1973). As far as I can determine, this was the first film treatment of demonic possession, a state that really opens up the world of special-effects wizardry.

Showcasing the work of such artists as Dick Smith and Rick Baker, *The Exorcist* took full advantage of the potential of the premise, and served up some of the most spectacular — and spectacularly messy — effects that had ever been seen. In terms of the movies in this festival, it also established and defined what has become a mini-genre.

The narrative line of the post-*Exorcist* possession movie is about as basic and stripped down as you can get: a person is taken over by a nasty spirit of some sort; the spirit causes all kinds of havoc; the spirit is dispatched; the end. Since the character at the center of the movie — the possessee — is essentially a bystander, there's a curious absence of real conflict, and little possibility for the kind of plot twists that are necessary for an engaging, well-structured story.

In this respect, the possession movie most resembles the psycho-killer epic (see Section III). The psycho's demons are internal rather than imposed from the outside, and, lacking telekinetic power, he has to physically wield his weapon, but otherwise there is little difference, and the focus of the movie is clearly on the havoc the psycho causes. With the slice-and-dicers, though, there is at least the possibility of adding some mystery with regard to the identity of the killer, an element that is not available in the possession movie.

In my view, the most interesting and successful possession movie of the 1980s is not a horror movie at all, but a comedy. The Steve Martin - Lily Tomlin *All of Me* (1984) is essentially a comic variant of *The Hands of Orlac*, and it works because the central character is not merely a passive vessel, but is actively involved in the conflict going on within his body.

With *The Exorcist*, the lavish spectacle and the quality of the production made it easy to overlook the fundamental hollowness at the center. In most of the movies that follow — without much spectacle, energy, wit, or originality — there is little to distract us from the mechanical emptiness of the exercise.

It seems clear that unless someone figures out a new variation on the form — or invests it with extraordinary energy, as Sam Raimi did (see **EVIL DEAD**s, above) — the possession movie is really a dead end, and we can hope that this most unprepossessing form will soon fade away.

The Presence in Residence

AMITYVILLE II: THE POSSESSION *(1982, U.S./Mexican)*
wr Tommy Lee Wallace; dir Damiano Damiani

Based, no doubt very loosely, on *Murder in Amityville* by Hans Holzer, this is a prequel to *The Amityville Horror*, and concerns the brutal murders that occurred before the hapless Lutzes moved into their dream house. As the subtitle indicates, the movie is less about the haunted house — though there are lots of movings, shakings, and other weirdnesses — than about Sonny's (Jack Magner) takeover by the resident evil spirit. First he grows sullen, then he commits incest with his sister, then his complexion gets shot to hell (so to speak) as the demon starts to manifest itself, then he blasts the other five members of his family with a shotgun, then he gets exorcised by the local priest (James Olson) who, having learned a trick or two from Father Jason Miller, invites the demon to possess him instead. With Burt Young as the abusive loutish father and Rutanya Alda as whimpering wimpish Mom, this one starts out being overwrought then really cranks up the emotional intensity. Some good effects and makeup, some very flashy camera work and direction, and a good dose of gratuitous nastiness just to keep things moving make this, while not a good movie, the best one in this festival. It's so vigorously and relentlessly sensationalistic that those with slightly warped sensibilities might well find that it holds their attention. I know I did.

MAUSOLEUM *(1983)*
wr Robert Barich and Robert Madero; dir Michael Dugan

For several centuries, for reasons not explained, the first daughter born into each generation of the Nomed family is possessed by a demon. ("Nomed" is "demon" spelled backwards. Clever huh?) As family traditions go, this one sucks, especially since the demon isn't likely to win any awards for congeniality. The current generation's possessee is a blonde bimbo named Susan who periodically displays the usual symptoms — glowing green eyes, echo-chamber voice, and a fondness for levitating people and ripping their faces off. Bobbie Bresee plays Susan, and although she's just as wooden as everyone else in the cast, she spends most of the time in revealing negligées (or out of them), so it's not nearly as noticeable. For a low-budget job, the effects aren't bad, but they're scarce, and you don't see much of the demon until the very end. Aside from the fact that the demon has a pair of carnivorous breasts, there's probably nothing here you haven't seen before. I'll leave it up to you to decide if those are enough of an inducement.

KILLER PARTY *(1986)*
wr Barney Cohen; dir William Fruet

This opens with a movie-within-a-movie-within-a-video-within-the-movie, thus expending the bulk of its creativity and cleverness before the credits roll. For the longest time, it seems like we've got yet another psycho on campus here, as a bunch of fraternity bozos and sorority bimbos hold a party in a frat house that's been vacant for 20 years, ever since an initiation prank resulted in the death of a pledge. Sound vaguely familiar? This very deliberately trots out almost every slasher cliché from *Halloween* to **HELL NIGHT**, but what might have been an amusing pastiche if done with some wit, ends up a pointless exercise. After more than an hour without producing a body count, the story takes its final meaningless twist and becomes a tale of possession, as Joanna Johnson gets taken over by the spirit of the dead pledge and wipes out everyone at the party. The possession sequence is kind of fun, but not worth the wait, and the mayhem is entirely off-camera. Some not-bad bits and pieces here, but they add up to nothing. (The director repeated this kind of unfunny catalog of genre clichés the following year in **BLUE MONKEY**, but not to any greater effect.) With five minutes of Paul Bartel that contributes nothing to nothing.

HELLO MARY LOU: PROM NIGHT II *(1987, Canadian)*
wr Ron Oliver; dir Bruce Pittman

The characters in this one all have the last names of horror directors, but they left out the only one that matters — De Palma — because this is much less *Prom Night II* than *Carrie* again. The spirit of Mary Lou — school slut circa 1957 — has been waiting 30 years in a trunk in the school basement for a chance to take revenge on those who caused her to burst into flames just before she was to be crowned prom queen. When virginal Vicki (Wendy Lynn) opens the trunk, she is possessed by the spirit and becomes Mary Lou Maloney, prom queen from Hell. She takes off her clothes and crushes a friend in a gym locker, then causes the usual telekinetic mayhem at the big dance. Large chunks of the script have been lifted whole from *Carrie*, but the flair, energy, and excitement were left behind. There's lots of teen chatter, but little suspense, and although there are a couple of decent effects, most are limp, bloodless, and very familiar. Another wimpish wallflower.

POSSESSION
No possession; amorous tentacled entity; see Festival 8.

> "Some people get fever blisters when they're sick. I get a long tail and lizard skin."
>
> MY DEMON LOVER

Crypto Egyptos

THE AWAKENING *(1980)*
wr Allan Scott, Chris Bryant, and Clive Exton; dir Mike Newell

Despite warnings to the contrary, an obsessed archaeologist (Charlton Heston) opens the tomb of the "Unnamed Queen," enabling the queen's evil spirit to travel from tomb to womb, and take possession of his newborn daughter. Cut to 18 years later: Chuck now has a beard, the baby has turned into Stephanie ("I don't feel like me anymore") Zimbalist, and it's time to perform the ritual that will fully reincarnate the 3000-year-old queen. Based on a Bram Stoker novel, this is basically *The Omen* with an Egyptian twist: anyone who tries to interfere with the queen's plans meets a violent death, but very little else happens, and the script fails to develop any real tension or suspense. Teetering on the brink camp humor, it doesn't quite have the vigor to get there, and remains strictly soporific.

MANHATTAN BABY *(1982, Italian, dubbed)*
wr Elisa Livia Briganti and Dardano Sacchetti; dir Lucio Fulci

From the writers of **1990: BRONX WARRIORS** and the director of two outrageous Italian zombie flicks comes this slow, muddled, badly dubbed supernatural nonsense. It takes about 80 of its 90 minutes to reveal that it's ripping off **THE AWAKENING** (of all things!), and gives us a little girl who gets taken over by an amulet known as the "Eye of Evil" — an ancient Egyptian mood ring that can "open the infernal gate." Lots of slow, portentous camera work, suspicious looks, and suspenseful music, but virtually nothing happens. There is a scene in which a taxidermist is pecked to death by his stuffed birds, but it's the final sequence and not worth the wait. The title, by the way, has no apparent significance, except perhaps to suggest some unjustified connection to Rosemary's offspring.

MIRROR OF DEATH *(1987, made for video)*
wr Gerry Daly; dir Deryn Warren

For those who have been keenly awaiting the next slow, dull, ultra-cheap, amateurish, shot-on-tape, backyard possession opus, this one delivers the goods. Sarah (Julie Merrill), a mousy airhead with no self-esteem, lights some candles and recites voodoo chants in the hope of becoming beautiful. Selecting the wrong chant to recite, she summons a really cheap optical effect out of the title looking glass. Empress Sura, apparently some kind of goddess left over from ancient Egypt, makes Sarah beautiful; then makes her pick up men; then makes her rip a throat open, put a dagger in an eye, and tear out a heart (none of which is likely to satisfy even the least discriminating gorehound). At one point, Sarah's sister tells her, "You are dealing with something you know nothing about," and the same might be said to the filmmakers, who are clearly clueless as to what constitutes conflict, suspense, tension, or an interesting story. Upon reflection, there seems to be no reason to look into this one.

Indian Invaders

DEMONOID *(1981)*
wr David Lee Fein, Alfred Zacharias, and F. Amos Powell; dir Alfred Zacharias

There's this ancient Mexican devil (or something) that lives in the left hands of those it possesses. In the first half of this one, Samantha Eggar, assisted by priest Stuart Whitman, pursues a series of hands, each of which is eventually severed from its owner ("This hand wasn't meant for you"). In the second half, Sam is pursued by a series of hands, each of which is eventually severed from its owner. The special effects, limited to a few shots of crawling hands, are pathetically shabby, but superior in quality to the script, direction, and performances. Naturally, anything this cheap and ridiculous can't help but provide a couple of laughs, but nothing justifies the effort required to slog through the tedium.

THE POWER *(1983)*
wr and dir Jeff Obrow and Stephen Carpenter

The spirit of Destacatyl, an evil Aztec deity, possesses all those who own a small clay figurine of the god, giving them the power to move objects telekinetically and to grow large rubber noses. A rather slow, routine possession effort, rambling and unfocused in its plotting, this one is slightly enlivened by some not terribly original or impressive effects. All in all, this is very familiar stuff — neither gripping nor gross — about twenty-five watts worth.

SCALPS *(1983)*
wr and dir Fred Olen Ray

Some jerky collegiate anthropologists go into the desert to dig up a sacred Indian burial ground, and one of them is possessed by the spirit of Black Claw, a renegade Indian magician with a serious complexion problem. Soon the others are being shot with arrows, hacked, or bopped with a rubber tomahawk. (Despite the title, there is only one scalping, and that has all the impact of an orange peeling.) If this weren't so dull it might have been laughable, but, as it is, the only thing that distinguishes this no-budget effort is some of the worst day-for-night photography you're ever likely to see. Midway, the spacey girl D.J. remarks that "something horrid is going to happen." It does: the closing credits threaten us to "watch for *Scalps II* — The Return of D.J." With Carol Sue Flockhart as the bimbo who gets her shirt ripped off.

A Possessive Parent

BLOODSPELL *(1988, direct to video?)*
wr Gerry Daly; dir Deryn Warren

When a nice kid named Daniel (Anthony Jenkins) gets taken over by the spirit of his evil father (or, more precisely, by the evil spirit that has taken over Dad), bizarre accidents and horrible deaths befall the resident "teenagers" at the St. Boniface Group Home for Emotionally Disturbed Bad Young Actors. Of course, being just a step or two above basic backyard, this one doesn't offer much in the way of graphic mayhem, other than a couple of decent makeup effects and a nicely handled chewing-up in a woodchipper that might catch your attention. What's more likely to catch your attention, though, are performances so painfully overwrought that they become the acting equivalent of fingernails scraped across a blackboard. By no means classic stuff, but for those with a taste for turkey, this is dumb and silly enough to provide the odd laugh (if you enjoy the wood-chipper, the *very* odd laugh). And laughably bad is an improvement for the writer/director team who perpetrated the deadly dull **MIRROR OF DEATH** the year before.

Nine Tenths of Nothing

THE RIPPER *(1986, made for video)*
wr Bill Groves; dir Christopher Lewis

Oklahoma's home-grown goremeisters (**BLOOD CULT**, **REVENGE**) are back with another piece of shot-on-tape backyard sludge. The title refers, of course, to Jack, the original slice-and-dicer, who, via a magic ring, takes possession of a very drippy English professor (Tom Schreier), and starts carving up young women in Tulsa. This cross-genre premise might have worked, but not with this numbingly amateurish execution. There are five so-so throat slittings, followed by three lackluster disembowelings, but the main distinction (?) of this is effects wizard Tom Savini's brief appearance as Saucy Jack, a performance that demonstrates why he wisely spends most of his time behind the camera. Marginally more competent than the earlier Tulsa witch shit, but still utterly unwatchable.

FESTIVAL 10

* * *

TROUBLED SPOTS
A Refrain of Hauntings

> "No, I won't — I won't leave this house!"
> — *The Nesting*

For over a century before the birth of the motion picture, old, dark, scary houses — whether or not actually haunted by resident spirits — had been a familiar subject and setting of popular literature and drama. It is thus not surprising that haunted-house movies have been turning up on the screen ever since the silent era.

What is surprising — at least, it was to me — is that before the 1960s the haunted house was hardly ever treated as either supernatural or horror. There were supposedly haunted houses, but the mysterious goings on were eventually shown to have perfectly natural, if nefarious, origins. Also, the subject was almost invariably played for a mixture of chills and comedy, with the latter winning out in the end. That this combination is still popular can be seen in **HOUSE**, the most financially successful movie included in this festival, the big hit *Beetlejuice* (1988), and *Ghostbusters* (1984), the most successful supernatural movie ever made. (It's interesting to note that *Ghostbusters* seems to be a comic version of *The Sentinel* (1976), and that its title is almost certainly derived from *The Ghost Breakers* (1940), a haunted comedy starring Bob Hope, that was itself a remake of *The Ghost Breaker* (1924), which appears to be the very first screen treatment of a haunted-house story.)

In the 1960s, with the growing interest in paranormal phenomena, haunted-house movies finally entered the realm of the supernatural proper. Such films as *The Haunting* (1963) and *The Legend of Hell House* (1973) employed the common formula: a team of occult investigators checks out a house reputed to be haunted and discovers that, like the fabled monsters of Festival 2, the legends have substance. The movies of this period used special effects, but mostly they strove to create suspense and atmosphere, and the story generally focused on the unraveling of the mystery as to why the house was so inhospitable.

Following the megasuccess of *The Exorcist*, the emphasis shifted, and troubled houses more often came to be seen as a natural venue for the provision of supernatural spectacle. This trend produced such movies as *House of the Seven Corpses* (1974), *Burnt Offerings*, *Suspiria*, *The Sentinel* (all 1976), *The Evil* (1978), and, in 1979, *The Amityville Horror*.

Based upon the best-selling account of a "true" occurrence, *Amityville*, like *The Exorcist*, treated its subject with considerable seriousness — what the *Aurum Film Encyclopedia* describes as "coffee-table horrors" — but did not stint on the big effects. It promptly took in something around $70 million at the box office, making it easily the most successful haunted-house movie and the second-biggest supernatural horror film to that date. Then, the Haunted '80s were upon us, and the success of such movies as *Ghost Story* (1981) and more especially *Poltergeist* (1982), with an even bigger box office than *Amityville*, has done nothing to diminish the appeal of the form.

Hauntings, of course, are not limited to houses. While that is certainly the most common variety, the condition can also apply to other structures and tracts of land, and to inanimate objects (the best-known example being a '58 Plymouth Fury named Christine). To some extent, movies about hauntings are the supernatural equivalents of the movies in Festival 5, movies concerned with the rebellion of Nature and the disruption of the natural order. Hauntings, too, are concerned with things (objects or environments) that should be unexceptional, predictable and safe, but that turn menacing and deadly. Even more cruelly ironic than the situation in the slasher flicks, in which a victim is menaced in what should be the safety of his or her own home, is a haunting in which one is menaced *by* one's home.

Regardless of locale, most of the movies that follow treat their hauntings essentially as possessions. The point of the exercise is, more often than not, the weird, messy, and/or spectacular havoc caused by the controlling entity.

However, unlike human-possession movies, where the who, why, and how are incidental, the haunting movie gives the viewer questions. The answers most commonly are that the haunting spirits are anguished ones seeking rest or justice, angry ones wanting revenge, or just plain evil entities out to cause as much misery as inhumanly possible. The specific spiritous reason or motivation is less important than the fact that there is *something* for the characters and/or viewer to discover. Thus, even though the *raison d'être* may be the mayhem, there is at least the possibility of a real narrative, with mystery and conflict, to engage one's attention between effects. Because of this, movies about hauntings tend to be somewhat less mechanical than the entries in Festival 9.

That's not to say that the movies that follow are an especially distinguished group. Some equate slowness with suspense and murkiness with mystery, while others try to substitute atmosphere for action and eeriness for effects, and still others, lacking both brains and budgets, don't do anything at all. And of course, a number flounder on what is one of the chief problems of the form — namely, making plausible the characters' determination to linger in a location that is clearly hostile to their best interests. Some come up with satisfactory reasons, but others rely on the utter stupidity of the comatose dolts involved — a rationale of its own, of course, but one that often undermines the rest of the proceedings.

That said, a few of the movies that follow do have a sense of what the form requires and energetically try, at least, to deliver some scares and spectacle, occasionally with a touch of style or wit or cleverness. Even more, as some of the most recent entries suggest, there seems to be a movement away from the traditional spooky house, which was, after all, already a cliché when the movies were young. Other sorts of locations are starting to be used, and with these, some exploration of the possibilities to be found by injecting hauntings into other traditional, non-supernatural film genres, such as the prison movie or the coming-of-age story. Not all of these cross-genre hybrids are completely successful, but it does strike me as a promising trend, and the sort of variation that is necessary to keep a genre fresh. If the trend continues, there may well be some very spirited efforts coming our way in the future.

Domestic Haunts

INFERNO *(1980, Italian, dubbed)*
wr and dir Dario Argento

Various strange people who live in a strange apartment building in New York City are killed in various strange ways when they try to find out what's behind the numerous strange occurrences. No shortage of strangeness here, but neither it nor the slick and stylish direction is nearly enough to compensate for the absence of plot, suspense, and comprehensibility. The building belongs to a mythical creature known as the "Mother of Darkness," apparently Death in drag, but by the time that revelation is made, the viewer has long since ceased to care. Had the slaughter — various hacking and choppings, a devouring by rats, and another by cats — been perpetrated with any of the usual *giallo* gusto, the many shortcomings would have been much less significant, but this inferno generates somewhat less heat than a hand-warmer.

THE NESTING *(1980)*
wr Armand Weston and Dario Price; dir Armand Weston

Like many haunted-house movies, this one hinges on the corporeal inhabitant — here, an author of gothic mysteries (Robin Groves) — refusing to get the hell out. It seems the house, about which she has previously had visions, was once a brothel where a slaughter occurred. After several grisly and mysterious deaths, our heroine adamantly insists, "No, I won't — I won't leave this house!" There's little here we haven't seen before, including the cadaverous presence of John Carradine.

THE HOUSE BY THE CEMETERY *(1982, Italian, dubbed)*
wr Dardano Sacchetti, Giorgio Mariuzzo, and Lucio Fulci; dir Lucio Fulci

A professor and his family rent the title property, which, after lots of eerie music and peculiar camera work, turns out to need more than a bit of renovation. The house is haunted by the family of the original owner, mad scientist Dr. Freudstein who, bearing more than a passing resemblance to a decomposing zombie, is still in the basement happily slaughtering anyone who enters his home. The usual offering, if more subdued, from one of the masters of *giallo* cinema — slow, dull, murky, dreadfully dubbed, enlivened by the occasional moment of messy excess. There's a knife through the head, a ferocious battle with a plastic bat, the impaling of a real estate agent, several ripped and slit throats, and a couple of spurting arteries. And of course, there are maggots — a truly disgusting stream of them oozes out from the body of Dr. Freudstein

All in all, a rather half-hearted effort from the director of **THE GATES OF HELL**.

SUPERSTITION *(1982)*
wr Donald G. Thompson; dir James W. Roberson

Somewhere on the outskirts of Amityville, an alcoholic minister, his remarkably stupid family, and most of the rest of the cast meet bloody ends when they move into a house built on the site where a witch was executed in 1692. The demon who possessed the witch is still around, pissed at being drowned in the pond 300 years earlier. We get a stake through a head, a crushing in a wine press, a hanging, a kid cut in half by a window, an exploding head in a microwave oven, a priest bored through by the runaway blade from a circular saw — and a number of laughably bad performances and a script that makes the characters seem somewhat less intelligent than root vegetables. However, there is suspense, a decent jolt or two, and a few bits of enthusiastic splatter, so you've probably done worse.

AMITYVILLE II: THE POSSESSION

Possessive prequel; see Festival 9.

AMITYVILLE 3-D *(1983)*
wr William Wales; dir Richard Fleischer

Professional psychic-debunker Tony Roberts gets a good deal on the notorious Long Island house, then gets debunked himself when it kills the real estate agent with flies, incinerates Candy Clark, drowns his daughter, and coughs up a demon to gobble Robert Joy. This has nothing to do with the first two Amityvilles, which claimed to have some factual basis, or with much of anything except the purported lust of the movie public for 3-D effects. Whatever minimal value these effects might have had is, of course, lacking for the viewer at home, leaving us with ample opportunity to wonder how these normally respectable actors were cajoled into participating in this exercise in haunted pointlessness. Besides about 10 seconds of marginally decent effects, the good news is that the house blows up: unless someone gets the bright idea to rebuild, this series has finally reached its much-belated conclusion. (Sigh. Between writing and printing this book, there's been a TV movie, *Amityville: The Evil Escapes*. What's next — "Jason Goes to Amityville"?)

HOUSE *(1985)*
wr Ethan Wiley; dir Steve Miner

Mystery writer William Katt, having bad Vietnam flashbacks, moves into the house where his aunt recently hanged herself and where his young son mysteriously disappeared a few years before. Needless to say, strange things soon start to happen. This tries to combine laughs with creepiness, and generally succeeds. There are three quite effective creatures, a good helping of genuine humor, and a couple of bits of inspired silliness, all of which elevate this a good deal above the average. With an amusing George Wendt (Norm on "Cheers") and a decomposing Richard Moll, this is a nice bit of fun, which is more than can be said for . . .

HOUSE II: THE SECOND STORY *(1987)*
wr and dir Ethan Wiley

Wiley's writing and direction and Sean Cunningham's (*Friday the 13th*) production are the only connections this puff of juvenile flatulence has with the original, besides a big old house filled with strangeness (including a crystal skull — a piece of Aztec magic junk — that opens up alternate universes, a pair of ambulatory mummified outlaws from the Old West, a cutesy baby pterodactyl, and a reptilian-puppy handpuppet). Early on, the inheritor of the house, noticing a space on the mantel, says, "It looks like something's missing." I'll say! — the wit, humor, cleverness, energy, and good effects that distinguished its predecessor. John Ratzenberger (Cliff on "Cheers") has a nice bit as an "Electrician/ Adventurer," but otherwise, strictly "House II: The Septic Tank."

WITCHBOARD *(1986)*
wr and dir Kevin S. Tenney

There are no witches and the board in question is a ouija, through which the nasty spirit of a psycho killer enters the house where the wonderfully named Tawny Kitaen lives. Uninteresting characters and a tiresome love triangle make it hard not to root for the spirit. Tawny takes a quick shower, but there's little else in this dull and predictable affair that you haven't seen many times before (and if you've seen **THE PERILS OF GWENDOLINE**, you've seen a lot more of Tawny than you get here). About the only genuine energy or fun in this one is a nice bit by Kathleen Wilhoite as a punk medium, but all she really accomplishes is to demonstrate how flat everything else (other than Tawny, of course) really is.

GHOSTHOUSE *(1987?)*
wr Cinthia McGavin; dir Humphrey Humbert

Various young, and apparently stupid, people keep going back into the title residence to be slaughtered, one by one, by a spirit bearing a 20-year-old grudge. We eventually learn what the issue is, but neither it nor the process of discovery that fills most of the movie is at all interesting or original. There is, of course, the occasional splash of mayhem, but it too is very uninspired, mostly just mediocre renditions of effects borrowed from other movies. You've probably seen worse semi-pro efforts, but that's still no reason to bother with this edifice constructed from dead wood.

Haunts of the Very Stupid

SATURDAY THE 14TH *(1981)*
wr and dir Howard R. Cohen

The title is the best thing about this labored, limp, sophomoronic mess. And even the title is misleading: this is not a slasher parody, but an unfunny send-up of the demon/haunted house genres. Richard Benjamin and Paula Prentiss inherit a house, and with it *The Book of Evil*. When they open it, they find themselves seriously infested with a variety of monsters that look like they came off the rack at a costume supplier. Benjamin and Prentiss offer stunned deadpan easily mistaken for brain death. Perfect for a double bill with **TRANSYLVANIA 6-5000**.

CARNAGE *(1982)*
wr, dir, photo Andy Milligan

A decade after he gave us *The Man with Two Heads* and *The Rats Are Coming! The Werewolves Are Here!*, Andy Milligan, Staten Island's favorite backyard filmmaker, is still at it, and still making dull, cheap, and shoddy movies. An extraordinarily boring pair of newlyweds (Michael Chioda, Leslie Den Den Dooven) move into a house that was the site of a murder-suicide, and the previous occupants, still in residence, are not at all pleased to have company. They axe and pitchfork a couple of intruders, but contrary to what the box exclaims, we do not "See home appliances slice and dice . . . people!" What we see is home-movie lighting, sound, and performances and some of the cheesiest non-effects on record. Too deadly dull even for unintentional humor.

Haunted Ground

NIGHT OF HORROR *(1981?)*
wr Tony Malanowski, Rebecca Bach, and Gae Schmitt; dir Tony Malanowski

You'll have the title evening if you get suckered by the nifty drawing on the box and bring home this utterly unwatchable Maryland home-movie piece-o-shit about a haunted Civil War battlefield. The copyright says 1981, but it looks like it was shot ten years earlier and forgotten until the video revolution disinterred it from well-deserved obscurity. The closing credits thank Don Dohler (**FIEND**), and say that the "film was processed and printed at Pete's Quality Film Labs" in Baltimore (tel. 305-435-1212). Any questions?

EYES OF FIRE *(1984)*
wr and dir Avery Crounse

Set on "the American frontier" some time in the 18th Century, this one concerns the discovery by a small and peculiar religious sect of a haunted valley somewhere in the Louisina Territory. The valley is populated with an assortment of tree people, mud people, various demons and naked spirits, and a lot of solarized optical effects. I don't have a clue what this one's all about. It moves so slowly and is so murkily meaningful it defies you to pay attention, and I confess I was not up to the challenge. Maybe it's supposed to be artsy and symbolic, but it sure ain't a good time.

THE SUPERNATURALS *(1985)*
wr Joel Soisson and Michael Murphey; dir Armand Mastroianni

The South rises again as the spirits of Confederate soldiers take revenge on the modern-day descendants of the Yankees who cruelly slaughtered them. A platoon of eight young army recruits, led by crusty sergeant Michelle Nichols (*Star Trek*'s Uhura) go on maneuvers in the Alabama woods and make the mistake of setting up camp on a haunted battlefield. Considering what must have been a fairly small budget, this has a good slick look and some competent performances. What it doesn't have is much of the suspense or eeriness that hauntings require, nor any of the big shocks or effects. There are some briefly glimpsed ambulatory corpses and a lot of chat and very pedestrian plotting. Not really a bad movie, just a dull one.

GHOSTRIDERS *(1987)*
wr Clay McBride and James J. Desmarais; dir Alan Stewart

A hundred years after outlaw Frank Clements was hanged, he and his ghostly gang return to lethargically menace a handful of very uninteresting actors in this slow and sluggish Texas backyard cheapie. Unless you're collecting a complete set of Lone Star lameness, mosey on by.

CONTAGION *(1987, Australian)*
wr Ken Methold; dir Karl Zwicky

After narrowly escaping from a band of Outback psychopathic louts, a yuppie real estate agent (John Doyle) stumbles into a magnificent isolated mansion occupied by a wealthy older man (Ray Barrett) and two slinky kinky blondes who have trouble keeping their clothes on (Nathy Gaffney, Pamela Hawksford). The yup is invited to join their ménage — promised both riches and sensual pleasures — if he can demonstrate that he is ruthless and determined enough to be worthy, which he attempts to do by bumping off a few people. But there is no mansion, only a decaying shack where some brutal murders took place — a site, the voice-over narrator informs us, so evil that all who come upon it are infected with the contagion. This is very slickly made — displaying the strong visual sense seen in so many Aussie movies — but it can't make up its mind if it wants to be a haunted gothic filled with violence and perversity or a Pirandelloesque study of madness and delusion, and consequently misses on both counts. Not without effective moments, but more interesting for what it might have been.

SCARECROWS *(1988)*
wr Richard Jeffries; dir William Wesley

A commando group of bandits, on the run with $3.5 million stolen from the army, find themselves trapped at a very weird farm and spend what turns out to be the "Night of the Living Scarecrows" as the title entities go after them with knives and pitchforks. Apparently the cornfield is haunted by the spirits of some Black Magicians, although no explanations are offered — a lacking that extends to shocks and suspense. Most of the movie is devoted to these uninteresting louts stumbling around in the dark. Other than slick production values, there's not much reason to land in this field. (Note: Unfortunately, I saw the R-rated version; apparently the unrated version does, in fact, deliver some striking splatter.)

STONES OF DEATH *(1988, Australian)*
wr Ian Coughlan; dir James Bogle

The high-schoolers who live in a fancy housing development built on an aboriginal burial site start to have bad dreams in which they're given the title crystals, and soon after they die in horrible and mysterious ways. In other words, it's "Poltergeist on Elm Street" or "Nightmare in Kangaloola." Although this is decently made, it's all so familiar that enthusiasm flags. Despite a few good moments, this one never manages to sustain its suspense for long, nor is there much in the way of effects to generate shocks. Unless you're really desperate or really curious about down under versions of the old sacred-ground setup, I can't see much reason to get weighed down with this one.

> *"In the Yik Yak, isn't there an enormous crevice with smoking gas coming out of it?"*
> THE PERILS OF GWENDOLINE

THE OFFSPRING
Troubled-town mini-weirdness; see Festival 14.

Imprisoned Phantoms

SLAUGHTERHOUSE ROCK *(1987)*
wr Sandra Willard, Nora Goodman and Ted Landon; dir Dimitri Logothetis

A demon, the embodiment of "pure Evil," called up by a satanic calvary commandant a century earlier, is loose on Alcatraz Island, where it had been imprisoned long before there was a prison there, and it's up to five collegiate types to put it back in its place. This one passes through virtually every type of supernatural horror — from hauntings, ghosts, demons, and possessions to bad dreams, Black Magic, and out-of-body experiences, omitting vampires, but including a cannibal to compensate — with stops along the way for a hand-severing, a torso-ripping, a human-barbecuing, a worm-vomiting, a levitation, a fist through a skull, a minor transformation, and a de-shirted (several times) Hope Marie Carlton. As in **THE EVIL DEAD**, the narrative is only a vehicle for throwing a steady stream of weird stuff at us, and it does that, if not quite as relentlessly as did Sam Raimi, with a fair amount of energy and a real desire to please. The effects are not bad but the budget pre-empted a knockout punch. Unfortunately, the stuff between the effects — the dialog and its delivery — leaves an awful lot to be desired, but at least it never goes on too long before something else happens. Ignore the chat and the acting, and don't try to figure out what's going on, and this serves up enough brisk, slick, mindless fun to hold your attention, and to make you curious about what these folks will do next.

PRISON *(1987)*
wr C. Courtney Joyner; dir Renny Harlin

Overcrowding in the Wyoming prison system has forced the reopening of a derelict facility, out of use for twenty years. A full complement of prisoners and guards are moved in, along with the vicious, hard-line warden (Lane Smith) who used to run the place. It soon develops that there is Something Else in the prison, and it's not exactly benign. While there's nothing terribly original about either the haunting stuff or the prison stuff, both are really nicely presented and work very well together. This has a good slick look with dramatic lighting, and effective use is made of the visually interesting setting. The script and the direction keep things moving briskly, the performances are all quite acceptable, and there are some good poltergeist effects and some very messy corpses (courtesy of John Buelcher). In style and setting, this is somewhat reminiscent of **THE KEEP**, but is a tighter, more successful effort. If you're looking for some solid supernatural fun, this one does a pretty good job of delivering the goods.

Assorted Haunted Habitats

DEATH SHIP *(1980, Canadian/British)*
wr John Robins; dir Alvin Rakoff

After a mysterious German ship left over from the Second World War rams and sinks a passenger liner, the ten survivors (including George Kennedy and Richard Crenna) climb aboard. The ship appears deserted, but is actually possessed by the psychic residue (or something) of the Nazi atrocities once perpetrated on board, and it starts to claim the intruders, one by one. A few mouldering skeletons are eventually discovered, but scarcely any suspense or shocks, and the viewer is subjected to some rather excruciating torture by tedium. For horror on the high seas, you're better off with reruns of "Love Boat."

THE BOOGEY MAN *(1980)*
wr Ulli Lommel and Suzanna Love; dir Ulli Lommel

The title, opening music, and prolog, in which a young boy kills someone with a big knife, lead you to the conclusion that this is not just a *Halloween* clone, but a remake. Somewhere along the way, though, it takes an abrupt turn and becomes a story about a haunted mirror. As one of the characters helpfully explains, "When you break a mirror, you free everything that it's seen." In this case, it's the psychopathic nasty who was

> *"We'll follow Emergency Plan H, and keep Plan B in reserve in case things get out of hand."*
> CITY OF THE WALKING DEAD

murdered 20 years earlier, and he has not mellowed with age. Fragments of the mirror possess considerable telekinetic power and are capable of making windows crash down on necks, pitchforks and knives fly through the air, and scissors seek out the throats of those who hold them. There are some moderately good gory effects, and enough silliness to keep you going. Naturally, just when you think it's safe to look at your reflection again, it turns out that a fragment of the malicious mirror remains, setting us up for . . .

BOOGEYMAN II *(1982)*
wr Ulli Lommel and Suzanna Love; dir Bruce Starr

The shard of glass is transported to Hollywood where it wipes out a bunch of movie types at a party, but whatever cheap vitality the original possessed is completely absent here. In fact, this is barely a movie. At least a quarter of the 80 minutes is given over to clips from the first effort, and most of the rest is spent on static scenes made up of clichéd chat about Hollywood. Even when the mirror finally gets down to business, the effects are shabbily done. We are, however, treated to some extraordinarily peculiar murders, including death by garden hose, barbecue tongs, electric toothbrush, and an aerosol can of shave cream. Obviously not meant to be taken seriously, this one seems to be an unfunny in-joke about how to make a movie with as little effort as possible (Lommel once worked with Fassbinder).

THE LIFT *(1983, Dutch, dubbed)*
wr and dir Dick Maas

Stephen King creates murderous cars and trucks; Dick Maas, a psychopathic elevator. Vehicles, at least, can move around, but elevators can only go up and down. That's more than can be said for this movie, which kind of just sits there. Still, there certainly aren't many Dutch horror movies, and few give us an elevator repairman as hero — sounds like something out of "Monty Python" — so I guess there's some marginal curiosity value here.

MOVIE HOUSE MASSACRE *(1984)*
wr, prod and dir Alice Raley

A bunch of pathetically amateur actors get the chop in bloodless and uninteresting ways when they attempt to open a haunted movie theater. A spoof of sorts, but too sophomoronic and leadenly unfunny to work. With Mary Woronov, who, you can bet, has not put this one on her résumé.

BLOODY NEW YEAR *(1986, British)*
wr Frazer Pearce; dir Norman J. Warren

First off, the action here takes place in July, and there's not much blood to speak of. Six supremely stupid and unresourceful young people find themselves stranded in Horror Hotel. Sinister things start to happen — at various times, the kids are attacked by a hostile Hoover, a psychotic fishing net, a pile of seaweed, and a carnivorous newel-post ornament. The victims don't really die, but turn into ghoulish creatures wearing unpleasant face makeup. Sound familiar? Despite its slice-and-dice title, this turns out to be a bargain-basement version of **THE EVIL DEAD**. But where Sam Raimi's exercise in excess was lively and lurid, this one is lumpen and lame, with no suspense and cheap, dull effects. Near the end, one of the chorus of bimbos shrieks, "I don't think I can take much more of this!" and by that point, we're in complete agreement.

NIGHTFLYERS
Haunted spaceship; see Festival 24.

Electromagnetic Mayhem

MAXIMUM OVERDRIVE *(1986)*
wr and dir Stephen King

Basically *The Birds*, with household appliances and motor vehicles taking the place of our feathered friends. When the earth passes through the tail of a "rogue comet," machinery takes on a life of its own and attacks people. The action here centers on the usual mixed bag of jerks who get trapped in a truck stop, surrounded by menacing semis. There are a few good bits — a rabid carving knife, a psychotic vending machine — but mostly the movie is a lot of crashes, people getting smeared by trucks and steamrollers, and more explosions than I could count. The big problem is that the machines are much more intelligent and animated than the victims. Even King admitted this was a stupid movie. Probably only for those who find high drama in Destruction Derby. With Emilio Estevez, Pat Hingle, and music by AC/DC.

PULSE *(1988)*
wr and dir Paul Golding

A suburban family (Cliff De Young, Roxanne Hart) is menaced by what seems to be mutant, intelligent, goal-oriented power surges that reprogram the appliances and turn their house into an enemy. So what we have might be described as a cross between "Poltergeist Gets Wired" and "The Birds Go Electric". The first half is a little slow, especially since we know where it's heading, but it eventually delivers a few moderately effective moments. This makes exceptionally good use of sound and has good low-budget production values, and director Golding manages to create a sense of creepy menace in everyday things, but doesn't bother to write in an explanation, leaving us with what is essentially a possession movie. That aside, this is well enough made to be an acceptable time-waster.

Auto Haunts

THE WRAITH *(1986)*
wr and dir Mike Marvin

This one's about drag races, car chases, and exploding automobiles. The rest of the movie concerns some vague, largely undeveloped story of supernatural revenge in which Charlie Sheen returns from the dead in order to blow up the gang of young thugs who killed him before the picture began. One of the thugs calls him a "wraith," thereby giving us a more evocative title than, say, "Blazing Barracudas," but it might have been more appropriately called "High Plains Dragster." The real star here, however, is a one-of-a-kind beast made by Dodge called the

Turbo-Interceptor, a sort of interplanetary fighter, which, without competition from the cast, easily provides the most charismatic performance. Sherilyn Fenn plays the well-built bimbo, and we get a couple of brief glimpses of what earned her the part; the race/chase sequences are competently done, but more than a little repetitive; and lots of stuff blows up. Mainly for those who enjoy watching Daytonas and Tornados go over the edge of cliffs.

DARK OF THE NIGHT *(1984, New Zealand)*
wr Gaylene Preston, Geoff Murphy, and Graeme Tetley; dir G. Preston

After a retiring young woman (Heather Boulton) buys a magnificent old Jaguar that had belonged to a murdered woman, things turn peculiar for her. She has visions of the victim and then is menaced by a mysterious man whom no one else sees. The car is haunted by the spirit of the dead woman who wants revenge, and the mysterious man is, of course, the murderer (though how or why he happened to show up is just one of a number of gaping holes in the plot). Boulton does a nice job and the production values are decent, but after the first half hour, the rather fragile suspense and intrigue collapse. With a few more twists and a couple of jolts this might have been passable, but as is, it's as pointless as its title.

Restless Spirits

LADY IN WHITE *(1988)*
wr, prod, dir Frank La Loggia

Clearly modeled on *Stand By Me*, this one gives us a best-selling horror novelist returning to the small town where he grew up, and thinking about what happened in 1962 when he was ten years old and looked like Lukas Haas (*Witness*). As the result of a Halloween prank, he's locked overnight in the school cloakroom and witnesses the murder of a little girl — the first in a series of unsolved child-slayings in the small town that had taken place ten years earlier. The girl is, in fact, a spirit and appears to him, and eventually to his older brother, leading the two boys to try to solve the case. This is quite ambitious in its reach — part ghost story, part murder mystery, part small-town nostalgia, part coming-of-age — and while it succeeds occasionally, it attempts too much. The minimal ghost effects are cheap and unimpressive, the pace is far too leisurely, and the viewer figures out the solution to the mystery early on. Still, it does a good job of presenting the child's view of the world and there is some intelligence on display. Too flawed to be anything really special, this is the kind of honorable effort that one would like to like better, but you could easily do worse.

GOTHAM *(1988)*
wr and dir Lloyd Fonveille

An archetypally seedy private eye, wonderfully named Eddie Mallard (Tommy Lee Jones), is hired by a wealthy client to stop the man's wife (Virginia Madsen) from bothering him. The twist is that she died thirteen years earlier, and the troublesome woman is actually a ghost. Despite having a contemporary setting, this movie is in the style of '40s *film noir*, part suspense thriller, part steamy romance. A *film noir* ghost story is a terrific concept, and this falls just short of being a terrific movie. As an exercise in style it could hardly be better, and is a wonderfully clever and very fine re-creation of the look, feel, structure, and attitude of the form. The leads give strong performances, and the production values are great; but the script has too many rough spots and doesn't quite generate the impact it should. Still, this is an extremely well done, interesting, and entertaining effort, brimming with talent and panache, and well worth checking out. As a bonus, and not a trivial one, Virginia Madsen takes several showers and baths.

NOMADS
Evanescent neo-vamps; see Festival 12.
GHOST WARRIOR
No ghost; flash freezing; see Festival 25.
GHOSTKEEPER
No ghost; windigo; see Festival 2.

FESTIVAL 11

* * *

SORCERORS, WITCHES, AND MAGIC
An Exhibition of the Black Arts

"My guess is that someone or something is sucking the lifeforce out of these people."
— *Necropolis*

Magic in its many forms — Black, White, shamanism, voodoo, witchcraft, alchemy, sorcery — has been around since prehistoric times. Tribal peoples have had their medicine men, and monarchs, their mediums, soothsayers, and necromancers. Magic has been used as a tool for healing, a means of expressing dissent, and an instrument of oppression. It is an extremely diverse and complex subject — part religion, part science, part psychology, part politics — and in various places and ages, people have killed for and died because of it. Without getting into the issue as to whether or not there is a reality behind the rituals and beliefs, there is no question that a great many people have taken, and still do take, magic very, very seriously.

With perhaps two exceptions, the same cannot be said about the movies in this festival. As is true of most supernatural-horror movies, magic and witchcraft are less the subjects of these movies than convenient, shorthand devices for conjuring up a wide range of special effects, creatures, and splatter. Most of the themes here — witches returning for revenge, ancient curses, raising the dead, satanic cults, and dark practices — are familiar ones and part of a long cinematic tradition that includes such movies as *Witchcraft Through the Ages* (1922), *The Mummy* (1932), *The Devil-Doll* (1936), *I Walked with a Zombie*, *The Seventh Victim* (both 1943), *Black Sunday* (1960), *Rosemary's Baby* (1968) and *The Wicker Man* (1973).

During the 1980s, the biggest hits to present these subjects have been *The Children of the Corn* (1984) — the worst-ever adaptation of a Stephen King story — and *Angel Heart* and *The Believers* (both 1987 and stylish enough to be worth checking out). George Miller's flamboyant version of *The Witches of Eastwick* — also 1987 — while hardly typical, became the most successful witch movie yet made.

This festival is a very mixed bag, in terms of both approach and quality of the movies in it. There are the usual low-budget stiffs, but there are also quite a few that, if not entirely successful, offer up enough of the good stuff and are sufficiently entertaining to be worth the price of a rental. If nothing else, several of the entries below will show you things that you definitely have not seen before.

Witch Bitches

THE DEVONSVILLE TERROR *(1983)*
wr Ulli Lommel, George T. Lindsey, and Suzanna Love; dir Ulli Lommel

It's 1683 and the good God-fearing folks of Devonsville (just down the road from Salem) savagely execute three young women for being witches. Apparently, at least one of them was guilty as charged since she vanishes in a lightning bolt, then reappears in a tacky optical effect to curse the town. Cut to the present and, as the town nears the 300th anniversary of the witch hunt, strange things are starting to happen. A mild-mannered storekeeper (Paul Willson) smothers his wife. Donald Pleasence, a descendent of the executioner, finds his body infested with worms that are eating him from the inside out. And three young women (including Suzanna Love as the new schoolteacher) arrive in town. The townspeople decide that the curse has arrived with them — "They're back. The legend is true" — and that the only way to deal with the problem is to do what their ancestors did: burn the newcomers. Nothing very exceptional here, but it is better than you'd expect from the dreary-looking box. There are lots of really cheap effects, but also a couple of decent ones, including a melting head and Donald Pleasence's creepy worms. Performances are generally acceptable, the script is reasonably intelligent, and some suspense is generated. With a little more on repressed sexuality and mob hysteria, this could have been quite an interesting little movie. As it is, if you're not feeling too demanding, there's probably enough going on to hold your attention. From the director of **THE BOOGEY MAN** and **BRAINWAVES**.

PLAY DEAD *(1985)*
wr Lothrop W. Jordan; dir Peter Wittman

"Not since *Cujo* has there been such canine terror." — or so the box says. If you take that to mean that this Texas cheapie is one of the biggest dogs to come along in some time, it's not far wrong. Forget foaming jaws, this is just Black Magic mumbo-jumbo. Rich witch Yvonne De Carlo (?!), for reasons never adequately explained, wants to drive her niece crazy. Working through her familiar — a Rottweiler named Greta — she kills various people around the girl. But there's no snarling or growling for this Hound of Hell. No, Greta manages an electrocution, a strangling, a poisoning, and a hit-and-run accident. As the detective on the case remarks, "Boy, that's some smart dog," which is not something one can say about the movie she's in. Bad acting does nothing to enhance a dull script, devoid of suspense and surprises; there are no special effects (gore or otherwise); and the shoddy production even features a classic microphone-in-the-frame shot. The title must refer to the standing instruction the director issued to the cast and crew. With art direction by Robert A. Burns, the director of **MONGREL**.

NECROPOLIS *(1986)*
wr and dir Bruce Hickey

Despite the title and the references on the box to *Night of the Living Dead*, this one has nothing to do with zombies. Instead, it concerns a platinum-blonde witch named Eva (Leeanne Baker) who returns to New York after an absence of 300 years in order to complete the ritual that will give her eternal life. The ritual seems to involve a magic ring, the sacrifice of a virgin, and a lot of awkward, bare-breasted dancing in a black-lace bodysuit. Eva also has a sweet tooth for human souls. (The soul — and I bet you didn't know this — is a clear, viscous fluid slurpable through the victim's forehead.) Eventually, Eva sprouts four additional breasts, through which she feeds the soul fluid to a litter of ghouls she has called up from somewhere. So far so good. Unfortunately, all this stuff, which is vigorously ludicrous, takes up only a couple of minutes. The other 75 or so minutes are filled up with brain-dead characters blathering about magic and reincarnation, and do not pass quickly. Still, despite its many shortcomings, this is unquestionably the finest movie ever made about a six-titted witch.

Raising the Dead

DEAD AND BURIED *(1981)*
wr Ronald Shusett and Dan O'Bannon; dir Gary A. Sherman

Undead and unburied is more to the point here: people savagely murdered in the small town of Potter's Bluff turn up, walking around as though nothing had happened. Sheriff James Farentino sure can't figure out what's going on, and neither can we, which is a good part of the fun in this one, so I'm not going to spoil it by saying too much. Although the pace is occasionally a touch slow, the script serves up enough jolts to keep us on our toes and enough surprises to hold our interest. The performances and production values are quite good, and there are some really striking makeup effects by Stan Winston, including burnings, batterings, acid injections, and a hypodermic needle jabbed into an eyeball that'll probably catch your attention. As a bonus, there's a nifty twist ending, and Lisa Blount briefly takes her shirt off. While there's nothing really great here, this does deliver a fair amount of the good solid mindless messy B-movie fun that we've learned to expect from co-writer O'Bannon (*Alien*, **RETURN OF THE LIVING DEAD**).

FRIGHTMARE *(1981)*
wr and dir Norman Thaddeus Vane

After the body of recently deceased hambone horror star Conrad Ragzoff (Ferdinand Mayne) is stolen by a group of film students, his widow calls up his spirit in a seance and encourages it to seek revenge for the prank. The spirit is willing and the body is re-animated, thus demonstrating that, for a true thespian, death is no reason to stop chewing the scenery. This starts off being mildly entertaining, but after Conrad walks again, it turns into a supernatural variant on the standard slice-and-dice formula — with the students being stalked and bumped off in their big spooky house — and a fairly routine rendition, at that. The effects are scarce and not impressive, but this is competently made and marginally livelier than some supernatural sludge.

DAWN OF THE MUMMY *(1981, U.S./ Italian/ Egyptian)*
wr Daria Price, Ronald Dobrin, and Frank Agrama; dir Frank Agrama

Your basic pharaoh's tomb, ancient curse, and bunch of dolts who desecrate the former and suffer under the latter. This very routine fare is enlivened slightly by some so-so splatter and by the fact that it was shot on location in Egypt. With a black-faced putrescent mummy and his army of decomposing minions who rise from the sand, this is basically a zombie movie in Egyptian drag. As such, there are the usual guts being ripped out and some zomboid cannibalistic munching, but nothing you haven't seen before, although it's shot so darkly and indistinctly that you might not be aware of that. A couple of decent moments, but nothing special, and very slow.

SPOOKIES *(1985)*
wr and dir Frank M. Farel, Thomas Doran and Brendan Faulkner

An utterly improbable assortment of lamebrains poke around an apparently deserted mansion, only to discover that the owner is a sorceror (Felix Ward, looking a lot like Martin Short's impression of Pierre Trudeau) who's not only in residence, but planning to sacrifice them in order to resurrect his long-dead wife. To accomplish his purpose, he calls up a variety of zombies and muck men, the Grim Reaper, a reptilian demon, a spider woman, and a tentacled pile of humanoid putrescence. The abundant effects and creatures range from unimpressive to pretty decent (if derivative). The problem is the actors and the script, both of which are firmly planted on the unimpressive side. Still, these guys were trying, and they do deliver a few effective moments. Certainly, I hope they try again, and maybe the next time, they'll have a bigger budget and a better script.

TRICK OR TREAT *(1986)*
wr Michael S. Murphy, Joel Soisson, and Rhet Topham; dir Charles Martin Smith

As far as I know, this is the first movie to be based on the idea that certain records, when played backwards, supposedly reveal satanic messages. Eddie (Marc Price) is a socially maladjusted "Metalhead" who is constantly tormented by the preppie assholes at his high school. When his idol, "Rock Warrior" Sammi Curr, dies in a fire, he is devasted, but then he receives the only copy of Curr's last record and discovers that Sammi is talking to him through one of those hidden messages. At first, it looks like Sammi is helping Eddie, but we — having seen a lot of these movies — know that Sammi's spirit has other fish to fry. Actually, it's a whole lot of people that Sammi fries, in bolts of sparking blue electricity, thereby demonstrating that Heavy Metal really is the devil's music. First-time director Charles Martin Smith (star of *Never Cry Wolf*) worked hard to make the most of some fairly thin, very familiar material and a limited budget. This could use a lot more tricks, but it's not without a few treats: Marc Price does a good job, and there are some nice humorous touches, especially a bit with Ozzy Osbourne as a conservative, anti-rock evangelist.

Simpering for the Devil

EVILSPEAK *(1981)*
wr Joseph Garafalo and Eric Weston; dir Eric Weston

Lumpy cadet Clint Howard is continually shat upon by the sadisitic staff and his classmates at the West Andover Military Academy. Then, when he discovers a secret basement filled with Black Magic paraphernalia left there by a 16th-Century sect of satanists, he uses his computer to call up the spirit of Esteban (a brief appearance by Richard Moll), and the nerd turns ... with a vengeance. Clint levitates; heads are cleaved, severed, and rotated; a heart is ripped out; and a pack of carnivorous porkers goes on a rampage. Sort of "Carrie Carries On at Military School," this is not badly done, but too slow in developing. Howard makes his character sympathetic, the implausibilities can be overlooked, and the effects, while not very spectacular or abundant, are acceptable. Keep your expectations modest, and this will hold your attention. With Lynn Hancock as the nasty bitch eaten by pigs while taking a shower.

BLOOD CULT *(1985, made for video)*
wr Stuart Rosenthal; dir Christopher Lewis

A Black Magic coven in Tulsa, Oklahoma, is killing coeds at Central State College and cutting off bits of them as part of their ritual worship of the dog-god Caninus, patron of worldly success. Not since **COPPERHEAD** has the Midwest produced such a cheap, amateurish, and dull piece-o-shit. Don't even think about this one.

REVENGE *(1986, made for video)*
wr and dir Christopher Lewis

The folks from Tulsa, apparently thinking they were on to a good thing, are back with the further adventures of everyone's favorite dog-worshipping coven. More young women are chopped up, off-camera, and this time the cult succeeds in raising Caninus himself for a brief appearance at the very end. Slightly better made than **BLOOD CULT**, this offers a few seconds of so-so makeup, but there's still no reason to watch. With Patrick Wayne, John Carradine, and a title of no discernible significance.

Family Curses

SKULLDUGGERY *(1982)*
wr and dir Ota Richter

Adam (Thom Haverstock), the latest inheritor of a 500-year-old curse, bloodlessly bumps off a bunch of people while playing a "Dungeons and Dragons"- type fantasy game. As he remarks, "It's hard to say where the game begins and life ends"; after about half an hour of this labored ponderousness, it's even harder to say why it was made. This kind of role-playing confusion could work, but here the supernatural overlay just gets in the way. Matters are not helped by the disco soundtrack, the tiresomely jokey attitude, and the seriously inadequate performances. The title promises deviousness, but this one delivers only muddle.

> "You don't understand. In America, exploitation is an art form."
> BOOGEYMAN II

THE ALCHEMIST *(1985)*
wr Alan J. Adler; dir James Amante

There is no alchemist here, and not much of anything else either, so I suppose it's as good a title as any. A curse has been put on Robert Ginty, dooming him to an unpleasant eternal life, and he attempts to release his soul by exchanging it for another in a Black Magic ritual. As it conveniently turns out, the sacrificial victim is a young woman who's the double of Ginty's long-dead wife (whom he accidentally killed 80 years earlier). This has something of the old-fashioned feel of British horror films of the 1960s, but none of their style. The lame script is not helped by the cheapness of the production. Talk about unlavish! Five actors, one set, a lot of cheap traveling shots, a couple of splashes of unconvincing gore, inferior optical effects, and as crummy a melting-head stunt as you're likely to come across this side of the "Late Show." Alchemy was the conversion of base metal into gold, but this one undergoes no transformation and remains resolutely leaden.

BESERKER *(1987)*
wr and dir Jef Richard

The usual six-pack of tiresome collegiate jerks and bimbos goes camping, but discovers that the legend of the title creature has substance, and that the spirit of an ancient psychopathic cannibalistic Viking warrior inhabits the body of his descendant, roaming Rainbow Valley, dressed up in a bear suit and clawing anyone he comes across. Very lackluster maulings do nothing to disguise the fact that not only is there no plot, suspense, or surprises here but, except for trained bear "Bart," who saves the day, there's scarcely a creature to be seen. This sluggish Utah semi-pro paint-by-numbers effort soon makes you think fondly of such efforts as **THE PREY** and **DON'T GO IN THE WOODS**. Subtitled "The Nordic Curse," you'll curse more than nords if you get suckered by this one. With Beth Toussaint as the bimbo who takes her clothes off.

MAUSOLEUM
Toothed-titted demonic family tradition; see Festival 9.
THE CURSE
No curse; alien mutagen from outer space; see Festival 3.

Miscellaneous Magic

DARK FORCES *(1980, Australian)*
wr Everett DeRoche; dir Simon Wincer
Originally released as *Harlequin*.

This hopelessly muddled and confusing mess seems to involve sleazy political machinations and a mysterious, Rasputin-like stranger with supernatural powers. Whatever's going on, it's not only not worth the effort it would take to figure it out, it's not worth the electricity it takes to run the tape. With Robert Powell, David Hemmings, Broderick Crawford — and Alison Best as the girl who gets a nasty surprise when she takes a bath.

TROLL *(1985)*
wr Ed Naha; dir John Carl Buechler

Michael Moriarty, Shelley Hack, and their two kids move into an apartment building complete with all the modern conveniences, including a troll in the laundry room. The troll, explained here as a sort of malevolent fairy, looks just like the Scandinavian rubber dolls sold in tacky airport giftshops. Before the family's even unpacked, the title creature has assumed the form of the daughter, and transforms the various apartments in the building into different fairy worlds, each peopled with nasty little creatures that might have been left over from **GHOULIES** (also from Empire Pictures). Although somewhat better than that misbegotten lump, this is still seriously stupid, and not redeemed by the fact that some of that stupidity is supposed to be funny. There are lots of special effects, but most are not very impressive. We do, however, get to see Sonny Bono transformed into a giant pod, then into a troll-infested forest, so it's not a total waste. Maybe for the kids, if they're not very fussy.

THE NIGHT STALKER *(1986)*
wr John Goff and Don Edmonds; dir Max Kleven

A large, muscular psycho is murdering L.A. prostitutes as part of an Asian ritual in which he gains immortality by stealing their souls. Since we see him on several occasions absorb bullets without ill effect, the ceremony is apparently successful, but the movie sure isn't. The script ignores entirely the potentially interesting supernatural angle and focuses instead on the trials and tribulations of alcoholic tough cop Charles Napier. What thus could have been an effective cross-genre hybrid turns out to be an extremely routine and mechanical cops-and-hookers shoot-'em-up. Too bad: the production values are slick, the direction and cast are competent, and there are quick glimpses of a couple of nice bodies. (Not to be confused with the fine 1971 Darren McGavin TV movie of the same name, which was exceptional in combining genres.)

DOLLS *(1987)*
wr Ed Naha; dir Stuart Gordon

Six travelers take shelter from a storm in an isolated gothic mansion that belongs to an old dollmaker and his wife. As we eventually learn, the elderly couple are witches of some sort, and the toys he makes are what you might call "living dolls." It seems these creations have a low tolerance for jerks so when four of the visitors prove to be just that, the dolls go after them with knives, miniature saws, and a toy-soldier firing squad. Homicidal dolls and puppets are hardly an original concept (*Devil Doll*, 1932, etc.), and beyond presenting them in battalion strength, this one gives us nothing very new or interesting. We're treated to lots of lingering shots of the dolls sitting on the shelf, but they don't seem particularly creepy or menacing, and when they're moving, the effect is nothing at at all special. While there are a few inspired moments — an attack by an eight-foot-tall carnivorous teddy bear, for instance — this is mostly very flat, cheap, predictable stuff. A real disappointment from the director responsible for the outrageous excess of **FROM BEYOND**.

HELLRAISER *(1987, British)*
wr and dir Clive Barker

At the center of this directorial effort by the writer who's being touted as the next big name in horror is a magic box that opens the door to the realm of the Cenobites. These are singularly unpleasant fellows — kind of S&M demonic mutants — who introduce their visitors to brand-new sensual experiences by ripping their flesh with giant fish-hooks then reducing them to constituent body parts. Not much plot or characterization here; this follows the Italian *giallo* tradition, sacrificing all for the effects, and doesn't skimp — flayed flesh, internal organs, slime, corpses vomiting maggots, weird beings, and blood by the bucket. Some of the effects are pretty good, especially the Cenobite makeup, while others are ho-hum. Ultimately this one is flat and mechanical and the striving to be unpleasant turns slightly rancid, making this neither all that horrific nor very much fun. While it probably delivers enough to be worth the price of a rental, it's a disappointment from the guy Stephen King is quoted on the box as calling "the face of horror." (The sequel, *Hellbound: Hellraiser II*, was released too late for inclusion, but it's exactly the same movie, with all the same faults and slightly grosser effects.)

FOREVER EVIL
Necronomiconjurations; see Festival 8.

The Real Thing?

APPRENTICE TO MURDER *(1987)*
wr Allan Scott and Wesley Moore; dir R.L. Thomas

This one probably doesn't belong in this section, but it's packaged like it does, and I don't know where else to put it. In fact, it's clear from the copy on the video box that New World (the distributor) also didn't know what to do with this rather curious movie about a supernatural episode that may or may not have happened. Set in a poor and primitive farming community in western Pennsylvania, in 1927, this tells the story of 16-year-old Billy (Chad Lowe) who falls under the sway of Dr. Reese (Donald Sutherland), a "powwow doctor" (apparently a combination of faith healer, herbalist, and fundamentalist preacher). Billy helps the healer in his work, and Reese educates Billy so he'll be able to leave the village. Along the way, they become convinced that a local hermit is a some sort of sorcerer who's put a curse on them. In the course of trying to break the spell, they kill the hermit, and the movie ends with them being convicted of murder. Was it real? A delusion? This potentially fascinating situation is lost in the movie's structure, and our interest is never captured. It's too bad, because this is really quite well done in other respects. It has a very effective gray, dreary look and good performances all around. What could have been an intriguing psychological study or account of a most peculiar incident is defeated by its own ambivalence and creates just that in the viewer.

THE SERPENT AND THE RAINBOW *(1987)*
wr Richard Maxwell and A.R. Simoun; dir Wes Craven

Dr. Dennis Alan (Bill Pullman), hired by an American research company, goes to Haiti in 1985, just before the fall of Duvalier, to try to find the drug used to create actual zombies. He and Haitian psychiatrist Cathy Tyson (*Mona Lisa*) soon find themselves in over their heads in the steamy stew of mysticism, voodoo, and politics that informs most aspects of life in one of the world's poorest and strangest societies. Based upon Wade Davis's factual account of his experiences, the adaptation is rather loose, since this medical mystery/anthropological thriller is dressed up like an Indiana Jones adventure, with a very generous infusion of frightening hallucinations like those in Craven's earlier *Nightmare on Elm Street*. The subject and the country are so fascinating in themselves that the overlay of Hollywood hokum severely diminishes the interest and impact of the story, and one wants to go to the source to find out what really happened. However, it's slickly made, briskly paced, and filled with some quite striking dream-sequence effects. Although this doesn't end up going anywhere, the journey is fast and furious enough to hold your attention if you're in the mood for some mindless cheap thrills.

FESTIVAL 12

* * *

DOWN FOR THE COUNT
A Coagulation of Vampiric Variations

"There's lots worse things than being a vampire."
— *My Best Friend Is a Vampire*

Of all the supernatural entities in film, none has appeared more frequently than the vampire. Numerous books have been written analyzing the appeal of the vampire myth, but, for whatever reasons, this ultimate creature of the night — ageless and undead, sustaining his immortality through the lifeblood of others — seems to hold a lasting fascination shared by no other monster.

The vampire's first screen appearance was in *Nosferatu* (1922), F.W. Murnau's unauthorized adaptation of Bram Stoker's *Dracula*, which may still be the best and the creepiest vampire movie ever made. The best-known version, of course, is the 1931 *Dracula*, starring Bela Lugosi and based on the stage-play based on the novel, which had enjoyed a two-year Broadway run with Lugosi in the lead. Considering its fame, it is not, with the exception of a few effective moments, a very good movie at all, and probably has more camp appeal these days than anything else. Nonetheless, it was a huge success at the time for Universal Pictures. (A far more interesting film is Carl Dreyer's bizarre, dream-like *Vampyr*, produced the same year as *Dracula*, but it was a commercial failure and without much subsequent influence.)

Following on *Dracula*'s success, there was *Mark of the Vampire* (1935), which is not in fact a real vampire movie, and *Dracula's Daughter* (1936) and *Son of Dracula* (1943), which are. By this point, after more than a decade of considerable popularity, the horror genre was starting to run out of steam. In an effort to juice things up, Hollywood started cranking out the rather pathetic series of multiple-monster movies, the first of which was *Frankenstein Meets the Wolf Man* (1943). The next year Lugosi, playing a different vamp, met a werewolf himself in *Return of the Vampire*, and Dracula (played by John Carradine) joined the Wolf Man and Frankenstein's Monster in *House of Frankenstein*, and then the threesome got together yet again in *House of Dracula* (1945). This process reached a logical conclusion of sorts when Lugosi's Dracula turned up in *Abbott and Costello Meet Frankenstein* (1948).

Serious bloodsucking resumed in 1956 with an Italian production, *I Vampiri*, and the 1958 Hammer remake of *Dracula*, directed by Terence Fisher and starring Christopher Lee, which introduced a full-color Count to a new generation of moviegoers. With the growing permissiveness of the movies, the 1960s saw a string of increasingly sexy vampires, a very partial listing of which includes: *The Vampire's Lover* and *Playgirls and the Vampire* (1960); *Kiss of the Vampire* (1962); *Queen of the Vampires* (1967); *The Vampire's Niece* (1968, also known as *Fangs of the Living Dead*); and *Taste the Blood of Dracula* and *The Naked Vampire* (1969).

In 1970, vampirism reached epidemic proportions. In a feeding frenzy that nearly rivaled the slice-and-dice mayhem of the early 1980s, that one year saw the following titles produced: *Dracula 71*; *Count Yorga, Vampire*; *Countess Dracula*; *Curse of the Vampires*; *Sex and the Vampire*; *The Vampire Happening*; *Bloodsuckers*; *Lust for a Vampire*; *The Scars of Dracula*; *The Vampire Lovers*; *Lesbian Vampires*; and *The Horrible Sexy Vampire*. Naturally, this pace could not be sustained, and the next year saw only *The Curse of the Vampyr*; *Sex Vampires*; *The Return of Count Yorga*; *Virgin Vampires*; *Vampire Circus*; and *The Velvet Vampire*.

By the time we got to *Blacula* (1972) and *Deafula* (1975, performed in sign language), it was clear that anemia was setting in, a condition that was not alleviated by the production of *Dracula's Dog* in 1977 (available on cassette as *Zoltan, Hound of Hell*). The Slurping Seventies ended with the release of Werner Herzog's tired and pointless remake of *Nosferatu*, and the making of a New Jersey backyard vamp epic about a mortician named A. Lucard, with the very appropriate video title, *Dracula's Last Rites*.

Compared to the preceding decades, the 1980s have not been especially kind to vampires. Besides the entries that follow, the only other notable vampire movies are the stylish but silly version of Whitley Streiber's best seller *The Hunger*, and *The Lost Boys*, which took in more (inflated) dollars than any vampire movie ever made. (However, North American rentals did not make up the estimated $18 million it cost to make.)

With the exception of **FRIGHT NIGHT**, which is one of the decade's best B-movies, and one of the best-ever vampire movies, none of this festival's efforts can be regarded as a significant or complete success. Quite a few of them, however, are interesting in the ways in which they work variations on the vampire myth — using and changing one of the most durable icons of the horror film.

The traditional aristocratic vampire — suavely sinister, creepily elegant — modeled on Lugosi's has become as passé and impoverished as the rest of the aristocracy. It's hard to see how this figure could be presented absolutely straight nowadays, and thus he turns up only as a subject for heavy-handed parody or, as was the case in *Fright Night*, as a foil for our familiarity with six decades of vampiric villains. In place of the Count, we have such creations as the even more ancient entity that lies behind the vampire myth (**THE KEEP**) or, in *The Lost Boys* and **NEAR DARK**, very contemporary versions who, instead of dragging through the centuries with the curse of immortality, revel in the intoxicating power of eternal youth.

Although the execution of most of the movies that follow may not be up to the quality of their premises, the fact that they offer some interesting and original conceptions suggests that there may still be some blood left in the form.

Playing with the Form

THE BLACK ROOM *(1981)*
wr Norman Thaddeus Vane; dir N. T. Vane and Elly Kenner

A kinky brother-and-sister team rents the title chamber in the Hollywood Hills as a love nest for swingers. They take pictures of the occupants at play, then they take the occupants' blood, draining it out with some medical apparatus. It seems the brother suffers from a rare form of anemia that requires frequent infusions of the red stuff, and they've arrived at this scheme to ensure a nice fresh supply. There is the germ of a successful contemporary vamp variation here, but it is killed by a script that focuses on the boring marital relations of the swingers and not on the draining duo. Still, despite itself, this does provide a couple of brief

> *"First we get attacked by bandits, then those damn zombies. What's next?"*
> DEATHSTALKER II

moments of genuine creepiness, and there is blood by the bottle-and bathtub-full. With Geanne Frank as the hooker who briefly takes her top off before being exsanguinated, and an extremely young Linnea Quigley.

THE KEEP (1983)
wr and dir Michael Mann

One expects a lot of high style and strong visuals from Michael Mann ("Miami Vice", "Crime Story", *Thief, Manhunter*) and we have them here in abundance. Unfortunately, that's about all we have: as great as the look of this movie is, it can't take the place of interesting characters and a driving narrative. Based on a novel by F. Paul Wilson, this is set during the Second World War at a remote mountain pass in Rumania. A company of German soldiers is stationed at the title structure, a mysterious stone fortress that was apparently built, not to keep something out, but to keep something in. Of course, the something — the actual entity behind the vampire myths — is released, and goes on a real tear, either biting the heads off its victims or else sucking out all their energy and leaving only a dry husk behind. To this situation, add a thoroughly nasty SS troop, a fatally ill Jewish historian, his lovely young daughter, and Scott Glenn as the ancient supernatural warrior who is the guardian of the Keep, and we end up with enough style to make it fun to watch and to hold your attention reasonably well, although ultimately it becomes mechanical and fails to grab or jolt in the way it should. The something itself is kind of a cross between a Frazetta drawing and the video creatures in *Tron*, and similarly never quite makes it.

FRIGHT NIGHT (1985)
wr and dir by Tom Holland

Charlie Brewster (William Ragsdale), a teenage horror-film buff, sees his new neighbor arrive... in a coffin. Only Charlie understands that the neighbor (Chris Sarandon) is a vampire, and — naturally — no one believes him. The first half of the movie is very funny, playing the conventions of the classic vampire film off against the mundane reality of suburban life. The second half takes the conventions and raises them to new heights with some really striking scary effects as Charlie, assisted by Peter Vincent (Roddy McDowell), a has-been actor from old vampire movies, attempts to save his girlfriend and destroy the monster. Like **RETURN OF THE LIVING DEAD**, which was released at virtually the same time, this manages to simultaneously work within the genre and have fun with it — no small achievement. The result is good, scary, entertaining fun, and one of the best horror films of the 1980s. Highly recommended.

NOMADS *(1985)*
wr and dir John McTiernan

Revenge of the flashback. This opens with a badly injured French anthropologist (Pierce Brosnan) dying in a hospital emergency room. Before he does, though, he somehow transfers his memories of what happened to the mind of the doctor attending him (Lesley-Anne Down). Thus most of the movie consists of Down's "recollections" of the events of the past week, during which the anthropologist discovered a "tribe" of violent punk bikers who roam the wastelands of Los Angeles just like the nomadic tribes he has studied in other parts of the world. It became clear to him that these are not really people, but legendary evil spirits in human form, alien predators (not really vampires) who move, unrecognized, through the fringes of society, and are very similar in both style and attitude to the outlaw punk vampires in *The Lost Boys* and **NEAR DARK** (both of which may owe a slight debt to this one). There's a lot of potentially very interesting stuff here, almost none of which is developed. The two stories — Brosnan's and Down's — don't really hang together, and each might have worked better on its own. Decently made, and not without some good moments (especially Mary Woronov as a motorcycle Black Madonna), but there's just not enough of them. The first feature from the director of *Predator* and *Die Hard*.

GRAVEYARD SHIFT *(1986, Canadian)*
wr and dir Gerard Ciccoritti

A breast-biting vampire cab driver (Silvio Oliviero) does his thing on a number of his despondent female passengers, thus giving them a lift, so to speak, before they go off, bare-breasted, to slash the throats of assorted horny men. Thus, we get a number of attractive women in various stages of undress, some sex, and blood dripping over naked bodies — all of which are nothing to complain about — as well as a vampiric self-sucking, which is kind of an interesting concept. Unfortunately, what we don't get is a story with any discernible conflict, or a character to root for (the vamps are murderers and the non-vamps are jerks). There is some potentially interesting stuff here — the vamps have a psychic link between them, and there's the suggestion that the cabbie is a kind of Christ figure, taking his victims' trouble and despair into himself and giving them a new life — but it's left largely undeveloped. This low-budget first effort has the usual flaws, but also some style, visual drama, and exploitative flair. While certainly nothing special in itself, there's enough here to make one curious about the director's next effort.

VAMPIRE AT MIDNIGHT *(1987)*
wr Dulaney Ross Clements; dir Gregory McClatchy

A hypnotist vampire, Dr. Victor Radkoff (Gustav Vintas), who wears a wrist knife like Olivier did in *Marathon Man* and who talks like a bad mimic's Ricardo Montalban, is draining folks all around the L.A. Basin, and the cops are baffled. Of course, it wouldn't take anything more complicated than a serial jaywalker to stump these dolts and, from the shambling structure and totally lethargic pace, it looks as though the good doctor put folks on both sides of the camera into trances of near comatose depth. In other words, this is not a bright movie or a zippy one (and, based on the ambiguous conclusion, may not even be a vampire movie). Lesley Milne, Esther Alise, and Jeanie Moore all take their clothes off, but neither gratuitous nudity nor the occasional inadvertent laugh is enough to keep your eyes from glazing over in company with the characters'.

NEAR DARK *(1987)*
wr Eric Red and Kathyrn Bigelow; dir Kathryn Bigelow

A group of young vampires cruise the southwest in a van. When May (Jenny Wright) bites farmboy Caleb (Adrian Pasdar), he has a week to decide if he wants to join them, which means killing nightly, or to suffer a painful death. A potentially interesting premise and the locale is a nice variation — but the script doesn't deliver. Likewise, although this has great production values, a terrific look, and some strong performances, the pace is slow, and the ending unsatisfying. Ultimately, despite some good and original elements the movie is as flat as its landscape.

A RETURN TO 'SALEM'S LOT *(1987)*
wr Larry Cohen and James Dixon; dir Larry Cohen

When anthropologist Michael Moriarty and his son go up to the old house he inherited in a small town in Maine, the boy remarks that "this town sucks." It does, indeed, since this is Jerusalem's Lot, the vampire community chronicled in Stephen King's 1975 best seller. This is more Larry Cohen doing another of his slightly off-center variations on a standard horror genre than a sequel. It seems the vamps want Moriarty to write a history of their ancient race, which has been grievously misunderstood and persecuted over the years. As they tell it, they are actually upstanding citizens who drink human blood only on special occasions. They are opposed to alcohol and drugs, and don't take any money from the government. In other words, these bloodsuckers are good, solid Middle Americans. As is true of most of Cohen's films, the narrative rambles and there isn't much in the way of effects, but the vision is quirky enough to keep you curious about the proceedings, if not absolutely engrossed. A minor effort that may be of most interest for the presence of Sam Fuller, the famous B-movie director, as an ancient Nazi hunter who dispatches vampires in his spare time.

MY BEST FRIEND IS A VAMPIRE *(1987)*
wr Tab Murphy; dir Jimmy Huston

From the title and the first half hour or so, as Jeremy (Robert Sean Leonard) gets bitten by hot lady vamp and starts to change, this looks like a reprise of **ONCE BITTEN** — not as leadenly bad, but still labored and unfunny. Then, René Auberjonois shows up as Jeremy's vampire mentor and this unexpectedly turns into a quite amusing depiction of vampirism as just another alternative lifestyle. As René says, "There's lots worse things than being a vampire." The conceit here is that there's a huge vampire underground whose members drink bottled pig's blood — "This blood's for you" — purchased from similarly inclined butchers, and only rarely are converts to the persuasion sought out. Similarly, the fearless vampire hunter (David Warner) turns out to be a demented bigot, not unlike rabid, born-again homophobes. While not completely successful — too much stuff falls flat — this is a pretty cleverly worked-out reversal of the form, with a lot of attention to detail, a pleasant attitude, some quite nice performances (especially by Leonard, and Cheryl Pollack

> *"Your family? It's not even human!"*
> THE FUNHOUSE

as his girlfriend), and a good number of genuinely funny moments. An enormous improvement from the director of **FINAL EXAM**.

ETERNAL EVIL
Astrally projected soul-suckers; see Festival 13.
EVILS OF THE NIGHT
Cheapshit alien platelet-poppers; See Festival 1.
BLOODSUCKERS FROM OUTER SPACE
Alien-virus vamp zoms; see Festival 7.

Vampire Queens

THE TOMB *(1985)*
wr Kenneth J. Hall; dir Fred Olen Ray

After her tomb is opened and vandalized, a legendary Egyptian vampire queen is released from her imprisonment, then immediately hops a plane to Los Angeles in order to retrieve the stolen magic junk that ensures her immortality. While not quite as cheap, shoddy, and amateurish as the director's earlier **SCALPS**, this is no less ridiculous and no more entertaining. It seems to want to be both funny and scary, but doesn't have a clue how to be either, and settles for painfully dull. Even Sybil Danning's presence, so prominently featured on the box, is a cheat since she appears only in a brief segment before the titles that has nothing at all to do with what follows. As far as ancient Egyptian curses go, few could be more deadly than what you'll experience if you open this tomb. With Kitten Natividad as the extraordinarily top-heavy topless dancer.

ONCE BITTEN *(1985)*
wr David Hines, Jeffrey Hause, and J. Roberts; dir Howard Storm

The "Countess" is a 390-year-old vampire who needs the blood of a virgin male in order to keep looking like Lauren Hutton. Of course, virgins are hard to come by in L.A. these days, but she manages to find a horny high-school student (Jim Carrey) whose long-time girlfriend still refuses to put out. This combines the vampire movie with the tiresome teen comedy about getting laid, and adds nothing to either form. There's no skin, no sex, and both the "plot" and the "humor" consist of a leaden series of predictable clichés. Not worth a nibble.

DRACULA'S WIDOW *(1985, direct to cassette)*
wr Kathryn Ann Thomas and Christopher Coppola; dir C. Coppola

For reasons never explained, the wife of the late, lamented Count (Sylvia Kristel) arrives at the Hollywood House of Wax in a crate, then proceeds to do her thing across Los Angeles (or at least around Dino DeLaurentiis's North Carolina studio, which sits in for the Big Orange). Let me tell you, Sylvia's no dainty bloodsucker. She sprouts taloned hands like the original vamp in *Nosferatu* (which is remembered cinematically several times), undergoes some serious facial alterations, and leaves her victims looking like badly prepared steak tartare. Although this casts lots of knowing winks at the vampire tradition, it's not done to much point or especially cleverly. Still, it's brisk and mildly amusing, and there are some very silly effects (including a bat transforming itself into Sylvia). Also, Rachel Jones takes a bath, and Candice Sims is toplessly sacrificed to Satan. (I have no idea if the director is any relation to Francis Ford.)

VAMP *(1986)*
wr and dir Richard Wenk

Grace Jones as a vampire queen? Great! In fact, let's have lots of sexy female vampires. Even better! And how about making them exotic dancers at a very weird after-hours club? Wow! With concepts like these, I guess the folks responsible for this one decided they didn't need anything else — such as an intelligible script, decent acting, or genuine humor. Three collegiate types — a hustler asshole (Robert Rusler), a wimp asshole (Chris Makepeace), and a comic relief asshole (Gedde Watanabe) — head to the sleazy part of town to hire a stripper for their fraternity party, only to discover that they're the liquid refreshment in a vampire bar. This combines elements from *The Hunger,* **FRIGHT NIGHT**, and *An American Werewolf in London*, but it's a lame mélange, without any energy or originality of its own. Only when Grace and the girls are on does this come to life. Grace does a fairly exotic dance number, a pretty hot vampire sex scene, and looks good with a mouth full of fangs. But that's

> "Everyone knows that my snake stew seasoned with
> cactus is the best in the forbidden lands."
> EXTERMINATORS OF THE YEAR 3000

about all she does, and there's even less to say about the other girls. Another high concept shot to hell.

LIFEFORCE

Naked alien vamp queen; see Festival 1.

Parodies that Suck

TRANSYLVANIA 6-5000 *(1985)*
wr and dir Rudy DeLuca

An absolutely dreadful, sophomoronic attempted spoof of old horror movies that includes a Frankenstein monster, a mad scientist, a vampire, a mummy, and a wolfman, but not one single laugh. Indeed, considering the talent in the cast, this one is worse than you could imagine. Jeff Goldblum and Ed Begley, Jr., the two leads, embarrass themselves mightily, but that's nothing compared to what Joseph Bologna, John Byner, and Carol Kane accomplish. Jeffrey Jones doesn't fare too badly, but only Geena Davis, awesome in a spectacularly low-cut vampiress outfit, manages to avoid public humiliation. A wrong number all the way.

THE MONSTER SQUAD *(1987)*
wr Shane Black and Fred Dekker; dir Fred Dekker

A hundred years after Dracula was cast into the void, he returns, bringing with him the Mummy, the Wolfman, Frankenstein's Monster, and the Creature from the Black Lagoon. Only the title team of 12-year-olds stands between the forces of darkness and total global domination. This horror-comedy was obviously made for the peers of the juvenile heroes, and while I have no idea if it works for that group, I am reasonably confident that the only adults who could watch this with any enjoyment are those who thrill to *The Goonies*. Absurdly expensive ($14 million), this returned barely a tenth of its cost in theatrical release, which shows that there is, after all, some justice in the world.

FESTIVAL 13

* * *

MINDLESS OVER MATTER
A Medium of Visions, Psychic Phenomena, and Dream Sequences

"You're letting your mind run away with you."
— *Cassandra*

The entries in this festival comprise several different, often overlapping, subject areas, all of which are, in some way, centered on the mind. While perhaps not "supernatural" in quite the same way as the movies in the preceding festivals, the material they deal with is also clearly not "normal" or "real."

Parapsychobabble: Although a wide range of psychic powers — telepathy, precognition, déjà vu, astral projection, telekinesis, and so on — have long been the subjects of speculative fiction, mystical works, and supposedly true accounts of unexplained parapsychological phenomena, until recently they were only infrequently given film treatment. The best-known titles are Roger Corman's *X — The Man with the X-Ray Eyes* (1963), George Pal's production of *The Power* (1967), and Nicholas Roeg's *Don't Look Now* (1973).

The situation changed in 1976 when a director who was still looking for a breakthrough movie adapted a novel by a writer who was not yet well known. The director was Brian De Palma, the writer, Stephen King, and the movie that moved both their careers into high gear was *Carrie*. This effectively demonstrated that you didn't need a demonic possession to send things flying, and that hi-tech telekinesis could provide the kind of spectacle that would bring in an audience.

After *Carrie* the movies developed a new interest in the world of parapsychology. De Palma followed up with *The Fury* in 1978, a year that also saw the unintentionally hilarious *Medusa Touch* (with Richard Burton managing to make his performance in *Exorcist II* seem subtle), and the telepathic thriller *The Eyes of Laura Mars* (co-scripted by John

Carpenter who, himself, turned out a little movie that same year, which, as we see in Section III, was not without some small influence). David Cronenberg moved from the horrors of the body to mental monstrosities with *Scanners* in 1981, and in 1983 directed one of the best screen treatments of a Stephen King novel, the precognition thriller *The Dead Zone*. And yet another King novel, the pyrokinetic *Firestarter*, did respectable business in 1984.

Most of the movies in this festival, not surprisingly, are concerned with the less-flamboyant forms of psychic phenomena for the obvious reason that it's a lot cheaper and easier to have a telepathic vision than a telekinetic fit. While there are a couple of fairly entertaining little psychic numbers below, most offer up visions that are really not worth seeing. (Note: Those interested in serious movings and shakings will find some of the demonic variety in Festival 9, and the haunted variety in Festival 10.)

Dreamstuff: The most common metaphor applied to the motion picture is that of the dream. Not only is a movie, any movie, a kind of dream in itself, but the medium is ideally suited to the depiction of dreams and hallucinations. Almost from the earliest days of the motion picture we have been shown exercises in Freudian symbolism, fantasy reveries, and surrealism, and, in the 1960s, we were taken on various LSD excursions. Almost always though, the movie would let the audience know they were watching a dream, either through the nature of the images or because a framing device of some kind — the screen going all wavy, say — indicated entry into a dream state.

Today's horror cinema has found a much more effective way to use dreams. Just as what we see and experience in a dream state seems "real," so too does what we see on the screen. Because we cannot be sure if what we're seeing is really real, as opposed to dream real, a skillful filmmaker can use the blurred distinctions to manipulate an audience, and in the process deliver some very high-grade surprises and shocks. We are led to believe that what we are seeing is actually happening and then, when we least expect it, something — usually something disturbing and unpleasant — occurs to make us realize that we have been POV:Dreamer all along.

In 1965, Roman Polanski used this approach to take the audience on a terrifying descent into madness in *Repulsion,* and such movies as **THE SENDER** and **DREAMSCAPE** (below) have also used it to good effect. The movie everyone thinks of when it comes to bad dreams is, of course,

Wes Craven's *Nightmare on Elm Street* (1984). It, and its sequels, demonstrated how the dream sequence could be one of the more efficient and effective devices for generating shocks and thrills. Its utility is obvious: you don't have to be concerned about logic or cause-and-effect; literally anything goes; and it can be inserted at almost any time to juice up a flagging narrative. It may not always contribute to suspense or narrative coherence, but when it comes to mindless sensationalism and special-effects spectacle, the dream sequence is mighty hard to beat.

As of this writing, it's too soon to tell if *Elm Street* will spawn enough clones to make up a full Dream Movie subgenre, but I have the feeling that it might. Although there are not yet many direct descendants, its influence and techniques are starting to show up in the alarming dream sequences that are intruding with increasing frequency into a wide variety of movies across the horror spectrum. In other words, the Nightmare Nineties may be coming...

Mental Murderers

INVISIBLE STRANGLER *(1983)*
wr Arthur C. Pierce; dir John Florea

Don't be fooled by the cast, which includes Robert Foxworth, Stephanie Powers, and Elke Sommer, who themselves must've been fooled into being parties to this lame lump (apparently shot sometime in the '70s and given a few years to mature). Perhaps this was modeled on *The Psychic Killer* (1976), but the title says it all: a convicted murderer develops the power to make himself invisible, then escapes from the mental hospital and sets about strangling the four or five bimbos (for some reason, identical blondes) who testified at his trial. Since the guy's invisible, the filmmakers were cleverly able to eliminate the need for special effects — there's nothing to see, right? — and make do with the various victims looking wide-eyed and short of breath. They likewise seemed able to eliminate the need for logic, suspense, and pacing. Simultaneously dumb and dull, this does nonetheless manage to exercise a peculiar mind-numbing fascination.

"The five senses weren't enough for him — he wanted more."
FROM BEYOND

ETERNAL EVIL *(1985, Canadian)*
wr Robert Geoffrion; dir George Mihalka
Also released as *The Blue Man*.

Paul Sharp (Winston Rekert) has been practicing astral projection, but when people close to him start to be killed off in mysterious ways, he, we, and a police detective suspect he may be doing it unawares. It turns out he's not; in fact, the soul responsible has been moving from body to body — kind of a spiritual vampire — for a thousand years (hence the title). This is not badly done and not nearly as stupid as it could have been, but it could have used a few more twists, a zippier pace, and a couple of special effects (there virtually are none). Passing mediocrity from the director of **MY BLOODY VALENTINE**. (Not to be confused with **FOREVER EVIL**.)

MIND KILLER *(1987, made for cassette?)*
wr Dave Sipos, Curtis Hannum, and Michael Krueger; dir M. Krueger

Warren (Joe McDonald), a terminally nerdy librarian, has tried every self-help technique in the manual to learn how to pick up girls, but nothing works for him. Then he discovers a manuscript in the archives that tells how to unleash the full power of the mind, and soon he's able to make those around him do his bidding. As a method for getting laid, it proves quite effective, but, once unleashed, Warren's mind decides it doesn't need him any longer, eventually exiting the cranial confines and striking out on its own. Made in Denver, this seriously low-budget movie is not nearly as amateurish as a lot of backyard efforts. McDonald is pretty good, as is Christopher Wade as his even-nerdier fellow librarian; the pace is brisk; the script has a nice sense of fun and manages to keep you interested; and there are even a few good messy creature effects. Nothing more than a cheap and cheerful time-passer, but there is energy and enthusiasm on display here, and this is definitely the finest film featuring a homicidal out-of-body brain since *Fiend Without a Face* (1958).

Telepathic Twins

THE LOST TRIBE *(1983, New Zealand)*
wr and dir John Laing

Okay, let's see if I can get this straight. There's an anthropologist, Max Scarry, who disappears in a remote area of southern New Zealand while searching for a legendary lost Maori tribe. And there's a murdered woman, back in the city, with whom Max was apparently having an affair. And there's Max's identical twin, Edward, over whom he seems to be able to exercise some kind of telepathic power. And there's Max's wife, who once was Edward's girlfriend. And there's Max's young daughter, who also seems to have some telepathic connection with her father. And there are the spirits of the dead Maoris, who apparently don't like having their graves interfered with. All of this stuff, though, doesn't add up to anything since you're never sure what the hell's going on. Except for some nice scenery, this one's a lost cause.

BLOOD LINK *(1983)*
wr Theodore Apstein; dir Albert De Martino

A nerdy doctor (Michael Moriarty) starts to have visions of murders, and realizes he's seeing them through the eyes of his identical Siamese-twin brother, who he had long believed was dead. He hurries to Germany to track him down before he kills again, but himself becomes the number-one suspect for the crimes. This has lots of boring chat, but virtually no suspense or surprises. The dual role and bad script give Moriarty the opportunity to give two dull performances for the price of one, and he takes advantage of it. Four well-endowed young women display their endowments, but otherwise this lame thriller doesn't connect with anything.

CASSANDRA *(1987, Australian)*
wr Colin Eggleston, John Ruane, and Chris Fitchett; dir Colin Eggleston

Cassandra (Tessa Humphries), a troubled young woman, is having bad dreams about a suicide. It turns out she's remembering something she saw as child, and the woman who killed herself was her real mother. The

> *"These aren't just kids — these are clean-cut, all-American kids."*
> SPACECAMP

woman she thinks is her mother is actually her father's sister, but her real mother was also her father's sister. (Are you following this?) Then she starts to see murders being committed, and it turns out she's also got a twin brother, whom she didn't know about, and he just got out of the loony bin and wants to kill the rest of his family as a punishment for the incest, and she's seeing it through his eyes. At least I think that's what's going on here. This one can't decide if it wants to be a psycho thriller or a psycho killer, so it settles instead for being long, slow, dull, and stupid. There are no thrills, chills, blood, or surprises, and no reason that I can think of to watch it.

BASKET CASE
Pint-sized mutant telepathic Siamese twin; see Festival 3.
IDENTITY CRISIS
Escaped psycho loony twin; see Festival 18.
SORORITY HOUSE MASSACRE
Telepathic psycho loony older brother; see Festival 16.

Seeing Things

DARK SANITY *(1981)*
wr Phillip Pine and Larry Hillman; dir Martin Green

The box for this one proudly exclaims "Pre-cinema release!" In other words, it will be a brisk day in Hell before this dull, dreary, pointless, plotless piece-o-shit gets a theatrical showing. It has something to do with ESP, visions, and a grisly murder, but it's so slow and amateurish that it all but defies you to try to follow it. Aldo Ray lends a welcome note of ponderous stolidity to the proceedings, but as the hysterical, on-the-wagon alcoholic bimbo who's seeing things puts it, "It's too terrifying even to visualize."

BRAINWAVES *(1982)*
wr, prod, dir Ulli Lommel

After receiving a head injury, Suzanna Love (the director's wife) falls into a deep coma, and the only hope for her is a radical process developed by

Dr. Clavius (Tony Curtis) that involves the transfer of electronic impulses from the brain of a dead woman. The procedure is a success, but once she recovers, Suzanna starts to have disturbing visions, and it turns out that the impulse-donor was actually murdered. This starts as a medical drama with a futuristic twist then turns into a psycho thriller as Suzanna and her husband (Keir Dullea) try to unravel the visions. The medical half is a little bit better done than the thriller half, which is badly structured. Still, this is competently made and, with the exception of Dullea — who creates a histrionic vacuum on the screen — decently acted. If you're not feeling very demanding, it's probably interesting enough to pass some time.

THE KILLING HOUR *(1982)*
wr B. Jonathan Ringkamp; dir Armand Mastroianni

A serial murderer called the "Handcuff Killer" is menacing New York City. A cop who'd like to be a night-club impressionist (Norman Parker) is trying to track him down, and an ambitious TV newsman (Perry King) is using the case to further his career. In the middle is a young art student (Elizabeth Kemp) who's a clairvoyant, and whose impressions of the murders are revealed through her drawings. This could easily have been very mechanical and silly, but turns out to be something of a pleasant surprise. It's quite competently made, generally well-acted (notably by Kemp), and nicely plotted, with enough complications to keep you guessing. By no means a great thriller — there are some holes and some awkward bits — but it does move right along and holds your interest.

SHADEY *(1985, British)*
wr Snoo Wilson; dir Philip Saville

Shadey (Antony Sher), the owner of a bankrupt garage, has a unique talent: he is able to visualize things that are happening anywhere in the world (and sometimes in the future), and then transfer those images to film. In order to raise money for a sex-change operation, he offers to sell his services to a wealthy industrialist (Patrick Macnee). Instead, Macnee trades him to British Intelligence in exchange for some office space, despite the fact that Shadey specifically stated he did not want his talents used by the government. Soon, word of Shadey leaks out, and agents from other countries are after him. Also involved are Macnee's seriously loony wife (Katherine Helmond), his daughter (Leslie Ash) with whom he may be having an incestuous relationship, and a cold-as-ice government psychologist (Billie Whitelaw). A lot of strange things happen, but there is some question as to whether or not it's all a dream or a hallucination. In the end, I don't have a clue what this is about — or even if it's a good movie for that matter — but the performances are good (especially by Sher and Helmond), there are a few laughs, and it's intriguing enough to keep you interested. If you figure it out, let me know.

NIGHT VISION *(1987, made for video?)*
wr Michael Krueger, Nancy Gallanis, and Leigh Pomeroy; dir M. Krueger

Naive, would-be writer Andy Archer (Stacy Carson) leaves Kansas and heads to the big city (Denver) to get some experiences to write about. He gets more than he bargained for when he acquires a videocassette stolen from a sect of hi-tech satanists and starts to write stories about violent occurrences that soon take place. Fairly slickly made, this starts off promisingly and humorously — Carson does a nice job, as does Shirley Ross as his wise-cracking girlfriend — but it doesn't go anywhere. A bit more polished than the director's earlier **MIND KILLER** (about which a little joke is made in passing), but it's not nearly as energetic or as much fun. Still, there is some real talent here that may yet get the budget and the script needed to produce something pretty good. Stay tuned.

JACK'S BACK *(1987)*
wr and dir Rowdy Herrington

From the description on the video box, it's obvious that the distributor didn't how to say much about this one without spoiling the fun, and neither do I. It involves telepathy and a hunt to find a killer who's duplicating Jack the Ripper's murders in Los Angeles a hundred years later. The Ripper provides the title and a convenient hook, but is really incidental to the proceedings. What this is really about is misdirection, keeping the viewer guessing, and two of the best-executed plot twists you are ever likely to see. As a thriller, it is slickly made, decently acted (especially by James Spader in the lead, showing that he can do much more than the preppy asshole roles for which he is best known), and briskly paced. Most of all, it could serve as a textbook example of how to structure a script for maximum impact. This doesn't pretend to be more than an entertaining little B-movie, but it is a nifty, intelligent, and effective one, and well worth checking out.

NOMADS
Memory dump; spirit vamps; see Festival 12.

Moving Things

KISS DADDY GOODBYE *(1982)*
wr Alain Silver, Patrick Regan, Ron Abrahams, and Mary Stewart; dir Patrick Regan. Also released as *Revenge of the Zombie.*

Beth and Michael, two young, blond kids, possess a variety of psychic powers, so when their father is murdered by a group of bikers, they re-animate his corpse and send him out to get revenge. An entertaining piece of nonsense could have been fashioned from that premise, but it wasn't. Severely cheap, badly plotted, and lethargic, this has virtually no special effects, suspense, or any reason to be interested unless you happen to have a real weakness for stupefyingly dull dialog and wooden acting. With Fabian (!) as the local deputy sheriff.

MAKING CONTACT *(1986, German, dubbed)*
wr Roland Emmerich, T. Lechner, and Hans Haller; dir R. Emmerich

At the center of this dull effort is a telekinetic kid who talks to his dead father on a toy telephone. There's also a haunted house, an evil ventriloquist's dummy, and enough stuffed animals and mechanical toys for two or three Steven Spielberg movies. In fact, there's virtually nothing in this lame piece-o-shit that wasn't plundered whole from something that S.S. either directed or produced, and the only possible interest lies in trying to identify the sources. Very definitely avoid the title activity with this one.

> *"If she were any quieter, she'd be dead."*
> SLEEPAWAY CAMP

Making Dreams Come True

DEADLINE *(1980, Canadian)*
wr Mario Azzopardi and Dick Oleksiak; dir Mario Azzopardi

Stephen Young plays Steven Lessey, a successful horror writer with artistic pretensions, who wants to do more than turn out the usual crap, seeking to reveal the Ultimate Horror. This he discovers when his children — whom he is too busy to pay attention to — act out a scene from one of his movies and the youngest girl is accidentally hanged. Not surprisingly, Dad then goes a good distance around the bend. The narrative is interrupted a number of times with scenes from the story he's working on, and a good thing too, since there's some pretty effective splatter in it — a blood-from-the-shower gag, a torching, cannibalistic nuns, an exploding-intestine stunt, and (the highlight) a guy getting chewed up real good in a giant piece of farm equipment. The problem here is that this movie should have stuck to dishing out the usual crap — which it does quite effectively — but itself seems instead to have artistic pretension. So, we're treated to lots of angst, discussions about Art and Commerce, and scenes from a disintegrating marriage, all overwrought enough to induce dyspepsia. Personally, I don't have a lot of interest in the artistic torment of a writer who drives a Mercedes, but if you hurry through all that shit, this does deliver a few good moments. (Not to be confused with the 1987 movie with the same title that stars Christopher Walken and is set in Beirut.)

THE SLAYER *(1981)*

There was no credit here for the writer and director (who I've seen elsewhere identified as J.S. Cardone) but, given some of the things in this book to which the filmmakers proudly attach their names, the folks responsible for this one have no reason to be especially ashamed. Not a slasher flick (despite the title), it concerns a young woman (Sarah Kendall) who's having very disturbing violent nightmares. When she goes with three of her friends to an isolated island off the coast of Georgia, the dreams and premonitions intensify, and then start to come true — a neck is crushed in a trapdoor, a fishhook is lodged in a throat, and a woman is pitchforked in the chest. This does get you mildly curious but the material is stretched too thin to hold your interest (it would have played much more effectively as a half-hour segment in an anthology). Still, this is not badly made and there are a couple of decent effects. If your VCR has a double-speed mode, you could probably do worse.

THE SENDER *(1982)*
wr Thomas Baum; dir Roger Christian

Two years before Freddie started to intrude on Elm Street's slumber, there was The Sender. Zeljko Ivanek, the title character, is a disturbed, telepathic young man with the ability to transmit his dreams and visions into the minds of those around him, and Shirley Knight is his mother, a religious crazy very similar to Carrie's demented mom. This is a modest but well-made little thriller that generates a fair bit of suspense and makes good use of the blurred line between dreams and reality. Although not truly exceptional, this has a decent script, solid performances, and a number of quite good effects — an intriguing little movie that deserves to be better known.

DREAMSCAPE *(1983)*
wr David Loughery, Chuck Russell, and Joseph Ruben; dir Joseph Ruben

This is not great, but it's a competently done, generally interesting sci-fi/parapsychology combo. The plot concerns a top-secret experiment in which certain psychics (including Dennis Quaid) are able to enter and participate in the dreams of someone else. The scientist in charge (Max Von Sydow) sees this as a great therapeutic tool, but the government spook who's funding it (Christopher Plummer) sees its value as a tool for political manipulation. The script is only so-so — never totally dumb, but a bit too mechanical and predictable to be a real grabber — but the quality of the cast gives the proceedings a credibility that movies with smaller budgets have difficulty achieving. The fantasy effects, while lacking the punch of those in *Nightmare on Elm Street*, are not too bad. A commendable first effort from the director of **THE STEPFATHER**.

DEADLY DREAMS *(1988 direct to cassette)*
wr Thom Babbes; dir Kristine Peterson

Ten years after his wealthy parents were blasted away by a disgruntled business associate wearing a wolf mask — and shortly before he's due to inherit his share of the estate — Alex (Mitchell Anderson) is having the title reveries (by my count five, plus one hallucination) about the hunter coming after him, and he's rapidly losing his grip. Now, anyone who's read more than two mystery novels knows that when strange things start to happen to someone about to come into a sizable sum of money, chances are there's a nefarious scheme afoot. It will not be difficult for the perceptive viewer to predict well in advance the two twists this laboriously delivers. Even the missing logical link between the scheme and the dreams could be forgiven if the latter, which are apparently the point of the exercise, had some of *Elm Street*'s flamboyance, but they don't. Juliette Cummins sheds her clothes twice.

BAD DREAMS *(1988)*
wr Andrew Fleming and Steven E. de Souza; dir Andrew Fleming

Awakening from a 13-year coma after surviving a mini-version of the Jonestown cult massacre, Cynthia (Jennifer Rubin) is placed in a therapy group for "borderline personalities," apparently in the belief that associating with a bunch of suicidal losers will somehow ease her into the '80s. Only Cynthia starts to have visions of the dead cult leader (Richard Lynch), now understandably with a serious complexion problem, who wants her to join her fellow culties and starts to kill off members of the therapy group when she resists. Kind of a cross between **SOLE SURVIVOR** and *Nightmare on Elm Street*, this has a decent premise that goes nowhere. Although quite slickly made, the direction is pedestrian and the only twist in the script is the concluding "explanation," which, far from making sense of the situation, serves to render everything that preceded it totally nonsensical. There are quite entertaining performances by Susan Ruttan ("L.A. Law") and Dean Cameron as two of the borderline personalities, and some nice tastes of graphic gore, but otherwise it's flat and slumberous.

SLUMBER PARTY MASSACRE II
Dream-sequence driller killer; see Festival 15.
STONES OF DEATH
Nightmare in Kangaloola; see Festival 10.
SLAUGHTERHOUSE ROCK
Bad-dream supernatural stew; see Festival 10.

FESTIVAL 13: PSYCHIC PHENOMENA

NIGHTMARE
Psycho-loony bad dreams; see Festival 19.
NIGHTMARES
No dreams; mini-ripoffs; see Festival 14.
FRIGHTMARE
No dreams; resuscitated hambone; see Festival 11.

Really Bad Dreams

A DAY OF JUDGEMENT *(1981)*
wr Tom McIntyre; dir C.D.H. Reynolds

Set in the 1920s (probably because the filmmakers had access to some old cars), this lame piece-o-shit has the Grim Reaper — yes, complete with cloak and scythe — arriving in a small North Carolina town to dish out a little divine retribution to assorted sinners. Most of the movie is spent establishing, in considerable tedious detail, just why these semi-pro actors are deserving of punishment. Then it sends them to Hell, or rather to a really shabby painting thereof. Then, in the only "twist" that could have rendered the proceedings even stupider and more pointless, it all turns out to be a dream, and the sinners reform and go to church. A message picture scripted by the author of **DOGS OF HELL**.

VIRGIN AMONG THE LIVING DEAD *(198?, dubbed)*
wr Jess Franco, Peter Kerut, and Henry Braid; dir Jess Franco

Yeah, I know, this is one of the all-time great titles. And considering it was made by a director known for his relentlessly tawdry exploitation you'd think this would dish up a large helping of shocks and sleaze. Jess, though, displays good taste here and delivers only yawns. A young woman (presumably the title virgin, though her sexual experience, or lack thereof, never figures in the story) arrives at an isolated castle for the reading of her father's will. She finds an assortment of weirdos living there, and starts to have dreams about being attacked by a half-dozen zombies who have bad teeth but are otherwise undecomposed. Ah, it's only a dream — the same dull, unfrightening one, over and over. From some of the dubbed dialog, there's a chance this is all supposed to be a joke, but it'll be on you if you get suckered by this one.

> *"She's back from the grave, Eddie, and she knows things we don't know."*
> GOTHAM

THE APPOINTMENT *(1982, British)*
wr and dir Lindsey C. Vickers

Before renting this one, I had never seen Edward Woodward (*Breaker Morant*, "The Equalizer") in anything really crummy and discovered there's a first time for everything. A vaguely supernatural story about dark dreams and dark forces, apparently this is supposed to be subtly eerie and quietly menacing. In practice, what you get here is a series of the slowest pans possible over inanimate objects and suspenseful music, but no payoff. The blurb on the box warns you not to see this movie alone . . . probably because, misery loves company.

THE DUNGEONMASTER *(1984)*
Various writers and directors from the stable of Empire Pictures

Through circumstances too dumb for the movie to attempt to explain, a computer whiz named Paul (woodenly acted by Jeffrey Byron) enters the fantasy dream world that comprises almost the entire picture. There he meets Mestema (Richard Moll), an incarnation of Satan, who gives Paul a series of tests that he must survive if he is ever to get back to what passes for the real world. Each of the test sequences was written and directed by a different person, but the paucity of imagination and cheesiness of special effects provide a certain stylistic unity. Amongst the monsters Paul must defeat in his trials are a stone giant, demons, zombies, a psycho killer and, maybe most terrible of all, the Heavy Metal band Wasp. With the exception of Richard Moll, who's pretty entertaining, this is less a dungeon than the absolute pits.

DREAM LOVER *(1986)*
wr Jon Boorstin; dir Alan J. Pakula

Kristy McNichol is a musician who is attacked in her apartment, and has terrible nightmares about the incident. A sleep researcher gives her an experimental drug, hoping to help her, but it goes wrong, and she starts to physically act out her dreams as she's having them. I guess it's supposed to be tense and scary, but it's not, and in the absence of any real conflict the movie just kind of meanders. The credits cite Yale University and other sleep-research centers, suggesting that, if nothing else, it's accurate. So what?

GOTHIC *(1986, British)*
wr Stephen Volk; dir Ken Russell

This purports to tell the story of how Mary Shelley (wife of the poet) came to write *Frankenstein* after a dark and stormy evening drugfest at Lord Byron's Swiss chateau. Ken Russell has made a career out of the depiction of madness and outrageous excess, and this one's no exception. However, despite the most intriguing premise, it doesn't work here. While there are a few grotesquely striking images, it's mostly just all loud, overwrought, and muddy — confusing rather than hallucinatory, hysterical rather than energetic. Worst of all, the characters are so pompous and unappealing that we wish they'd just go to bed.

FESTIVAL 14

* * *

MORE IS USUALLY LESS
A Compendium of Anthologies

> "Being told a really wierd tale is better
> than getting no tale at all."
> — *Really Weird Tales*

The movies in this festival, with the exception of the compilations, are anthology or omnibus films, each of which consists of a number of short stories linked in some way, often quite tenuously. Since the individual stories tend to have some supernatural component, these movies have been included in this section.

The stories usually end with a twist, and most frequently resemble those made popular in the late '50s in television anthologies such as "The Twilight Zone," "The Outer Limits," and "Alfred Hitchcock Presents." Although the omnibus horror film apparently goes back to a 1919 German silent movie called *Tales of Horror*, it was not until the 1960s that it started turning up fairly frequently. (Note, though, *Dead of Night*, from 1945, which may have the best segment-linking device seen to date.) In 1961, following his success with three adaptations of Poe, Roger Corman made a collection of Poe stories called *Tales of Terror*. In 1964, a small British studio, Amicus, produced *Dr. Terror's House of Horrors*, which became the first of a series of anthology films that includes *Torture Garden* (1967) and *From Beyond the Grave* (1973), most of which periodically show up on late-night TV.

In terms of box office, the two most successful anthologies of the 1980s are the ill-fated *Twilight Zone — The Movie* (1983) and the Stephen King-George Romero tribute to '50s horror comics, *Creepshow* (1982). (This was not the first movie inspired by William Gaines's famous comicbooks. Ten years earlier, Amicus had produced *Tales from the Crypt* and *Vault of Horror*, both of which were based on stories that had appeared in E.C. Comics.)

Besides the movies included here, there have been video packages of stories originally made for TV, such as *Tales from the Darkside, Ray Bradbury Theater*, and the absolutely unwatchable *Mania*. Generally, television is television, and I don't believe in renting it. Thus, with one exception, this sort of anthology has been omitted.

Personally, I'm not a big fan of the omnibus film, for much the same reasons that I prefer the extended narrative of the novel over the much slighter short story. The short story or its movie equivalent usually requires a good kick of some kind at the end — indeed, the conclusion is often the whole point of the exercise — and if it's not sufficiently strong or surprising, the whole thing falls flat. That is exactly what happens in a good number of stories included in the movies that follow. Still, there are a couple that are definitely worth checking out, and a couple more that might do if you're desperate.

* * *

NIGHTMARES *(1983)*
wr Christopher Crowe (Chaps. 1,2,3) and Jeffrey Bloom (chap. 4); dir Joseph Sargent

The four short chiller-thrillers presented here are linked by the fact that each is a mini-ripoff of an earlier, more successful movie. In the first chapter, a woman is threatened by an escaped psycho with a carving knife *(Halloween)*. In the second, a very young (and very blond) Emilio Estevez gets caught in a real-life battle with a video game *à la Tron*. The third is modeled on *Duel* (Steven Spielberg's famous 1971 TV movie), in which a priest with a crisis of faith finds himself being attacked by the Devil in the shape of a huge black pickup truck. And the fourth is a lot like *Poltergeist*, only instead of a spirit menacing the suburban family, it's a giant "Devil Rodent." The stories are rather predictable and the "twists" don't have much of a kick, but the production values aren't bad, the performances are professional and generally competent, and the director worked hard to energize some pretty thin material. While there's certainly nothing very special about this one, it's well enough done to be watchable, and the transparency of the "inspiration" for the stories is not without a certain fascination.

> *"I haven't had anything this pure since the Vienna Boys' Choir hit town."*
> ONCE BITTEN

SCREAMTIME *(1983, British)*
wr Michael Armstrong; prod and dir Al Beresford

I don't know the story behind this one, but from what we see, I'd guess that the producer somehow acquired (very cheaply, no doubt) the rights to three short scary/supernatural stories that were probably originally made for television, and added about ten minutes of framing/linking material. The cast is servicable, but not likely to turn up on "Masterpiece Theatre," and the stories are humdrum, familiar, and predictable. The middle one, about a haunted house, has the kind of surprise twist that this kind of story requires, but for 20 seconds of effectiveness out of 90 minutes, it's hardly worth the effort.

DEAD TIME STORIES *(1985)*
wr Jeffrey Delman, Charles F. Shelton, and J. E. Kiernan; dir J. Delman

The title pun indicates the level of the wit and humor operating in this thoroughly lame reworking of such bedtime stories as "Little Red Jogging Suit (and the Werewolf)" and "Goldi Lox and the Three Baers." This is a movie that strives to be sophomoric, but falls a good deal short. The 90 minutes spent with this are totally dead time.

CAT'S EYE *(1985)*
wr Stephen King; dir Lewis Teague

Adaptations of three very different types of short stories from Stephen King, loosely linked through the presence of a brave and intelligent cat. The first features James Woods, who wants to quit smoking, and Alan King, who's developed a harsh but effective aversion-therapy. The second involves Robert Hays in a harrowing journey around the ledge of a high-rise apartment building. The third is pure fantasy as the title feline battles one of the all-time great little creatures (created by E.T.'s Carlo Rambaldi) in order to save Drew Barrymore. Although there's no thematic or stylistic unity here — the first two are quite nasty, while the third is heroic — each episode is extremely well done. This is easily the best collection in this festival, and may be one of the most successful of all the adaptations that have been made of King's work. The third story alone makes this an absolute must for cat fanciers.

THE OFFSPRING *(1986)*
wr C. Courtney Joyner, Darin Scott, and Jeff Burr; dir Jeff Burr

Four episodes of violence and weirdness that have occurred over the years in the small Tennessee town of Oldfield. As narrator Vincent Price repeatedly tells us, "Oldfield's history is written in blood," and there's something in its atmosphere that inspires its inhabitants to do violent and weird things. The stories are of the *Creepshow*/horror-comics variety, each building to a moderately gruesome conclusion — a monster baby rises from the grave to exact revenge, a man discovers the secret of eternal life and then has to spend it without arms or legs, a carnival glass eater is cut to ribbons from the inside, and a *Lord of the Flies* community of savage children does some nasty things to Cameron Mitchell. This is basically TV fare with the addition of a little so-so splatter, but it's competently made and delivers a couple of decent moments. If you're really desperate, you could do worse.

REALLY WEIRD TALES *(1986, made for Pay TV)*
wr Joe Flaherty, David Flaherty, Catherine O'Hara, and John McAndrew; dir John Blanchard, Don McBrearty, and Paul Lynch

Anyone who's discovered "SCTV" — the wonderful Canadian-made spoof of television now showing all over the place in late-night syndication — probably wishes they were still making new programs. They're not, but this anthology reunites four of the "SCTV" alumni — Joe Flaherty, Catherine O'Hara, John Candy, and Martin Short — and is similar in style and humor. Flaherty is the rather clumsy and inept host who introduces and comments on the three stories, which are basically extended "SCTV" routines, modeled on old "Twilight Zone" and "Outer Limits" programs ... except, as the title indicates, these tales are *really* weird. Given the talent involved, there are, of course, a lot of good bits, but it seems the humor gets stretched a little too thin in order to fill 85 minutes (and almost entirely evaporates during the final segment with Martin Short as a fourth-rate lounge singer). That said, it's always a treat to watch Catherine O'Hara, and there is some quite funny stuff here — especially a white-pompadoured John Candy as a man "cursed with charisma" and doomed to preach no-down-payment-real-estate. Most of all, for those of us who think that "SCTV" represents some of the best comedy that's ever been on television, even a minor-league version is better than none at all.

> *"I never killed anyone before. What'll I say to Father O'Brien when I go to confession?"*
> I WAS A TEENAGE ZOMBIE

CREEPSHOW 2 *(1987)*
wr George Romero (from Stephen King stories); dir Michael Gornich

Like its predecessor, this is another live-action horror comic, but neither the stories or the production values are nearly as good as the original (and I thought the original was only intermittently effective). Here we have a wooden Indian that comes to life to avenge a murder, a man-eating oil slick, and a hit-and-run victim who won't stay down. George Romero, who's a much better director than a writer, provides dialog and characterization that might well have come from a comicbook; the effects are cheesy; and there are far too few twists or shocks. Hard-core Stephen King fans may want to see their author in another brief acting role, but there are not a lot of other reasons to watch this one.

Two Compilations

That's Entertainment! (1974) demonstrated that people like watching bits from their favorite old movies, and it was just a matter of time until the horror film was given the treatment. It's a good idea that is apparently quite difficult to do well. *It Came From Hollywood* (1982) managed to remove all the appeal from some of the most wonderfully lame movies ever made, and the first entry below accomplishes the same for some of the scariest. Other compilations that I regret I have not yet been able to locate are *Filmgore, The Best of Sex and Violence, Zombiethon*, and *Sleazemania: The Special Edition*. These are probably disappointing as well, but how can you not want to check them out?

TERROR IN THE AISLES *(1984)*
wr Margery Doppelt; dir Andrew J. Kuehn

Promoted as being nothing but good stuff — the best shocks from the best shockers, without any of the boring bullshit — you might wonder how this could not be a treat. As it turns out, it's easy. First, you don't show any of the great scenes in their entirety. Then you show very little of the truly good stuff. Then you always intercut three or four movies at once, just to show how spiffy your editing is. Then you make your definition so broad as to include such things as *Klute, Midnight Express,*

Nighthawks, and *Strangers on a Train*. And finally, you have lots of boring commentary delivered by Donald Pleasence and Nancy Allen about why we like to be scared, what scares us, blah blah blah. The result is that this only has value as a trivia exercise to see how many of the 75 or so movies you can identify. For a more entertaining compilation based on the same premise, check out . . .

TERROR ON TAPE *(1985)*
wr Philip L. Clarke; dir Robert A. Worms III

Cameron Mitchell is the comically ghoulish proprietor of the "Shoppe of Video Horrors," and he shows samples of his wares to prospective customers. This is basically the same format as the preceding entry, but it presents some of the bloodier highlights from the low end of the line. There are clips from **THE DEADLY SPAWN**, **SCALPS**, **CITY OF THE WALKING DEAD**, **NIGHTMARE**, **ALIEN PREY**, three ground-breaking splatter classics from Herschell Gordon Lewis (the "guru of gore"), and a bunch of cheapies from the '70s, including *Vampire Hookers*, *Cathy's Curse*, and *Madhouse Mansion*. Most of the clips, like the movies they came from, are not very good and mainly serve to satisfy whatever curiosity you might have had about these titles. Toward the end, though the material is edited into a number of fast montages — tits, sex screams, gore, etc. — that are quite clever and effective, and packed with some spectacularly messy mayhem, including a pitchforking, an eyeball-gouging, a tongue-extraction, limb-severings, two head-axings, and throat-cuttings galore. The montages alone probably make this one worth renting, and for all those who like to poke around the bottom of the video barrel, this could be quite useful in identifying titles to be either sought out or avoided.

III

SLICE AND DICE

An Asylum of Psycho Killers

You are cordially invited to the traditional Christmas New Year's Valentine's Day Graduation Birthday Slumber Party Hell Night Prom Massacre. Festivities will take place in the dark, and entertainment will be provided by an unseen strange prowler in the hospital mortuary mall who's watching and knows you're alone in the sorority-house summer-camp backwoods motel. Masks will be worn, breasts will be bared, and a bloody good time will be had by all.

At the end of October 1963, in the small Illinois town of Haddonfield, six-year-old Michael Myers went up to his teenage sister's room shortly after she had made love with her boyfriend, and killed her with a large carving knife. For the next 15 years, Michael was confined in an asylum for the criminally insane, never speaking, never doing anything other than stare blankly at the wall. Then, on the anniversary of the murder, Michael escaped and, for reasons that can neither be explained nor understood, returned to his home town to celebrate the occasion in his own unique fashion.

The night he came back was Halloween. The year was 1978. Although still officially 14 months away, the slice-and-dice '80s had begun.

Aliens, mutants, demons, and zombies have sucked, slimed, and munched across the screen in the 1980s, but none as often as the stalking, slashing, sicko psycho killer. Since the start of the decade, this monster has appeared in more than a hundred movies, perpetrating many times that number of hackings, choppings, piercings, slittings, severings, impalings, sawings, torchings, forkings, dismemberments, and decapitations.

As a screen villain, the homicidal maniac, driven by uncontrollable subconscious urges, is certainly not anything new or unusual. The movies, like society in general, have long been fascinated by this twisted personality, as John McCarty makes clear in *PSYCHOS: Eighty Years of Mad Movies, Maniacs, and Murderous Deeds*.

The film that firmly and forever established this character as a horror subject was Alfred Hitchcock's *Psycho* (1960). Based on Robert Bloch's 1959 novel — which was inspired by the real-life case of Ed Gein, the Wisconsin murderer-necrophile-cannibal whose unimaginably grisly crimes were uncovered in 1957 — *Psycho* was the vehicle that Hitchcock used to demonstrate that the horror movie did not need grotesque creatures to scare the socks off the viewer. The worst nightmare was not necessarily some fantasy creature from a distant world or ancient legend; it could be as close as the quiet little guy down the road ... and as real as the morning headline.

Although *Psycho* was generally disparaged by critics when it was released, audiences ate it up, and were soon being offered a fairly steady procession of Norman Bates's deranged relatives. Today, *Psycho* is regarded as a contemporary classic — analyzed on a shot-by-shot basis in textbooks and film schools — and may well be one of the most influential of all modern films.

While Norman Bates is most definitely the godfather of today's slice-and-dicers, the actual progenitors are two extraordinarily successful low-budget movies: John Carpenter's *Halloween* (1978) and Sean Cunningham's *Friday The 13th* (1980). Few of the movies in this section would have been produced if these two films had never existed.

Of the two, *Halloween* is easily the better and more influential film. It is slickly and stylishly made, with a first-rate script and performances, and extremely good direction by Carpenter, who had already shown considerable skill and inventiveness in two earlier micro-budgeted genre efforts, *Dark Star* (1975) and *Assault on Precinct 13* (1976). Even after ten years and scores of imitations, *Halloween* still holds up — a wonderfully efficient, fast, and gripping piece of horror film-making.

As Danny Peary points out in his *Guide for the Film Fanatic*, John Carpenter drew upon a variety of sources and inspirations, from the menacing atmosphere of Val Lewton's '40s classics to the kind of tricks and jolts that master promoter William Castle put into his cheerfully gimmicky fright flicks, such as *The Tingler*, in the '50s and '60s. Carpenter acknowledged a further debt by giving Donald Pleasence's psychiatrist the same name — Sam Loomis — as that of John Gavin's character in *Psycho*, and by casting Janet Leigh's daughter, Jamie Lee Curtis, in the lead. And even *Halloween*'s focus on young people, making them both the protagonists and the prey (the now tediously familiar teens-in-jeopardy situation) had started to turn up in such movies as *Black Christmas* (1974), *The Texas Chainsaw Massacre* (1974), and *Kiss of the Tarantula* (1976).

In *Halloween*, Carpenter skillfully and imaginatively combined and utilized these various influences, spicing things up with a touch of contemporary sex and gore. He also provided a subtle and sophisticated subtext on the notion of vision — looking, seeing, voyeurism — in terms of the characters themselves and the audience watching them. Most of all, though, *Halloween* gave us a brand-new variant of the traditional screen psycho.

Whereas Norman Bates's madness was masked behind a perfectly unexceptional face, Michael Myers is faceless and has only a mask. Similarly, no attempt is made to account for his psychotic condition or to present a portrait of his madness; Michael just *is*. Driven by incomprehensible forces, he is an unstoppable killing machine — in fact, menace personified. Identified in the credits as "The Shape," *Halloween*'s psycho killer is stylized to the point of symbol — he is whatever scares us — and in the process he acquires more than a touch of the supernatural (even being frequently referred to in the movie as that ultimate childhood horror, "The Boogeyman").

In a stroke of brilliant simplification, John Carpenter was able to dispense with the need for explanations, sense, and logic, and cut right to the point of the exercise — the delivery of high-energy thrills and chills. *Halloween* was one of those all-too-infrequent occurrences — a horror movie that really was as scary as its ads suggested. It was also a record-breaker. Produced for an estimated $325,000, it had a box office world-wide in excess of $70 million. In terms of net earnings, it is considered to be the most successful independent picture ever made, and, of course, the rustle of cash triggered a response in asylums everywhere. Not quite two decades after we checked into the Bates Motel, psychos were again big business.

Profits aside, it's easy to see why the psycho flick was (and still is to a lesser degree) so popular with independent, low-budget filmmakers. As *Halloween* demonstrated, all you need is one or two primary locations, and that is cheap. The cast can be small, and that is certainly cheap. Since the characters, like their target audience, can be young, you can use unknown actors eager for credits, and they always come cheap. And because night is much scarier than day, a good part of the movie can be shot in the dark, and that can be very cheap to do. So what's left? A mask? Bare breasts? Blood? None of those is likely to strain the budget.

In short, it was a natural, and the fact that the form was solidly based on three of the central pillars of exploitation — sex, violence, and weirdness — was not exactly a deterrent. If anyone paused to consider that a significant part of *Halloween*'s success might have been the result of its genuine quality, it did not apparently slow them down unduly in the race to grab the available holidays, festivities, and venues.

Although some of the psycho flicks drew upon sources other than (or in addition to) *Halloween*, most saw no reason to deviate from the formula whose popularity had already been demonstrated so empahatically. Given that *Halloween* was quite stylized to begin with, it was hardly any trouble to extract the basic elements and then to replicate them with paint-by-numbers simplicity. Thus we see a good number of *Halloween*'s structural and stylistic features turning up in movie after movie, stamped out with a certain monotonous rigor. For instance:

- The movie takes place in a bland, nondescript Midwestern community, previously quiet and very safe.
- It opens with a prolog set in the past (established with titles), in which a violent episode occurs.
- It then cuts to the present, to the anniversary of the event, with the calendar triggering a new psychotic outburst.
- It gives us good looking, sex-obsessed teenagers and isolates them in a virtually deserted environment in which they can be stalked unawares

and picked off one by one, without any of the other characters realizing what's going on.
- It generates suspense through the extensive use of subjective, handheld camera work as we watch the victims from the killer's point of view.
- Because of the subjective viewpoint, we rarely see the psycho, and when we do, his face is hidden behind a blank, all but featureless mask, rendering him as something other than human.
- The killer is finally defeated — at least for the time being — by a spunky, resourceful heroine who's presented as the only character not completely preoccupied with getting laid.
- And, although the heroine survives, it's clear that she has been deeply and permanently scarred by her traumatic encounter with Evil.

If you've seen even a couple of the movies in this section — or virtually any of the calendar or campus ones — you've likely seen most of the above elements trotted out with scarcely any significant variation. However, the clone that was most successful, and that became influential in its own right, was *Friday the 13th*.

Quick enough off the mark to utilize the only other inherently ominous date, Sean Cunningham offered John Carpenter the sincerest form of flattery. Oh, he moved the kids out of town and isolated them at a lake. And he enlarged the cast and slightly upped the sex component. And the killer, while unseen, was not masked (that would wait for the sequel). In most other respects, though, *Friday* was simply *Halloween* with a woodsy scent.

Besides showing virtually no originality in terms of story and structure, *Friday the 13th* was not even particularly well done. The characters were undeveloped and uninteresting, the direction was extremely pedestrian, and there was very little genuine tension or suspense. What we got instead was lots of superior splatter. Where *Halloween*, like *Psycho*, had used very little on-screen violence, *Friday the 13th* — thanks to effects wizard Tom Savini — showed it all, including such highlights as a throat-slitting, an arrow-piercing, a head-axing, and a decapitation, and in explicit and amazing detail. (In all, there were eight violent deaths, plus two more in the prolog.)

Produced independently for an estimated $700,000, *Friday the 13th* was picked up by Paramount and became the first slice-and-dicer to be distributed by one of the major studios. In June 1980, at the end of its first month in wide release, it had pulled in something approaching $40 million at North American box offices. The body-count movie had arrived.

In terms of the things that ordinarily go into making a movie — a well-structured plot, characters to root for, mystery, suspense — it's hard to imagine an approach less demanding of skill and talent on the part of the filmmakers. And indeed, in the early '80s, it looked like every one with access to an empty building or a clearing in the woods, a young woman or two who would take off her shirt, a mask, and a couple of bottles of red corn syrup was getting in on the act. Few of the resulting efforts are what one would characterize as wildly creative flights of filmmaking. Derivative in the extreme, most faithfully reprise *Halloween the 13th* — with abundant nods to *Psycho* and that other classic of low-budget mayhem, *The Texas Chainsaw Massacre* — and "originality" means little more than using different weaponry and setting the mayhem in a new location. (Note: The chief exceptions to this — movies more concerned with suspense and psychology than with random slaughter — have been collected in the final festival of this section.)

When the psycho wave crested in the early 1980s, giving us what sometimes seemed to be the Slasher-of-the-Week, a lot of people got very exercised about the situation, bemoaning what was usually referred to as a "disturbing new trend." Most frequently, the critics, focusing in on images of scantily clad young honeys screaming as an unseen psycho approached them, deplored the preoccupation with violence against women. This criticism — often made by people who had not watched many, or even any, of these movies — has been repeated often enough to become a truism, but the genre, seen as a whole, does not entirely support this claim.

Yes, there are a number of nasty, reprehensible movies about sexually warped, misogynistic sickos who get their jollies by perpetrating acts of violence against women. The number of these sordid pieces-o-shit, however, is actually quite small. In the majority of slice-and-dicers, the killer is a firm believer in non-sexist slaughter, and he is just as likely to wipe out a boring bozo as he is an underwear-clad bimbo. Indeed, given the level of most of these efforts, the case could easily be made that the psycho, rather than expressing rage against women, is punishing stupidity and bad acting. In all, while female victims probably do outnumber male victims, the margin is not great, and the real goal of most psycho killers is

> *"The thing is using us for food."*
> CREATURE

not to do in males or females specifically, but to boost the body count as high as the budget for cast and splatter permits.

In other words, the spurt of psychotic mayhem in the early 1980s was not anything new or different, nor did it have sinister sociological implications. Although the psycho movie was produced in greater than usual numbers, it was merely the latest style in a long series of youth market exploitation films — creature features, beach party epics, biker flicks, etc. — designed to separate young moviegoers from the price of admission.

Like all fads and trends, styles of exploitation change, and by the end of 1982, the psycho flood had been reduced to a slow trickle. Since 1984, just about the only slasher flicks to earn the million dollars in rentals necessary to make *Variety*'s annual list of top money-makers have been a few sequels, most notably the endless *Friday the 13th* series (which has moved steadily deeper into the realm of the supernatural). Just as there was nothing ominous in the rise of the slice-and-dicer, so too its decline did not signify a resurgence of scruples and good taste, but only that the audience had grown exceedingly tired and disappointed with the form. And, as the reviews that follow suggest, not without good reason.

Taken as a whole, the psycho flicks are a depressingly dismal bunch of movies, with too few examples rising above the dreary norm and a great many sinking below it. Most do little more than mechanically reprise the formulas from *Halloween*, as though reciting a catechism by rote, and only infrequently is there an attempt to alleviate the staleness of the material with a few sparks of wit, humor, or irony. In fact, most of the time there isn't even any awareness on the part of the filmmakers that it's already all been done many times before.

At the high end of the line, there are at least decent production values and a certain professional sheen, but more often than not the movies that follow fail to display much energy, or even minimal filmmaking competence. Because the requirements of the form appear to be so simple — no elaborate creatures, no fancy sets, no complicated effects, no imagination or originality — it probably seemed like *anyone* could make a slice-and-dicer . . . and they have.

But the repetitiveness, the absence of genuine suspense, the lack of wit, and the shoddiness are not the worst failings of the genre. The real disappointment — and *this*, not alleged violence against women, is what the critics should have been upset about — is that so many of these movies are so pitifully pisspoor as exploitation. I mean, what is it one expects from a slice-and-dicer? Clinically accurate depictions of psychosis? Tender teenage traumas? Of course not. The genre stands for flesh and blood: naked bimbos; shower scenes; locker-room scenes; dressings; undressings; graphic gore; piercings and power tools; flying body parts; arterial geysers. While perhaps a quarter of the movies that follow do have some grasp of the fundamentals, the rest do little more than pay lip-service to them, and even then without much skill or real conviction. They skimp on the skin and offer up decidely sub-par splatter, and thus achieve neither vigorous sleaze nor enthusiastic excess. Just what, he asks with a touch of pique, do they think the damn point is?

In the reviews that follow, I've tried to indicate which movies deliver the goods, what those goods are, and their quantity and quality. I've also tried to point out which movies do more that just grind out the same old thing, and which of those that do grind it out do so with at least some degree of style or competence. (It should be noted that the judgments are very relative; saying that a slice-and-dicer is better than average in some respect does not necessarily mean that it possesses real quality, only that it is an improvement over a very inferior norm.)

If you can skirt the vast morass of psycho sludge out there — which I hope the following festivals will make easier for you to do — you should be able to satisfy your taste for slice-and-dice carnage without getting grossly ripped off. While there are not many "good movies" in this section, there are definitely a good number that, one way or another, are entertaining enough to be worth their rental cost.

Now, as someone brilliantly suggested in **THE DORM THAT DRIPPED BLOOD**, "Why don't we split up and look for him?

FESTIVAL 15

* * *

KILLERS BY THE CALENDAR
A Psycho for Every Occasion

> "... yet another Santa is slain."
> — *Don't Open Till Christmas*

It's well known that psycho killers are very temporally oriented. *Halloween* and *Friday the 13th* deftly snagged the two inherently spooky dates, but that only served to inspire filmmakers to scan the calendar for other events that could be fraught with menace. What's surprising is not that they found so many, but that so many have thus far been overlooked. It doesn't take much imagination to see the mayhem potential in such occasions as St. Patrick's Day, Good Friday, Father's Day, Passover, Labor Day, Yom Kippur (the Day of Atonement!), or the *eight* days of Hanukkah. While some of these might be considered to be in questionable taste, there's no evidence to suggest that such constraints have yet had any influence on the work of no-talent hacks, so maybe it's just a matter of time. As it is, I'm keenly awaiting the release of *Arbor Day*, the gripping tale of a deranged environmentalist who goes on a spree of planting lumberjacks.

MY BLOODY VALENTINE *(1981, Canadian)*
wr John Beaird; dir George Mihalka

Twenty years ago, on February 14, in the town of Valentine Bluffs, a deranged miner pickaxed those responsible for a mine explosion, then sent the victims' hearts to the annual dance with the warning that the town should never again hold another Valentine's Day party. As this movie opens, the townsfolk are preparing for their first forbidden dance since the tragedy and, even though the jerky young miners don't know what's going to happen, I trust you do. The killer wears black coveralls and a menacing-looking gas mask, and prefers to impale his victims on his pick, though he's not above poaching a head in water. It looks like a lot of the really explicit gore was cut, but we do get a few glimpses of some seriously messy corpses, as well as a couple of excised hearts ("It looks like a butcher ripped this thing out"). The last part of the movie takes place in the mine, and fairly good use is made of this creepy location, but the "surprise" ending isn't much of one. Eleven bodies; decent production values; no skin; a few good shocks; the usual number of plot stupidities.

APRIL FOOL'S DAY *(1986)*
wr Danilo Bach; dir Fred Walton

During spring break, three virtually identical blondes and five barely distinguishable collegiate bozos go out to an isolated island retreat owned by their friend Muffy. Soon, the strangeness begins: Muffy's behavior turns weird, dark secrets are revealed, and one by one the guests disappear. No skin and no gore, but the production values are quite good, the characters are slightly more appealing than the usual hopelessly brain-dead, and the script, if not a real grabber, does manage to generate some curiosity about what is going on. As to just what that is, the title here is more relevant than most. Depending on your point of view, this is either a refreshingly nonviolent variation on the well-worn formula or a total cheat. I don't mind being cheated cleverly, but this effort isn't clever enough and falls kind of flat.

MOTHER'S DAY *(1980)*
wr Charles Kaufman and Warren Leight; dir Charles Kaufman

It's not easy being a single mother, especially when your two sons are backwoods psychopathic louts whose hobby is brutally raping then killing young women. Still, boys will be boys, and what's a mom to do except join in the fun. The fun here takes the form of three women out on a camping trip. When one of them is killed, the two survivors decide to get even, and eventually do so by planting a hatchet in the groin of one good ol' boy and dumping a can of Drano down the throat of the other. Clearly a cross between *The Texas Chainsaw Massacre* and *Deliverance*, this one lacks the driving power of both, and the appeal of the slavering idiot sons (Holden McGuire, Billy Ray McQuade) quickly thins. Some reviewers considered this an effective black satire on the consumer society and the power of television — the TV is always on and the family's shack is crammed with brand-name products — but the humor is quite feeble and does not compensate for the streak of nastiness toward women. Three bodies (plus the psychos'); no blood; the girls go skinny-dipping; very cheap, heavy-handed, and sloppy. The associate producers, Lloyd Kaufman and Michael Herz, went on to form Troma Team, whose products tend to be even cheaper and sloppier.

PROM NIGHT *(1980, Canadian)*
wr William Gray; dir Paul Lynch

Six years after a little girl died as the result of a childish prank, someone is out to get those responsible. As it happens, the anniversary of the death coincides with the big school dance, making it convenient to borrow big chunks from *Carrie* (1976) for the characters, situations, and subplots. Although moderately successful when first released, this limp effort is bloodless in every respect. Talk about not delivering the goods! There's a gratuitous shower scene without breasts, the murders are so murky and indistinct as to be scarcely visible, and so much time is spent establishing what are obvious red herrings that more than two-thirds of the movie goes by before anything actually happens. The production values are good, but it's really starting to show its age. Four bodies; scant blood; Jamie Lee Curtis as prom queen; no skin; no suspense; no pace; lots of disco shit. Sit this one out.

HELLO MARY LOU: PROM NIGHT II
Prom queen from Hell; see Festival 9.

GRADUATION DAY *(1981)*
wr Anne Marisse and Herb Freed; dir Herb Freed

Wouldn't you know it: it's the title event at the local high school, and someone's sticking sharp objects through the bodies of the school track team. For reasons that are unusually vague and unclear, even for this kind of movie, it seems the team is being held responsible for the fact that one of the girls died from a blood clot after winning a race. The perceptive viewer will spot the signs of imminent psychosis in the opening sequence, and thus the identity of the person behind the fencing mask will not be much of a surprise, despite the presence of several red herrings dangled before our glazed eyes. Christopher George as the track coach maintains the overall tedium of the proceedings. With a young Vanna White as one of the victims. Nine bodies; a couple of so-so effects; lots of oral blood capsules; masked psycho; Linnea Quigley shows her breasts to the music teacher; stupider than usual. No diplomas for this dropout.

June Brides

HE KNOWS YOU'RE ALONE *(1980)*
wr Scott Parker; dir Armand Mastroianni

The title expresses one of the fundamental thematic elements of the genre, but the movie does little to expand upon it. "He" (Tom Rolfing) is a wide-eyed, wild-eyed slasher who, because he was jilted by his fiancée, now has it in for brides-to-be, as well as their friends and acquaintances. As he stalks an airhead co-ed named Amy (Caitlin O'Heaney), he's pursued by a very slow cop whose own bride-to-be was the first victim. Although directed with a bit of style, the script is very pedestrian — sluggish, filled with annoying characters, and even less engaging chat — and the movie ends up being a poor reprise of *Halloween*, down to the use of similar images and music. Tom Hanks makes a brief appearance in a supporting role and manages, even here, to show signs of his considerable comic charm. Six bodies; nongraphic gore; a severed-head-in-a-fish-tank gag; Elizabeth Kemp takes a very welcome shower; a seriously stupid twist ending; clonier than usual. Rent this one, and he'll know you're bored.

SLUMBER PARTY MASSACRE *(1982)*
wr Rita Mae Brown; dir Amy Jones

The title tells all as an escaped psycho killer stalks bimbos and their boyfriends with a giant power drill. This one has all the elements: a high body count, a fair amount of splatter (including a head lost and a hand chopped off), a most phallic weapon, lots of false shocks, and ample gratuitous bimbo flesh (i.e., a very bouncy girls' basketball game, a shower and locker-room sequence, and several other dressings/

> *"You mean the poor woman is dying while you're playing a waltz?"*
> VIRGIN AMONG THE LIVING DEAD

undressings). Given the writer and director, one might have expected that this routine material would have been given an edge of parody or irony, but it's played straight — an example, I suppose, of equal-opportunity exploitation. There's nothing new here, but there are a few sparks of fun; and although it's all pretty mechanical, it's not badly done, especially the last 20 minutes. With Robin Stille in the Jamie Lee Curtis role, and Andree Honore as the party-goer with the largest breasts. Eleven bodies; good gore; tits galore; lots of screams; a more stylish-than-usual, energetic clone.

SLUMBER PARTY MASSACRE II *(1987)*
wr and dir Deborah Brock

Just down the block from **SORORITY HOUSE MASSACRE**, the slumber party has moved to Elm Street in what might have been subtitled "The Revenge of the Dream Sequence." It's five years after the first party, and the youngest survivor is now in high school and a member of an all-girl rock band. Although played by a different actress, she's still having nightmares about the event, only now the killer has become a leather-clad rock 'n' roller with an even bigger drill bit emerging from his electric guitar. When the band and their boyfriends go to a deserted condo complex for the weekend, the nightmares intensify, then, quicker than you can say Black and Decker, the killer is among them, adding new orifices to their bodies. In the end, it all turns out to be — not surprisingly — a stupid cheat, but along the way there's lots of blood, two drills bursting out of chests (male), and some fairly good hallucination/dream-sequence effects. Five bodies; decent production values; a few shocks; lots of jiggle, but only Juliette Cummins briefly bares her soul; a severed hand on a hamburger bun.

THE LAST SLUMBER PARTY *(1988, made for video)*
wr and dir Stephen Tyler

Three boring high-school airheads and their loutish boyfriends spend the night yakking about sex (but doing nothing) as a psycho in a surgical mask slits their throats with a scalpel. It doesn't come as much of surprise that it all turns out to be a dream, nor much more of one when the psycho turns up for real for the "twist" ending. Of all the possible goods, slumber is the only one this backyard lump delivers. Ten dream-sequence bodies; pathetic throat-slittings; no skin; unwatchable; unlistenable. A shameful desecration of one of the sacred slasher occasions.

BLOODY BIRTHDAY *(1980)*
wr Ed Hunt and Barry Pearson; dir Ed Hunt

This is a really bizarre little number. The story is the basic psycho-on-a murderous-rampage, but, instead of one deranged killer, we have three . . . and they're all ten years old. Debbie, Curtis, and Steven were all born at the same time in the same hospital during a solar total eclipse. As an astrologically inclined character figures out, this peculiar conjunction of the planets has somehow left the kids without consciences or feelings. It has, however, given them a real taste for homicide, which they start to indulge in the week before their mutual tenth birthday. They begin with teen lovers making out in the cemetery, then quickly move on to friends, teachers, family, and anyone else standing in their way. In essence, then, this is a slasher version of *The Bad Seed* (1956), and quite decently done, clicking right along from stranglings to clubbings, to shootings, to an arrow in the eyeball, paced with a decent amount of gratuitous bimbo flesh. While none of the violence is very graphic or explicit, it is nonetheless quite effective, especially considering the smiling, angelic looking perpetrators. Seven bodies; sex; voyeurism; much nastier than usual. Definitely above average, and peculiar enough to hold your attention.

HAPPY BIRTHDAY TO ME *(1981, Canadian)*
wr John Saxton, Peter John, and Timothy Bond; dir J. Lee Thompson

Someone is killing rich, snobbish preppies at the Crawford Academy in some fairly inventive ways — a weight lifter crushed under his weights, a mouth-skewering, a nifty strangulation. Suspicion points to Melissa Sue Anderson — who suffered a serious brain injury in the accident that killed her mother five years earlier — but the script has more than a few surprises up its sleeve. Quite a few of them are rather silly and/or contrived, but at least try to keep us guessing and generally succeed. Competently directed by an old pro, this is a real movie and not just a compendium of random slaughter. By any objective standards it's no very good, but in terms of the slice-and-dice genre, it's way above average and does manage to keep you interested. Seven bodies; some fairly effective splatter; no skin; some mystery and suspense; less stupid than usual; lots of twists and turns.

SWEET SIXTEEN *(1982)*
wr Edwin Goldman; dir Jim Sotos

In a small redneck Texas town, sultry new arrival Melissa (Aleisa Shirley) is fifteen going on twenty-five, and is in hormone overdrive as she approaches the title occasion. After the first two boys who drool over her get the chop, Sheriff Bo Hopkins begins to wonder what's going on. He is diverted by an obvious red herring involving an Indian and the excavation of a sacred burial ground, but we aren't. As soon as we learn that Melissa's mother grew up in the town, we know that dark and terrible secrets from the past are filtering their way to the present. However, since this is boring, confusing, clichéd, and unsuspenseful, we don't care. Four bodies; inferior mayhem; surprise psycho; Melissa takes a shower and goes skinny-dipping. A decent cast and fairly slick production values are wasted in the service of a really inferior script.

TRICK OR TREATS *(1982)*
wr, prod, dir Gary Graver

Four years after his dragon-lady wife had him wrongly committed, Malcolm (Peter Jason) escapes from the loony bin on Halloween and heads home to exact revenge. Except the wife is out of town and he finds the babysitter (Jacklyn Giroux), who's just spent the whole evening being tormented by young Christopher (played by the director's son), a junior Houdini and a complete brat. I guess this is supposed to be a spoof of sorts, but it's resolutely unfunny. For a while, at the beginning, it keeps you wondering where it's heading, then ends up going nowhere. David Carradine, Carrie Snodgrass, Steve Railsback, and Paul Bartel all put in brief appearances for no particular purpose. Two bodies; no blood; no skin; decent production values; a few stupid tricks; no treats. As one of the neighborhood kids asks, "Why are the lights on if there's nobody home?" Not to be confused with **TRICK OR TREAT** (Festival 11).

HOME SWEET HOME *(1980)*
wr Thomas Bush; dir Nettie Peña

Eight years after bludgeoning his parents to death, a deranged bodybuilder escapes from the asylum on Thanksgiving Day, ready to carve up some turkeys of his own. Fortunately, he finds a flock of very stupid ones on an isolated ranch and proceeds to inflict some singularly bloodless mayhem, punctuated with a series of good maniacal laughs. Mr. Muscles is played by Jake Steinfeld — the hunk behind "Bodies by Jake," trainer to the stars — but that's about the only thing that's vaguely professional about this one. Even for a homemade slasher, this is cheap, slow, dull, and numbingly dumb. Nine bodies; seriously inferior gore; a chortling psycho; two seconds of Sallee Young's right breast; a hypodermic-in-the-tongue gag. This property is condemned.

CHRISTMAS EVIL *(1980)*
wr and dir Lewis Jackson. Also released as *Terror in Toyland.*

Terminally warped as a child when he saw Santa fondling Mommy in front of the tree, Harry (Brandon Maggart) is one of those folks who has trouble coping with the holiday season. He's been keeping lists, and checking them repeatedly. When he puts on his Santa suit, he rewards those who have been nice, but the naughty are treated to a bout with Claus the Avenger. Made before the slasher wave broke, this is more a study of the psycho than a menu of mayhem. Although not a very good movie — slow, cheap-looking, and starting to show its age — Maggart is not bad, and the premise is so loopily perverse that you can't help but be curious about where it's going. One of the side trips is an homage to *Frankenstein*, in which an angry torch-wielding mob chases a frantic Santa through the streets. Four bodies; traces of blood; an eyeball-puncturing; no skin; a nicely warped sense of humor. Certainly not for sentimentalists, but Christmas cynics could do worse.

TO ALL A GOODNIGHT *(1980)*
wr Alex Rebar; dir David Hess

The usual bunch of sex-obsessed bimbos and bozos stay behind at the Calvin Finishing School for Girls over the Christmas holidays while a killer in a Santa suit is stabbing, axing, decapitating, garroting, piercing, and smashing them one by one. The issue is revenge for a tragic accident that happened two years earlier, but this one's hardly into explanations. This is an archetypal body-count flick, and starts to dispatch its oversexed young folks without even bothering to tell us their names. Twelve bodies; insipid splatter; masked killers; lots of teen sex chat; some rolling around; scant skin; a stupid "surprise twist"; a severed-head-in-the-shower gag; clonier than usual; not a millisecond of originality or suspense. With Judith Bridges as the skinny girl whose shower is interrupted.

DON'T OPEN TILL CHRISTMAS *(1984, British)*
wr Derek Ford; dir Edmund Purdom

Near the beginning of this one, the BBC news reader solemnly intones "... yet another Santa is slain," and that about sums things up. Forty years after being traumatized by seeing Santa shove Mommy down the stairs, a psycho escapes from the bin to begin a campaign to eradicate Father Christmas from London. As two astonishingly stupid Scotland Yard detectives (including director Purdom as the painfully dull Chief Inspector) dither, Santa after Santa is stabbed, speared, burned, cleavered, castrated, and shot in the face. (Most of the abundant splatter is nothing very special, but this one certainly gets points for quantity.) With something around a dozen Santas getting the chop, the potential existed for a fair amount of absurdist black humor, but the script plays it very straight, and Purdom is as soggy and stodgy behind the camera as he is in front of it. Not as amusing as it sounds, but you can't completely dismiss a movie that piles up more Clauses than a roomful of lawyers. Besides, it's a pleasant change to hear the nonsense spouted with a refined accent. Fourteen bodies, unevenly executed; lots of messy excess; masked psycho; costumed victims; slight suspense; mediocre mystery. With Pat Astley as the model who keeps removing her top.

SILENT NIGHT, DEADLY NIGHT — PART 2 *(1987)*
wr Lee Harry and Joseph H. Earle; dir Lee Harry

I didn't get to see the original *SN,DN* (1984). That was the one about Santa the Ax Murderer that inspired lots of irate protests when it was first released, and that the Brain Police in Ontario, Canada, decided was too controversial for our tender sensibilities. Fortunately, nearly the entire first half of Part 2 consists of flashback highlights from the original. We get to see Ricky and Billy's parents brutally murdered by a guy in a Santa suit. We get to see Billy traumatized by the draconian Mother Superior of the orphanage at which they're raised. We get to see Billy, age eighteen, put on a Santa suit, pick up an ax, and turn into St.-Nick-with-a-vengeance. We see him dispatch nine naughty folks, a third of whom just happened to be bare-breasted young women. And we see him shot down just as he was about to give the Mother Superior the chop. This flashback is presented courtesy of brother Ricky (Eric Freeman), who is, himself, now in an asylum for the slaughter of a further eight naughties. Another set of flashbacks shows us these murders, mostly uninspired shootings, though there is a decent hot-wired-tongue/exploding-eyeball gag. Finally, for the last ten minutes, Ricky escapes to go on a brief rampage in the present tense. This is probably some kind of record for a flashback body count, and probably outdoes **BOOGEYMAN II** in its use of earlier material. Still, consisting almost entirely of "good stuff," it moves right along and includes a quite entertaining performance by Freeman that seems to be modeled on Jack Nicholson's in *The Shining*. This is certainly not a good movie, but it may be peculiar enough to hold your attention, and it's obviously a must for those collecting anti-Xmas flicks. Twenty-two (!) bodies; so-so splatter; flashback breasts; a decapitated-Mother-Superior stunt; no suspense, but no boring plot stuff — in fact, no plot at all.

NEW YEAR'S EVIL *(1981)*
wr Leonard Neubauer, dir Emmett Alston

As the psycho killer (Kip Niven) explains near the end, "This has been a bad year for me," so he decides to end it in style. On the stroke of midnight in each of the time zones, he strikes, stabbing or strangling a young woman or two. As midnight moves across the continent, he edges closer to his prime target, Roz Kelly, a fading celebrity who's hosting a televised New Year's Eve New Wave rock concert. I think there are more music/dance interludes than bodies in this one, which probably says it all. There are a couple of vaguely amusing sequences as the clockwise killer starts to fall behind schedule, but otherwise this is very routine stuff, very mechanically executed. Four bodies; fleeting bimbo flesh; a little splatter; mild suspense; heavily padded. This does not ring in anything new.

BLOODY NEW YEAR
July; haunted hotel; see Festival 10.
SATURDAY THE 14TH
No slasher; haunted-house ho-hum; see Festival 10.

FESTIVAL 16

* * *

A VERY LITTLE LEARNING
A Curriculum of Campus Killers

> "I wonder what the murderer wanted with the head?"
> — *Pieces*

The campus is clearly a natural habitat of the psycho killer — a self-contained community comprised almost entirely of young people with rampant hormones that is nearly deserted at certain times of the year. There are frequent ceremonies such as fraternity/sorority initiations in which sadistic behavior is customary. There are also numerous occasions on which the students traditionally let off steam, and thus out-of-control weirdness is not only tolerated, but expected. Most of all, there are a variety of buildings inhabited solely by coeds, a good number of whom have a tendency to undress without drawing the shades, pad around in their underwear, and take the odd shower. Yes, indeed, the campus has it all, and it is consequently more than a little disappointing that so few of the slice-and-dicers set there exploit the potential of the environment.

NIGHT SCHOOL *(1980)*
wr Ruth Avergon; dir Kenneth Hughes

A psycho in a motorcycle helmet is decapitating the night-school students at a Boston girls' college, and leaving the heads submerged in water (i.e., a sink, a toilet, a bucket). This one wants to put the emphasis on the mystery rather than the splatter, but once the connection to the amorous anthropology prof is made, early on, we know who's doing it, then have to wait about 70 minutes for the supposedly Harvard-educated detective (Leonard Mann) to catch up. There's a minor plot twist of sorts, but even that's familiar and anticipated. The production values are decent, but there's no zip or any reason to be interested in the proceedings. This was one of two slice-and-dicers Rachel Ward (*The Thorn Birds*) made early in her career (**THE FINAL TERROR** is the other), and the one in which she gets her body painted during a fairly sultry shower scene. Five bodies; off-camera decapitations; masked psycho; slow, mechanical, and predictable. Only for those who want to see Rachel get smeared.

THE PROWLER (1981)
wr Glenn Leopold and Neal F. Barbera; dir Joseph Zito

As a lengthy prolog establishes, a Second World War vet who took his "Dear John" letter especially hard pitchforks his jilter and her new boyfriend on the night of the graduation dance at a small college in Avalon Bay. Cut to the present, thirty-five years later, and it's the day of the first graduation dance since the tragedy. Care to guess who puts in an appearance? Obviously, there's scarcely a microsecond in this one that's original, but at least it's competently made and no dumber than usual, and there is a so-so twist at the end. What really distinguishes it are some quite good gore effects by Tom Savini. Besides more pitchforkings, there are stabbings, throat-slittings, a bayonet through the skull, and an exploding head, most shown in considerable detail. Seven bodies; superior blood; Lisa Dunsheath takes a shower (and gets forked); a masked psycho; a pathetic red herring; a little suspense; a couple of surprises. You've probably seen worse.

HELL NIGHT (1981)
wr Randolph Feldman; dir Tom DeSimone

For their initiation, four sorority/fraternity pledges in fancy dress have to spend the night in a supposedly haunted house that was the site of a brutal murder 12 years earlier. Three frat pranksters also turn up to play practical jokes and add to the body count. The joke's on them, though, as — who would've guessed? — the sole survivor of the massacre is still in the house, and he's not exactly pleased to have visitors. "Night" is apt here, as nearly every scene is so dimly lit that most of the screen is black. But that's okay, because there's nothing to see anyway — no blood, no explicit murders, and no skin, other than Linda Blair in a low-cut bodice and Suki Goodwin in her underwear. An exercise in gratuitous good taste from the director who went on to make *Reform School Girls*. Seven bodies; a severed head; an impaling; no suspense; no surprises; lots of boring chat.

THE DORM THAT DRIPPED BLOOD *(1981)*
wr Stephen Carpenter, Jeffrey Obrow, and Stacey Grachino; dir Stephen Carpenter and Jeffrey Obrow

Five young people stay behind to close up a large dormitory scheduled for renovation, but someone has plans to do some major alterations on them and on the other people who drop in to boost the body count. The killer here is of the unseen variety, meaning we're supposed to wonder who it is, but the revelation is neither very surprising nor interesting. Indeed, except for a rather neat twist at the end, there's not much in this one beyond the thoroughly routine. The killer's rather eclectic, treating us to a couple of hackings, a garroting, a drilling, a crushing, a burning, and a boiling, but what must have been a minuscule budget didn't permit anything very dramatic or explicit. An early backyard effort (though marginally better done than some) by the team that went on to make **THE KINDRED**. With Chandre in the role of the woman who bares her breasts because they were there. Ten bodies; ten seconds of gratuitous Chandre; little blood; a dismembered corpse.

FINAL EXAM *(1981)*
wr and dir Jimmy Huston

It's the end of the semester at Lanier College and someone's bumping off the bozos and bimbos still around for the title test. The problem is that it takes at least an hour before we start to get rid of these jerks — an hour filled with numbing chat and stupid frat pranks. This monotony is not lifted by the unseen psycho and off-camera mayhem, and the killer is never identified or explained. Six bodies; bloodless; brainless; boring; Deanna Robbins takes off her dress. That dull clunk you hear is this North Carolina piece-o-shit hitting the bottom of the Bell curve.

BLOODY MOON *(1981, West German, dubbed)*
wr Rayo Casablanca; dir Jesus Franco

In a Spanish-language school for oversexed bimbos, someone is expelling the students in fairly dramatic ways — a knife in the breast, a knife through the throat, a decapitation via circular saw. Considering the otherwise shoddy production values, the splatter effects are a lot better than you'd expect, but nothing else is. After two decades largely spent showing nasty things happening to scantily clad young women, old Jess has reached the point where he can effortlessly make nudity and violence seem boring. Seven bodies; graphic mayhem; abundant blood; a severed-head-in-the-bed gag; a masked psycho; bountiful breasts; a stupid and tedious mystery; terrible acting; worse dubbing; lots of shots of an unbloody moon.

STUDENT BODIES *(1981)*
wr and dir Mickey Rose

A satire on the genre that delivers a few smiles, but misses the big comic punches. The style is a lot like the humor of *Airplane!* (1980), but not nearly as fast, dense ... or funny. It deals with all the clichés — sometimes amusingly — but the targets are so large and so easy that much more should have been done with them. As it is, this is more like an extended TV skit that quickly wears very thin. Thirteen bodies of sorts; no blood; no skin; not much.

THE HOUSE ON SORORITY ROW *(1982)*
wr and dir Mark Rosman

Just before the big graduation party, a stupid prank goes awry, and seven sorority sisters kill their housemother. Thinking quickly, they borrow a touch from *Diabolique* (1955) and dump her body in the swimming pool, to be dealt with after the festivities. However, the body disappears, as do the girls ... one by one. Strictly standard fare, and pretty tepid at that, but it is professionally made and acted, which I guess is worth something. Eight bodies; mild gore effects; very brief breast exposure courtesy of Eileen Davidson; masked psycho; a couple of jolts; a severed-head-in-the-toilet gag; occasional brief suspense; not significantly stupider than usual.

SPLATTER UNIVERSITY *(1983)*
wr Richard W. Haines, John Michaelson, and Michael Cunningham; dir Richard W. Haines

The title's the best thing about this one. Your standard-issue sexually warped psycho is killing coeds at St. Trinian's, a Catholic college for brain-dead louts. Eight stabbings/slashings, mostly off-camera; fake blood, mostly after the fact; no bimbo skin; no suspense; no humor; no talent; no intelligence; no point. This is the kind of trash that gives cheapshit, amateurish, homemade slasher-exploitation flicks a bad name.

PIECES *(1983, Spanish/Puerto Rican, partly dubbed)*
wr Dick Randall and John Shadow; dir J. Piquer Simon

Forty years after he planted an ax in his mother's skull because she wouldn't let him keep a nudie jigsaw puzzle, the psycho is assembling a new puzzle for himself, using parts cut off of co-eds at at small New England college. The movie thus consists of scenes of the unseen sicko psycho stalking semiclad women with a chainsaw, interspersed with the tedious investigation into the serial murders by some stupid police officers (Christopher George, Linda Day). It would be easy to dismiss this as utterly nasty and reprehensible — which its premise certainly is — but, in fact this is not well-enough made to incite any real indignation. Indeed, it's such an inept and heavy-handed distillation of the genre — psycho kinky chainsaws on campus — that it almost becomes interesting. *Nothing* here is anything but dull and stupid, including the brainless script, the leaden direction, the lousy dubbing, the cheap splatter, and the typically lifeless performances of Chris, Linda, and Edmund Purdom. Six bodies; lots of phony blood; one decapitation; several topless co-eds; ridiculously obvious red herrings; unseen psycho; no sense, suspense, or surprises. For those who can find amusement in relentlessly mechanical filmmaking and uncompromising inertness, this really supplies something to ponder.

GIRLS NITE OUT *(1983)*
wr Gil Spencer, Jr., Kevin Kurgis, Joe Bolster, and Anthony N. Gurvis; dir Robert Deubel

Posing as the mascot for the basketball team at Dewitt University, someone is rather bloodlessly ripping out the throats of co-eds on the night of the big scavenger hunt. Campus cop Hal Holbrook, looking intensely puzzled, has to wade through a school of red herrings (including his son David), and we have to listen to the endless nattering of a flock of airheads. Seven bodies; inferior slaughter; a psycho in a bearsuit; no skin; lots of Golden Oldies on the soundtrack; much duller and dumber than usual. Proper punctuation is not all that this one's missing.

SILENT MADNESS *(1984)*
wr Robert Zimmerman and William R. Milling; dir Simon Nuchtern

Seventeen years after he dispatched four sorority bitches with a nail gun, a mute psycho is inadvertently released from the mental hospital and returns to the Delta Omega house during spring break to do some more home repairs with a hatchet, a sledgehammer, a crowbar, a vise, and a drill press. The sleazeball shrinks try to cover up their mistake, but a spunky shrink (Belinda Montgomery) heads to Barrington College to try to find the loony. Then, in what passes for a subplot, the nasty shrinks send two sadistic attendants after her in order permanently to keep her from spilling the beans. I don't believe there's thirty seconds of originality in this one — even the "surprise revelation" at the end is tired, familiar, and predictable — and despite all the machinations, hardly anything seems to happen. The theatrical release was juiced up with a few tacky 3-D effects, but this one's so flat it barely exists in two dimensions. Eight bodies (plus four nailings in flashback); inferior mayhem; a sorority sister flashes her breasts in flashback; considerably duller and stupider than usual.

THE INITIATION *(1984)*
wr Charles Pratt; dir Larry Stewart

As the result of a stupid sorority initiation prank, seven collegiate bimbos and bozos find themselves locked in a Dallas department store/shopping mall. In a completely unexpected turn of events, an escaped psycho killer is in there with them. The usual sharp implements (knives, arrows, spear guns, gardening forks, axes) enter bodies, but this one tries to add a bit of mystery about the killer's identity, but does it so badly as to make things even dumber than they would have been otherwise. Ten bodies; pedestrian splatter effects; fair production values; brief breast exposure; a shower sequence barely worthy of the name; slight suspense. With Daphne Zuniga as the girl with bad dreams, and Deborah Morehart in the role of the shirtless sorority pledge.

SLAUGHTER HIGH *(1985)*
wr and dir George Dugdale, Mark Ezra and Peter Litten

Ten years after an April Fool's Day gag played on the school nerd goes tragically awry, the jerks responsible are invited to a reunion in the now-deserted school, where the permanently scarred victim has a few tricks of his own to play. These include an electrocution, a piercing, an impaling, a crushing, an acid bath, and a belly-bursting, which are marginally acceptable, but unlikely to make you forget Tom Savini. The filmmakers felt no need to acknowledge the fact that this movie had been made several times before they got around to it, and the twist ending in which it all turns out to be a dream (oops!) is not exactly what I'd call an interesting variation. Eleven bodies; serviceable splatter; Donna Yeager and Josephine Scandi take their clothes off; somewhat slower, duller, and dumber than usual; not a millisecond of wit or originality.

SORORITY HOUSE MASSACRE *(1986)*
wr and dir Carol Frank

Just when you thought it was safe to go back on campus... Beth goes to spend the weekend with three friends in an otherwise deserted sorority house. Only it turns out that this is the house where her older brother brutally slaughtered the rest of her family 14 years earlier, an event of which she is somehow unaware until the house triggers dreams about what happened and is going to happen. Beth's psychic psycho brother picks up on her dreams and escapes from the bin, returning home to perpetrate the title in the form of seven fairly bloodless and unconvincing stabbings. So, we have a psycho slasher, weird dreams, and a troubled house. In other words, he came back to Elm Street in Amityville on Halloween night. Nothing for originality here, but three points for recombinant chutzpah. Decent production values; brief bimbo exposure; lots of psychic mumbo-jumbo; weak suspense; mediocre dream sequences. Angela O'Neill is not bad as Beth, and Nicole Rio plays the sorority sister with the largest breasts.

FATAL PULSE *(1987)*
wr James Hurdhausen; dir Anthony J. Christopher

A campus killer is doing in a bimbo a night from the A-OK sorority house (the only decent joke in this one) in bloodless but eclectic ways

> *"What about that thing you keep in the freezer? You call that normal?"*
> MACABRE

(strangulation, throat-slitting with an LP, drowning in a bathtub, electrocution, defenestration, and a plastering-to-death). Is it hostile Brad, weird Ernie, intense Jeff, or the troubled chemistry professor, each of whom does his best to look suspicious as all get-out? This certainly keeps us guessing. Why do the survivors continue to stay in the house as the body count rises? And where are the police? What, almost a decade after *Halloween*, made these folks want to trot out the same tired old stuff with nary a trace of skill, wit, ingenuity or irony? Mechanically lurching from cliché to inanity, this doesn't deliver much in the way of suspense or splatter; it does, however, have a grasp of at least some of the essentials of the form, and thus partially undresses each of the seven attractive young women involved. Six bodies; low-impact mayhem; an assortment of bare breasts; spot-the-loony; decent production values; sleazier than usual; faint pulse; no brainwaves.

RETURN TO HORROR HIGH (1987)
wr Bill Froelich, Mark Lisson, Dana Escalante, and Greg H. Sims; dir Bill Froelich

A low-budget film company returns to Crippen High School to make a movie about the brutal massacre that took place there five years earlier. Of course, the psycho was never caught, and history repeats itself. The idea here was to do *The Stuntman* as a slasher movie, playing with the idea of illusion and reality, having some fun with the conventions of the genre, and keeping the audience guessing. The surprise is that it works fairly well. This displays an understanding of the clichés, makes good use of shifting frames of reference — flashbacks, dreams, the movie-within-the-movie, the making of the movie-within-the-movie — and provokes quite a few laughs. Old pros Andy Romano and Vince Edwards deliver wonderful, deliberately overdrawn performances, but the highlight is Alex Rocco as the sleazeball producer who strives to up the gore quotient because, as he says, "Everybody loves a good gross-out." Although it doesn't quite hang together — too much doesn't make sense in retrospect — there's more than enough cleverness here to make it easily the best satire thus far of a genre sorely in need of an injection of wit, humor, and fun. Six murders, mostly off-camera; lots of movie blood and body parts; Vince Edwards gets his heart ripped out and shoved into his mouth; breasts provided by Alison Noble; lots of twists.

DEADLY OBSESSION *(1988)*
wr Jeno Hodi, Paul Wolansky, and Brian Cox; dir Jeno Hodi

There is no discernible obsession, deadly or benign, in this one. Instead, we've got a disgruntled maintenance man (Joe Paradise) at a university, threatening to kill co-eds with rat poison unless he's paid a million dollars, and the spunky, resourceful young woman (Darnell Martin) whom he stalks for most of the picture. This is one of those movies in which everyone — the extortionist, the heroine, the police — are required to act stupidly at virtually every turn in order to keep the story moving and provide the opportunities for the suspense, action, and violence that are the point of the exercise. That point is, in fact, pretty well handled here, with slickness, style, and energy, as well as a couple of bits of high-impact brutality. Also, Paradise gives a very energetic — and frequently quite amusing — performance as the psycho janitor. If you're willing to overlook the inadequacies of the script and some of the actors, this delivers a number of effective moments. Four bodies; several splashes of splatter; six or eight gratuitous breasts; a seriously abused heroine; some variation on the form; much zippier than usual.

KILLER PARTY
Haunted frat house; see Festival 9.
GRADUATION DAY
Cap and groan; see Festival 15.
PROM NIGHT
Disco disaster; see Festival 15.

FESTIVAL 17

* * *

THE KILL OF THE WILD
Psychos in the Great Outdoors

> "Our trip is a complete disaster."
> — *The Final Terror*

The unfamiliar is always a source of uneasiness, and as modern life grows steadily more urban — though hardly urbane — the wilderness becomes more distant and consequently more forbidding. The sidewalks and back alleys of the city may be packed with shambling, wild-eyed, doped-up crazies, but mostly they're just after the same thing as everyone else — a piece of the action. Once you get away from concrete, though, you never know what or who you'll find, but there's a good chance it'll be some backwoods, inbred, devoluted, degenerate louts who only want a piece of you.

Deliverance (1972), based upon James Dickey's action tribute to the Southern Gothic literary tradition, was not the first to exploit these fears, but it was, and remains, one of the most effective and successful expressions of what can happen when city folks make the mistake of leaving the pavement. Three years later, a young regional filmmaker named Tobe Hooper burst into prominence with a low-budget horror movie based on essentially the same theme. Inspired, like *Psycho*, by the story of Ed Gein, the Wisconsin ultra-weirdo, *The Texas Chainsaw Massacre*, with its demented family of homicidal cannibals, quickly became a cult classic.

While some of the movies in this festival draw upon *Halloween/Friday the 13th*, the most seem to owe more to *Deliverance* and *Massacre*. The focus is thus more on action and survival than on mystery, but none of the movies that follow achieves anything approaching the power of the precursors. Indeed, even Hooper's muddled, sloppy, and stupid 1986 sequel to *Massacre* seemed to have not a clue how to do it.

If the back country is peopled with psychos, it's also the natural habitat of amateurish, backyard filmmakers. A few friends, an ax, a couple of pints of blood, and a 16 mm camera, and you're all set. Unless you happen to be using an isolated cabin, everything takes place outdoors, mostly in natural light (or natural darkness), and since the "action" consists primarily of happy campers hiking through the woods, you can really crank out the footage.

If you're wondering how this process could possibly result in anything worth watching ... it can't. While a couple of the movies that follow provide a few unintended laughs, they mostly represent the kind of product that brought about the decline of the genre.

Arboreal Assassins

JUST BEFORE DAWN *(1980)*
wr Mark Arywitz and Gregg Irving; dir Jeff Lieberman

Ignoring the advice of Ranger George Kennedy, five young campers go into the Oregon mountains and discover that a pair of wheezing, inbred, psychopathic identical twins (John Hunsaker) armed with saw-toothed machetes have declared open season on jerks from the city. It's always darkest, as they say, at the title time, and this underlit exercise in backwoods gloom does nothing to disprove it. Indeed, this one's so murky that it's often hard to tell what's going on ... and even harder to stay curious. Four bodies; no blood; scarcely seen psychos; Jamie Rose goes skinny-dipping; lots of waterfalls. In no respect a bright movie.

THE PREY *(1980)*
wr Summer and Edwin Brown; dir Edwin Scott Brown

It's pretty hard to resist a movie with the tagline "It's not human ... and it's got an ax," but this ultra-cheapie from the Brown family deserves the effort. Three young couples go into the woods and discover that "It" is, in fact, human, the hideously mutilated survivor of a forest fire that raged 30 years earlier who doesn't take kindly to visitors in his domain. This one is made up almost entirely of filler, including numerous close-ups of insects and reptiles that are far more interesting than any of the characters. Eight bodies; a couple of splashes of second-rate splatter; no skin worth mentioning; a human "monster," unseen until the last few moments and hardly worth the wait; lots of walking-in-the-woods footage; virtually no action; less suspense or tension. Minimalist filmmaking at its sparsest.

HUMONGOUS *(1981, Canadian)*
wr William Gray; dir Paul Lynch

The usual collection of young jerks and bimbos are stranded on an island whose only inhabitant is large, deformed, and hungry. Stupidly scripted, sluggishly paced, and woodenly acted, this one's main distinction is that we never get to see the monster. (Indeed, we don't see much at all in the darkness and murk.) With Joy Boushel as the girl who likes to show off her large breasts. Five bodies; a little blood; bimbo flesh, courtesy of Joy; no suspense; no shocks; no light; no sense.

THE FINAL TERROR *(1981)*
wr Jon George, Neill Hicks, and Ronald Shusett; dir Andrew Davis

The usual bunch of guys from the Forest Service and their dates go into the wilderness and discover that the campfire stories about the wild woman of the woods are true. Originally produced as *The Campsite Massacre*, this sat on the shelf for a couple of years before being released under this pointless and even less-accurate title. Although surprisingly well photographed and acceptably acted, this delivers none of the goods. The girls keep their clothes on; there is no explicit mayhem, no blood, and an utterly pathetic body count. Aside from the total absence of anything that might get your attention or hold your interest, this one's sole distinction is that it features early appearances by Daryl Hannah and Rachel Ward. Neither embarrasses herself, though Rachel, in a mini-fit of hysteria, comes close. Two bodies (plus two before the titles); nonexistent effects; a severed-head-in-the-outhouse gag; a mother-son psycho combo; two seconds of wild woman; no terror.

THE FOREST *(1983)*
wr Evan Jones; prod and dir Don Jones

Another backyard object-lesson as to why city folks should probably stay home. Here, a pair of bimbos and matching bozos (married but travelling separately for some stupid reason) discover that they have to share their idyllic spot in the wilderness with a backwoods loony (Michael Brody) who, after killing his wife and her lover, retired to a cave to subsist on whatever hikers happen to wander through. It takes a real talent to make cannibalism boring, and the Jones boys rose to the challenge. Sensing that story was missing something — characters, plot, and action, for instance — the filmmakers threw in the ghosts of the loony's dead kids to offer assistance to the campers. It didn't help. Six bodies; trickles of blood; no munching worth mentioning; no skin; lots of walking-through-the-forest footage. Dead wood.

MASTERBLASTER *(1986)*
wr Randy Grinter, Glenn Wilder, and Jeff Moldovan; dir Glenn Wilder

A dozen or so assorted dull clichés head to the Florida woods for the grand final of the "Masterblaster" survival game, only to discover that someone is playing the game for real and is prepared to wipe out the lot of them in order to exact revenge on one person. A small step above basic backyard, this is still seriously boring and, except for a brief but impressive shower by Tracy Hutchinson, provides absolutely nothing worth watching. Seven bodies; off-camera mayhem; one of the all-time dismal decapitations; inert action; no suspense; no sense.

DON'T GO IN THE WOODS
Class assignment at EDWACA; see Bonus Festival.

Summer-Camp Slaughter

THE BURNING *(1981)*
wr Peter Lawrence and Bob Weinstein; dir Tony Maylam

Five years after an adolescent prank left Cropsy the caretaker hideously burned and deformed, you'll never guess who's come back to Camp Blackfoot with his garden shears to do a bit of pruning. I'm a little confused as to who it is that gets snipped. If these bozos and bimbos are the counselors, they never do any work; and if they're the campers,

> *"He said he'd kill you or anyone else who tried to cut out part of his brain."*
> THE LAST SLUMBER PARTY

Blackfoot is a retreat for out-of-work 23-year-old actors. This issue is easily the only interesting one here. Tom Savini's effects are nothing very special, and the briefly seen Cropsy is merely unpleasant. With Carrick Glenn as the girl who takes a shower and Carolyn Houlihan as the girl who goes skinny-dipping. Nine bodies (and five of those go in one swell foop); low-impact splatter; misshapen psycho; a severed-arm-on-a-raft gag; no tension, suspense, or interest; duller and dumber than usual.

MADMAN *(1981)*
wr and dir Joe Giannone

The usual bunch of counselors at a summer camp discover that the campfire stories about Madman Marz, a deranged killer said to still prowl the woods, are more than legend. Although it's established early on that it's dangerous to go into the woods alone, each counselor does just that, making it easy for the title loony to ax, hang, impale, decapitate, and rip them real good. While not quite as cheap-looking as a lot of backyard efforts, this one is no more entertaining or original. Indeed, in most respects it's a fairly accurate facsimile of *Friday the 13th*, lacking only the sex and the spectacular mayhem (and, what else is there, after all?). Seven bodies; sub-par splatter; a psycho in coveralls; a severed-head-in-a-truck-engine gag; no skin to speak of; scant suspense; slightly dumber and more mechanical than usual.

SLEEPAWAY CAMP *(1983)*
wr and dir Robert Hiltzer

Someone is killing kids and counselors at Camp Arawak, the very place where, eight years earlier, a camper was responsible for a fatal boating accident. Technically fairly competent, but everything else is a little stupider, nastier, and more heavy-handed than usual. The violence is generally not explicit, but we do get to see the rather gruesome remains of victims of such things as a scalding, a drowning, a decapitation, and a fatal attack by wasps. The makeup effects are good, but the only real shocker (bizarre and perverse) occurs at the very end, and the trip there is too tedious to be worth it. Ten victims; no breasts; some seriously bad acting; an unsavory surprise.

SLEEPAWAY CAMP 2: UNHAPPY CAMPERS *(1988)*
wr Fritz Gordon; dir Michael A. Simpson

From high on the list of least necessary sequels comes this exercise in summer-camp somnambulism to remind us why they stopped making movies like this several years earlier. The sexually confused psycho from Camp Arawak has grown into Pamela Springsteen (Bruce's sis), had shock therapy and a sex change, and is now a counselor at Camp Rolling Hills, where she dispatches a large bunch of painfully bad young actors in the usual ways — drilling, chainsawing, stabbing, barbecuing, throat-ripping, tongue-removal, outhouse-drowning, etc. — none of which is very explicit, realistic, or impact-laden. Maybe it's supposed to be a spoof, but if so, it's not funny. With Valerie Hartman as the bimbo camper who keeps removing her shirt in order to show why she's justifiably proud of what's underneath. Fifteen bodies (I think); mediocre mayhem; numerous exposures of Valerie; decent production values; brainless and boring; paceless and suspenseless. Rent this, and the campers will not be the only unhappy ones. Sleep away.

Waterfront Wackos

THE MUTILATOR *(1983)*
wr, prod, dir Buddy Cooper

The standard six-pack of college types go out to an isolated North Carolina island to close up Ed's father's beach house. Dad's still around, though, and still kind of pissed off that Ed, years before, accidentally shot and killed Mom. This one shows us an inventory of sharp objects, but pointlessly (as it were) since — unless I saw a seriously cut version — it studiously avoids actually showing us any of them in use. Five bodies; off-camera mayhem; scant blood; Frances Raines goes skinny-dipping; seriously underlit; characters and dialog even dimmer; significantly more inept and inane than usual.

DEADLY INTRUDER *(1984)*
wr Tony Crupi; dir John McCauley

A psycho killer (who is carefully kept from view) escapes from the asylum and bloodlessly bumps off folks around Midvale. Meanwhile, a weird drifter (writer Crupi) holds Jessie (Molly Cheek) hostage in her isolated house. The big twist here is that the drifter isn't the killer, and that the psycho turns out to be the clean-cut guy who was Jessie's blind date. Oops! I've given it away. Eleven bodies; shabby, off-camera mayhem; a psycho and a loony; Molly's body double takes a bath; music lifted from *Halloween*; no blood; no originality; no energy; no interest. Keep the doors locked.

TERROR AT TENKILLER *(1986)*
wr Claudia Meyer; prod and dir Ken Meyer

Apparently undeterred by the fact that the golden age of cheapshit, amateurish, backyard slasher flicks had ended about four years earlier, the Meyer family of Oklahoma offer up an unusually lame and minimalist contribution to the canon. Two bimbos arrive at a cottage on Lake Tenkiller where, in an unexpected turn of events, they are menaced by a psycho who manages to live up to only 50 per cent of the title. Five bodies; a surprisingly good throat-slitting and arm-severing; the briefest possible flash of Stacy Logan's considerable charms; no mystery; no suspense; absolutely godawful sound, plotting, dialog, and delivery. Could a movie with a title like this one be anything other than a dead fish?

AMERICAN GOTHIC *(1987, British/Canadian)*
wr Burt Wetanson and Michael Vines; dir John Hough

The title notwithstanding, engine trouble forces six yuppies to land their seaplane near an isolated island in British Columbia. There they encounter a family that's been out of touch with the world since the 1920s. These people make the *Texas Chainsaw* folks seem positively mainstream. Yvonne De Carlo and Rod Steiger are the Bible-thumping Ma and Pa, and their three "kids" all behave like preadolescents, but are, in fact, decidedly middle aged. (No explanations are given for this arrested development . . . or for anything else.) Needless to say, the number of the visitors is quickly reduced to one, in bloodless and uninteresting ways. The box claims that this offers both horror and humor, but unless Michael J. Pollard cast as a ten-year-old is your idea of either, it lies. Even worse — and quite disappointing considering the grotesque situation and the presence of Rod and Yvonne — it's all too dull and dreary to have even camp appeal. Five bodies (plus five loonies); off-camera mayhem; a little after-the-fact dried blood; various mummified corpses; no skin; no suspense; labored and tiresome creepiness.

Dementia in the Desert

DEATH VALLEY *(1981)*
wr Richard Rothstein; dir Dick Richards

A divorcée and her young son go to Arizona for a vacation with an old beau from her high-school days. While cruising the wide-open spaces, they happen upon a murder, then find themselves pursued and menaced by the pair of psycho brothers responsible. Somehow, the decent production values and the presence of real actors (Paul LeMat, Wilford Brimley, Stephen McHattie) only serve to emphasize the utter paucity of everything else. The plotting is contrived, there are no surprises or suspense, the dialog is unlistenable, and the little kid is cutesy enough to make your teeth hurt. Five bodies; scant mayhem; less blood; two psychos for the price of one; Gina Christian takes her top off; no style; no pace; no point. This one's as vibrant as the setting.

THE HILLS HAVE EYES — PART II *(1984)*
wr and dir Wes Craven

This has almost nothing to do with the original *Hills* (1977) — which had a certain raw energy if not much finesse — than with coughing up yet another limp clone of *Friday the 13th*. The eight slow members of a motorcycle racing team, who literally can't tell time or read a map, get lost in the California desert and discover that Pluto (Michael Berryman), one of the cannibal sons from the original, is still alive and has been joined by a large, chortling psycho called The Reaper (John Bloom). Directed without style, sense, or even any decent splatter, this is the kind of inert lump that gives sequels a bad name — a pointless exercise that has nothing to do with making movies and everything to do with making a buck. Deservedly, it didn't make many, thereby, I hope, sparing us a Part III. Five bodies; cheapshit, low-impact mayhem; Penny Johnson takes her shirt off; scarcely better than backyard. Another dismal mess from Wes, who's made more than a few.

BLOOD FRENZY *(1987)*
wr Ted Newsom; dir Hal Freeman

SCHIZOID goes camping. The six variously disturbed members of an encounter group go into the desert with their doctor to engage in "confrontational therapy." After 45 minutes of serious soul-baring and neurosis-flaunting, one of them finally gets his gullet slit, and we discover that the pre-title sequence in which an unseen child takes a garden tool to Dad's throat is, in fact, relevant. The remaining members of the group then get to demonstrate that they're not only crazy, but also stupid as they do their best to boost the body count. Naturally, this is slow and cheap, completely lacking in shocks or suspense, but the general tedium is at least occasionally enlivened by some hammily overwrought performances, thoroughly ridiculous psychologizing, and a totally ludicrous finale. While this falls short of being really amusing, those who collect laughably unskilled, unsubtle portrayals of mental imbalance will find more than a little to savor here. Seven bodies; very tacky but graphic mayhem; a couple of real spurters; unseen psycho; spot-the-loony; no skin; lots of psychobabble.

THE HITCHER
ROAD GAMES
Highway stalkers; see Festival 20.

FESTIVAL 18

* * *

HOME SWEET HOMICIDE
A Suburb of Psychos in Residence

"There's something wrong in that house . . . something evil."
— *Funeral Home*

Statistically, more than 40 per cent of North American homicides occur in the home, which suggests that, while you can go home again, you probably shouldn't. Certainly, the movies that follow, along with the residential rampages from other festivals in this section, do nothing to contradict that recommendation. It seems that the psycho killer, besides a fondness for masks and sharp implements, possesses a well-developed homing instinct, especially for isolated houses whose power and phone lines can be easily severed. For the filmmaker on a tight budget, this is a rather welcome trait since considerable economies can be realized by confining the action to one primary location (not to mention the built-in dramatic irony of having the victims menaced in what should be the safest of all places). So, wouldn't you know it: No sooner do you get the furnace fixed and new wiring put in, then you have to contend with an infestation of psycho killers.

It's enough to make one become a bagperson.

Forbidding Abodes

DON'T GO IN THE HOUSE (1980)
wr Joseph Ellison, Ellen Hammill, and J. R. Masefield; dir J. Ellison

Donald's mother severely abused him as a child by roasting his arms over the gas burner. When she dies at the beginning of the movie, he flips out and, listening to the voices in his head, decides to return the favor to the rest of the world. He lures a series of women (who obviously were unaware of the title of the movie they were in) into his house, where he

> *"I don't know what it is — I'm usually not such a putz with the girls."*
> I WAS A TEENAGE ZOMBIE

strips them, douses them with gasoline, and blasts them with a flamethrower. After they're charred black, he dresses them in his mother's clothes and leaves them sitting around her bedroom, where he talks to them (i.e., Norman Bates has a barbecue). Sick though this is, it's not quite as vile as it sounds. We actually see only one flame-broiling; most of the movie is concerned with his inner torment. Do we really care? Three murders; one nude; cheap production values; terrible lighting; a decent performance by Dan Grimaldi as the sicko; lots of flames.

HOUSE OF DEATH *(1981)*
wr Paul C. Elliott; dir David Nelson

Another lump of regional slasher sludge dredged up by the video revolution. A unseen killer is doing some major body work with a machete to the usual bunch of bozos and bimbos in Shelby, North Carolina. First, however, the B&Bs spend a long, long time at a two-bit carnival, trying to establish their indistinguishable characters. Then they go down to the river, where Judy Kay goes skinny-dipping, then to a cemetery where someone tells a creepy story. Finally, it starts to rain, so they take shelter in the title abode, where heads and hands are chopped off, and Ramona, the town slut, gets cut in half, all of which is fairly explicit and utterly ridiculous. Even with the insatiable demand of video distributors, it took seven years for this tiresome effort to make it to cassette. Nine bodies; laughable splatter; one of the shabbiest exploding heads on record; unseen psycho; significantly dumber and duller than usual.

FEAR *(1981, French/Italian, dubbed)*
wr Antonio Cesare Corti, Fabio Piccioni, and Riccardo Freda; dir Riccardo Freda

A disturbed young actor and some of his friends go out to his mother's isolated villa where the friends meet with common household accidents, such as an ax in the skull and a chainsaw in the throat. Is it the actor, who apparently killed his father years before? Is it Oliver, the all-purpose servant who is always lurking around? Or is it the loony mother, wracked with incestuous yearnings and practicing witchcraft in the basement? To save you the trouble, it's Mom, for reasons that are no stupider than any of the incredible idiocies that precede the ludicrous conclusion. This would be hilarious if it weren't also so drearily cheap and dull. Four bodies; laughable splatter; ample bare breasts; a grindingly slow pace; grating electronic soundtrack. Fear not. (Not to be confused with the 1988 piece-o-shit with the same title featuring Frank Stallone.)

TOO SCARED TO SCREAM *(1982)*
wr Neal Barbera and Glenn Leopold; dir Tony Lo Bianco

Somebody is chopping up the residents of a fancy New York apartment building, but fortunately tough cop Mike Connors ("Mannix") is called in on the case, so only three more vacancies occur before he figures it out. So much suspicion points to the weird, Shakespeare-quoting doorman (Ian McShane) that we assume he must be a red herring, but by the time the big concluding revelation rolls in, we're too bored to care that it's rather arbitrary and uninteresting. Produced by Connors, this is decently made, but very plodding, without any zip or suspense. Indeed, except for some coarse language and the fact that Victoria Bass takes off her dress and Karen Rushmore takes a lengthy sauna, this feels exactly like a made-for-TV effort. Seven bodies; off-screen slaughter; unseen psycho; obscure motivation; inferior mystery; no thrills or chills.

ALONE IN THE DARK *(1982)*
wr and dir Jack Sholder

Shortly after a new doctor starts work at a mental hospital, a power blackout disarms the security system in the psycho ward, and the patients escape to lay siege to the shrink's house. With four psychopaths, a slightly mad psychiatrist, and a young woman (the doc's sister) with a history of mental illness, you need a scorecard to keep track of the loonies here, and that's part of the fun. Another part is provided by the psychological chat, which, for once, tends to be amusing rather than boring or stupid. And yet more fun is provided by old hams Jack Palance and Martin Landau as two of the psychos and Donald Pleasence as the crazed, dope-smoking director of the clinic. The mayhem includes a strangling, an arrow-piercing, a broken back, several stabbings, a ripping with a garden tool, and a meat cleaver in the back, all decently done if not very explicit, bloody, or powerful. All in all, this is fairly standard stuff enlivened with some wit and skill (which, considering the competition in the genre, is enough to

> "You know — it's kind of weird having Jack the Ripper in our town."
> THE RIPPER

make this a good bit above average). Eight bodies; a few seconds of bimbo flesh; good production values; a little suspense; a couple of twists; music by the Sic F*cks, including a spirited rendition of "Chop Up Your Mother."

A BLADE IN THE DARK *(1983, Italian, dubbed)*
wr Dardano Sacchetti and Elisa Briganti; dir Lamberto Bava

A rather dumb, bland composer goes to an isolated villa to write the score for a horror movie, but these young women keep turning up for no particular reason except to get the chop from "Linda," the unseen psycho-in-residence. The identity of the killer is supposed to be something of surprise, but the perceptive viewer will recognize that the villa is located in that crowded subdivision just behind the Bates Motel. Some reviewers claim to find this atmospheric and suspenseful, *à la* Hitchcock, but I thought it was slow and contrived, with dubbing so bad as to be distracting. Six bodies; rather subdued splatter; trace bimbo exposure; lots and lots of corridor footage. From the director of **DEMONS** and the son of Mario Bava, the godfather of Italian horror cinema.

IDENTITY CRISIS *(1985, Canadian)*
wr John Sheppard, Peter Colley, and Bruce Pittman; dir Bruce Pittman
Originally released as *The Mark of Cain*.

Robin Ward plays Sean and Michael, very dull identical twins. Fifteen years earlier, Michael brutally murdered a young woman, apparently as part of some satanic ritual, and was confined to an asylum. Now, Sean is married and wants to sell the isolated family home, but Michael objects, then escapes to visit the old homestead. He is easily recaptured but, in an unexpected turn of events, the wrong twin is sent back, leaving the loony alone with the wife. The abundant possibilities for Pirandelloesque twists and surprises inherent in the premise are ignored here with a total lack of style, pace and interest. Four bodies; off-camera mayhem; a few drops of blood; no skin; no suspense; almost painfully stiff, tedious, and predictable.

HORROR HOUSE ON HIGHWAY FIVE *(1985)*
wr and dir Richard Casey

From the description on the box — two psycho brothers, one of whom has maggots in his brain, and their deranged father who bumps off folks while wearing a Richard Nixon mask — you might well think this is "filled with strange humor and wild action." It's not. While there are three or four mildly amusing moments, mostly it's just a painfully labored, dreadfully amateurish exercise in backyard incoherence — an apparent parody with all the failings of its targets and none of their minimal virtues. Six bodies; seriously inferior gore; no skin; much stupider and duller than usual. Another condemned property.

OPEN HOUSE *(1987, direct to cassette)*
wr David Mickey Evans; dir Jag Mundhra

A homeless psycho is doing in Beverly Hills real estate agents (all blonde, bimbous airheads), and only realtor Adrienne Barbeau and her radio-psychologist boyfriend (the ever-bland Joseph Bottoms) stand between him and a significant reduction in commissions. Now, anyone who's had dealings with the type of agent presented here can certainly sympathize with the desire to exterminate the breed. The yuppie angle aside, though, this is more of the same, maybe even a bit more tired and mechanical than usual, with just enough nastiness to turn the whole thing slightly rancid. Five bodies; basically bloodless; a severed-head-in-the-swimming-pool gag; Roxanne Baird goes skinny-dipping; lots of tedious chat. Primarily for those collecting the complete works of Adrienne, who not only shows us a quick glimpse of things when she slips off her bathrobe, but offers so much intense brow-wrinkling that her brain, as well as her hair, seems to have been overpermed.

NIGHT SCREAMS *(1987)*
wr Dillis Hart II and Mitch Brian; dir Allen Plone

The usual bunch of high-school jerks have a party after the big game, and they start to be picked off, one by one — a stabbing, a crushing, an electrocution, a barbecuing, etc. Red herrings — including a pair of homicidal escaped convicts hiding in the basement — abound, but the big revelation at the end will come as a surprise only to those who managed to sleep all the way through this dull, dreary, Kansas backyard piece-o-shit. Don't be fooled by the high body count: the mayhem is inferior and lackluster. This does, however, boast some of the most completely gratuitous bimbo flesh on record through the clever device of having a

> *"I'm the monster you've heard about."*
> THE TOXIC AVENGER

couple of the jerks watch a porno tape. Since these clips are easily the best part of this one, you have to wonder why you're wasting prime viewing time with this bullshit. Sixteen bodies; no blood worth mentioning; no jolts; no suspense; lots of teen chatter.

Accommodating Killers

THE UNSEEN *(1980)*
wr and dir Peter Foleg

When there are no motel rooms available in the cutesy California town of Solvang, the three members of an all-bimbo TV news team are invited to stay with a strange little man (Sydney Lassick), and discover that there's something nasty in the cellar. The "something" is a severely retarded young man — the product of Syd's incestuous relationship with his sister — who has been raised like an animal in the basement. Obviously, creepy Syd is the real monster here, and the unfortunate down below is just as much a victim as the two women he kills, no doubt accidentally. Well played by Stephen Furst, "Junior" becomes something of a pathetic figure, and the movie as a whole takes on a rather unsavory quality. Although this is competently made, it is a little too gratuitously unpleasant to be much fun, and thus suggest that you leave it in the title state. Two victims; little blood; lots of filth; Lois Young takes a bath; psychosexual creepo; human "monster"; minimal suspense and tension.

MOTEL HELL *(1980)*
wr Robert Jaffe and Steven-Charles Jaffe; dir Kevin Connor

Besides running the Motel Hello (the neon "O" is burned out), Vincent (Rory Calhoun) and his sister Ida (Nancy Parson) have dedicated themselves to serving humanity. Concerned as they are about world hunger and overpopulation, they have come up with an ideal solution — including motel guests and other passers-by as the secret ingredient in Farmer Vincent's Smoked Meats, acknowledged to be the "best in the whole world." Like other animals, Vincent's have to be fattened up; the sausages-to-be are buried up to their necks, their vocal cords cut, and are force fed ("I treat my stock better than most farmers treat their animals"). Obviously located midway between the Bates Motel and the Texas Chainsaw Barbecue, this one can't decide if it wants to go for shocks and chills or grotesque black humor, and doesn't quite achieve either. Still, the deadpan, matter-of-fact style delivers a few chuckles, Calhoun has a number of funny lines, and the concluding chainsaw duel, with Calhoun wearing a pig's head, is worthy of note. Four bodies; numerous body parts; surprisingly subdued mayhem; Nina Axelrod takes a quick bath; decent production values; some satiric touches. While this could do with a lot more spice, it does at least have some flavor.

FUNERAL HOME *(1981, Canadian)*
wr Ida Nelson; dir William Fruet

Two years after Mr. Chalmers the embalmer mysteriously disappeared, Grandma Chalmers (Kay Hawtry), with the logic typical of the genre, decides to turn the mortuary into a tourist home. She's assisted by her pudgy granddaughter (Lesleh Donaldson) who hears strange voices in the locked basement and eventually decides that "there's something wrong in that house — something evil." It will take the perceptive viewer about 10 minutes to recognize that the tourist home is just down the road from the Bates Motel; the remaining 75 minutes rewards you with dreary production values, dismal dialog, and dull performances of a lot of actors familiar from Canadian TV commercials. Four bodies; no blood; no skin; no mystery; no tension. This one's deader than the mortician's clients.

NEXT OF KIN *(1982, Australian)*
wr Michael Heath and Tony Williams; dir Tony Williams

Upon the death of her mother, whom she apparently had not seen for many years, Linda (Jackie Kerin) returns to the isolated family estate that's being run as a retirement home. Soon, there are dark, mysterious goings-on that seem to echo events of twenty years earlier. This one's so damn dark and mysterious (as well as slow and ponderous) that it's hard to tell who's who, and what, if anything, this is about. For the longest time, it looks like nothing is going to happen; then, abruptly, bodies start to fall and Aunt Rita (long believed to be dead) turns up, for good measure accompanied by an unidentified homicidal maniac. The last third

> *"According to these readings, he should be dead."*
> THE HOWLING III

or so of this is not badly done, if utterly brainless, but it's hardly worth the struggle to get there, and the abundant use of slow motion does nothing to speed the journey. Five bodies; off-camera mayhem; surprise psychos; murky mystery; a few good moments; portentousness up the wazoo.

MOUNTAINTOP MOTEL MASSACRE *(1983)*
wr and dir Jim McCullough, Jr.

Evelyn (Anna Chappell), a frumpy middle-aged woman recently released from a mental hospital, runs a seedy little motel in the Bates chain, complete with stuffed animals. Shortly after she takes a sickle to her daughter's guinea pig, and then to her daughter, she has seven guests spending a stormy night in her cabins. The rooms cost seven dollars, and come with rattlesnakes, rats, and cockroaches, and later with Evelyn herself; armed with her sickle, she makes sure her guests enjoy a long rest, if not a very peaceful one. Seven bodies (not counting the guinea pig); nonexplicit violence; after-the-fact blood; wet T-shirts, but no skin; surprisingly good production values and decent performances. A touch slow and nothing very special, but better than you'd think from the title.

FESTIVAL 19

* * *

A PLACE FOR MURDER, EVERY MURDER IN ITS PLACE
The Omnipresent Psycho

"No checkup is ever just a simple formality, Miss Jeremy."
— *Hospital Massacre*

Okay, let's see where we stand. You should avoid most major holidays and festivities, educational institutions, the great outdoors, and home visits. That leaves lots of places where you're not likely to get the chop from a psycho killer, right? Not quite, as the entries below suggest. Supermarkets, restaurants, and City Hall seem safe. On second thought, scratch restaurants (see **BLOODY WEDNESDAY** in the next festival), and I'm far from certain that politicians are to be preferred to psychos. That still leaves the supermarket, where all you have to worry about is carcinogenic additives, though it is probably just a matter of time until someone gives us *Checkout Line*, about a boxboy with bloodlust. That leaves hot-air ballooning — solo.

Medical Mayhem

SCHIZOID (1980)
wr and dir David Paulsen

Someone is poking holes with big scissors in the members of Dr. Klaus Kinski's encounter group, and there's no shortage of suspects. There's Craig Wasson who blames the group for the breakup of his marriage to lonely-hearts columnist Mariana Hill. There's group member Christopher Lloyd who's strange and creepy and ever-present. There's Klaus's hysterical, rage-filled adolescent daughter (Donna Wilkes). And, of course, Klaus himself has more than a couple of kinks and is always suspect. This one emphasizes the mystery — often with a fairly heavy hand — and while the revelation is not much of a surprise if you've been paying attention, Paulsen does at least play fair with the viewer, as well as tossing out a couple of decent red herrings. Of course, it's all ridiculous and not exactly gripping, but at the same time, there are a couple of entertainingly overdrawn performances and, as usual, producers Golan and Globus give a professional sheen to the proceedings. Three bodies; bloodless; Donna Wilkes takes a shower and Flo Gerrish performs a topless dance; very stupid police; a plethora of loonies; a soupçon of kinkiness; a touch more stylish than usual.

HOSPITAL MASSACRE *(1981)*
wr Marc Behm; dir Boaz Davidson

As an asshole doctor tells ex-Playmate Barbi Benton, "No checkup is ever just a simple formality, Miss Jeremy," and she discovers he's right when she stops by the Sisters of Perpetual Malpractice Hospital for some test results. It seems a psycho in a surgical mask, still smarting over a Valentine's Day slight 19 years earlier, intends to win her heart and is prepared to perform a fair amount of unnecessary surgery to do so. Tapping into the fact that hospitals are inherently sinister places, verging on the sadistic, this one subjects poor Barbi to a steady stream of medical indignities, including a full-frontal examination. Indeed, this lays it on so thick that the doctors here make Ilsa the She Wolf seem like Florence Nightingale. Produced by Golan and Globus, this combines a certain slickness with an awesome lack of subtlety, and delivers some pretty brisk nonsense in the process. Eight bodies; bloodless off-camera surgery; a decent acid facial; a severed-head-in-a-hatbox gag; Barbi shows why she was a Playmate of the Year and why she never had much of an acting career; the entire cast of suspicious actors acts suspiciously. No shocks or chills, but this is a bit livelier than most and delivers a couple of laughs.

VISITING HOURS *(1981, Canadian)*
wr Brian Taggert; dir Jean Claude Lord

A sicko psycho with a grudge against the world (Michael Ironside) goes after a crusading TV commentator (Lee Grant). When his attack only injures her, he stalks her in the hospital, dispatching a few innocent people along the way. Ironside is believable, with intensity, and this is decently produced, but otherwise it's just another mechanical exercise in women-in-jeopardy. Lee gets to whimper and have hysterics, nurse Linda Purl gets to be spunky, and William Shatner appears for five minutes as a boring stuffed shirt. Three bodies; trickles of blood; no skin; somewhat nastier than usual. Perhaps useful as a general anesthetic.

DOOM ASYLUM *(1983, direct to cassette)*
wr Rick Marx; dir Richard Friedman

Ten years after he came to in the middle of his own autopsy, famous palimony lawyer Mitch Hanson (Michael Rogan) now lives in the ruins of the hospital where the terrible mistake was made. His face is hideously scarred, and he has a thing about using surgical instruments to slaughter everyone he sees — two characteristics that don't get him invited to many parties. Fortunately, the party comes to him in the form of an all-girl punk trio and five assorted bimbos and bozos out for a picnic. Obviously, this backyard New Jersey cheapie is not meant to be taken seriously and it has enough of a sense of its own silliness — and that of the genre — to provide a few smiles and maybe even a laugh or two. Lots of blood and a few good makeup effects but, no doubt for budgetary reasons, most of the mayhem takes place off-camera. To compensate, the action is intercut with clips from campily dreadful Tod Slaughter mysteries from the '30s, presumably to show us how little has changed. Seven bodies; passable gore; a flash of punkette breasts, courtesy of Ruth Collins; a rather cheerful tackiness. Nothing at all special, but there are much worse fates than an hour or so in this asylum.

Backstage Blood

TERROR ON TOUR *(1980)*
wr Dell Lekus; dir Don Edmonds

The "tour" is that of a band aptly named The Clowns, who wear KISS-like makeup and whose performance features a lot of simulated violence against women. The "terror" is someone dressed up as a Clown who's stabbing bare-breasted groupies backstage in punishment for their sins.

> "We use men to breed with us to create future warrior
> women, then we dispose of them."
> ROBOT HOLOCAUST

Given that the movie consists almost entirely of sex, drugs, rock 'n' roll, and wild parties, you'd think it would at least be energetically sleazy, but this is so cheap and inert that it only manages to be seedy and nasty — par for the course from the director of *Ilsa, She Wolf of the S.S.*, a schlockmeister whose delicate touch can make even nudity and violence seem boring. Eight bodies; seriously crummy gore; four or five topless groupies; a disguised sicko psycho; bottom-of-the-barrel script, acting, direction, and production values. Another example of the kind of misogynistic mess that gives sleaze a bad name.

CURTAINS *(1982, Canadian)*
wr Robert Guza, Jr.; dir Jonathan Stryker (Richard Ciupka)

Six actresses go out to a sleazy director's isolated country house to audition for the lead in his next movie, and it turns out that one of them will, as they say, kill for the part. Although technically professional and fairly slick, this is remarkably shoddy and amateurish in most other respects. Dreadfully paced and confusingly plotted, it generates no tension or suspense, although the vigorously hammy performances do occasionally provide some unintentional humor. Eight bodies; no gore; masked killer; no skin; unusually stupid; only for those who want to see a bunch of Canadian actors (including John Vernon) really devour the scenery.

STAGE FRIGHT *(1983, Australian)*
wr Colin Eggleston; dir John Lamond

Upset at seeing her mother fondled by a lover, a young girl causes a car accident that kills Mom. Twenty years later, she's grown into a schizophrenic actress (Jenny Neumann) who's phobic about sex and who slashes with shards of glass most of the people connected with the artsy-fartsy play she's in. Although not too badly done, this seems singularly pointless. The killer is unseen, even though we know who it is; there is no attempt to create a portrait of madness; and there is no suspense in the random slaughter of the series of hackneyed theatrical types. Not surprisingly, the writer went on to direct **SKY PARTIES** and **CASSANDRA**, two other pointless exercises. Nine bodies; mostly off-camera slashings; lots of blood; Sue Jones and Rossana Zuanetti bare all before being sharded; unusually senseless. Don't get this one confused with . . .

STAGE FRIGHT *(1987, Italian, dubbed)*
wr Lew Cooper; dir Michael Soavi

While rehearsing an artsy horror-musical about a symbolic psycho killer called "The Night Owl," the cast members find themselves trapped in the empty theater while a real psycho killer dressed in the owl suit picks them off one by one. Except for the owl suit, this is not exactly a wildly original situation; the big surprise here is that this actually manages to bring a little vitality and freshness to the familiar formula. It's stylishly lit and shot, the performances are decent, and there are a number of quite flashy and effective sequences. The slaughter is varied — a pickax in the mouth, a drill through the stomach, various stabbings, several serious chainsawings — enthusiastic, and very, very messy. This one's also distinguished by it's sense of fun with regard to some of the form's sillier conventions, and a few bizarre touches (the chainsaw-wielding giant owl, for one). According to the box, this was the winner in the "Fear Category" at the Avoriaz Film Festival, and you sure could do a lot worse. Ten bodies; a masked killer; no skin; but an interesting "fat suit"; good production values; decent dubbing; abundant blood; a dismemberment; a decapitation.

ANGUISH *(1987, Spanish)*
wr Bigas Luna and Michael Berlin; dir Bigas Luna

This one's set in a movie theater showing a sicko psycho slice-and-dicer called "The Mommy." The movie-within-the-movie features Michael Learner as the seriously disturbed son of Zelda Rubinstein (the weird midget de-haunter from *Poltergeist*), who, through post-hypnotic suggestion, has him kill people and cut out additions to her eyeball collection. Meanwhile, the movie is starting to have a strange effect on the audience. When Learner goes into a theater to get more specimens (a movie-within-the-movie-within-the-movie), the two movies begin to echo each other as a psycho in the audience for "The Mommy" starts to pick off people with his .38. This is thus kind of a cross between **DEMONS** and *Targets* (1968), but it's not quite as interesting as it sounds. We spend more time watching "The Mommy" than *Anguish*, and, even though the former is the more entertaining of the two, the device of the double feature eventually wears thin. Still, this is not badly done, and not without a few good moments, and at least makes an attempt to play with the form. Fourteen bodies (seven in each movie); inferior gore; superior eyeball removals; two psychos for the price of one; no skin; some style and ambition; a twist ending that shouldn't come as much of a surprise; less stupid than usual.

MOVIE HOUSE MASSACRE
Haunted cinema; see Festival 10.

A Rolling Psycho

TERROR TRAIN *(1980, Canadian)*
wr T. Y. Drake; dir Roger Spottiswoode

Three years after a nasty frat prank went tragically awry, the usual bunch of collegiate bimbos and jerks hires a private train for a rolling costume party, the last big fling of their college days. And it will be just that for some of them since — are you ready? — the traumatized victim of the stunt is also along for the ride. The setting is about the only original thing in this one, and first-time director Spottiswoode (*Under Fire*) makes good use of the confining environment and the fact that everyone is masked, as well as keeping the identity of the killer a surprise (though not one with a lot of punch). What he can't compensate for is a script that provides unappealing characters, terrible dialog, and little in the way of either shocks or suspense. Five bodies (and several disappearances); off-camera mayhem; after-the-fact blood; a severed-head-in-the-upper-berth gag; two seconds of large exposed breasts; masked psycho; masked victims; lots of frat chat; lots of train chat; lots of magic tricks; not significantly stupider than usual. With Ben Johnson, magician David Copperfield, and Jamie Lee Curtis precisely reprising her role from *Halloween*.

A Rambling Psycho

NIGHTMARE *(1981)*
wr and dir Romano Scavolini

When young George walked in on his parents engaging in a little mild S&M, he promptly picked up an ax and lopped off Mom's head, then buried the hatchet in Dad's skull. Twenty years later, supposedly cured of his psychosis by experimental drug therapy, it seems that George (Baird Stafford) still has a few problems. He keeps dreaming about the incident, which means we get to see Mom's severed head and spurting torso more than once. Then, after a literal foaming-at-the-mouth fit in a Times Square porno palace, George heads to Florida for reasons that are eventually explained but far from interesting. This loses its sicko-sleazo conviction early, and turns into a feeble *Halloween* clone, with a script and acting scarcely better than basic backyard. Still, there are a few decent splatter effects from Tom Savini, and Stafford is energetically demented, so this does catch your attention at least occasionally. Seven bodies; explicit mayhem; buckets of blood; two foaming fits; various topless bimbos; very stupid doctors; even stupider psychology. Plan to fast-forward.

A Carnival Killer

THE FUNHOUSE *(1981)*
wr Larry Block; dir Tobe Hooper

While visiting a seedy travelling carnival, four young people decide to spend the night in the funhouse, where they witness a murder and then are tracked by the killer, the horribly deformed son of the funhouse operator. Although not entirely successful, this has considerably more going on than the average teens-in-jeopardy flick. There are interesting references to other movies, including *Frankenstein* (the creature wears a Frankenstein monster mask to disguise his own, far more terrible appearance), and a great parody of the shower scene from *Psycho*. Good use is made of the carnival setting, and there's an intriguing subtext concerning masks, illusions, and voyeurism. Unfortunately, the central story is not as strong as the peripheral material, and, despite some effective moments, it's slow in developing and never pulls us in the way it should. As always, a "monster" who's at least as sympathetic/pathetic as he is menacing is a problem, and, while parts of this are good, the whole is not really satisfying. Five bodies; standard gore; good creature design by Rick Baker; glimpsed breasts; stylishly shot; more ambitious than usual. Reflexive horror from one of the founding fathers of the contemporary form.

Psycho in Stir

DESTROYER *(1988)*
wr Rex Hauck and Peter Garrity; dir Robert Kirk

A low-budget film company is shooting "Death House Dollies," a standard bimbos-behind-bars epic, in the now-abandoned prison that was the site of the worst-ever riot 18 months earlier. As it develops, the last convict executed there — a 300-pound mass of muscle and homicidal meanness named Ivan Moser (an entertaining Lyle Alzado) — somehow managed to survive and is steadily reducing the size of the crew. This has a good slick look, a high-quality cast (Anthony Perkins, Deborah Foreman, Clayton Rohner), a little humor, and passes the time in a fairly lively fashion. What it doesn't have is a script that could decide if it wants to play with the form or merely replicate it, and thus this kind of rambles around, never being quite funny or suspenseful or violent enough to hang together or have much impact. Double-digit body count, mostly discovered after the fact; a little splatter, including Tony Perkins getting his eyeballs popped; a standard prison shower scene featuring six buxom bimbos; a couple of good dream sequences; very little sense.

A Dubious Undertaking

MORTUARY *(1983)*
wr Howard Avedis and Marlene Schmidt; dir Howard Avedis

A guy in a mask and a black cloak is skewering people with an 18-inch embalming needle. Utterly lacking in tension or even the occasional shock, this one's as stiff and lifeless as the clients of the title institution, which is what you expect of any movie starring the Georges, Christopher and Linda Day, cinema's most consistently tedious couple. If you slog through this one, the big revelation is that the murderer turns out to be the person we suspected on first sight. Five bodies; a little blood; lousy effects; one nude corpse; a masked psycho; no suspense; no pace; no brains; and the only point is on the embalming needle.

FUNERAL HOME
Now a tourist trap; see Festival 18.

Shop 'Til You Drop

CHOPPING MALL *(1986)*
wr Jim Wynorski and Steve Mitchell; dir Jim Wynorski

Eight sex-obsessed Valley girls and boys are trapped in the Sherman Oaks Galleria and menaced by a trio of heartless, unstoppable killers. The three killers happen to be the mall's malfunctioning robot security force, but that's the only variation on the theme that you're going to find here. This could have been fun if they'd played with the familiar formulas instead of merely trotting them out unchanged. However, the psycho killers are not the only things that are totally mechanical in this one. From the director of **DEATHSTALKER II**; with Suzee Slater in the part of the bimbo with the largest breasts. Nine bodies; a little blood; two seconds of skin courtesy of Suzee; a couple of laughs; no tension; a lot of shattering glass; one so-so exploding head. Only if you're really desperate.

THE INITIATION
Department-store psycho sorority prank; see Festival 16.

An Aerobics Assassin

KILLER WORKOUT *(1986)*
wr and dir David A. Prior

Because of a tragic accident at a tanning salon five years earlier, somebody is wiping out the young honeys in an aerobics class at Rhonda's

> *"His fermented buffalo milk will be your fermented buffalo milk."*
> SHEENA

Workout. Besides the rather unique motivation, the only thing that's surprising about this one is that it took so long for a psycho to get into a gym. Showers, locker rooms, and lots of bouncing exercisers should have made it one of the natural habitats of the psycho killer. Considering the potential, this one's disappointingly light in terms of nudity, but there's enough exercise footage to make up a "Twenty Minute Workout." In between the scenes of aerobicized jiggle, there are lots of hackings, stabbings, and jabbings with a giant safety pin, mostly off-camera. This one had the potential to be vigorously sleazy, but it lacks conviction, so what we've got is very routine, mechanical stuff, perhaps a touch stupider and more amateurish than usual. Twelve bodies; inferior blood; Teresa Vander Woude briefly unzips her top; no tension or suspense; a phenomenally stupid policeman; several boring fistfights; lots and lots of disco music.

Bargain-Basement Bloodletters

DON'T ANSWER THE PHONE! *(1980)*
wr Robert Hammer and Michael D. Castle; dir Robert Hammer

An overweight psycho (sexually hung-up, misogynistic variety) with a penchant for strangling lingerie-clad young women terrorizes Los Angeles, while a stupid cop and a radio psychologist try to catch him. The first 15 minutes or so of this display a certain ugly energy, then everybody starts to talk — macho police chat, psychoanalytical babble, psychotic raving. It's all badly written, woodenly delivered, cheaply shot, and very tedious. That we see the stranglings, but only get to hear about what the psycho does to the bodies afterwards is an uncharacteristic lapse into good taste, as this one tries hard to be nasty and unpleasant, and generally succeeds. This is the kind of violence-against-women movie everyone complains about, and only an overriding ineptitude keeps it from being completely repugnant. Five bodies; breasts; no blood; no suspense; no production values; no interest. Strictly a wrong number.

THE DEMON *(1981)*
wr, prod, dir Percival Rubens

No demon, but there is a completely unidentified psycho who wears a glove with steel claws on it and who likes to put clear plastic bags over the heads of his victims. After he bloodlessly bumps off a couple of folks, he stalks a pair of topless nursery-school teachers. In an unrelated subplot, Cameron Mitchell is on hand as a psychic investigator who takes a bullet in the forehead. The only interesting thing here — besides the gratuitous breasts — is the location. They drive on the left, and there's a curious mix of accents, which suggests that it has been shot in Australia or New Zealand. *Why* it was made, and what Mr. Ruben thought he was doing, are much more difficult issues. Cam, of course, is always good for a few unintended laughs, but nothing that makes this one worth the trouble. Five bodies; bloodless; braless; much stupider, shoddier, and duller than usual.

WATCH ME WHEN I KILL *(1981, Italian, dubbed)*
dir Anthony Bido

Not a psycho-slasher flick, and the only point of the title is to sucker you into thinking it is one. In fact, this is a wretchedly dubbed, terribly made, thoroughly stupid mystery about revenge for some wartime atrocity. Tedious even at fast-forward.

EVIL JUDGEMENT *(1984, Canadian)*
wr Victor Montesano and Claudio Castravelli; dir Claudio Castravelli

What should have been a straightforward little slasher opus about a psycho judge who escapes from the asylum to mete out some capital punishment got all muddled up in a confusion of plots concerning the Mafia, a crooked cop, a would-be dancer who thinks about turning tricks, her petty-thief boyfriend who's phobic about hookers, and the double for the judge who's apparently been taking his place in an important trial. Golly! What a dull, dreary, amateurish mess this one is. Six bodies; marginal mayhem; no skin; no blood; no brains; much stupider than usual.

BLUE MURDER *(1985, Canadian, made for TV)*
wr Charles Wiener and Geoffrey Pico; dir Charles Wiener
Also released as *The Porn Murders*.

From the description on the box — a psycho is wiping out porno filmmakers — you'd think this would have all the elements for some serious sleaze, but it turns out to be an appallingly bad, numbingly dull movie made for Canadian television, and tame even for TV. No skin; no gore; no brains; no pace; no point.

NAIL GUN MASSACRE *(1985)*
wr and prod Terry Lofton; dir Bill Leslie and Terry Lofton

Six months after a young woman was raped by a crew of louts from a construction company, someone is using the title tool to attach construction workers, their girlfriends, and miscellaneous passersby to trees, the highway, and each other. The killer wears a motorcycle helmet, drives a hearse, and speaks through Darth Vader's echo chamber to make little jokes after each nailing. As the box says, "It's cheaper than a chainsaw," and this little backyard Texas number certainly is just that, but it's rather cheerfully so and it does show a good grasp of some of the essentials. While the splatter is nothing special and the stuff between the nailings is worse than clunky, the body count is significant, as are the considerable charms of Staci Gordon, Shelly York, and Kit Mitchell. Fifteen nailings; a fair amount of blood; a severed hand; a crotch-spiking; ample breasts; seriously stupid police; no suspense, but silly enough to keep you interested.

TRUTH OR DARE *(1986)*
wr Tim Ritter; dir Yale Wilson

There's certainly no shortage of mayhem in this one. There's a finger chopped off, a chest cut open, a tongue ripped out, and a facial performed with a hunting knife (all self-inflicted); there's an eye skewered out, a hand cut off, and an exploding head (all in dream sequence); there's the old pencil-in-the-eyeball, several hit-and-runs, some machine-gunnings, two explosions, a chainsawing, a clubbing, and a bullet in the forehead. I think it's all supposed to be in fun — kind of a slasher version of **THE EVIL DEAD** — but I'm not entirely sure, since it's so badly made that the only real laughs are unintentional. As for the abundant gore, there's probably nothing you couldn't do just as effectively yourself with things commonly found in the kitchen. Looking as though its budget were in the high three figures, this one's strictly for those who collect awesomely cheap movies. Innumerable bodies; glimpsed breasts; a variety of loonies;

no plot to get in the way. Filmed in Jupiter, Florida, home to Burt Reynolds.

CRAZY FAT ETHEL II *(1987, made for video)*
wr and dir Nick Philips

Thirteen years after the title character gave the chop to a bunch of people who stood between her and the refrigerator, she is released from the asylum, and while she's older and somewhat slimmer, she's still hungry. You really want to like a movie with this title, put out by a company called "Chop-Em-Ups Video," which identifies its product as being "schlock horror video at its best." Unfortunately, you can't. About half of the 70 minutes here consists of flashback footage from the original, which isn't listed in the reference books but looks like it was made in the early '70s. At the time, it must have been a contender for cheapest and cheesiest — a position that was secure until this sequel, which makes all of the bargain-basement efforts noted above seem lavish and professional by comparison. The original might have been vigorously awful enough to be worth a couple of laughs, but this one is just painfully dreary. If you're really perverse, you're going to want to see for yourself, but don't say I didn't warn you. Four bodies (plus seven in flashback); blood as phony as any on record; no skin.

THE RIPPER
Jack is back . . . in Tulsa; see Festival 9.
THE SLAYER
Nightmare psycho; see Festival 13.

FESTIVAL 20

* * *

THE KILLER NEXT DOOR
Friendly Neighborhood Madmen

"If you could see inside my head . . . you'd run."
— *Bloody Wednesday*

The movies that follow all focus on psychopaths, but in somewhat different ways than the descendants of *Halloween* and *Friday the 13th* in the preceding festivals. Here the goal tends to be suspense rather than mayhem (though there may still be a fair amount of that) and/or an attempt to present the descent into madness in a plausible way. (Most of these could just as easily have been included with the Chiller Thrillers in the second volume, but I decided to keep all my loonies in the same bin.) These movies are not really clones, and might well have been produced even if *Halloween* had never been made, and are thus much less formulaic in their approach. While the quality is decidedly uneven — from quite effective to flat, to hilarious — the variety in the way the material is handled is welcome. The era of the masked slice-and-dicer may be over, but the friendly neighborhood madman, whose cinematic roots go back decades farther, will continue as long as his real-life counterparts turn up in the news.

Innocuous Killers

EYES OF A STRANGER (1980)
wr Mark Jackson and Eric L. Bloom; dir Ken Wiederhorn

A sicko scuzball is rape/murdering young women in Key Biscayne, and a feisty TV reporter (Lauren Tewes) gets the idea that the psycho is a nondescript nerdo living in her apartment building. She has something of a personal stake, because her younger sister Tracy (Jennifer Jason Leigh) is now psychosomatically blind, deaf, and mute as the result of a childhood assault. Acting on her hunch, Lauren turns the tables and phones the killer; when he figures out who the caller is, he goes after Tracy, thus reprising *Wait Until Dark* (1967). There are some interesting possibilities in this that should have been more fully developed and it sorely needs a few twists, but it is efficiently and professionally made, and the two women are more than simply passive screamers. Despite the fact that Tom Savini is credited with the special effects, almost all the mayhem is off-camera and there's scarcely any blood. To compensate, there are a number of topless women. (The movie showing on the television, by the way, is *Shock Waves*, the director's 1977 high-concept opus about underwater Nazi zombies.)

MANIAC *(1980)*
wr C. A. Rosenberg and Joe Spinell; dir William Lustig

Co-writer Spinell, a familiar character actor, plays Frank Zito, a schizo sicko who gets even with his dead mother by savagely killing women, scalping them, and then nailing their hair to the mannequins he keeps in his room. Banned in parts of Canada, this is one of the more notorious slasher flicks and one of the grimmest. There is no suspense surrounding the series of victims being stalked, and while Spinell is plausible as the creep, that doesn't mean we want to watch him or give a shit about what makes him tick. Instead, this features what Tom Savini calls some of the goriest effects he's ever done — stabbings, throat-slittings, a head blown apart by a shotgun blast, a scalping, and a head ripped off in a dream sequence — but he doesn't have anything good to say about the film as a whole. Far too sordid to be any fun, this is the kind of movie that justifies the criticism of the genre, and that even die-hard psycho fans don't bother defending. Seven bodies; explicit mayhem; abundant blood; Gail Lawrence takes a very quick bath; lots of psychotic ramblings and interior monologues; much nastier than usual.

HONEYMOON *(1985, Canadian/French co-production)*
wr Philippe Setbon, Patrick Jamain, and Robert Geoffrion; dir P. Jamain

A young French woman (Nathalie Baye) arranges a marriage of convenience in order to stay in New York, then her nominal husband (John

Shea) turns up at her apartment with other ideas. Although innocuous-looking, he turns out to have more than a few problems . . . which means Nathalie does, too. And given the illegality of what she's done, there's no one she can go to for help. The situation contains the elements for a nice taut little thriller, but it's too leisurely in developing, and too slowly paced and predictably plotted to generate the necessary tension. Likewise, although Baye gives a believable performance, Shea doesn't manage to convey the bland, smiling menace that his character should have. While this is not really bad, it's all rather plodding and flat, and thus nothing very special.

MURDERLUST *(1986, direct to cassette)*
wr James Lane; dir Donald James

Steve Belmont is your typical guy next door — he has a job, hoists a few beers with the boys, teaches Sunday school at his church, and, when he has a little spare time, kills prostitutes and dumps their bodies in the Mojave Desert. There is no question that serial killers are fascinating subjects, and that they can sometimes work in a low-budget movie, even one without good production values or competent acting. Indeed, a degree of amateurishness can add an effective gritty edge to things, if there's energy and we can believe in the killer. This one comes close to turning its inadequacies into assets, but doesn't quite manage to pull it off. Eli Rich does a good job as Steve, suggesting the deeply buried insecurities that lie behind his murderous rage, but we never get to see him act out his compulsion, and thus the movie lacks the necessary edge. (Either I saw a heavily cut version, or else the filmmakers showed an excess of "good taste" by never presenting the actual murders; for once, violence against women would not have been gratuitous, as it's central to the understanding of this character/personality type.) As it is, we never quite get grabbed by this guy, and thus it's hard to overlook the many shortcomings of the script and the acting.

VIDEO MURDERS *(1987, direct to cassette)*
wr and dir Jim McCullough, Jr.

A troubled mama's boy (Eric Brown) with more than a couple of problems strangles women in Bossier City, Louisiana, recording the proceedings with a video camera for his later enjoyment. Most of the movie is devoted to the second victim-to-be, the hostage situation that results, and the efforts of the police detective (John Fertitta) to find them before it's too late. Unfortunately, the psycho, the victim, and the cop are so bland, dumb, and boring that it's impossible to work up interest in any of them, nor do several lengthy chase sequences do much to enliven the tedium. Although this doesn't look too bad for a real cheapie, whatever minimal vitality the director's earlier **MOUNTAINTOP MOTEL MASSACRE** possessed is sadly lacking here.

THE STEPFATHER (1987)
wr Donald Westlake; dir Joseph Ruben

Jerry Blake is another typical, likable guy-next-door who only wants to have one of those happy, perfect families just like you see on television . . . and he keeps marrying widows with children in a effort to get it. But the kind of relationships about which Jerry fantasizes don't exist outside of sitcoms. So, when the reality fails to live up to the ideal, Jerry solves the problem by hacking his adopted family to pieces and moving on to try again. There are a lot of really good things in this movie, most especially Terry O'Quinn's chillingly plausible portrayal of the title character. Although there is some fairly explicit violence, the primary aim is suspense rather than gore, and this generally manages to deliver a fair amount of it. While I don't think this is as good as some early reviews suggested — it falls short of building the really hard edge of tension it needs — this is still a pretty nifty little thriller, well worth checking out.

Flipping Out

FADE TO BLACK (1980)
wr and dir Vernon Zimmerman

Wimpish outsider Eric Binford (Dennis Christopher) is obsessed with the movies to the point that he tries to make his reality match up with his film fantasies. Inspired by Richard Widmark in *Kiss of Death*, he pushes his wheelchair-bound aunt (who's actually his mother) down the stairs. Then he dresses up like Dracula, Hopalong Cassidy, the Mummy, and James Cagney to get even with those who have been nasty to him. There are a number of fairly good things in this one. Christopher does a decent job with the descent into madness, managing to make the character sympathetic, and Linda Kerridge is really fine as the Marilyn Monroe look-alike; clips from old movies and references to others are used to good effect; and there is some wit and intelligence. However, I don't find this as clever as it might have been; the pace often drags and too many of the secondary characters are badly written and poorly acted. Still, while I don't think this is as successful as some reviewers do, it's certainly more ambitious than most psycho slasher flicks, and not without some elements of interest. With an early appearance by Mickey Rourke as a lout.

MACABRE *(1980, Italian, dubbed)*
wr Pupi Avati, Roberto Gandus, Lamberto Bava, and Antonio Avati; dir Lamberto Bava

Considering the elements that are at the heart of this one — a nasty pubescent girl who drowns her younger brother, and her mother who nightly makes love to a severed head she keeps in the freezer — you'd think that it would have a good chance of delivering some energetically creepy kinks. Instead, in the tradition of the Italian psycho-thriller, it turns out to be remarkably boring — all portentous atmosphere and excruciatingly slow pace, with no logic, sense, or suspense. Some reviewers claim to have liked this one, also known as *The Frozen Terror*, but it left me cold.

DEMENTED *(1980)*
wr Alex Rebar; dir Arthur Jeffreys

Released after confinement in a sanitarium following a traumatic gang rape, wealthy suburbanite Linda (Sallee Elyse) is having a little trouble coping. She whimpers, screams, and has bad dreams — as her psychiatrist tells her, in the argot of the trade, "You went through a very trying ordeal and your mind is bogged down with a closetful of memories." Well, it gets more and more bogged down, until four teenage assholes from the neighborhood sneak into her house, then it breaks free with a vengeance. Thinking the boys are the original rapists, she goes after two of them with a meat cleaver, shotguns one, and castrates and stabs the fourth. Everything about this one is cheap and unconvincing, from the mayhem to the interminable dull conversations and wooden acting, to the static and mechanical direction. About the only bright spot in it all is Sallee Elyse, who's so far out of her histrionic depth that we watch her descent into dementia with a certain painful fascination. While it is not up to the classic status of the following entry, collectors of ridiculous cinematic crackups will find this one a minor, but none the less welcome, addition.

NIGHT WARNING *(1981)*
wr Stephen Breimer; dir William Asher

This is a somewhat curious effort, very much in the school of *What Ever Happened to Baby Jane?* with the injection of some contemporary splatter at the end. When three-year-old Billy's parents are killed in a car accident — a spectacular stunt that opens the movie — he is raised by his possessive, repressed Aunt Cheryl (Susan Tyrrell). Fourteen years later, Billy (Jimmy McNichol) is talking about going away to college and Auntie is going seriously around the bend. Early on, in a fit of sexual frustration, she kills a homosexual TV repairman, then says he was trying to rape her. Bo Svenson, the homophobic police captain, isn't buying it, believing instead that Billy is both gay and the murderer, and then spends most of the movie trying to prove it. Meanwhile, Aunt Cheryl runs through the textbook of sexual pathologies and grows battier by the minute, building to a homicidal rampage in which she kills most of the principal actors. This movie is almost laughably overwrought, heavy-handed, and contrived, with a centerpiece — Tyrrell's mad act — the likes of which has not been seen since the scenery-chewers of Joan Crawford's late period. Indeed, she makes Bo's painfully overdrawn portrayal of rampant redneck homophobia seem positively understated. The Academy of Science-Fiction, Fantasy and Horror Films named this the best horror flick of 1982, which suggests the pickings must have been pretty slim. Still, Tyrrell keeps it from being dull, and it's not every day that you get to see an actress rev it up to full rolling dementia. As a bonus, those curious about the customarily hidden assets of Julia Duffy (Stephanie on the "Newhart" TV show) will have their questions answered.

> *"Oh, my God! We're going to spend the weekend there?"*
> APRIL FOOL'S DAY

THE BOYS NEXT DOOR *(1985)*
wr Glen Morgan and James Wong; dir Penelope Spheeris

"TWO YOUTHS ON KILLING SPREE!" — that's the way the tabloids might headline this story about a seemingly unmotivated murderous rampage. But these reports, after the fact and based on observation from the outside, do not address the real issues: How could something like this happen? What are the killers thinking of? What was it like for them? This compelling little movie answers those questions, from the killers' perspective. Bo (Charlie Sheen) and Roy (Maxwell Caulfield) — the title boys — are alienated and disaffected, facing what they see as a bleak and pointless future in their central California town. Bo has a slightly better grip on things, but Roy carries so much rage and violence that it is only a matter of time until he explodes. Detonation occurs on the night of their high-school graduation as they head for Los Angeles for some fun, which for them turns out to be steadily escalating levels of violence. The first third of the movie, establishing their mindset, is a little stiff, but once they get on the road, it becomes completely engrossing. The two leads are frighteningly believable, especially in the way they regard their casual violence as though it were no more real than a Saturday-morning cartoon. Very potent stuff.

BLOODY WEDNESDAY *(1985)*
wr Philip Yordan; dir Mark G. Gilhuis

No doubt inspired by the massacre at the McDonald's in San Diego, this traces the not-so-gradual disintegration of Harry Curtis (Raymon Elmendorf) that culminates in his taking a Uzi and wiping out everyone in a neighborhood café. As presented here, Harry is an average, nondescript guy for whom things no longer fit. His marriage ends, he loses his job, he's arrested for indecent exposure. He doesn't know what's happening to him — and has no one to turn to for help and support. As he becomes increasingly disconnected from reality, he begins to hallucinate, and then picks up the gun. Harry's isolation and descent into violent madness is a little heavy-handed and contrived but is made somewhat plausible by Elmendorf's surprisingly competent, sympathetic, and low-key performance. However, the movie is neither all that interesting nor very well done in any other respect, and, since we know where we're heading, we eventually grow impatient for Harry to get down to it. While this has a few good moments, the whole ends up being rather flat and pointless.

WHITE OF THE EYE *(1986)*
wr China and Donald Cammell; dir Donald Cammell

In a small Arizona town near Tucson, someone is ritually sacrificing young women. Suspicion points to Paul White (David Keith), a likable guy with a family and a thriving business in customized audio equipment. We start off thinking that Paul will be proving his innocence here, then, through an odd turn, he is exposed as the psycho killer. Eventually he flips out entirely, paints his face, straps dynamite to his chest, and menaces his wife (Cathy Moriarty) in the long concluding segment. There may, in fact, be a decent little thriller lurking somewhere in here, but at an extremely leisurely 2½ hours, it has little chance to show itself. Some reviewers quite liked this one, comparing the director to Nicolas Roeg (with whom he once worked), but I'm not a big Roeg fan and felt that, despite a few decent moments, there was too much film-school self-consciousness and sophomoric self-indulgence.

THE HOUSEKEEPER *(1986, Canadian)*
wr Elaine Waisglass, dir Ousama Rawi

This "thriller," based on Ruth Rendell's novel *A Judgement in Stone*, could have been an interesting and subtle psychological study of how a handicap — illiteracy caused by dyslexia — can lead to shame, isolation, and ultimately violent rage. Or it could have been an amusingly heavy-handed treatment of scenery-gobbling dementia. I suspect the filmmakers were aiming for the former, but kind of ended up with the latter, then didn't know what to do with it. The tagline on the box — "She cooks ... she cleans ... she kills" — suggests that someone decided to push its camp appeal, but it's really too stiff to have much of that. Rita Tushingham as Eunice, the title dyslexic, settles for being strained, intense, and withdrawn, and only Jackie Burroughs really lets 'er fly with her awesomely overwrought performance as the religious loony who befriends Eunice. Some regional curiosity value in the fact that the featured players include Shelley Peterson, the wife of the premier of Ontario, and Jonathan Crombie, the son of a former mayor of Toronto, but, as Eunice says before she blows away one of her employers, "You never really cared for me." Indeed.

Stalked and Chased

DEADLY GAMES *(1980)*
wr and dir Scott Mansfield

Someone is bumping off young women in Fresno . . . but not nearly fast enough, considering how they yammer away. This one's nothing but chat — on telephones, in restaurants, alfresco — about sex, about relationships, about feelings. After about twenty minutes, you want to throttle them yourself. And the worst offender is the nominal heroine (Jo Ann Harris) who chirps nonstop through the whole damn movie. There is a feeble little mystery buried beneath the great lumps of gab, but it may be even dumber and less interesting than the conversation. With Alexandra Morgan as the bimbo who takes her shirt off. As cat-and-mouse games go, this one's strictly a dog.

A STRANGER IS WATCHING *(1982)*
wr Earl MacRauch and Victor Miller; dir Sean S. Cunningham

Sean Cunningham follows *Friday the 13th* with a different kind of psycho, based on a Mary Higgins Clark novel. Two years after eleven-year-old Julie (Shawn Von Schreiber) saw her mother brutally murdered, the killer (Rip Torn) returns and kidnaps the girl and TV reporter Kate Mulgrew, taking them to his hideout in the tunnels under Grand Central Station. Meanwhile, the man Julie mistakenly identified as the murderer is scheduled to be executed. I'm not sure why this doesn't work. The cast is good, it's well produced, and it has some interesting locations. But the subplot concerning the impending execution of the wrong man is so undeveloped that it just gets in the way, and the main focus — the kidnapping and the hostages' attempts to escape — never manages to generate the tension necessary to really grab our attention. While not really bad, this is just a little too flat and straightforward to have much impact at all, and thus it's not too surprising that hardly anyone was watching when this first came out.

TORMENT *(1985)*
wr and dir Samson Aslanian and John Hopkins

A menopausal madman (William Witt), filled with middle-aged rage against young women, kills a couple of them off-camera in San Francisco. As it turns out, he's the father of Jennifer (Taylor Gilbert), the perky, young fiancée of the detective who's investigating the crimes. As it further turns out, Jennifer is spending the weekend at the large isolated house of her future mother-in-law (Eve Brenner), a tough old bat in a wheelchair. Care to guess who shows up to play a game of cat-and-mouse with the two women? If you think the setup sounds a touch contrived, the way in which it plays itself out manipulates the hapless characters far more cruelly than anything loony Dad is capable of. Lacking in any real tension and suspense, this one's main distinction may be that its psycho — who is slashed, stabbed, shotgunned, clubbed, banged, and stepped on — receives far more punishment than he dishes out. Although this does eventually get silly, hammy, and/or hysterical enough to provide a few unintended laughs, the title gives a good sense of what the unwary viewer is likely to experience.

THE WIND *(1986)*
wr Niko Mastorakis and Fred C. Perry; dir Niko Mastorakis

In this completely formulaic "thriller," Meg Foster (of the bizarre light blue eyes) plays a successful mystery writer trapped alone in a house and menaced by a psycho killer (Wings Hauser doing a Bruce Dern imitation). The problem here is not that the situation is so familiar, but that the execution is every bit as mechanical as the premise: there are no twists, the violence doesn't jolt, the shocks fail to surprise, and, for all the prowling through shadowy, back-lit corridors, no suspense is generated. The setting is the Greek village of Monemvassia, but for all the use made of this exotic locale, the movie might just as well have been set in the traditional isolated house in the woods. The title breeze blows incessantly (the credits list four wind-machine operators), but other than rattling the shutters, it has nothing to do with the story. Indeed, very little in this limp effort seems to have anything to do with anything. As the village police chief says, "Anyone who goes up there in this wind is either stupid or crazy." The choice is yours.

> *"Why should nature suddenly break its own laws?"*
> NIGHT OF THE ZOMBIES

PERFECT VICTIMS *(1988)*
wr Shuki Levy, Joe Hailey, and Bob Barron; dir Shuki Levy

Infected with AIDS and consumed with rage against women, a psycho loner stalks, then drugs and rapes, attractive young women in order to pass the disease along to as many people as he can. Despite what is obviously not a fun subject, this movie is pretty decently made and generally avoids exaggerating what is already quite grim and sensational. Dividing its time among the rapist, the two young models who are the first victims we see, the woman who runs the modeling agency, and the police officer in charge of the investigation blurs the focus somewhat, but otherwise this is briskly paced and moderately intriguing. Tom Dugan does a good job as the sicko, and the movie builds to quite a tense and suspenseful concluding sequence with the three women being trapped and menaced by the creep. While not an absolute grabber, this is an acceptable little thriller and — for what it's worth — the first that I'm aware of to treat this most uncomfortable subject in this way.

Highway Stalkers

ROAD GAMES *(1981, Australian)*
wr Everett DeRoche; dir Richard Franklin

A psycho is killing young women as he moves across the vast, empty deserts of Western Australia. On his trail is a self-educated, poetry-quoting trucker (Stacey Keach) carrying a load of pig carcasses, and the runaway heiress (Jamie Lee Curtis) who hitched a ride with him. Keach suspects the driver of a green van, but — through a number of coincidences — he, in turn, is suspected by the police of being the killer, while the real murderer plays cat-and-mouse "road games" with him. Both the script and the direction are a little flat and could have offered more twists and surprises, but an attempt is made to develop characters, and we do get interested in Keach and Curtis. While not an absolute grabber, this does deliver enough genuine suspense to make it a better-than-average thriller.

THE HITCHER *(1986)*
wr Eric Red; dir Robert Harmon

A Lone Star version of the preceding entry that, although flashier and much better known, is much less engaging. While driving across the barren expanse of Texas, C. Thomas Howell gives a ride to Rutger Hauer who, for no particular reason, has been chopping people up along the highway. He quickly finds himself playing violent and sinister games with the psycho, trying to elude both Hauer and the police, who think Howell is responsible for the carnage. The extended chase that ensues is right out of a nightmare, as is the movie's logic. Events happen randomly, without regard for time, space, or common sense, and while there are certainly plenty of shocks and surprises, the absence of any recognizable reality keeps us from getting involved in what's going on. If this were just another slasher cheapie, none of this would make much difference. However, because this is so well made in other respects — slickly and stylishly shot, well acted, quickly paced, and with some really spectacular chases and car stunts — it's shortcomings end up seeming that much more disappointing. Sure, pick this one up, but be prepared to be taken for a bit of a ride.

IV

GREAT QUESTS AND DANGEROUS JOURNEYS

Fantasy Adventures in Strange New Worlds

If you've spent any time exploring the video fringe, you've probably come across quite a few fantasy adventures. They might be defined, most simply, as action movies set in worlds that, if not completely unreal or imaginary, differ in significant ways from our own.

The fantasy adventure has to be considered one of the predominant genres of the 1980s. Its popularity — for filmmakers, at least — is directly traceable to the success of a handful of movies, the most obvious and influential being *Conan the Barbarian*, *Raiders of the Lost Ark*, *Road Warrior*, and *Star Wars*. In these movies, form counts for almost as much as content — the look and the style can be as important as the plot and the characters. Indeed, the success of these movies may have been due, in no small part, to the skill with which they created their imaginary worlds. In other words, they achieved one of the things that only movies can do — they showed us things we'd never seen before, perhaps never imagined. And we ate it up.

Filmmakers have been happy to keep dishing out more of the same in the hope that we still have this appetite. As a result four very specific and distinct types of fantasy adventure have emerged, each clearly derived from one of those four hit films. These four are virtually mini-genres in which the same world, the same look and style, the same characters and conflicts appear again and again. (One clone is a ripoff; ten ripoffs are a mini-genre.)

Sometimes the imitation is so blatant, slavish, or inept as to be comical. Occasionally something new and original may be added, but most often what we get is essentially what we've seen before, executed with varying degrees of skill and, perhaps, with enough variations on the basic conventions and formulas to keep things moderately interesting. In all cases, however, there is rarely any possibility of mistaking the type of fantasy adventure presented or its origins, influences, and models.

Although most of the fantasy adventures in your video store are likely to be descended from *Conan, Raiders, Road Warrior,* or *Star Wars,* not all are; the last two festivals in this section present other varieties of the form. Regardless of the particular style, though — whether an original or a ripoff — there are certain distinguishing characteristics shared by nearly every fantasy adventure.

To begin with, these movies are set in imaginary worlds, worlds that are distant in space and/or time from our own, that never were or never will never be. In these settings the logic of our world does not necessarily apply; if it does, it's been altered, often by the addition of supernatural or technological forces.

This is not to suggest, however, that a fantasy world is a world without logic. On the contrary, it has to be internally consistent with the rules established for it; it has to follow its own logic.

A lot of the movies in this section blithely ignore this necessity. They borrow at random from their sources but ignore the kind of reasoning that makes the fantasy vision cohere. So, what we get is style without sense and lots of unanswerable questions: "What do these people eat?" or "Why are they wearing such bizarrely impractical outfits?" A fantasy will work even if we don't believe in the reality of what we're seeing, but not if that reality has no innate plausibility. Failure to establish this — and believe me, there are a lot of failures — results in the creation of a world that is not so much imaginary as ridiculous. (Of course, ridiculousness has its own rewards, and what it fails to provide in terms of satisfying fantasy, it can more than compensate for with outright hilarity.)

In fantasy adventures, the setting, or the imaginary world — its landscape, its social order, its lifeforms, its technology — provides the "fantasy" and the characters and plot, the "adventure." All but a few of the movies in this section share a narrative structure. The story that they all tell is based on the quest romance — one of the oldest and most pervasive narrative terms that provides the underlying structure for

> *"Your cassettes are destroying innocent people."*
> REMOTE CONTROL

countless myths, heroic legends, and fairy tales, as well as the more contemporary versions of these forms, such as the Western and the James Bond-type thriller. ("Romance," as used here, does not refer to a love story, but is the medieval term for a narrative about chivalry and epic adventures.)

The world of the quest romance is one in which good and evil are clearly delineated, a world of black and white with very few shadings in between. Whether evil is represented by a fearsome creature such as a dragon or a snake god; a powerful, sinister sorceror; or the armies of a brutal tyrant, it has very nearly triumphed in the world, and only one man stands between it and total domination. That man is the Hero.

The Hero may assume his mantle as though born to it (as indeed he often is), or he may be coerced into reluctantly accepting his role. In either case, he possesses exceptional powers — great strength and endurance, great knowledge and resourcefulness — that both elevate him above mere mortals and isolate him from them. He may need companions and colleagues to fulfill his mission, but the final confrontation with evil is his alone, and he always remains a man apart.

In allegorical terms, the classic quest romance is a story of death, redemption, and rebirth. The forces of evil have enslaved the world (or threaten to), rendering it barren and sterile, a desolate place oppressed by brutality, fear, and despair. The hero is the redeemer. By defeating the evil, often at great personal risk, he releases the world from its bondage. The darkness lifts, and the world is free, reborn to flourish once again.

In practical terms, the quest romance involves the hero in a great adventure. The ultimate goal of the quest could be a fabled treasure or an instrument of great mystical power, the exacting of revenge or the rescue of a captive princess, a crusade to overthrow a usurper and restore the rightful ruler, or the search for a Promised Land. Whatever the goal is, it's a long way off and the journey to it is a perilous one, marked by terrible obstacles and harrowing encounters.

This may seem an inflated way to introduce what are, for the most part, cheap ripoffs of big box-office hits, but even trash has form, structure, and antecedents. A filmmaker who wanted only to make a few bucks from a low-budget *Conan* or *Road Warrior* ripoff still ends up producing a movie that fits into a much larger tradition. In this regard, it is worth noting that George Lucas acknowledges that Joseph Campbell's studies of the hero in myth and legend played a significant role in the creation of the *Star Wars* saga. Clearly, Lucas feels that this is a potent narrative form. And several hundred million movie goers around the world would seem to agree with him.

As the reviews that follow make clear, I'm rather partial to the movies in this section. Through an energetic display of imagination — or an energetic lack thereof — fantasy adventures can, I've found, much more often than not be relied upon to provide a fair amount of entertainment. So, whether you're on a quest for good, solid, mindless action or a healthy shot of vigorous silliness, you'll find plenty of both in the 100-plus titles included here.

FESTIVAL 21

* * *

PECS AND FLEX
Sagas of Sword and Sorcery

"I will have no peace until the last damned Ungat will have paid
for this infamous deed with his life."
— *The Invincible Barbarian*

There's no mistaking the movies in this festival when you come across them in your video store. The titles nearly always indicate what kind of fantasy adventure they are, and the hyperbolic illustrations on the boxes leave no doubt.

Yes! It's pecs and flex to the max, as pumped-up pieces of beefcake hack and chop their way through savage hordes in titanic combat with evil wizards in a distant — and much weirder — age. These are the sagas of sword and sorcery — a genre in which the look is much more important than the logic. And the look is that of a Frank Frazetta drawing in which a leather-and-fur-clad behemoth wields an enormous broadsword as he battles a fearsome and fantastic opponent.

Conan the Barbarian (1982) was the movie that brought the look to life. Although it is clearly descended from the sword-and-sandal epics and the mythological fantasies (*Hercules, Sinbad*, etc.) that briefly flourished in the late '50s and early '60s, *Conan* gave us a different world — a world older than those of our myths, a world that lies outside our knowledge of history and tradition. Based on the fantasies of Robert E. Howard, it is a world of magic and strange creatures, a harsh and brutal age in which everything — the landscape, the architecture, and, above all, the warriors — is of legendary proportions.

In the massive frame of Arnold Schwarzenegger, the fantasy warrior became flesh, and in the huge sets and lavish productions, Howard's Hyperborean Age was given detail, shape, and substance. While not exactly wildly original, *Conan* was still not quite like anything we'd ever seen before in the movies. And since we indicated through box-office receipts that we liked it, we have been given lots of opportunities to see it again.

Like *Conan*, all but a few of the movies in this festival present a version of the quest romance that is very close to that found in medieval epics and classical myths and legends. As always, it is a story of Good vs. Evil, but here everything is considerably larger than life — including the Hero, who most frequently turns out to be an enormous slab of beefcake, waving a sword that most people couldn't even lift.

Although the Hero's quest can take many different forms, the Beefcake, taking his lead from Conan, goes into action either to effect a rescue or to exact revenge. Most typically, a princess will need rescuing or the slaughter of the Beefcake's family or village will need avenging. Quite often, the quest is multipurpose — saving the princess, exacting justice, placing the hero on the throne, and restoring order and prosperity to the land.

If you watch more than a couple of the movies in this festival, you'll realize that not only the stories but the telling of them are identical.

Frequently, they begin with a narrator — usually a pompous and portentous voice-over — briefly establishing the world ("In the Fourth Millennium of the Third Illumination . . ."), and setting the stage for the conflict to come. The narrator can also be used to explain periodically what's going on or to bridge awkward gaps in the story line.

Sometimes we join the hero in mid-career, but more often than not, as in *Conan*, we begin with his birth. If this is the case, you can be sure that within minutes of the opening credits, savage hordes will descend upon our hero's village and slaughter everyone in it. Sometimes the carnage is exacted for the sheer sport of it; other times, it's an attempt on the part of the evil ruler to thwart a prophecy that foretells the end of his reign at the hand of a child born in the village. Naturally, the infant Beefcake-to-be survives, but he has been brutally stripped of his parents, his people, and his place in society.

Now, we jump ahead a few years, during which time evil has flourished throughout the land and the Hero has grown into a great rippling bruiser. He may not yet be aware of his heritage or heroic destiny, but you can bet all those muscles won't go to waste. Sure enough, before too long, something happens — often another massacre in the Hero's village, usually on his wedding day, with his bride-to-be being kidnapped in the process — that starts the Hero on his great quest.

Any quest worthy of the name necessarily involves many stages. To begin with, the Hero may acquire a mentor, someone who knows the

> "He's less than a man...and more than a man."
> THE DEMON

Hero's real background or will give him the martial-arts training he needs for the battles ahead. Then, before the Hero can challenge the forces of evil, he usually needs to acquire some vital piece of equipment (a sword or shield or some other bit of magic junk) and/or some vital piece of information.

These stages, of course, involve many different adventures, giving the Beefcake ample opportunity to flash his sword and flex his dramatic assets. The stages also involve a hell of a lot of traveling footage — a cheap and easy way to fill the spaces between sword fights. Along the way, the Hero acquires some faithful companions — animals, comic-relief, wise old men, and/or sword-wielding bimbos — until, finally he is kitted out for the ultimate confrontation.

Not every movie in this festival tells precisely this story in precisely this way. Some were made without reference to *Conan*, and thus present a different vision of the fantasy world and a slightly different version of the basic quest. Most, though, are clearly descended from *Conan*, and in these we see the same narrative elements and formulas repeated from movie to movie with almost metronomic precision. Indeed, a number of the shoddier efforts, if approached the right way, can be quite fascinating in the inept and heavy-handed ways with which they utilize the basic components.

Of course, in a genre like this one, the story really only exists as an excuse for swordplay and spectacle, and the details of the narrative are far less important than the way they are executed. *Conan* spent about $21 million on it, and that buys a lot of style. Trying to reproduce giant spectacles for a small fraction of the cost results in, shall we say, a certain loss of impressiveness. Some of the movies that follow use a bit of ingenuity and creativity within their constraints. Others try to compensate for the diminished grandeur with other things, for example, sleaze and prurience. Still others, resolutely refusing to recognize their many and varied limitations (in terms of money, talent, and imagination), really let fly, and provide us with some of the tackiest and most hilariously ludicrous extravaganzas ever captured on celluloid.

Taken as a whole, not many of the sagas of sword and sorcery in this festival are what you'd call good movies, but quite a few of them do manage, one way or another, to be very entertaining ones.

Classic Quests

DRAGONSLAYER *(1981)*
wr Hal Barwood and Matthew Robbins; dir Matthew Robbins

The classic fable: a huge, ancient, leather-winged, fire-breathing dragon holds a kingdom in thrall, pacified only by the periodic sacrifice of a virgin chosen by lottery. An old magician (Ralph Richardson) is called upon to kill the dragon; when he dies, the task falls to his young apprentice (Peter MacNicol). Only things don't quite go the way you'd expect — for instance, MacNicol only serves to make matters worse — and the script has some dark shadings and complexities, as well as a few effective twists. This had a big budget, and it's beautifully shot, making good use of some stunning scenery in Wales and Scotland. The dragon, too, once we finally get to see him, is fairly impressive, as are some of the other visual effects. A subplot concerns the end of magic and superstition and the coming of Christianity; while more might have been done with this, the fact that it's there at all gives this one a bit more substance than this sort of fantasy usually has. While this is not a completely successful movie (the narrative doesn't really have much driving force), there are some interesting things about it; it's often spectacular to look at, and it's always a pleasure to watch Sir Ralph, even in a small part.

THE BEASTMASTER *(1982)*
wr Don Coscarelli and Paul Pepperman; dir Don Coscarelli

The Beefcake here is Marc Singer, who's out to avenge the murder of his parents and the extermination of his village. The gimmick is that he can communicate with animals, and he's accompanied on his quest by an eagle, two comic ferrets, and a very elderly tiger who's been dyed black. This one came out about six months after *Conan*, and while it only did about 20 per cent of the business, you could do a lot worse. It's dramatically shot (by the photographer of *Barry Lyndon*), and the sets, though cheesy, are grandiosely so, making it, and Singer, who brings some humor to the role, kind of fun to look at. We get a brief glimpse of Tanya Roberts's significant assets, and Rip Torn as Maax, the evil priest, gives a ludicrously hammy performance, in one of the most ridiculous putty noses you're ever likely to see. For the rest, it's the usual mix of swordplay, strange creatures, weird warriors, and costumes out of a leather freak's fantasy. At 120 minutes it goes on way too long — and seemingly refuses to end, building in series to several not-so-dramatic climaxes — but that's why you have fast-forward. Keep your expectations low, and this one's not too bad.

THE SWORD AND THE SORCEROR *(1982)*
wr Tom Karnowski, John Stuckmeyer, and Albert Pyun; dir Albert Pyun

The sword is a three-bladed affair that can shoot two of its blades like projectiles from a spear gun; it's wielded by a beefcake mercenary warrior with a steel glove, Talon (Lee Horsley), who's out to overthrow the evil king and restore the rightful heir. Xusia the sorceror (Richard Moll) is a greenish, decomposing creature raised from the dead, who also plans to seize the kingdom. He's easily the best thing in the movie but, since he can assume other shapes, he only appears in all his slimy splendor at the beginning and the end. In between, there's a very confusing jumble of plots and counterplots, punctuated with a lot of swordplay and a little dungeon torture. There are also some breasts from the royal harem, a few good effects (including a heart bursting out of a chest and a transformation scene involving Xusia), decent production values, and some really hammy performances. Above average, if only for Richard Moll and the fact that it's not dubbed.

KRULL *(1983)*
wr Stanford Sherman; dir Peter Yates

Instead of some earlier Heavy Metal Age, the setting for this one is the planet of Krull, but the look is still your basic medieval/studded leather, and the story, your basic young king/hero rescuing his princess/bride from the foul clutches of "The Beast" and saving the world from the army of the "Slayers." Naturally, the king and his companions have lots of adventures-encounters on the way, including a volcanic cavern, quicksand, a cyclops, a giant spider, and battles with the Slayers, whose helmets make them look like giant rhinoceros beetles. An estimated $27 million was lavished on this one, to the point that the movie is buried under the weight of its own overblown ponderousness. The conspicuous spending does not make up for the lack of creative energy here or the reliance on mechanical borrowing. While there are a few good effects — the Beast is not bad — the only fascination lies in trying to identify the sources for all the different bits stuck together to fill a long two hours. Too harsh? Perhaps, but this bloated lump cost more than many of the other movies in this festival combined, and for that I figure you should get something more than just the same old thing.

THE BARBARIANS *(1987)*
wr James R. Silke; dir Ruggero Deodato

Orphan twin boys are adopted by a troupe of entertainers who possess a magic ruby and who travel the weird lands, spreading pleasure. The queen of the troupe is captured by the evil tyrant (Richard Lynch, with long blond braids), the ruby is hidden, the performers are put out of business, and the twins are conscripted as slave labor. Ten or fifteen years later, no one else has aged, but the boys have turned into the Barbarian Brothers (Peter Paul and David Paul), identical twin slabs of well-oiled beefcake who promptly set about rectifying various problems. Before they can rescue the queen, they need to get the ruby . . . which is guarded by a dragon . . . which can only be killed by a magic sword . . . and so on. Along the way, they meet a wolfman and a reptileman and arm wrestle with George Eastman. Produced by Golan and Globus in Italy, this obviously had a decent budget, and consequently the production values are way above those typically found in the bargain basement. This has a good slick look, with lots of stuff filling the screen and entertaining costumes from Frederick's of Anachronia. It is also fast-paced and cheerful, and displays a good sense of its own silliness. Indeed, the Barbarian Boys are played as engaging buffoons, always squabbling among themselves, and take on their sacred quest much as they would a Saturday at the beach. Now if only someone would team them up with the Harris girls from **SORCERESS** . . .

Sagas of Swords and Sleazery

SORCERESS *(1982, partly dubbed)*
wr Jim Wynorski; dir Brian Stuart

After their mother is savagely murdered by an evil wizard, twin infant girls are endowed with fighting skills and powers of sorcery to enable them to exact revenge. Twenty years later, they have grown into the Harris sisters (Leigh and Lynette), the cheesecake avengers. When the wizard slaughters their adoptive parents, the girls bounce on a quest for revenge, accompanied by Beefcake Bob (Nelson), a bearded Viking, and a satyr. Along the way, they encounter guys in ape suits, a zombie army, and something that looks like a stuffed toy lion with batwings. They also discover the difference between boys and girls, and some of the interesting possibilities therein. This doesn't have much swordplay or action of any kind, but there is a lot of bimbo flesh, a few really tacky special effects, and some ludicrous dialog. Unfortunately, the jokey tone tends to be annoying rather than amusing. Still, there are a few real laughs, mainly in Leigh and Lynette's delivery. As possibly the first attempt to exploit the sleaze potential of the genre, this is not without some historical significance.

THE WARRIOR AND THE SORCERESS (1984)
wr and dir John Broderick

This presents the basic *Conan* world, but goes to other sources for its story. David Carradine plays a mysterious black-clad warrior who's referred to only as "The Dark One." He comes to a remote desert town, where two opposing factions — armies of hired thugs — contend for the control of the only well. Carradine hires on with one side, then the other, then plays them off against each other for his personal benefit. Remind you of anything? This is a fairly precise rendering of *A Fistful of Dollars*, with swords instead of six-guns; but since *Dollars* was itself a precise rendition of *Yojimbo*, maybe this marks something of a return to the samurai roots. Whichever, the end result is much better structured than is usually the case in this genre. With David Carradine in the lead, this is low on beefcake, but, to compensate, there's a welcome sense of fun and they've really upped the sleaze quotient. Lots of naked slave girls; Maria Socas, as the title sorceress, bares her remarkable dramatic assets throughout; and there's a striptease by a four-breasted exotic dancer that itself may be worth the price of the rental. There's also some pretty good swordplay (in one fight Carradine wipes out twenty-five opponents) and a couple of interesting creatures, including a telepathic monitor lizard. All in all, it looks like everyone involved with this one had a pretty good time, and it shows on the screen.

DEATHSTALKER *(1983)*
wr Howard Cohen; dir John Watson

Boy! This one has it all! There's beefcake galore; vast expanses of nubile slave flesh; gladiatorial combat; female mud wrestling; a giant boar-headed warrior; a carnivorous handpuppet that eats eyeballs and fingers; a body count in the upper twenties, including three decapitations, an arm-ripping, and a drawing-and-quartering; dwarfs; and enough magic junk — a sword, an amulet, and a chalice — for three movies. There's also a plot — something involving an evil wizard and a captive princess (Barbi Benton, amply demonstrating her qualifications for Playmate of the Year) — but you hardly notice it. Rick Hill is not bad as the beefcake hero, known to his friends as "Deathstalker," but when it comes to bare-chested warriors, Lana Clarkson steals the show. With virtually nothing in this one that's not gratuitous, it's pretty hard to resist — very definitely upper-echelon Sword and Sleazery.

DEATHSTALKER II *(1987, direct to cassette)*
wr Neil Ruttenberg; dir Jim Wynorski

Don't get taken in by this one. Other than the title, the only connection this has to the above-cited classic is some brief spliced-in footage from the original. The story concerns restoring a princess to the throne that is currently being occupied by her vampiric phantom double who's the creation of an evil sorceror. Like **SORCERESS** (which director Wynorski scripted), this one is almost entirely played for laughs (it's jokey and deliberately camp), which means that it's unfunny. John Terlesky, as this incarnation of 'Stalker, might have walked out of a beach-party movie, and Monique Gabrielle, as the dual bimbo princesses, gives an awesomely stiff performance, for which she is forgiven later in the movie when she reveals the qualities that earned her this demanding role. There's some bloodless swordplay, zombies that would embarrass even the Italians, a large lady wrestler, Maria Socas (**THE WARRIOR AND THE SORCERESS**) as the leader of your basic band of Amazon bimbos, and a lot of third-rate sitcom dialog. The only really good bits in this one are the out-takes that are run with the closing credits. They're very funny and would have made an enjoyable movie.

> *"We've got to stop the movie."*
> DEMONS

Warrior Women

RED SONJA *(1985)*
wr Clive Exton and George MacDonald Fraser; dir Richard Fleischer

Brigitte Nielsen (the ex-Mrs. Stallone) made her film debut in the title role, another mighty swordsperson from the novels of Robert E. Howard, creator of Conan. The central issue here is the same as that in **THE BLADE MASTER**: the "Talisman" — a glowing green hunk of magic junk — has fallen into the hands of an evil queen (Sandahl Bergman), and Sonja has to destroy it before it destroys the world. Arnold Schwarzenegger turns up periodically to help, and together they hack their way across the landscape. The sets are imposing and the costumes, fairly bizarre, but there is no narrative, just one long sword battle after another, none of which is exciting or effective. There's also a fight with a large reptilian creature and an earthquake with lots of tumbling chunks of papier-mâché, but not a microsecond of humor, intelligence, or energy. Brigitte, Arnold, and Sandahl all keep their shirts on, thus eliminating any possible interest... except for trying to decide which of them has the most trouble delivering the minimal lines.

BARBARIAN QUEEN *(1985)*
wr Howard R. Cohen; dir Hector Olivera

This is your basic slaughter-of-the-villagers-on-the-wedding-day with one of the newlyweds being taken prisoner. The variation here is that it's the prince who's the hostage, and it's his bride who, accompanied by two warrior bimbos, must avenge her people and rescue her lover. Considering that this was made by the folks who gave us **DEATHSTALKER**, and that the title character is played by Lana Clarkson — she was mighty impressive in her earlier appearance, carving a D-cup swath through the forces of evil — I came to this with pretty high expectations. Unfortunately, despite a fairly decent complement of sleaze — mostly an orgy of slave flesh in the harem set from *'Stalker* — it seems more concerned with swordplay than skin; even Lana and her companions only rarely unloose their dramatic assets (that's not to suggest that Lana doesn't look fetching in her spandex body armor). However, what this lacks in sleaze, it nearly makes up for in silliness. Our warrior honeys make their sacred mission of rescue and revenge seem more like an expedition to the mall to buy mascara. If bimbos with broadswords is what you want, you could do a lot worse.

SHE
Post-apocalyptic Amazons; see Festival 23.

Bargain-Basement Imports

THE INVINCIBLE BARBARIAN *(1983, Italian, dubbed)*
wr Peter Lombard; dir Frank Shannon

Unless you collect dreadful dubbed dialog ("I will have no peace until the last damned Ungat will have paid for this infamous deed with his life"), this one is so mind-numbingly awful it can actually destroy brain cells. A warrior named Zucan, who's not so much beefcake as a slab of suet, was born the "Chosen One." The people of his village were slaughtered at his birth and he was raised by a tribe of Amazon bimbos until it became time for him to fulfill his destiny and rid the world of a singularly unimpressive oppressor. Along the way, he hooks up with a breeder slave played by Sabrina Siani ("Get her ready for copulation"), who spends a good part of the time with talents on display. How stupid is this one? Well, pompous voice-over narration opens with the creation of the world, then shows us a couple of minutes of stock footage of tussling plasticine dinosaurs. Talk about starting at the beginning! We then jump ahead to "the Fourth Millennium of the Third Illumination" blah, blah, blah.... They don't come any cheaper, duller, or dumber than this one. Strictly for laughs.

THRONE OF FIRE *(1983, Italian, dubbed)*
wr Nino Marino; dir Franco Prosperi

Morrock, the smirking son of Belial, wants to rule the world, but before he can sit on the title piece of furniture, he must marry the princess and rightful heir. (The throne is so named because any usurper who sits on it is flame-broiled.) Of course, the princess (Sabrina Siana, quite fetching in a string bikini) tries to escape, assisted by a chunky piece of beefcake named Sigfried (Peter McCoy). Sig, it seems, is not the most adept warrior, since he makes three rescue attempts, each of which ends in his own capture. (Had he been less inept, the movie would've lasted only 30 minutes, so it's just as well he's not more efficient.) This has lots of hilarious dialog — including the classic, "Stop that friar!" — but for the rest, it's rather lethargic and lackluster, no more than routinely cheap and stupid. Still, it does provide a few laughs, as well as several opportunities to see Sabrina wave a sword around, so it's not a total loss.

CONQUEST *(1984, Italian-Spanish-Mexican, dubbed)*
wr Gino Capone, Jose A. De La Loma, Sr., and C. Vasallo; dir Lucio Fulci

This one, from the director of several of the messier Italian zombie flicks, is so peculiar in so many ways, I hardly know what to make of it. Most of the movie looks like it was shot through gauze, sometimes through so many layers the image nearly disappears. There's also a lot of haze, smoke, sepia filters, and lens flare. Except for the two warrior heroes, most of the characters wear either featureless masks or strange makeup, and the women rarely wear any clothes. And there's almost no dialog, but there is a lot of weird electronic music. The effect is very dreamlike — a surreal sword-and-sorcery hallucination that kind of floats along. What little plot there is concerns a tribe of guys in wolf suits and the sorceress they worship (Sabrina Siani, naked except for a gold mask) who, when she's not sucking the souls from severed heads, caresses her body with a snake. I don't think this is very good, but it is frequently interesting to look at despite its serious cheapness, and it is certainly a most bizarre variation on the form. Maybe for curiosity value?

LIONMAN II: THE WITCHQUEEN *(1983, Turkish)*
wr Johnny Byrne; dir Michael Arslan

If you're in the mood for wooden acting, absurd dialog, remarkably unexciting action sequences, and an inanely jumbled plot, this English-language Turkish production should do quite nicely. According to an inserted montage of highlights from *Lionman I*, the title hero was raised by lions, but was actually the rightful king of Thracia. Wearing steel claws — kind of studded boxing gloves — Lionman reclaimed his throne from the evil Antoine, who had earlier killed his father. As this chapter opens,

Lionman is pining to return to the forest, while Bellesarius, Antoine's equally evil brother, is plotting revenge. Bellesarius (played by Erich Akman, the movie's producer) is assisted by a slinky sorceress bimbo (Dee Taylor) who has a magic ring and who likes to wear a very kinky metal brassiere. Dee — or rather her bizarre outfit — is kind of fun, but everyone, and everything, else is stiff to the point of rigor mortis. There are lots of dull fights and flights through the Turkish countryside, and titanic battles with a man-eating plant and a giant rubber reptile tail. Just how cheap and lame is this one? It makes the Ator cycle seem positively lavish and exciting. For trash collectors only.

REVENGE OF THE BARBARIANS *(198?, Icelandic/Swedish coproduction, dubbed) wr Hrafn Gunnlaugsson, Emmet Murphy, and Paulette Rubinstein; dir Hrafn Gunnlaugsson*

No pecs, flex, swords, or sorcery. What we do have are some Vikings in Iceland in A.D. 907, and a young Celt on a quest to avenge the murder of his family that took place twenty years earlier. This he accomplishes by pitting two clans against each other, and the story eventually turns out to be an Icelandic Dark Ages version of *A Fistful of Dollars*, even including the use of concealed armor for the final showdown. I guess this has some curiosity value, but the movie itself is so long, tedious, and confusing that there sure is no entertainment value here. Even the spectacularly brooding and rugged Icelandic landscape soon grows boring as we see the same few locations over and over. For a much livelier rendition of the source material, check out **THE WARRIOR AND THE SORCERESS**.

VIKING MASSACRE *(undated, Italian, dubbed) dir John Hold*

Just when you think you've hit rock bottom, the sub-basement opens up to reveal this piece-o-shit. Forget the picture of the he-man on the box; there's no pecs and flex in this one, not unless a bleached-blond Cameron Mitchell is your idea of a beefcake hero. No massacre, and the "Vikings" are bozos in fake fur who hail from the fjords of southern Italy. Murky, cheap, and dull, this one's not even lively enough to be funny. Take a second look at **LIONMAN II** instead.

YOR – THE HUNTER FROM THE FUTURE
Post-apoc primitivism; see Festival 26.
IRONMASTER
Cave beefcake; see Festival 26.

The Saga of Ator

Miles O'Keeffe, who was introduced to the world when he went chest to chest with Bo Derek in **TARZAN, THE APE MAN**, has the pectoral territory pretty much to himself in this Italian-made series of *Conan* clones. While not quite as cheap as **THE INVINCIBLE BARBARIAN**, these are all ultra-low-budget efforts, and it shows. The costumes and sets are really tacky, the "monsters" are laughably cheesy, and the dubbing is truly terrible. When the characters are not traveling across the countryside (jogging seems to be the preferred method) or engaged in tedious swordplay, they have a tendency to stand absolutely still in interminable two-shots as their lips move randomly to some nonsensical blather on the soundtracck.

To be fair, though, Miles certainly is a hunk, a Frazetta drawing come to life. There is lots of flexing and posing with huge swords, and the camera positively drools over his massive frame, as do the female characters, most of whom handle him as though he were, in fact, a piece of meat. Furthermore, these movies are all so totally dumb, so thoroughly mechanical, so relentlessly low-budget, and so uniformly shoddy that they manage a certain mindless fascination.

ATOR – THE FIGHTING EAGLE *(1982, Italian, dubbed)*
wr and dir David Hills (Joe D'Amato)

The saga opens during the Age of Darkness in the Kingdom of the Spider. The baby Ator, whose coming has been prophesied, is the sole survivor of the slaughter of the village populace. Unaware of his true background or destiny, he is raised in another village, where he grows into Miles O'Keeffe, complete with shoulder-length tresses, eyeliner, and fun-fur boxer shorts. On his wedding day, this village is similarly wiped out by the armies of the Spider God, and his bride taken prisoner. Ator hurries after her, pausing only long enough to learn his history and some useful martial arts, then to have some exciting adventures with Amazons, witches, blind warriors, magic shields, shadow swordsmen, and numerous other budget hokum. He's accompanied by a bear cub and Sabrina Siani.

THE BLADE MASTER *(1983, Italian, dubbed)*
dir David Hills (Joe D'Amato)

If you happened to miss the opening installment, don't worry: this one helpfully provides us with a five-minute recap of highlights from **ATOR**. Then we get this story: an instrument of great power called the "geometric nucleus" must not fall into the wrong hands. Just as the armies of the Snake God (the wrong hands) seize the castle, the good wizard sends his daughter (played by Lisa Foster, with astonishing woodenness) to fetch Ator, the only one who can save the day, from beyond "the ends of the earth." It only takes Lisa a couple of minutes to get there and find that his hair is as long as before, but he now affects studded-leather jockey shorts. It seems to take a long time to make it back to the castle — for everyone, since this sequel is even duller and cheaper than the original. Highlights include a fight with a giant rubber snake and — in a bit of awesome ludicrousness — an aerial attack by Ator from a hang glider. At one point, dubbing provides "The dividing line between goodness and stupidity is very, very fine." It's clear which side this one comes down on.

THE IRON WARRIOR *(1986, Italian, dubbed)*
wr Steven Luotto and Al Bradley; dir Al Bradley

The hero here is again named Ator, but he seems to have a different background (Miles now has hair in a braided bun, and he's wearing leather bermuda shorts) so I'm not sure this is a proper sequel. However, as everything else is the same, let's assume it is. The story concerns the battle between two witches for the control of the kingdom. Ator is accompanied by a bimbo princess (Savina Gersah) who wears a series of gauzy, see-through cocktail togas, but as far as pecs go, she's a poor second to Miles. The title refers to the evil witch's super-warrior, who wears a silver skull-shaped hockey helmet that must have cost five dollars to produce. Largely shot in some interesting Maltese fortresses, this one

> *"All that emptiness makes you crazy after a while."*
> STAR CRYSTAL

looks a little better than the first two. Its I.Q., though, is no higher, and falls well below Miles's chest measurement.

Two Sword-and-Sandal Throwbacks

HERCULES *(1983, Italian, dubbed)*
wr and dir Lewis Coates (Luigi Cozzi)

The original hunk is back and the Incredible Hulk (Lou Ferrigno) is playing him. Those of you who fondly remember the utterly shoddy Steve Reeves spectacle-epics of the early '60s won't want to miss this one. Freely (and hilariously) mangling Greek mythology in an effort to juice things up, we've got Herc on a mission to rescue Cassiopeia, the love of his life, from the clutches of Minos, the evil sorceror-king. But before he gets there, he's got to contend with characters from other Greek legends (Circe, Daedalus, etc.), and to confront every special effect in the book. He fights a giant robot moth, a giant robot centaur, and a giant robot version of Ghidrah, the three-headed monster. He uproots trees and tosses boulders around as though they were papier-mâché. He flies through space, diverts rivers, and journeys to Hell. In addition we get to see the creation of the universe, the cataclysmic destruction of several miniature cities, and Sybil Danning sheathed in spandex (apparently, the preferred fabric of the Bronze Age). In short, this one's got it all, and it's all wonderfully chintzy. The first hour or so is awesomely ridiculous, displaying a depth, variety, and flashiness of ineptitude rarely seen. Of course, it does eventually run out of new ways to amaze us, and the last third seems to drag a bit, but that's a minor quibble. Besides spandex, Sybil has a fondness for the nectar of the black lotus, which, she says, "numbs the mind." For the same sensation, take a swig of this one. From the director of **ALIEN CONTAMINATION**.

THE SEVEN MAGNIFICENT GLADIATORS *(1983, Italian, dubbed) wr Claude Fragass; dir Bruno Mattei*

You just can't keep a good story down. First there was *The Seven Samurai*, then *The Magnificent Seven*, then it moved to outer space with

BATTLE BEYOND THE STARS. And here we have a sword-and-sandal version, set in what is apparently one of the stupider periods of the Roman Empire. After an evil tyrant killed the men in their village, four bimbos travel to Rome to recruit some heroes to defend them. They get Lou Ferrigno and Sybil Danning, but the other five are less magnificent than undistinguished and nondescript... as is the rest of the movie, with its boring swordplay, absence of effects, and lethargic pace. That's not to say that there aren't moments of astonishing dumbness — especially some of the costumes and dialog — but mostly it's too drab and ponderous to be anything other than routinely silly. As she was in the space version of the tale, Sybil — here in a black leather gladiatrix outfit — is the most exciting aspect of this one, and if there'd been six more like her, the title might, in fact, have been apt.

Parallel Worlds

PRISONERS OF THE LOST UNIVERSE *(1983, made for Pay TV) wr Terry Marcel and Harry Robertson; dir Terry Marcel*

A spunky TV reporter (Kay Lenz) and a resourceful electrician (Richard Hatch) inadvertently fall into an interdimensional transport device and emerge into a parallel universe that, though English-speaking, is of the sword-and-sorcery persuasion. When spunky Kay is captured by Kleel (John Saxon), the evil warlord who rules this world, resourceful Richard goes to the rescue. He's joined in his quest by a comic-relief thief, a friendly giant, and a guy in light green makeup. Together they have lots of tedious adventures involving mudmen with glowing eyes, a gillman, and a few zombies. Had this been made with any skill or wit, the situation of strangers in a weird age might have been an amusing variation. But everything is so lethargic, mechanical, and shoddy — utterly unfunny and lacking in any imagination — that it's just a dull bore whose TV origins are very evident. This universe wasn't lost — it was deliberately abandoned, and better left that way.

> *"The knife is a phallic symbol."*
> SORORITY HOUSE MASSACRE

GOR *(1987, partly dubbed)*
wr Rick Marx and Peter Welbeck; dir Fritz Kiersch

A magic ring transports a nerdy physics professor (Urbano Barberini) to the alternate world of the title, and he finds himself on a quest to retrieve a piece of magic junk called the Homestone from evil tyrant Sarm (Oliver Reed), and to release the people from Sarm's brutal regime. This is a rather plodding and ponderous version of one of the series of fantasies by John Norman, but except for some rather extravagantly tacky costumes, it's seriously lacking in either imagination or energy. Even more disappointing — considering that this also stars former *Playboy* centerfold Rebecca Ferratti as a battling bimbo and takes place in a society where all women are slaves — is the curious dearth of nudity and significant sleaze. There are some intriguingly skimpy costumes and some energetic chorines, but the obvious potential was smothered by the rather pointless infusion of good taste. While those who have been avidly following Oliver Reed's declining fortunes will want to check this out, I don't see much reason for anyone else to rush to be transported. (There is apparently a sequel with Jack Palance that was not yet released at the time of writing, but unless the filmmakers got their priorities straight, I see no reason for optimism about that one either.)

A Futuristic Variant

ROBOT HOLOCAUST *(1986, direct to cassette)*
wr and dir Tim Kincaid

The holocaust of the title — a rebellion of the robots — occurred long before this story begins, and left the earth all but uninhabitable. The human survivors in the one remaining city are slaves of the evil master known as "The Dark One," but there are a handful of free men in the wasteland, ready to fight against the tyrant. Technically, I guess, this is a post-apocalyptic fantasy, but aside from the futuristic setting, the nonsense in this one is strictly sword-and-sorcery. A band of rebels — including an Amazon bimbo, a wasteland warrior, a Conan look-alike, and a guy in a robot suit along for comic relief — take a perilous journey to the Power Station whence The Dark One rules. Along the way they encounter many dangerous opponents, including ferocious handpuppets disguised as sewer worms, the claw of a giant spider, and a toothy little belly-burster. It's difficult to say whether the vigorously feeble imagination, the ridiculously cheap effects, the absurd dialog, or the astonishing performances are more laughable, but almost every moment gives you something to ponder and to savor. Especially worthy of note is Angelica Jager who, as Valaria, the Ilsa-like sadistic bitch-assistant to The Dark One, not only bares her bounty, but gives a performance the likes of which has not been seen since *Queen of Outer Space* (1958). I mean, we're talking the stuff that classics are made of here, and turkey-hunters will definitely want to track down this frisky little gobbler from the director of **BREEDERS**.

A Futuristic Timewarp Plastic Toy Cartoon Variation

MASTERS OF THE UNIVERSE *(1987)*
wr David Odell; dir Gary Goddard

In case you're unaware of the antecedents involved here, this is the big-budget, live-action version of the Saturday-morning cartoon that is, itself, a half-hour promotion piece designed to sell various plastic figures and paraphernalia. As a general rule, you can probably pass on any movie that contains the credit "Based on the toy line developed by Mattel" without feeling you're missing very much, and this does little to refute the principle. Indeed, the most interesting aspect of this one may be the way it combines three different styles of fantasy into one quest adventure. From sword and sorcery, you've got the broadsword beefcake hero, He-Man (Dolph Lundgren), a wily dwarf, and an evil sorceror, Skeletor, with a nefarious plan to rule the universe. To this add a *Star Wars* technological gloss — flying surfboards, laser guns, and soldiers remarkably similar to those of Darth Vader. Then, through a piece of hi-tech magic junk called the "Cosmic Key," everyone gets transported to the present-day Midwest, thus giving us a *Terminator*-like time warp, complete with a teen couple on the run from the forces of darkness. About all they missed was the post-apocalyptic era (see Festival 23), but they did throw in an evil mercenary dressed right out of *Road Warrior*. Some $20 million was spent on this one, and it frequently shows, but the look and the effects are no less derivative and familiar than the narrative. Mainly for young kids, and older viewers with an interest in recombinant eclecticism. With Frank Langella, hidden behind a rubber skull face, as Skeletor, and a very funny Meg Foster as Evil-Lyn, his dragon-lady assistant.

Two Big-Budget Variations

HIGHLANDER *(1986)*
wr Gregory Widen, Peter Bellwood, and Larry Ferguson; dir Russell Mulcahey

"The Immortals," a breed of indestructible warriors, have battled with broadswords through the centuries for "The Prize." Few are left by the time they gather in New York for the final confrontation, and soon there are only two: a Scot played by Christopher Lambert with a perpetual four-day growth of beard; and an evil being known as The Kurgan (Clancy Brown), whose current incarnation is as a monster punk in leather, with a shaved head, a huge scar on his neck, and a voice that comes through an echo chamber. In flashbacks to 16th-Century Scotland, we get Sean Connery as another Immortal who teaches Lambert about his true identity and trains him to be a warrior. Lambert looks good but is a little too blank to hold our interest, and thus the film does not quite manage to engage and pull us along the way it should. However, this had a big budget ($17 million), and it shows — in its spectacular look, some stunning effects, nonstop action, violent swordplay (including a bunch of decapitations), and the most impressive villain since *The Terminator*. Despite its shortcomings, this is one of the most stylish and interesting of the movies in this festival.

FLESH + BLOOD *(1985)*
wr Gerard Soeteman and Paul Verhoeven; dir Paul Verhoeven

This doesn't really belong in this festival, but it's packaged like it does, and it frequently turns up in video stores next to other sword-and-sorcery titles. Besides, I don't know where else to put a costume saga about love, lust, swordplay, and slaughter in the feudal world of 1501. The story centers on the leader of a band of mercenary soldiers (Rutger Hauer), the princess he kidnaps (Jennifer Jason Leigh), and her betrothed (Tom Burlinson), who is the son of the lord who betrayed Rutger and his men. This one is 50 per cent of a really great movie. It has a fantastic look, a great gritty texture, and truly abundant quantities of the two title elements. In its graphic depiction of a world ruled by brutality, revenge, and self-interest, it's kind of medieval Sergio Leone — very strong, powerful, highly charged stuff. Unfortunately, the other 50 per cent comprises a plot that rather mindlessly lurches forward, clunky dialog and acting, and characters that tend to be either too stupid or too nasty to really engage us. Still, 50 per cent is not bad, and this one really does try to deliver the goods. (The Dutch director went on to make *Robocop*.)

FESTIVAL 22

* * *

THE CLONES OF INDIANA JONES
Old-Fashioned Adventures in the Land of the Lost Golden Raiders of the Sun

"He was always ready to go off at the drop of a legend."
— *Allan Quartermain and the Lost City of Gold*

It seems unlikely that any of the movies in this festival would have been made had it not been for *Raiders of the Lost Ark* (1981). Just as *Star Wars* revived interest in science fiction, *Raiders* brought back the good, old-fashioned, thrill-a-minute, cliff-hanging adventure.

Modeled on the cheap and silly action serials from Saturday matinees in the '30s and '40s, *Raiders* distilled the major elements of the form and combined them with a very contemporary sensibility. It added a generous helping of wit and intelligence, then delivered the goods with a skill and a lavishness never before seen. The result was a truly great adventure fantasy — a rollercoaster ride of a movie filled with some of the most spectacular action sequences ever filmed — and a box office of hundreds of millions of dollars, making *Raiders* one of the biggest money-makers of all time. Needless to say, success like that does not go unnoticed . . . or uncopied.

In their attempts to tap into the new market for old-fashioned adventures, the Jones Clones have drawn on various period sources, such as Victorian novels and wartime comic strips. Regardless of the ostensible source, though, the real inspiration has always been *Raiders* itself.

Like the other varieties of fantasy adventures, the *Raiders* formula is essentially that of the quest. A macho, soldier-of-fortune hero seeks, often at the behest of an attractive young woman, a great prize, and there are usually bad guys trying to get there first, and always obstacles to be overcome and mini-adventures to be had along the way.

All of this takes place in an exotic locale, most frequently a jungle, and often in the past. Wherever and whenever it is set, the world of these movies is generally sufficiently distant and remote to a acquire an aura of fantasy — a world of high adventure in which there is still unexplored territory and great unexplained forces. The things that happen don't always make a lot of sense, but since the tone is usually kind of jokey, we're not meant to quibble about the logic.

Raiders invested its borrowings from tradition with energy and imagination to give us a creation that was exciting, fresh, and new. Unfortunately, the same cannot be said of its imitators; the movies that follow are not what you'd call a real inspired (or inspiring) group. The debt most of them owe to *Raiders* is abundantly clear, and often includes the characters, plots, structures, and even specific action sequences. The influence, though, didn't seem to extend as far as quality or entertainment value, which means that the only real interest in a number of these clones is the blatancy and ham-fistedness of their wholesale pilfering.

At the high end of the line, there's a willingness to spend money, not that it is put to very good use. Even the best of these are not all that good, and they mainly serve to enhance our appreciation of *Raiders* and to remind us how virtually no one approaches Steven Spielberg when it comes to constructing breakneck action sequences and nonstop adventures. Thus, the real fun in this festival seems concentrated at the other end.

At the low end, insufficiencies of budget and inadequacies of talent combine to produce results that can be quite astonishingly heavy-handed, stupid, and tacky. Of course, not all of these dreadful failures are amusing, but a few are aggressively ridiculous enough to rate as significant discoveries for connoisseurs of trash and shoddiness.

Three Shots from Cannon

KING SOLOMON'S MINES *(1985)*
wr Gene Quintano and James R. Silke; dir J. Lee Thompson

This is the third version of H. Rider Haggard's classic tale of "Darkest Africa," but it's Golan and Globus's (Cannon Films) first go at *Raiders*, and they certainly gave it a good try. In fact, they put in some of the same action sequences and jokes, some evil Germans, *déjà-vu* theme music, and John Rhys-Davies (in a burst of originality, this time he plays a Turk).

> *"You woulda thought — with all they must know — those rocket guts could've done something for Joey."*
> ZONE TROOPERS

Jessie (Sharon Stone, who's cute, blonde, and wooden) hires famous explorer Allan Quartermain (a bearded Richard Chamberlain) to find her father who's gone in search of the legendary title mines. The evil Germans and Rhys-Davies are also in on the chase. There are lots of adventures on the way, and certainly no skimping on *stuff:* a cast of thousands, lots of chases, machine guns and explosions, wild animals and strange natives, vast treasure, and molten lava. What there is little of here is originality, logic, effective humor, characters interesting enough to root for, and reason to suspend our disbelief. A lot of money was spent, but there's no energy; whereas *Raiders* grabbed us by the throat and pulled us with it, this one just ambles along in front of us. Wait for the 1950 version to turn up on the "Late Show."

ALLAN QUARTERMAIN AND THE LOST CITY OF GOLD *(1986) wr Gene Quintano; dir Gary Nelson*

This is G & G's sequel to their first shot at *Raiders*. Richard Chamberlain and Sharon Stone are back, but he's no more charismatic and her acting hasn't improved. This time, they're looking for Allan's brother, who's disappeared in quest of the title metropolis ("He was always ready to go off at the drop of a legend"). James Earl Jones is also along, presumably for the salary. On their quest, they encounter many obstacles, but none of them advances the story, or is interesting in itself. The Lost City looks like a Southern California health spa, and the only marginal interest there is Cassandra Peterson ("Elvira") as the evil queen, awesome as she bounces around in a golden brassiere. This sequel is so inert it almost makes the first one seem exciting. At one point, our hero says, "I've seen some amazing things in my life, but never anything to compare with this." Indeed.

FIREWALKER *(1986)*
wr Robert Gosnell; dir J. Lee Thompson

This is G & G's third run at *Raiders*, and they seem to be getting the hang of it. While hardly anything very special, this does at least have a little energy, and the touch, if not exactly light, is not completely leaden. This time, the story is contemporary and the setting is mostly the jungles of Central America. Chuck Norris and Lou Gossett are Max and Leo, two soldiers-of-fortune who have never managed to claim one. They team up with Melody Anderson (another cute blonde, but more sprightly) who has an ancient map to some legendary Indian treasure. Sonny Landham (the Indian heavy in *48 Hours*) plays an Indian heavy who's also after the treasure. Along the way, our heroes encounter the usual obstacles, Chuck has three karate fights, and John Rhys-Davies turns up for no particular reason. (Some movies have gratuitous sex and violence, this one has gratuitous Rhys-Davies.) The plotting is very mechanical, the adventures, mundane, and the second half of the movie really loses steam. Still, there is a smattering of humor, and Lou Gossett sure does light up the screen. There is, by the way, no firewalking.

Two Comic-Strip Heroines

JANE AND THE LOST CITY *(1987, British)*
wr Mervyn Haisman; dir Terry Marcel

"Jane" was a popular British comic-strip character from the '30s, who apparently had a lot of adventures in which she lost her dress but never her plucky spirit. The story here, owing more than a little to *Raiders*, is set in Africa in 1940, and concerns a race between the British and the Nazis to find the fabled "Lost City," with its storehouse of fabulous diamonds, in order to finance the war effort. But where *Raiders* was a nonstop hurtle, this one is a stroll through quicksand. The flat characters and the inane narrative line betray the cartoon origins; all the action happens off-camera (cheaper and easier that way); and what I suppose was meant to be a certain campy charm doesn't make it. Jane (Kirsten Hughes) does lose her dress five times but, contrary to the promo copy on the box, never her silk underwear. About the only distinction this one enjoys is that it may well be the worst movie ever to quote from Hemingway. Strictly a lost cause from the director of **PRISONERS OF THE LOST UNIVERSE**.

"It doesn't look like anybody lives here yet."
SLUMBER PARTY MASSACRE II

THE PERILS OF GWENDOLINE IN THE LAND OF THE YIK YAK *(1984, French, dubbed)*
wr and dir Just Jaeckin

This one is based upon the adventures of a '40s comic-strip heroine; the box claims that it has "More thrills than *Raiders*, more romance than *Romancing the Stone*, and more action than *Temple of Doom*." If you believe that, I can probably get you a really good deal on some vacation property in the Everglades. What this actually has is a pretty good helping of sleaze and a remarkable dearth of intelligence. Tawny Kitaen, who was somehow overlooked in the Golden Turkey nominations for "the most ludicrous professional name in movie history," plays Gwendoline. She's supposed to be a virginal convent girl, and it looks like she modeled her performance on Bo Derek's stunning protrayal of Jane (see **TARZAN, THE APE MAN**). For reasons not explained, she arrives in the Far East in a packing crate, hoping to find her father who disappeared while searching for a rare butterfly. (I'm only reporting this, not making it up.) She teams up with a loutish soldier-of-fortune named Willard (Brent Huff) and a bimbo named Beth, and together they head off for the legendary land of Yik-Yak, from which, we are told several times, "nobody ever came back." To get there, they make a river journey, a desert journey, a jungle journey, and are captured by strange natives. Somewhere along the way, it starts to rain, and Willard tells Tawny, "Take your clothes off, quick!" and she does, giving us the first of several glimpses of the apexes of her dramatic range. Yik-Yak turns out to be a kingdom of bald, bare-breasted Amazons dressed only in string-bikini bottoms and leather helmets that might have come from an S&M football team. Before we're done, there are tits galore, a few dollops of violence (including an impaling and one guy getting his ears ripped off), a *papier-mâché* crocodile, and some of the most hilariously dumb dialog ever dubbed over randomly moving mouths. How can you resist?

Two Time Warp Variants

BIGGLES — ADVENTURES IN TIME *(1985)*
wr John Groves and Kent Walwin; dir John Hough

Jim Ferguson (Neil Dickson), yuppie entrepreneur, gets caught in a time warp and keeps flipping back and forth between the present and the front lines of the First World War in 1917. There he meets his "time twin," ace pilot James Bigglesworth (Alex Hyde-White) — "Biggles" to his friends — who was the hero of a series of boys adventures written by W. E. Johnson that were popular in the '20s. Together they destroy a German secret weapon that could have changed the outcome of the war and all subsequent history. The tagline on the box says that Ferguson had "one foot in the 20th century and the other in World War I," but while the copy writer obviously has no sense of history, this movie does have a pleasant sense of fun. It's fast-paced, with good production values and a number of nice bits of humor as our hero keeps changing periods at most inopportune moments (and in most inappropriate costumes). This is not much more than a piece of fluff, but it is at least well-made, generally entertaining fluff, and as far as old-fashioned adventures go, you could do a whole lot worse.

SKY PIRATES *(1985, Australian)*
wr John Lamond; dir Colin Eggleston

At the end of the Second World War, a hotshot Australian pilot (John Hargreaves) flies into a time warp, comes out near Easter Island, gets court-martialed, and then chases after some magic stone tablets that are the source of unimaginable power and must not fall into the wrong hands. The production values here are good, Hargreaves is an acceptable Jones clone, and, like so many Australian movies, this has some decent action sequences and a good strong look. What it doesn't have are pirates of any milieu, or a narrative that makes much sense. We hop from exotic locale to exotic locale, but despite nearly constant traveling, we never seem to get anywhere. There are lots of chases, races, and fights, but not much excitement and even less suspense. Interesting to look at but that's about it.

Another Variation on the Theme

JAKE SPEED *(1986)*
wr Wayne Crawford and Andrew Lane; dir Andrew Lane

The title character is the hero of a series of macho paperback adventures like those starring Mack Bolan or Remo Williams. Only Jake is not just a fictional hero: he's real, and his novels are based on actual adventures. (In this case, he appears to help a young woman — Karen Kopins — whose sister has been kidnaped by white slavers in Africa.) Not a bad premise, with the potential for some interesting and amusing interplay between the fictional world and the real world, much like what Woody Allen did in *The Purple Rose of Cairo*. However, very little of the potential is realized, leaving us with nothing but a piece of third-rate pulp filled with cardboard stereotypes, mechanical plotting, and a lot of things blowing up. Jake is clearly modeled on Indiana Jones, but, as played by co-writer Wayne Crawford, he has absolutely no charisma and no more depth than his books. I was told that this is quite popular at one of my local video stores, but I don't have a clue why. The attempts at humor are labored and flat, explosions take the place of any genuine energy, and, for all the things that happen, the only speed here is in the character's name.

The Bottom of the Barrel

TREASURE OF THE FOUR CROWNS *(1982, Spanish, dubbed) wr Lloyd Battista, Jim Bryce, J. Lazarus; dir Ferinando Baldi*

The crowns in question date from the 6th Century, and are the source of potentially awesome power for good and evil. They have fallen into the hands of the leader of a fanatical religious cult, and it's up to a soldier of fortune (Tony Anthony) to steal them from the mountaintop fortress where they're kept. The opening and closing sequences are right out of *Raiders* — though much longer, cheesier, and far less exciting — while the heist itself is ripped off from *Topkapi* (1964). But the plot is incidental; since this dubbed piece of nonsense was filmed in 3-D, the only point of the exercise is to provide a context in which lots of things leap and fly at us. And they do continuously — swords, spears, arrows, flames, dogs, snakes, pterodactyls — often with their suspending wires clearly visible. Of course, these effects don't mean much in 2-D, and we're left with lots of opportunity to ponder the staggering cheapness of it all, as well as the total absence of characterization, plot, and coherence. And speaking of cheapness, judging from the incredible number of black spots that appear on the flim — the result of dirt and crud on the camera lens

— the budget evidently did not permit the purchase of cleaning tissues. This one's only for those with a fondness for ineptitude, which it delivers in spades. There are, by the way, only three crowns.

ROBBERS OF THE SACRED MOUNTAIN *(1982, Canadian, made for Pay TV)*
wr Olaf Pooley and Walter Bell; dir Bob Schulz
Also released as *Falcon's Gold*.

Somewhere in the mountains of Mexico is a lost treasure consisting of crystals that, when put into lasers, have the potential to alter the balance of power of the world. Only a crusty old archeologist (John Marley) and a brash, resourceful young journalist (Simon MacCorkindale) can prevent them from falling into the wrong hands, which in this case belong to an evil arms merchant (George Touliatos). While not the lowest of the low, this is definitely the slowest of the slow. It crawls through a series of lame action sequences, and rarely has empty dialog been delivered with more painful deliberation: Marley croaks, MacCorkindale banters leadenly, and Touliatos sounds as though he is under heavy sedation. Only for those who want to see Simon in a loincloth. With Blanca Guerra as the woman who takes her clothes off three times.

YELLOW HAIR AND THE FORTRESS OF GOLD *(1984)*
wr John Kershaw and Matt Cimber; dir Matt Cimber

This is a familiar story of a search for lost Aztec treasure. The variations are the Old West setting and the title heroine (Laurene Landon, who looks a little like a young Linda Evans), a blonde bimbo raised by Apaches. Actually, considering the way she delivers flying dropkicks and other wrestling maneuvers, it looks like she was raised by the WWF. Just as *Raiders* was modeled on Saturday-afternoon serials, a framing device establishes that this movie is in fact one chapter of an ongoing adventure. But whereas *Raiders* was the matinee we always wanted to see, this one is all too reminiscent of the ones we actually got to see — which means lousy production values (a lot of expense was spared on this one), wooden acting, a nonsensical plot, and lots of riding around on horseback, blasting six-shooters. And since there's no sense of irony or playing with the form, what we end up with is very faithful replica of a cheap, dull movie. Quite an achievement.

> *"We've got to cut off their hands!"*
> THE CHILDREN

THE MINES OF KILIMANJARO *(1987, Italian, dubbed)*
wr and dir Mino Guerrini

Set in the 1930s, the Jones Clone here is named Ed Barclay and he's a professor at Berkeley. I suspect this was a little joke on the part of the dubbers, and it's one of the very few, intentional or otherwise, to be found in this tired, routine effort. Barclay goes to the dark continent to try and find the "Secret of Africa" — fabled diamond mines that the Germans are using to finance their rearmament. Also in on the chase are the British, the Dutch, a Chinese merchant, and assorted assassins and villains. Barclay is accompanied by a bimbo who loses her skirt midway, and thus ends up trekking halfway across the continent, wearing only a safari shirt. Along the way they encounter fierce natives, Coptic monks, a tribe of Amazons, and lots of cheap stock footage of African wildlife. This might have been as amusing as it sounds if it had been sleazier and/or more energetic. As it is, it's just cheap and dull, and of interest only to those who look for that particular combination of qualities in their ripoffs.

THE ARK OF THE SUN GOD *(1982, Italian, dubbed)*
wr Giovanni Simonelli; no dir credit

Aside from some spectacular Turkish scenery, the only interesting thing about this cheapo clone is the fact that there is neither an ark nor a sun god in it. Instead, everyone's after the "Sceptre of Gilgamesh," which is — who would've guessed? — some kind of ancient source of tremendous power that must not fall into the wrong hands. In this case — the year being 1982 — the wrong hands are not Nazis', but your basic fanatical Arabs'. But why go on? This is the kind of total stiff that gives ripoffs a bad name, and anyone gullible enough to fall for a title like this one probably deserves to sit through it.

FESTIVAL 23

* * *

FUTURE SCHLOCK
A Program of Post-Apocalyptic Adventures

"It's a new world with new rules."
— *Warlords of the Twenty-First Century*

In the early 1980s, two futuristic movies came out whose impact was almost immediately felt in the video fringe. The first was John Carpenter's *Escape From New York* (1981), in which the island of Manhattan has been converted to the world's biggest maximum-security prison. The same year saw the initial Australian release of *The Road Warrior,* George Miller's post-apocalyptic adventure that knocked out critics and audiences alike, and became a big hit when it arrived in North America in 1982.

Road Warrior is easily the better film — and may well be one of the greatest action movies ever made — but both have a number of features in common. Each presents a bleak vision of a near future in which things have seriously deteriorated. Each presents a wasteland — one urban, one desert — where there are only predators and prey, and life has been reduced to a violent (make that ultra-violent) struggle in which only the strongest can survive. Each has a very forceful look — a studded-leather, nouveau-punk, Heavy Metal style that's a lot of fun to look at. And each bears certain interesting similarities to a 1974 movie called *The Ultimate Warrior* (also available on cassette).

Most of all, though, the two films were very obviously influenced by Sergio Leone's westerns, both thematically and stylistically. In the dog-eat-dog societies depicted it would be hard to come up with two heros more like The Man With No Name than Snake Plissken and Mad Max. And, in the case of *Road Warrior*, the barren landscape and the desolate world is virtually identical to Leone's vision of the West.

In other words, the world after the apocalypse has become the next frontier, and most of the movies in this festival — particularly those descended from *Road Warrior* — can thus most properly be seen as the '80s version of the Western. A few details have changed — muscle cars instead of horses, black leather instead of white hats, maybe mutants instead of Indians — but none of the essentials.

Cataclysm and catastrophe have returned the world to a more primitive state. In the classic Western, one of the central themes was the bringing of civilization to the wilderness, with the conflict coming from those who opposed the change. In the post-apocalyptic world, things have already changed enough, thank you very much. Therefore the central conflict is between those attempting to preserve or reconstruct civilization as we knew it, and the hordes of slavering louts who find that the brutal anarchy of the wasteland suits them just fine.

In between these opposing camps stands the Hero, who differs from his traditional Western counterpart only in his transportation and his weaponry. He's a solitary man — a loner, perhaps with a painful past. He's a reluctant man of action, a supreme warrior tired of killing. He's too civilized to accept the lawless rule of the wasteland, but he's been out there too long to fit into society. And he's a knight errant, willing to fight for the right side, even though he can never be part of it.

In the post-apoc world, the hero generally undertakes a quest for two reasons. In the urban wasteland (*Escape From New York*), he is generally on a mission of rescue and/or escape that is not that different from the rescue of the princess in the pecs-and-flex epics of Festival 21. In the wide-open spaces, the quest is nearly always some version of a search for a Promised Land (as defined here, a place that possesses whatever is lacking in the wasteland — usually water, fuel, and/or civilization — but when the hero reaches it, like Moses, he rarely enters, and remains the solitary outsider).

While many of the *Road Warrior* descendants do little more than recycle the progenitor's basic narrative, it's interesting to note that a number of the movies in this festival draw upon and borrow from several classic Westerns for their plots or plot elements. *A Fistful of Dollars* and *The Magnificent Seven* are easy to spot (and were themselves Western versions of Japanese samurai films), but nowhere is this clearer than in one of the most recent entries, **STEEL DAWN**, which very faithfully reprises *Shane* in the post-apoc frontier. Maybe we're seeing a trend developing, and more classic Westerns will be remade with a futuristic setting. *High Noon* has already turned up in *Outland*, but such movies as *Stagecoach* and *The Searchers*, among many others, would seem to be naturals for the post-apoc world. (Note: for a sword-and-sorcery version of a *Fistful of Dollars* see Festival 21's **THE WARRIOR AND THE SORCERESS**.)

There's no way of knowing if this genre is going to continue to flourish and develop in the future. Thus far, though, of all the fantasy adventures only the *Conan* clones rival it in terms of numbers, and it's not hard to figure why the form has proven so popular with low-budget filmmakers around the world.

To begin with, since you're dealing with a wasteland, you don't have to worry about expensive sets. Any piece of rubble or barren land will do the trick, and once the filmmakers find a suitable patch, you can be sure they'll treat us to seemingly endless sequences of running over the rubble or driving through the desolation. It's rarely well-enough done to be interesting, but it is cheap and easy footage, and in the world of low-budget movies, that's often a much more important consideration than whether or not all this traveling is utterly tedious.

Next, since the post-apoc world is a brutal and savage place, it's the perfect setting for nonstop action. Thus, about the only thing that'll get people to stop traveling is a good firefight, and in the movies that follow there is much blasting away, many explosions, and body counts that often reach the upper double digits. Of course, it's hard to do this well, but once again, action — especially outdoors — provides bargain footage. Besides, if you blow up enough stuff, maybe no one'll notice that nothing really happening.

Finally, and maybe most important of all, the look and style that was so distinctive and striking in *Escape* and *Road Warrior* is fairly easily approximated. Indeed, it can conveniently be purchased off the rack in the local S&M emporium, and in some of the movies that follow, it probably was. But in *Road Warrior*, it was not solely style for it's own sake; the details that it showed us — the outfits, the vehicles, the structures — were not only interesting in themselves, but also made sense in terms of the fantasy world as a whole.

Some filmmakers have given some thought to the logic behind the look and have come up with some interesting and plausibly coherent variations. However, more than a few of the movies that follow borrow the style but jettison the sense, with results that can be very peculiar . . . and often quite amusing.

As with other genres, most of the movies in this festival are essentially the same movie executed with varying degrees of skill and creativity. Nor of them is as good as the model it follows, and certainly none comes close to delivering *Road Warrior*'s impact. Many are pure ripoffs — cheap, mechanical, and completely imitative. Some, though, do add a new wrinkle or two, and do it with enough skill, style, creativity, and energy to make them interesting to watch, if not absolutely engrossing.

At their best, several of these movies deliver decent entertainment. Most are, not surprisingly, hardly anything special, but have some interest if seen as exercises in formula and style or as extensions of the Western. And at their worst, if you're in the right mood, a few can be absolutely wonderful. (Note: Other variations of post-apocalyptic themes can be found in Festival 25.)

Welcome to the wasteland.

Urban Decay

1990: THE BRONX WARRIORS *(1982, Italian, partly dubbed)*
wr Dardano Sacchetti, Elisa Livia Briganti, and Enzo G. Castellari; dir Enzo G. Castellari

The Bronx has been declared a high-risk area, law enforcement has been removed, and rival gangs rule their respective territories. The heiress to the world's biggest arms manufacturer has taken refuge in the Bronx, and a sadistic Manhattan cop (Vic Morrow) has been hired to bring her back. So what we have here is *Escacpe From New York*, only from the gang's point of view. There's young beefcake aptly named Trash (Mark Gregory) who's the leader of a curiously clean-cut motorcycle gang. He joins forces with Fred Williamson, another gang leader, and together they battle Vic, the Scavengers (a gang of guys in rags and whiteface), and the Zombies (guys on rollerskates with metal hockey sticks). This one mostly consists of endless sequences of traveling across rubble or through crumbling basements, interspersed with frequent duels, fights, and explosions. Despite all the stuff going on — impalings, shotgun blasts, flamethrowers, and a head blown off — everything is mechanical and sluggish. There's also very little style here, with the "futuristic" look already seeming boring and dated. Displaying virtually no originality or energy, this one's strictly 3-D — derivative, dumb, and dull.

ESCAPE FROM THE BRONX *(1983, Italian, dubbed)*
wr Tito Carpi and Enzo G. Castellari; dir Enzo G. Castellari

Trash, the rubble, and the crumbling basements are back. The title acknowledges the debt to John Carpenter, but the story is actually about fighting to *stay* in the Bronx. Seems some big corporation is planning to level the place in order to build a new super-city. The inhabitants, though, are reluctant to leave their hovels, so "Disinfestation Squads" are sent in. These consist of guys in spiffy silver jumpsuits, armed with flamethrowers. After they fry Trash's parents, he decides to kidnap the president of the company, ransoming him for a promise that the company will drop the development and return the Bronx to the good old days when the gangs ruled. (What a swell idea, Trash!) The rest of the movie makes about as much sense as his objective, and mainly consists of blowing up large numbers of the disinfestation guys. (Actually, I think they blow up the same six or eight guys over and over.) Despite all the explosions, this one's strictly inert matter, though it does succeed in making the first Bronx effort seem like damn fancy filmmaking. With Henry Silva in the Vic Morrow role.

AFTER THE FALL OF NEW YORK *(1983, French/Italian)*
wr Julian Berry, Martin Dolman, and Gabriel Rossini; dir M. Dolman

In a fairly distant future, after a nuclear holocaust has rendered the world sterile, there is one fertile woman left on earth. She's hidden somewhere in the rubble that was once New York, and it's up to a leather-clad warrior named Parsifal (Michael Sopkiw, who looks remarkably like Kurt Russell) to find her so that the human race can have another chance on another planet. Parsifal's quest takes him through the usual basements, tunnels, and sewers, where he encounters rats, dwarfs, apemen, and lots of crazies with gooey radiation sores. Along the way, eyes are gouged out, a skull is axed, a head explodes, and intestines ooze out of a slit stomach, all of which are explicit but not the least bit realistic. For what it's worth, this is one of the better Italian clones, with decent production values, a moderately interesting look, acceptable dubbing, and an attempt to keep the strangeness coming. Not quite enough to make this much of a grabber — it's ultimately too flat, mechanical, and uninvolving — but if you're in a tolerant mood, this one will waste 90 minutes with a certain briskness.

> "Do you think the dead can come back to life?"
> FRIGHTMARE

CITY LIMITS *(1984)*
wr Don Opper; dir Aaron Lipstadt

About "15 years from now," a plague has killed most of the adults, leaving Los Angeles in the hands of two gangs of young bikers who wear striking costumes and weird masks. Their not-so-peaceful coexistence is disrupted by the arrival of a sinister corporation with plans to take over L.A. This seems to borrow elements from both Italian Bronx epics, but is considerably slicker and more stylish. That's not to say, though, that it's good. It's not; the narrative lacks focus and the driving forward motion it should have. Oddly the writing/directing team that gave us **ANDROID** omitted the wit and cleverness here. Still, it has some good actors (Darrell Larson, John Stockwell, John Diehl), is kind of fun to look at, and offers enough goings-on to hold your interest, at least for a while. Given the talent involved, it should have been better, but you could easily do worse.

WIRED TO KILL *(1986)*
wr and dir Franky Schaeffer

A plague wiped out a large part of the population, leaving behind, in 1998, only good decent folks trying to make a go of it and bands of marauding psychopaths whose only goal seems to be to act as slaveringly goonish as possible. Naturally, our heroes — Rebecca and Steve, two bland, blond teenagers — come into conflict with the thugs and are forced to learn how to defend themselves. The variation on this very familiar theme is that Steve is something of electronics whiz and battles back with clever little gadgets and deadly boobytraps — kind of *Short Circuit* meets *The Road Warrior*. The writer-director has no idea how to generate interest or tension, and the two leads, emotive to point of catatonia, give us no reason to care about the plight of their characters. These shortcomings, coupled with a budget that stretched to about three locations, make for rather slow, dull going.

ROBOT HOLOCAUST
Urban post-apoc pecs-and-flex; see Festival 21.

Barren Wastes

WARLORDS OF THE TWENTY-FIRST CENTURY
(1982) wr Irving Austin, Harley Cokliss, and John Beech; dir H. Cokliss
Originally titled *Battletruck*.

Set "after the oil wars," this gives us familiar territory — a broken world in which survival is a struggle, and only the most brutal manage it. The story centers on a peaceful, idealistic commune attempting to rebuild a life, a band of thugs led by a power-mad survivalist (James Wainwright), and a lone biker-warrior (Michael Beck) who rallies the commune to defend itself. There's obviously nothing very original in any of this, but it is quite well done. The script moves right along, and the casually violent world of the movie is well-thought-out logically and is plausible. The performances are generally pretty good, and if Michael Beck is not quite imposing enough as the solitary hero, John Wainwright is very effective as the cold-blooded commander of the new order. The production values are high, and while the action sequences lack the raw power of George Miller's, they have a fair amount of energy. Filmed in New Zealand, it has some great stark scenery and is consistently quite interesting to look at. This was one of the first of Mad Max's clones, and remains one of the best.

WARRIORS OF THE WASTELAND *(1983, Italian, partly dubbed) wr Tito Carpi and Enzo Girolami; dir Enzo G. Castellari*

The year is 2019 and, as a title informs us, "the nuclear holocaust is over." On one hand, you've got your handful of survivors dedicated to finding a sanctuary in the post-apoc wasteland (as someone explains, "They believe in something called . . . God"). On the other, you've got the Templars, a merry band of highwaymen dedicated to killing everyone unlucky enough to have survived this long; as their leader eloquently puts it, "We have been chosen to make others pay for the crime of being alive." And in the middle, you've got two knights errant dedicated to blowing things up — cars, buildings, and people — which they do repeatedly. There is also a decapitation, several graphic impalings, an exploding head, and a body count in the middle double digits. The Templars wear white jumpsuits with enormous shoulder pads, giving them a spiffy, Joan Crawford kind of look, but that's about as "futuristic" as this cheesy effort ever manages to get. The final showdown, in what I guess is an homage to Sergio Leone, is lifted whole from *A Fistful of Dollars*. Often laughable, but rarely dull. With Fred Williamson as the archer with exploding arrows.

THE EXTERMINATORS OF THE YEAR 3000 *(1983, Italian/Spanish, dubbed)*
wr Elisa Briganti, Dardano Sacchetti, and José Truchado Reyes; dir Jules Harrison

A nuclear war has destroyed the ozone layer, thus rendering the earth an uninhabitable desert. It is a world without water (or logic) and the minimal plot concerns the struggle to find some, to preserve, the last remnants of civilization against a band of maurauding "barbarians" with other ideas. Although the title purportedly places us in the year 3000, the vehicles are all late '70s American cars (suggesting a durability that far exceeds the manufacturer's warranty), and there is no indication of where the characters get their fuel or food for themselves. The movie consists of lots of traveling and car chases across the empty landscape, interspersed with badly dubbed chat about how savage and brutal things are. The production values are slightly above the usual low level of the Italian ripoffs, but nothing else is. The most interesting feature of this one may be just how closely it borrows from *Road Warrior*, complete with a nihilistic, leather-clad lone-wolf hero who is redeemed, and a mohawked villain who's a deadringer for Vernon Wells's deranged Wez. With more energy this might have been funny, but aside from a few choice lines — the villain is dubbed into shouting, "Charge! Once more into the breach, you mothergrabbers! Let's purloin that water!" — this one's as barren as the landscape.

STRYKER *(1983, Filipino, dubbed)*
wr Howard Cohen; dir Cirio H. Santiago

After the nuclear holocaust, it's a world without water, but, judging from the near-constant gunfire, not without ammunition. And when the folks are not blasting away, they're riding around (and around . . . and around) the barren wasteland. The title character (Steve Sandor) is a slightly beefy, bargain-basement Mad Max in a cowboy hat and a leather vest. He effects a couple of rescues, then helps defend the "Secret Spring" from an army of thugs dressed in standard-issue S&M gear. The action is random and lethargic, never generating any excitement. Aside from a few enlivening bits of nonsense — a tribe of dwarfs, motorcycle bimbos with crossbows — it's very tedious stuff. If you've seen any of the other movies in this section, you've seen this one as well.

WARRIOR OF THE LOST WORLD *(1983)*
wr and dir David Worth

A long time from now (in a future resembling the early '80s), civilization as we know it has collapsed, and what's left of the world is ruled by an evil tyrant (Donald Pleasence) and his army of black-clad stormtroopers. Robert Ginty is the title warrior, a wise-cracking lone-wolf survivor who rides a "supercycle" complete with an annoying computer that talks like a Valley Girl. He reluctantly agrees to help Persis Khambatta rescue her father — the drippy leader of the "New Way" — from the clutches of the tyrant. They succeed, but in the process Persis is captured, which means Dad and Ginty have to go back, this time assisted by a band of strangely dressed "marginals" from the wasteland. There's a lot of "action" in this one — endless car chases, gun battles, and so on — but it's all mechanical and dull, lacking both rationale and energy. Yet another lost world better left that way.

2020 TEXAS GLADIATORS *(198?, dubbed)*
wr Alex Carver; dir Kevin Mancuso

It's cowboys and Indians in the Old West, post-atomic war variety. Dubbed (from the original Italian and Australian?), either something was lost in the translation or this one was always a mess. It starts out looking like a *Road Warrior* replica, but takes a surprising turn by killing the Mad Max character, then segues into *The Magnificent Seven* (or, in this case, the Magnificent Four), who overthrow the evil oppressor with the help of a local tribe of Italo-Apaches. There are hordes of kamikaze bikers, motorcycle black Madonnas, a Russian-roulette sequence out of *The Deer Hunter*, explosions, flamethrowers and machine guns galore, a staggering body count, and lots of lingering pans over the scenes of carnage. Donald O'Brien (**DOCTOR BUTCHER**) is very weird as the neo-Nazi oppressor, and Sabrina Siani (**THE INVINCIBLE BARBARIAN**) shows a bit of skin and waves a machine gun as fetchingly as she does a sword. But otherwise more of the same old thing, and less coherent than most. Ho hum.

SURF NAZIS MUST DIE *(1986)*
wr Jon Ayre; dir Peter George

After an earthquake flattens Los Angeles, anarchy rules the land and the Surf Nazis, led by Adolf and Eva (Barry Brenner, Dawn Wildsmith), rule the beach. Yeah, sure, it's tough to resist a movie thus titled — another attention-grabber from the folks at Troma Team (**TOXIC AVENGER**, *Fat Guy Goes Nutzoid*, etc.) — but once you get past the title and the inspired premise — a post-apoc surfer flick — this one runs out of wit, humor, and energy mighty fast. This probably could be edited down to make a very funny 10-minute parody of the genre, but as a feature it's a total bore. Deliberately cheap and shabby, it gives us heavy-handed and mean-spirited humor, a laden pace, and seemingly interminable surfing sequences, none of which is very spectacular. A very crummy movie, and and the fact that it's that way on purpose doesn't make it better or funnier. With Christina Garcia as the waitress who takes her top off.

SURVIVOR *(1987)*
wr Bima Stagg; dir Michael Shackleton

Set 10 years after an all-out nuclear war has left the planet an uninhabitable desert, this focuses on the quest of the otherwise unnamed title character to find a fabled "paradise" — a hidden enclave with water and the remnants of civilization. While the basic story line is certainly nothing new, this is very well done, especially considering what must have been an extremely low budget. Visually, it's really impressive, with striking desert scenes and a giant abandoned factory that may be one of the most spectacular interior spaces since the ship in *Alien*. The script, while not great, does provide a few surprises and some fairly intelligent dialog. Chip Mayer does a decent job in the title role, and if he doesn't quite have the presence necessary to grab us, Richard Moll ("Night Court") compensates with a fascinating performance as Kragg, the brilliant psychopath who's taken control of "paradise." Overly derivative and a little too predictable, this is not a great movie, but most of its other shortcomings

— too much reliance on voice-over narration, for instance — seem to be the result of budgetary rather than artistic limitations. It is, however, terrific to look at and should hold your interest — another case where talent, imagination, creative energy, and a sense of style are more important in making a movie than having a lot of money to spend.

STEEL DAWN *(1987)*
wr Doug Lefler; dir Lance Hool

This one clearly recognizes that the post-apocalyptic adventure is the Western of the 1980s, and returns to the classic tales of the frontier. More specifically, this is a fairly precise reworking of *Shane*, complete with a little boy (Brett Hool) who looks remarkably like Brandon de Wilde. Patrick Swayze plays "Nomad," a nameless warrior who comes out of the wasteland to assist a community of farmers struggling to build a new civilization out of the desolate frontier. At issue is control of the valley, currently ruled by a petty tyrant (Anthony Zerbe) and his army of hired thugs. Adding an element from yet another tradition, Swayze is not a gunfighter but a martial-arts expert, a post-apoc leather-clad samurai adept at swordplay, karate, and everything in between. The mix — futuristic martial-arts Western — turns out to be quite effective. The production values are high and it's stylishly shot; the cast is professional and quite competent; and the fight sequences rival those of the best ninja flicks. In other words, this is a good, solid, entertaining piece of genre filmmaking, well worth taking a look at.

WORLD GONE WILD *(1987)*
wr Jorge Zamacona; dir Lee. H. Katzin

In 2087, seventy-five years after the "final war," and fifty years since the last rainfall, water is the most precious commodity on earth. The tiny desert community of Lost Wells has water, but they are menaced by Derek (Adam Ant), the psychopathic leader of a zonked-out cult whose bible is *Wisdom of Charles Manson*. So, the community's stoned, neo-hippie guru (Bruce Dern) and the schoolmarm (Catherine Mary Stewart) go to the city to recruit warrior Michael Paré and various other hired guns to defend them, thus giving us a fairly faithful post-apoc reprise of *The Magnificent Seven/ Seven Samurai*. There's very little here we haven't seen lots of times before, and the humor is often strained, but in all, the movie is quite well made and generally manages to hold your attention. Disappointing in terms of the potential, but a perfectly watchable and acceptable addition to the post-apoc genre.

HELL COMES TO FROGTOWN *(1987)*
wr Randall Frakes; dir R.J. Kizer and Donald Jackson

The title burg is the wasteland home of mutant humanoids with a decidedly amphibian caste. Sam Hellman (Roddy Piper), one of the last fertile men left on the nuked planet, goes there on a government mission, accompanied by Sandahl Bergman, in order to rescue and impregnate the fertile women being held prisoner in Commander Toady's harem. Considering that co-director Jackson was responsible for the backyard epic **ROLLER BLADE**, this one turns out to be really pleasant surprise. Good production values, a lot of attention to detail, a nice sense of humor, and a fair amount of energy, cleverness, and originality save this from lapsing into a sophomoronic post-apoc sex romp. Piper, erstwhile the Rowdy wrestler, is not yet very skilled as as an actor, but he has an appealing screen presence that's appropriate to the casual attitude of the movie, and he's assisted by pros, including Bergman, William Smith, and a gaunter-than-ever Rory Calhoun. Striking a nice balance between humor and action, this is probably the most relaxed and cheerful of all the post-apocs, and while nothing truly special, it's a decent piece of genre filmmaking, brisk and inventive enough to deliver the entertainment goods.

Two Combos

ENDGAME *(1983, partially dubbed)*
wr Alex Carver; dir Steven Benson

In the year 2025, after the earth has been devastated by nuclear war, the most popular global TV program is "Endgame" — a lethal game of hide and seek in which three "hunters" stalk the "prey" through the tunnels and the rubble of a fallen city. (Note: This was made four years before *The Running Man*.) A gladiator named Shannon (Al Cliver), fresh from his triumph, next finds himself hired to lead a party of telepathic mutants across the wasteland. It seems the government wants to exterminate the mutants because it fears their power, but others feel they offer the only hope for the future of the human race. With the help of six other mercenaries (making a not-so-magnificent seven), Shannon battles the government's stormtroopers as well as other post-apoc weirdos such as apemen, fishmen, and blind homicidal monks. This one combines both the post-apoc models, and does so with a fair amount of vigor and some intelligence and creativity. This is quite well shot (despite evidence of budget constraints), with a good look and very decent production values. Although the episodic plotting is somewhat arbitrary and sloppy, the pace is fast, and there's always something new and strange being tossed our way. Although clearly derivative, some effort was made to work variations on themes, which is enough to make this game a decent post-apoc time-waster.

DEAD-END DRIVE IN *(1986, Australian)*
wr Peter Smalley; dir Brian Trenchard-Smith

This one takes both the pattern forms and throws in a touch of *Lord of the Flies*. This is set in Australia, in the near future, after a series of political, environmental, and economic disasters have severely weakened the social order. Anarchy is the rule, and drive-in theaters have become concentration camps for the containment of nihilistic punks. (The director's earlier **ESCAPE 2000** was also set in a futuristic prison camp.) They live in rusting cars, are given food and entertainment, and have no desire to leave, since there's nothing any better outside. The Australians really know how to make this kind of movie. While not nearly as strong as *The Road Warrior*, this has a really good look, a lot of style, some decent action sequences, and even a touch of satire and social comment. Hardly great, but there is some energy and imagination on display here.

Wasteland Juvenilia

SOLARBABIES *(1986)*
wr Walon Green and Douglas Anthony Metrov; dir Alan Johnson

Somebody must've figured there was a big pre-teen market just waiting for a post-apocalyptic fantasy of its own. What we have here is a distant future in which the world is a desolate, waterless desert controlled by a Nazi-like tyrannical state. Seven rollerskating kids, who play a game much like that in *Rollerball* (1975), escape from their orphanage/prison, and go in search of something better. They are led on their quest by a piece of magic junk called "Bohdi" — a glowing orb of great intelligence and power that functions as a kind of an inanimate, pearlescent E.T. The production values are quite high, giving this one a fairly good, if not very original, look. Everything else, though, is such a derivative jumble — mechanical, sloppy, and confusing — that it's all but impossible to get involved in the proceedings. Young viewers might be willing to overlook the deficiencies, but there's no reason for hardcore wasteland aficionados to make the effort.

IN THE AFTERMATH *(1988, U.S/Japanese, partly animated)*
wr Carl Colpaert and Mamoru Oshii; dir Carl Colpaert

This one looks like it might have started as a fairly artsy Japanese animated film about a nine-year-old angel who comes to a desolate and destroyed earth, bearing a magic egg that will give the planet a second chance. Into this they inserted live-action sequences of the two survivors, who demonstrate that they are worthy to receive the gift. Thus, the first angelic, semi-animated, post-apoc fairy tale, but I have no idea who they thought the audience would be for this one. It's so slow, dull, plotless, and conflictless, it's hard to imagine anyone, including kids, not starting to squirm pretty quickly. The animation's okay, I guess, but even it seems to lack flair and excitement. Who needs it?

Woodsy Wastelands

SURVIVAL 1990 *(198?, Canadian, made for TV)*
wr Peter McCubbin, Craig Williams, and Gina Mandelli; dir Peter McCubbin Also released as *Survival Earth*.

Don't get suckered by this backyard ultra-cheapie made for Canadian TV. Despite the title, it's set in 1996, ten years after "The Fall" — the collapse of the global economy that resulted in the disintegration of the social fabric. Supposedly, life's now just one big Darwinian struggle for survival, but this one's nothing but chat, chat, chat, and none of it interesting or well delivered. Our three survivors wander through the woods north of Toronto, reminiscing about the past, having philosophical discussions, and reciting Yeats. Wow! Talk about nonstop excitement! When they're not chatting, they spend about 90 seconds shooting their guns off at passing "Vandals." Hard though it may be to believe, this one makes **THE AFTERMATH** look like a real movie.

DEFCON-4 *(1985)*
wr and dir by Paul Donovan

Three astronauts on a secret defense mission have orbited the earth for over a year, during which time there is an all-out nuclear war. When they return, they find a devastated planet, contaminated with radiation and populated with crazed cannibalistic "terminals" and an army of brutal survivalists who have enslaved those unlucky enough to still be alive. The long opening sequence in space is really quite well done, but once the astronauts come down to earth, the movie does too. Filmed in the forests of Nova Scotia, the look is different, but the story is the same escape to freedom (here, anywhere as yet uncontaminated by radiation). The production values are decent for what was obviously a severely limited budget, and at least a little thought went into the vision of the world. The story, though, is neither exciting nor involving, and plays itself out in a very routine and mechanical fashion. The first 20 minutes or so are definitely above average, but the rest is nothing special.

Bimbos of the Wasteland

OSA *(1985)*
wr and dir Oleg Egorov

In a world without water, a young woman named Osa (Kelly Lynch) is out to avenge the death of her family, which took place ten years earlier at the hands of some very clean-cut wasteland thugs. This one's a total mess — rambling, styleless, cheaply made, badly written and acted, and utterly without action, energy, or even marginal coherence — and makes one long for shabbier Italian wastelands.

SHE *(1983, partly dubbed)*
wr and dir Avi Nesher

Post-apoc sword and sorcery. The credits say "Inspired by H. Ryder Haggard," but the real inspiration seems to have been a recipe for cash based on a stew of stuff stolen from a variety of sources, with a dash of sleaze. This is set in the 23rd year "After the Cancellation," which was apparently some great catastrophe that turned the world into a mutant heavy-metal Middle Ages. Sandahl Bergman is the title pronoun who, clad in a studded-leather loincloth, rules a society of similarly clad Amazon bimbos. Naturally, there's a quest to a distant land to rescue the sister of a minor wedge of beefcake (Tom Goss). And of course, adventure marks the way, including vampires, a mad scientist, a telekinetic man-god, psychopathic monks with axes, and chainsaw-wielding mutants ("Don't ever trust a mutant"). Oh, yes — Sandahl takes a bath. Made in Italy, this is slightly better photographed than many of the pasta post-apocs, but that only serves to give a certain gloss to what is otherwise unfaltering crudeness of techinque and shoddiness of execution. In other words, this is just what trash collectors avidly seek — a vigorously silly movie whose inept reach far exceeds its limited grasp. Or, as Sandahl says, "Shanda, this has nothing to do with sense."

ROLLER BLADE *(1986, dubbed, direct to cassette)*
wr, prod, photo, dir Donald G. Jackson

I'm just guessing, but I have the feeling that this one started as a very funny 20-minute student film and got bloated out into a very dull feature. This takes as its model, not *The Road Warrior*, but all the Italian ripoffs. During the "Second Dark Age," a mystic sect of rollerskating women with supernatural powers uses martial arts to combat the forces of evil in an attempt to bring order out of chaos. Like the Italian post-apocs, this is entirely (and atrociously) dubbed, even though it was shot in California with an American cast. About five people do all the voices, imitations that range from Dennis Hopper to Darth Vader, to Zsa Zsa Gabor. And the dialogue! "And now, nights are black as ebony and thou either skate or die!" / "Damn! The Roller Patrol." / "Don't cry. Tears will cause thy wheels to rust." So far so good. Throw in a little nudity, and you'd think this could be a winner. The problem is, it's much funnier to think about than to watch. What it does is demonstrate just how difficult it is to make an intentionally bad movie that will be as funny as the real gobblers, such as **SHE**. The jokes here are too few and spread too thin, with the result that, while it aims for parody, it only hits the dullness of its targets. Perhaps the funniest line in the whole movie appears on the screen at the end of the credits: "Watch for Roller Blade Part 2 — Holy Thunder." At least, I hope it's a joke.

PHOENIX THE WARRIOR *(1987)*
wr Robert Hayes and Dan Rotblatt; dir Robert Hayes

The only male child in a wasteland populated by large-breasted bimbos in skimpy outfits is sought by the hideously ancient priestess who rules the world (Sheila Howard), and only the title Mad Maxine (Kathleen Kinmont) stands between her and total global domination. If you want high-impact post-apoc action, you should probably look elsewhere, but if you wish they still made movies like *Untamed Women* or *Fire Maidens of Outer Space* — and who doesn't? — the sight of these honeys waving automatic weapons around might help to temporarily dull your sense of loss, as might their delivery of consistently inane lines. While not quite as inspired or uniformly amusing as the '50s classics, this is not without its laughable moments, as well as a lot of jiggle and a dash of gratuitous nudity. Although a little too dull and unambitious to be really memorable, this will help fill those long stretches between the all-too-infrequent broadcasts of *The Wild Women of Wongo*. With Persis Khambatta as the awesomely hammy henchbimbo of the evil priestess.

A Post-Apoc Curiosity

SPLATTER — THE ARCHITECTS OF FEAR *(1986, Canadian, direct to cassette)* wr *Janet Schacter; dir Peter Rowe*

I'm not sure this belongs here, but I don't know where else to put it. An alternative title might be *The Making of Amazon Queens Versus the*

> *"It appears your insect has gone through some kind of metamorphosis."*
> BLUE MONKEY

Mutants. Amazon Queens is the movie being shot, and it's clearly some kind of post-apoc fantasy. Except we only see the big scenes, the special effects, and how these effects are made. So the movie has it both ways — lots of skin, sex, and gore, but in a documentary format that eliminates the need to have a real story, and gets away with exploitation by explaining it. Actually, it's kind of a clever way to make an asset out of a ludicrously low budget. There are some moderately decent effects and some good bodies, but the attempts at humor are strictly sophomoronic. Shot on tape, this is strictly bargain basement, but may be worth a look.

The Post-Apoc Pits

THE AFTERMATH (1982)
wr, prod, dir Steve Barkett

After a year in space, an astronaut (Steve Barkett) returns to find a nuclear holocaust has wiped out civilization as we know it. That's the good news. The bad news is that this is the movie we've been left with. Shot some time in the '70s, this backyard piece-o-shit makes the dullest, cheapest Italian number seem lively and lavish. Don't even consider it.

FESTIVAL 24

* * *

FAR, FAR, AWAY . . .
Space Adventures in Distant Galaxies

> "What kind of planet have we landed on?"
> — *Escape from Galaxy 3*

For almost a decade after Stanley Kubrick's *2001* (1968) first entranced (or infuriated) audiences, scarcely any space adventures were made, the only notable exceptions being Douglas Trumbull's *Silent Running* (1972) and *Dark Star* (1974), the very funny, low-budget first effort from John Carpenter and Dan O'Bannon. (Both are available on cassette and well worth watching.) Despite *2001*'s considerable success, the conventional wisdom in Hollywood still held that science fiction was basically a low-budget genre with very limited audience appeal.

All that changed in 1977 when George Lucas's *Star Wars* exploded on the screen, becoming, almost immediately upon its release, the most successful movie ever made. (*E.T.* has since surpassed it, but the *Star Wars* trilogy occupies the next three places on the list of top money-makers, and the trio had an estimated box office of a *billion* dollars.) The point hit home with the force of an exploding Death Star, and the marginal genre suddenly became the new mainstream.

As Danny Peary writes (*Guide for the Film Fanatic*), *Star Wars* is "arguably the most influential film ever made." It refined and pioneered techniques that revolutionized special effects. It gave us a brand-new futuristic look. It showed the staggering amounts of money that could be made from ancillary rights. And most of all, it demonstrated, along with *Close Encounters* (released later that same year), that there was a huge market out there for fantasy and science-fiction films. *Star Wars'* success initiated a new era of the fantasy film and led, directly or indirectly, to such movies as *Superman* (1978), *Star Trek* (1979), *Alien* (1979), *The Black Hole* (1979), *Flash Gordon* (1980), *Outland* (1981), *Tron* (1982) *Blade Runner* (1982), *Dune* (1984), and probably most of the fantasy adventures in this section. Indeed, had *Star Wars* been the expensive flop

> *"What we have to do is destroy his brain."*
> I WAS A TEENAGE ZOMBIE

that a lot of "experts" had predicted, perhaps over a quarter of the movies in this book might not have been made.

Of all the movies descended from *Star Wars*, the space adventures in this festival are obviously the most direct ones. While not all of these movies are exact clones, most of them borrow stories, settings, attitudes, and styles from *Star Wars*.

Star Wars has to be regarded as science fiction but, although there is a lot of imagination on display, there is almost no science nor any of the kind of complex speculation that marks much of the best science fiction literature. Instead, it is a fantasy adventure that owes much more to the old Flash Gordon and Buck Rogers serials than to the Sci-fi subtleties of *2001*. It is, as discussed in the introduction to this section, very deliberately a version of the classic fairy tale quest romance, a point that its famous opening words make abundantly clear: we don't have "Once upon a time," but we do see "A long time ago in a galaxy far, far away..."

The space adventures that follow also take place on distant worlds in some indeterminate age, and are set in what is very much a frontier. There are no cities or complex societies, only isolated outposts on barren planets or solitary ships and space stations in the emptiness of the universe. Man is just one intelligent species among many, and aliens are a basic part of the environment. However, since these are fantasy adventures rather than monster movies, the alien lifeforms are relegated either to the background or to secondary roles — sometimes helpful, sometimes hindrances — serving much the same function as, say, elves and ogres in fairy tales.

The stories themselves, following on form *Star Wars*, are usually simple versions of the quest romance — episodic tales of rescue and escape and the defeat of the great forces of evil that threaten dominance. Far from being speculations on future societies, these are basically old-fashioned Saturday-matinee action-packed adventures that have been given a hi-tech gloss.

The heroes are often scruffy soldiers of fortune — charming rogues remarkably similar to Harrison Ford's Han Solo. Like him, they tend to have an ironic, what-the-hell attitude, infusing the proceedings with a sense of fun and instructing us that they're not meant to be taken too seriously. The hero usually has a coterie of companions, which often includes a cutesy robot and/or a friendly alien.

However, as is true of other types of fantasy adventure, the story and the characters in space adventures are rarely very complex or well developed, and primarily function to create numerous opportunities for action sequences and big effects.

The special-effects technology that *Star Wars* pioneered is now pretty standard; thus, we frequently see the same kind of shots and camera movements, the same use of miniatures and mattes, and nearly identical laser fights and space battles. As well, we repeatedly see similar designs in structures, spacecraft, and, above all, costumes (Darth Vader and his stormtroopers are the leading style-setters for the forces of evil). Indeed, with the exception of the movies that have adopted *Alien*'s working-class grittiness or *Road Warrior*'s studded-leather style, few movies — in this festival and elsewhere — seem able to envision distant worlds, times, and technologies that look significantly different from those in *Star Wars*. I believe it is this lack of originality that makes the space adventures as a whole seem rather disappointing, as more tired ripoffs than interesting variations on a generic formula.

One of the main reasons that *Star Wars* — like *Conan*, *Raiders*, *Alien*, and *Road Warrior* — was so successful is that it showed us things we'd never seen before. That's not to say that *Star Wars* was completely original. It borrowed heavily from many sources — from Japanese movies to Leni Riefenstahl's — but it did so with a lot of imagination and originality, which, combined with technological wizardry, added up to something that seemed slick and sleek and brand new. It was, as Lucas was often quoted as saying, the sci-fi movie he'd always wanted to see as a kid.

Now, thanks to his success in presenting his vision, we've gotten to see it again and again. Occasionally, there are sparks of creative energy, but mostly it's exactly what we've seen before — from space cruisers blasting through the void to space cantinas filled with strange aliens — though probably not executed with the same degree of skill. However, what seems fresh and exciting the first time rapidly grows stale with repetition. And since we're dealing with imaginary worlds, anything remotely mundane in their realization becomes an especially serious failure.

The movies that follow are not all terrible. Most are cheap and dull, but a couple have a some verve and are moderately entertaining. None, though, has the vitality of *Star Wars*, or delivers anything approaching its fun and excitement, which is not too surprising, since Lucas himself had trouble keeping things fresh. (*Return of the Jedi* seems more than a little fatigued.)

My guess is that this type of space fantasy has pretty well played itself out. Space may continue to serve as a movie setting or locale, but it will be for different types of stories, as was the case with *Outland* and this festival's most recent entry, **NIGHTFLYERS**. Certainly, the possibilities are far from exhausted, but it looks like it may take someone doing what George Lucas did — coming up with a new combination of elements — to revive the genre and keep it going for another decade.

Star Warriors

BATTLE BEYOND THE STARS *(1980)*
wr John Sayles; dir Jimmy T. Murakami

Produced by Roger Corman, this is a moderately clever rendition of the classic Western *The Magnificent Seven*, using spaceships and lasers instead of horses and six-shooters. When his planet of nonviolent pacifists is threatened by an evil tyrant (John Saxon), Richard Thomas goes off and recruits an odd assortment of intergalactic mercenaries to defend his world. They include a space cowboy (George Peppard), a reptileman, a group of three-eyed telepathic clones, and, best of all, Robert Vaughn reprising his role from the original and Sybil Danning as a Valkyrie in a costume so eye-popping it alone may be worth the price of the rental. Played largely for fun, it has a nice light touch, some wit, and some amusingly bizarre and imaginative characters. Budget constraints show in the sets, costumes, and special effects, most of which look pretty cheap and are starting to show their age. Still, the cheerful tackiness is not inappropriate to the casual feel of it all. This is by no means an entirely successful move: lots of it is dull, insipid, and chintzy, but it has some nice moments and some creative intelligence on display. Perhaps most interesting in its use of *Mag Seven* (which was itself based on *The Seven Samurai*), this is a modest — and modestly entertaining — bit of space fluff.

SPACE RAIDERS *(1983)*
wr and dir Howard R. Cohen

A 10-year-old boy inadvertently gets picked up by a small band of likable intergalactic bandits, and then has lots of adventures as they're pursued across the universe by the forces of the all-powerful Corporation. The first 20 minutes of this shows promise — a good look, a decent premise, and some intriguing characters — but it fails to develop the characters and the strong central conflict. Produced by Roger Corman, this ends up being nothing but a space shoot-'em-up with footage recycled from **BATTLE BEYOND THE STARS**. Maybe young kids will be amused, but that's about it for this one. With Vince Edwards as the leader of the raiders.

SPACEHUNTER – ADVENTURES IN THE FORBIDDEN ZONE *(1983)*
wr David Preston, Edith Rey, Dan Goldberg, and Len Blum; dir Lamont Johnson

Soldier-of-fortune Peter Strauss goes to an inhospitable quarantined planet in order to rescue three stranded space tourists. He teams up with Molly Ringwald, a street kid in the Forbidden Zone, and together they journey to the fortress of "Overdog," the half-man, half-machine psychotic who rules the territory. Although the narrative is kind of rambling and predictable, there's a fairly high level of weirdness on display here — human slugs and amphibian Amazons, for example — so their adventures do tend to hold your attention. The production values are generally pretty good, as are the performances, and there's also some nice wordplay in the slang that Molly uses. Had they gone for an R rather than PG, this could have been a potent piece of space trash. As it is, it's not great, but there's enough imagination and energy to provide some fast-moving mindless fun.

THE ICE PIRATES *(1984)*
wr Stewart Raffill and Stanford Sherman; dir Stewart Raffill

A futuristic swashbuckler in which sword-wielding buccaneers attack ships of the evil Templar Empire to steal ice, the only commodity of value in a galaxy without water. This would like to be a comic adventure, but the humor is flat and the persistently jokey tone undercuts the possibility of any real tension or excitement. Despite a few effective sequences, the narrative veers off in so many directions that it lacks focus and forward movement. With a decent cast (Robert Urich, Angelica Huston, John

Matuszak), an often interesting look, and the occasional touch of creativity, this had the potential to be a fairly entertaining piece of space nonsense. In the end, though, despite an arid universe, this is a very soggy effort.

THE LAST STARFIGHTER *(1984)*
wr Jonathan Betuel; dir Nick Castle

Alex Rogan (Lance Guest) is a wiz at the "Starfighter" video game, designed by the Star League to find pilots to defend the galaxy. When he beats the game, he's recruited by Robert Preston to pilot a real starfighter, and is taken far away to be trained. After all the other pilots are killed, Alex must defend against the enemy invaders alone. Although more than a little heavy-handed and hackneyed, this one shows some sense of fun. Not anything very special, but there are some good performances, some good effects, and enough energy to make this one of the more successful clones.

Grounded Space Adventures

METALSTORM: The Destruction of Jared-Syn *(1983)*
wr Alan Adler; dir Charles Band

On a barren, distant planet that bears a remarkable resemblance to the southern California desert, the evil tyrant Jared-Syn is using a magic crystal to collect souls while getting ready to conquer the ravaged land, and only a Ranger named Dogen (Jeffrey Byron) stands in his way. Although this is supposed to be another world, its look and style is essentially that of the *Road Warrior* clones, with the addition of a few strange creatures and some laser blasters. Except for a couple of nice (brief) bits by Richard Moll and Tim Thomerson, this one's a total stiff. No metal, no storm, no destruction of Jared-Syn since they were obviously hoping to make a sequel. Not content to be dull, cheesy, and stupid in two dimensions, this was originally released in 3-D, but it would take more than an optical effect to make this one watchable.

SPACERAGE *(1985)*
wr Jim Lenahan

This is subtitled "Breakout on Prison Planet," and that just about sums up the plot. Some time in the future, on a distant penal-colony planet called New Botany Bay, where convicted felons are exiled to work in the mines, the prisoners riot, escape, kill a lot of people, and get wiped out. End of movie. This one was shot in the southern California desert, and about the only "futuristic" elements are some minor cosmetic alterations to the dune buggies everyone rides around in. Michael Paré, as the leader of the convicts, is the only actor in this dismal effort with any energy or presence, and since he's a totally despicable psycho, we aren't left with much to identify with. Certainly not with Richard Farnsworth, looking more cadaverous than John Carradine, as the old bounty hunter coming out of retirement for one last assignment. Except for a few classic lines ("Nobody gets off of this planet" and "Home has changed. There's nothing there for people like us"), this tedious mess doesn't even offer the relief of unintentional humor. The fact that there is no director credit (the director of the reshoots is credited) suggests that the production had a few problems . . . all of which showed up on the screen.

STARSHIP *(1985, Australian)*
wr Roger Christian and Matthew Jacobs; dir Roger Christian

In the 21st Century, at a mining colony on the planet Ordessa, the android masters plan to kill the rebellious human workers and replace them with robots. Only three gallant rebel leaders and their faithful 'droid (a Nissan 4000) can prevent the mass extermination. Like most Australian movies, this has a lot of really strong visuals. Filmed at a large mining operation, it made good use of the vast interior spaces and the huge equipment — including a sequence involving a dumptruck the size of a two-story house — and thus is consistently interesting to look at, despite what must have been a fairly small budget. Unfortunately, the look is all that's interesting here. We get no real sense of the future social order that created the situation; the plotting is mechanical and often disjointed and confusing; and the characters are too sketchy and undeveloped to command our involvement. You could do worse, but, despite its title, this one's strictly down to earth.

> *"Whatever it is, it's getting bigger."*
> THE BLOB

Space Schticks

GALAXINA *(1980)*
wr and dir William Sachs

This movie is known primarily as Playmate Dorothy Stratten's last, made just before she was murdered; regrettably it has no other distinction. This is a low-budget, low-brow, labored comedy that takes off on a lot far superior movies — *2001*, *Star Trek*, *Star Wars*, *Alien* — but is too rarely funny in itself. The story has something to do with intergalactic policemen and a piece of magic junk called the "Blue Star," but it's just the flimsiest of hooks upon which to hang a lot of very tired and clichéd "comic" routines. Oh, every once in a while there's something amusing — a silly creature, a deliberately crummy effect — and there's a nice sense of cheerful tackiness, but it's not enough, since the rest is cheap, familiar, and dull. Dorothy, by the way, looks very pretty and did not embarrass herself in the title role of a robot who reprograms herself to feel love.

SPACESHIP *(1981)*
wr and dir Bruce Kimmel
Originally released as *The Creature Wasn't Nice*.

This is what you might get if you crossed *Alien* with *Airplane!* The five crew members of the spaceship *Vertigo* (Cindy Williams, Leslie Nielsen, Patrick Macnee, Gerrit Graham, Bruce Kimmel) discover a small alien organism on a previously unknown planet and take it aboard. Soon it grows into an omnivorous intergalactic lounge singer — a ravenous, one-eyed ambulatory pile of goo that sings "I Want to Eat Your Face." The good comic actors make the first half hour or so of this kind of amusing, with a few good laughs and a nice, low-key sense of humor appropriate to the tacky production. Eventually, though, the material runs very thin, as do the laughs. Funnier than **GALAXINA** or Mel Brooks's *Spaceballs*, but for real space laughs, check out **ESCAPE FROM GALAXY 3**.

A Variant Closer to Home

SPACECAMP *(1986)*
wr W. W. Wicket and Casey T. Mitchell; dir Harry Winer

The producers must have hoped that this movie about a group of kids accidentally blasting off in a shuttle was going to be its year's big space adventure. Then the *Challenger* disaster occurred, grounding in grimness this fantasy of amateurs in orbit. The setting is Spacecamp, a NASA-run summer program in which junior astronauts learn how to operate a space shuttle. Kate Capshaw plays an astronaut who was not picked to go into space, but was instead put in charge of five young campers, including Lea Thompson (*Back to the Future*). Through circumstances too inane to relate, they find themselves in earth orbit, running out of oxygen. The long concluding space sequence does have some good effects and some excitement, but everything that precedes it is so dumb, manipulative, and flat that it hardly matters. Twelve-year-old kids, like the camper who dreams of being Luke Skywalker, might be willing to overlook the deficiencies, but it's hard to believe anyone more discriminating would.

Real Space Camp

ESCAPE FROM GALAXY 3 *(198?, Spanish? Italian?, dubbed)*
wr John Thomas; dir Ben Norman

All those who wish they still made movies like *Fire Maidens from Outer Space* (1956) or *Queen of Outer Space* (1958) will want to seek out this contemporary variant. We open with a space princess and a rocket jockey narrowly escaping the clutches of the evil "King of the Night" after he's killed her father and destroyed her planet. This thus begins like *Star Wars* — complete with some of the tackiest miniature spaceships and cheapest optical effects you'll ever see — then takes a surprising turn. The fugitives flip into "deep space" and emerge close to earth, apparently long after some apocalypse has reduced the population to a tribe of peaceful primitive folk who wear mini-togas and make out a lot. Borrowing a touch from *Superman*, the space visitors, with their highly developed powers — great strength, the ability to shoot laserbeams from their fingertips — seem as gods to the tribe. But somewhere along the path of advancement, the spacers clean forgot about sex, a deficiency that the fun-loving earthlings are happy to rectify. This is not quite as amusing as it sounds, being a little too slow and dull to be consistently funny, but there are a number of bits of inspired ineptitude — especially a couple of dance numbers by a chorusline of primitive bimbos — that are easily equal of anything in the '50s classics. With topless Cheryl Buchanan as the princess who discovers sex in a couple of touching sequences.

A Haunting Variant

NIGHTFLYERS *(1987)*
wr Robert Jaffe; dir T.C. Blake

In the 21st Century, somewhere far away, a group of researchers — including a professional telepath — start off on an expedition on *Nightflyer*, a chartered ship. Soon, strange things start to happen, and they eventually realize they're being menaced by a computer that makes *2001*'s HAL seem user-friendly. In fact, the computer contains the consciousness of the captain's deceased mother, and she's not exactly what you'd call a gracious hostess. With its emphasis on ESP, parapsychology, and what is essentially a possession, this turns out to be less a space adventure than a fairly standard haunted-house tale with a hi-tech twist and an intergalactic setting. Not a bad idea, but not very well done. This never manages to generate the kind of mystery, suspense, or surprises that the form requires. Things move forward slowly and predictably, the characters are never developed, and a few of the abundant effects are anything more than routine. This is not an absolutely bad movie, just a rather dull disappointment. With Catherine Mary Stewart in the Sigourney Weaver role.

FESTIVAL 25

* * *

SPECULATIONS
Time Warps, Future Visions, and Techno-Fantasies

> "What's happening here?"
> — *Final Countdown*

This festival offers a mixed bag of movies that, while clearly containing elements of fantasy, are different in terms of style and/or subject from the other forms of fantasy adventure we've seen thus far. Most will probably be found on the science-fiction shelves of your video store, and they deal with subjects that have long been staples of sci-fi literature — time travel, visions of future societies, robots, and so on.

However, like the space adventures in the preceding festival, these speculative films are only rarely concerned with the kind of exploration of complex ideas and alternative worlds that mark their more sophisticated literary counterparts. In large part, this is probably a function of the film medium itself, which has always found it much easier to present straightforward action than complicated concepts that don't conveniently lend themselves to visual or dramatic treatment. Thus, with a few exceptions, the movies in this festival tend to be action movies given some sort of technological or speculative twist.

Although few of the movies that follow are absolute originals, neither are they all slavishly imitative. Where they do borrow from other films, most at least use models that have not yet been cloned to death, and this alone is enough to give them a certain freshness. Furthermore, most of these seem to be more than just mechanical exercises in pursuit of a quick buck. Enthusiasm for the material and energy are often in evidence, as well as a little creativity, imagination, and flair. These are not all good movies, but taken as whole, they do make up a fairly interesting and entertaining group.

> *"The fact that he dismembered his victims indicated we were dealing with a psychopath."*
> BLOOD CULT

Time Warps: Extra-Dimensional Adventures

Until the 1980s, time travel only occasionally turned up in movies, most notably in George Pal's version of H.G. Wells's *The Time Machine* (1960) and in *Time After Time* (1979), in which Wells himself arrives in present-day San Francisco in pursuit of Jack the Ripper. Now, with the decade's emphasis on fantasy, variations on the theme are much more common, and include such box-office successes as *Time Bandits* (1981), *The Terminator* (1984), *Back to the Future* (1985), and *Peggy Sue Got Married* (1986).

None of these hits, nor any of the time warps that follow, do much more than touch upon or acknowledge the fascinating problems and paradoxes inherent in the subject. Instead, they tend to focus on action — encounters with strange creatures, getting back to the proper time — or the comic and dramatic possibilities of a character who suddenly finds himself/herself stuck in some very different age.

Even with this simplified treatment, this kind of story seems to require a good shot of cleverness to be effective. Sending someone backward or forward in time cannot help but create a situation filled with interesting potential, but the situation itself is only the starting-point. It takes some wit and ingenuity to do something with it, and when those qualities are present, the result can be quite amusing and entertaining. When they're not, what you get is, so to speak, a waste of time.

THE FINAL COUNTDOWN *(1980)*
wr David Ambrose, Gerry Davis, Thomas Hunter, and Peter Pawell; dir Don Taylor

While on maneuvers near Hawaii, the aircraft carrier u.s.s. *Nimitz* gets caught in a freakish storm ("a phenomenon of nature that can't be explained") that transports it back to December 6, 1941, the day before the Japanese bombed Pearl Harbor. With their superior firepower, they have the ability to wipe out the Japanese fleet, thereby changing history and setting up what one character calls the "classic paradox of time." Kirk Douglas, Martin Sheen, James Farentino, Katharine Ross, and Charles Durning are along for the ride, but the real star of this movie is the *Nimitz*. This ship is a truly awesome construction, and a good part of the time is spent putting her through her paces. The rest is spent on the efforts of the cardboard characters to figure out what happened and what to do about it. The ship aside, it's all very dull and clunky, with the pedestrian script scarcely raising any of the fascinating issues that are central to the story. This could easily have been a much better movie; as is, its chief appeal is for those with an interest in military hardware.

TIMERIDER *(1983)*
wr William Dear and Michael Nesmith; dir William Dear

A hotshot motocross racer (Fred Ward) inadvertently rides through a secret experiment in time travel, and finds himself transported back to 1877 — a modern man in the Old West. While generally well done and pleasant enough, this one's script fails to develop much of the potential, comic and dramatic, inherent in the situation. Thus, aside from the motorcycle, what we have is basically a very traditional, straightforward Western, complete with outlaws and shootouts, and it's not quite enough. Had the script been a little more complex and the pace faster, this could have been a pretty neat little movie. As it is, there are some nice bits, some good performances — especially Belinda Bauer as one of the tougher Western heroines — and a clever time-warp twist ending that, a year later, *Terminator* also employed. Nothing special, but if you don't expect too much, this is a mildly entertaining way to fill 90 minutes.

THE PHILADELPHIA EXPERIMENT *(1984)*
wr William Gray and Michael Janover; dir Stewart Raffill

The reverse of **THE FINAL COUNTDOWN**. A secret Navy experiment in 1943 to develop a radar-masking device goes awry, and Michael Paré falls through a hole in the space/time continuum and comes out in 1984 Nevada, where a similar sort of experiment has also gotten out of control. As Paré tries to figure out what happened, he meets up with Nancy Allen, and together they're pursued by the military as a time tornado threatens to suck up everything on the planet. This is, for the most part, a reasonably entertaining piece of time nonsense. The numerous visual effects are not all that special, but the story clicks right along and exhibits enough humor and twists to keep things interesting. And for once, Paré's usual stiffness seems appropriate for a character who finds himself in a situation way beyond his experience. Not a great movie, but another decent-enough space/time-killer. (By the way, the movie showing on the television in the diner is **HUMANOIDS FROM THE DEEP**, an even better time-killer.)

TRANCERS *(1984)*
wr Paul de Meo and Danny Bilson; dir Charles Band

This opens 300 years in the future, in Angel City, all that remains of Los Angeles after it was destroyed by an earthquake. Tim Thomerson plays Trooper Jack Deth of the Angel City P.D., an archetypal loner who wears a trenchcoat and goes skin-diving in the ruins of L.A., looking for parts of old automobiles. His assignment is to get Martin Whistler, a super-villain who's gone back to 1985 to eliminate the Ruling Council by killing their distant ancestors. Jack follows him "down the line," where he enters the body of one of his relatives, Philip Deth. He teams up with Phil's girlfriend (Helen Hunt), and together they contend with Whistler's zombie-like army of "trancers." This is a cross between *Blade Runner* and *Terminator*, with a look/style somewhat reminiscent of *Repo Man*. Although the budget was obviously limited, there is a fair amount of ingenuity and imagination on display here, along with some good performances, lively action, and nice bits of humor. I've read some negative reviews of this one, but I think it's a pretty nifty effort, way above the usual standard for Charles Band and his Empire Pictures.

MY SCIENCE PROJECT *(1985)*
wr and dir Jonathan R. Betuel

John Stockwell, poking around an Air Force junkyard in the hope of finding something he can use for his high-school science project, comes upon a strange device left over from an alien spacecraft that crashed 30 years earlier. The device turns out to be a machine for generating space/time warps, and when it gets going, it fills the corridors of the high school with apemen, gladiators, mutants, and a tyranosaurus rex. A lot of money ($14 million) was spent on this one, and there are a lot of effects, but very few that we haven't seen before, and even fewer that are at all impressive. Worse yet, the pace is lethargic, the narrative and the characters uninvolving, and most of the numerous attempts at humor fall flat. Dennis Hopper, as the leftover hippie science teacher, is the best part of the movie, but he's only around for about 10 minutes. The science project got an A, which is at least three grades higher than this one deserves.

BIGGLES — ADVENTURES IN TIME
Time-warped Jones clone; see Festival 22.

Two Flash-Frozen Time Travelers

ICEMAN *(1984)*
wr Chip Prosser and John Drimmer; dir Fred Schepisi

The body of a 40,000-year-old Neanderthal man, discovered during oil exploration in the Arctic, is thawed and brought back to life. The first 10-15 minutes of this are absolutely terrific, then it quickly falls apart as earnest biologist Lindsay Crouse wants to dissect him and even more earnest anthropologist Timothy Hutton wants to communicate man-to-caveman. John Lone (*The Last Emperor*) gives a wonderfully sympathetic performance as the title character, the rest of the cast is good, and the production values are extremely high. The script, though, is kind of rambling and lethargic and takes itself far too seriously. Despite some very good moments, this one ends up being considerably less than the sum of its impressive parts.

GHOST WARRIOR *(1984)*
wr Tim Curnen; dir Larry Carroll

My guess is that this one was rushed into production as soon as plans for **ICEMAN** hit the Hollywood trade papers. A master samurai warrior, frozen in a glacier for over 400 years, is thawed and revived in contemporary Los Angeles. Since the guy's last recollection is of his fatal wounding, he's kind of puzzled by this turn of events, and his mystification is hardly diminished by the fact that the brilliant scientists who revived him don't think to have a Japanese interpreter around to explain the situation. Of course, if they had done so, we wouldn't have had this low-budget ripoff, which I found more entertaining than its model. That's not to say that this

> "*Every Ragnik will fight to the death before they give up that ruby!*"
> THE BARBARIANS

is a very good movie, but Hiroshi Fujioka does a nice job as the stranger in a very strange land, and the idea of an ancient samurai slashing a broad swath through downtown L.A. is not without a certain appeal. While this doesn't really exploit much of the potential inherent in its premise, it manages to tap a little of it and thus, despite being basically cheap and dumb, it does keep us interested in the warrior and his impossible situation.

Future Tense: The Shape of Things to Come

Whether a few years ahead, or a few millennia, future societies on earth have been one of the most common subjects of speculative fiction, but, like time travel, have relatively rarely been given cinematic treatment. Among the more significant efforts have been such movies as *Metropolis* (1926), *Things to Come* (1936), *Fahrenheit 451* (1966), George Lucas's first film, *THX-1138*, (1970), *A Clockwork Orange* (1971), *Soylent Green* (1973), and *Rollerball* (1975). During the 1980s, we've had *1984*, *Brazil* (1985), and one of the most splendidly realized visions of a future society, *Blade Runner* (1982).

These movies have not all been successful, either financially or artistically, but they are all quite interesting in their attempts to create large, complex, functioning societies. The main reason we've not had more of this sort of future vision is economic: when you're doing a movie like this, there's very little that can be taken off the rack, and it can be very expensive to create a new world, with new architecture, costumes, and technology. What we get instead are movies like Bertrand Tavernier's grimly curious *Deathwatch* (1979) — much more simplified visions in which the future world is essentially the present one with a couple of new elements.

By far, though, the most common form of futuristic speculation is that of the post-apocalyptic film, again for economic reasons. The most prevalent vision of the post-apoc world is found in Festival 23, but the movies that follow present some often interesting variations on the theme, in terms of both the style and the way the subject is treated. For the most part, these are not what you'd call optimistic visions. Or, as someone once said, "The future isn't what it used to be."

ESCAPE 2000 *(1981, Australian)*
wr Jon George and Neill Hicks; dir Brian Trenchard-Smith

Made the same year as *Escape From New York*, this is one of the few future visions that doesn't have the distinctive studded-leather look. Actually, as far as style goes, this has very little, and doesn't go much beyond issuing everyone a basic yellow jumpsuit. Borrowing from *A Clockwork Orange*, this one is set in a prison camp for re-education and behavior modification, where "deviates" (i.e., anyone who disagrees with the government) are taught to conform for the good society. The camp also provides the ruling class with their favorite sport — a hunt in which the prisoners are the prey. Thus, most of the movie is a chase in which four prisoners (including Steve Railsback and Olivia Hussey) are pursued across Australian terrain by a party of cruel and decadent hunters. This is yet one more ripoff of *The Most Dangerous Game* (first made 1932 and remade countless times since), and one of the less exciting and involving versions. About all this one adds, besides the vaguely futuristic setting, is a fair amount of semi-explicit violence — hackings, impaling, exploding heads — but it's all very phony and inferior stuff. This now looks very dated, and should have kept its original title, "Turkey Shoot." The director employed a similar setting, more successfully, in **DEAD-END DRIVE IN**.

KAMIKAZE '89 *(1982, West German, subtitled)*
wr Robert Katz; dir Wolf Gremm

This is a very curious movie based on *Murder on the 31st Floor*, a crime thriller by the late Per Wahlöö (co-author of the terrific series of Swedish police novels featuring Martin Beck). The setting is the near future in a Germany in which everything is perfect and perfectly managed . . . or at least that's what those in power would like to believe. In fact, it is a stultifying, smiling, fascistic state. The plot concerns a threat to the combine that controls all the media, but it's very confusing and never goes anywhere. However, the view of post-industrial decadence is quite amusing, as is the wonderful performance by the late German director Rainer Werner Fassbinder, who plays Jansen, the number-one police detective, and gets to wear a nifty leopardskin-patttterned suit and to carry a revolver with a leopard-skin handle, and who has lines like "Avoid unnecessary remarks" and "Avoid unnecessary questions." By no means a great movie, but certainly an interesting one.

THE NEW GLADIATORS *(1983, Italian, partly dubbed)*
wr Elisa Briganti, Dardano Sacchetti, Cesare Frugoni, and Lucio Fulci; dir Lucio Fulci

In the year 2072, a narrator informs us, the world's most popular TV programs are "based on pain, brutality, and human destruction." (Sounds like your kind of television, right?) In an effort to win the ratings war, one of the two main global networks mounts the ultimate sports spectacular — "The Battled of the Damned" in which condemned prisoners engage in gladiatorial combat, the winner gaining his freedom. This opens strongly, and promises to be a media satire and an ultra-violent death game much like those in *Rollerball* and *Death Race 2000* (both 1975). Unfortunately, the focus is soon lost as various uninteresting tangents, including that old favorite — a super-computer out to take over the world — are explored. This looks better than a lot of the Italian futuristic efforts, but is still very cheap, and the action — mostly jousting on motorcycles, with lots of explosions and one decapitation — is similarly routine. Although occasionally interesting, this one is mostly dull and disappointing. As far as death sports go, you might first check out **ENDGAME**, made the same year and starring Al Cliver, who also appears here as one of the minor gladiators.

RADIOACTIVE DREAMS *(1986)*
wr and dir Albert F. Pyun

How to describe this curiosity . . . well, it's the movie you might get if you cross *Road Warrior* with *Blade Runner*, throw in a little *Repo Man*, add mutants and a touch of Abbott and Costello, and give it all a '40s-private-eye overlay. On April 1, 2010, two young men (John Stockwell, Michael Dudikoff) emerge from the fallout shelter where they have spent 14 years, following an atomic holocaust. Apparently, they remember little of their origins, and the only books they had were works of Raymond Chandler. Consequently, they now call themselves Philip and Marlowe, and intend to be private eyes in the post-apoc world. They travel to Edge City (Alex Cox's name for Los Angeles), where they quickly find themselves in the middle of a frenzied hunt for the keys that will launch the one remaining nuclear missile. The narrative doesn't always make a lot of sense, but the pace is fast, there's always something weird going on, and the look of the brutal but vibrant urban world is compelling. Unlike a lot of the movies in this book, which try to stretch a thin 30 minutes of material to feature length, Albert Pyun (**THE SWORD AND THE SORCEROR**), tends to put in too much and to make things too complicated, and that's the main problem here. The whole private-eye business, while occasionally amusing, seems unnecessary, and the story of two innocents in a very weird land would have worked just as well without that element. Also, Michael Dudikoff's character, who seems partly modeled on Lou Costello's loud-mouthed dummy, quickly becomes quite annoying. Still, this is a movie that takes risks and that displays a hell of a lot of creative energy. If this ultimately has too many problems to be considered a success, then it is a lively, original, and frequently fascinating failure.

Other Apocalypses

NIGHT OF THE COMET (1984)
wr and dir Thom Eberhardt

In Los Angeles, a comet passes close to earth, disintegrating all those exposed to its deadly emissions. Two spunky but bubbleheaded Valley Girls (Mary Catherine Stewart and Kelli Maroney) are among the few survivors, and while they see this situation as an opportunity to do some really serious shopping, they first have to contend with a few crazed zombies and a group of scientists (headed by Mary Woronov) who want to drain their blood in the hope of finding an antidote to the condition. Meant to be something of a post-apoc comedy-thriller, this one is very bright and casual. The girls give nice performances, and there is some clever dialog and a few effective moments. I don't, however, think there's quite enough here to make it work, nor is there much in the way or effects or suspense to fill in the spaces. Still, it's not unpleasant, and a lot of reviewers liked this better than I did, so you might want to check it out for yourself.

THE QUIET EARTH (1985, New Zealand)
dir Geoffrey Murphy

At 6:12 A.M., Zac Hobson wakes up to discover that, while the physical world is apparently unchanged, all the people, but him, have vanished. It

> *"You'll never get there. On the way, you'll encounter the ultimate horror."*
>
> SHE

seems that an experiment to create a "global energy grid" has somehow shifted things to another dimension or a different universe. At first Zac copes with the deserted city, then starts to go slightly mad from loneliness until a young woman turns up. When a third survivor — a young Maori man — appears, a triangle is created, very reminiscent of *The World, the Flesh and the Devil* (1958) and *The Last Woman on Earth* (1960). Then it seems that whatever caused the dimensional shift is about to happen again. This New Zealand-made film is beautifully shot and well acted, but a little slow until the third survivor shows up, and we eventually learn why these three survived, which sets up a striking conclusion. If you don't expect too much, this is a curious, intriguing little movie.

The Real Thing

TESTAMENT *(1983)*
wr John Sacret Young; dir Lynne Littman

This movie is so beautifully made that it is almost impossible to watch. Focusing on Jane Alexander and her family, it depicts the slow disintegration of a community just outside San Francisco in the aftermath of a nuclear war. There are no big events here, no high drama, just the gradual death of the community from the effects of radiation. It's all done with a low-key matter-of-factness that is completely plausible ... and utterly devastating. This might be the saddest movie ever made — a gentle elegy on the passing of the human race. I hesitate to recommend a movie that can make you feel so utterly miserable, but this could well be the most eloquent, powerful statement ever made against nuclear arms. Made in conjunction with PBS's "American Playhouse."

THREADS *(1984, British, made for TV)*
wr Barry Hines; dir Mick Jackson

Originally broadcast by the BBC, this is Britain's version of *The Day After*. Told in a docu-drama style, it shows us what happens to the city of Sheffield (fourth largest in the country) in the aftermath of a 3,000-megaton exchange of weapons between the U.S. and the U.S.S.R.

Although overly long — more than half the movie is spent on the events leading up to the war — it is very well done, focusing on both the personal stories of two families and the big catastrophic picture. The accurate portrayal of current scientific thinking about what would happen — radiation poisoning, nuclear winter, the disintegration of society, etc. — needless to say, makes viewing this a rather grim experience. Not quite as potent as **TESTAMENT**, it is nonetheless moving and thoroughly depressing.

Techno-Fantasies: Robots, Androids, and Lethal Machines

Robots and their more human versions, androids, have long enlivened sci-fi films, with some of the more notable creations being those in *Metropolis*, (1926), *The Day the Earth Stood Still* (1951), *Forbidden Planet* (1956), *Silent Running* (1971), *Westworld* (1973), *Alien*, and of course, *Star Wars*. With the exception of those in *Westworld*, however these mechanical entities tended to occupy secondary roles, and it was not until the 1980s that they really became central to their stories, in such films as *Blade Runner*, *The Terminator*, *Short Circuit*, and *Robocop*.

Among the movies that follow, androids (and their man-machine bionic brothers) are by far the more popular forms for the simple reason that they don't require any actual constructions, but can be portrayed by actors specializing in stiffness, awkwardness, and/or relentlessness. As such, human machines offer considerable potential for both comedy and action, and my guess is that we're going to see more of them before the subject is exhausted.

ANDROID *(1982)*
wr James Reigle and Don Opper; dir Aaron Lipstadt

This modest little movie has something of a cult following that is largely deserved. The setting is an orbiting space laboratory, where Klaus Kinski is conducting illegal research on the creation of a new generation of android. With him is MAX 404, an earlier android scheduled to be disconnected. When three escaped convicts arrive in a hijacked spacecraft five radically different agendas (MAX, too, has his own plans and dreams) come into conflict and the fun starts. What distinguishes this movie however, is not the fairly standard SF story/situation, but the quality of the execution. The script clicks right along, with barely any lulls or dead spots, the performances and the direction are strong, and the production values are first-rate, despite what appears to have been a fairly small budget. Most of all, though, there is the wonderful performance of co-writer Don Opper as MAX, who is as scrawny and awkward as a gangly adolescent ... and just as sex-obsessed. MAX is frequently funny, often quite touching, and always engaging; he carries the movie on his very narrow shoulders and, although it probably won't ever happen, I'd love to see MAX 404 return in another movie. About the only quibble I have is the sense that there was comic potential that was not fully realized, but there's still enough good stuff here to make that a minor disappointment.

RUNAWAY *(1984)*
wr and dir Michael Crichton

In a near future with highly advanced robotic technology, Tom Selleck and Cynthia Rhodes are members of the police Runaway Squad, in charge of disconnecting robots that are out of control. A homicidal robot leads them into the middle of the scheme of techno-villain Gene Simmons to sell extraordinarily dangerous technology to terrorists and gangsters. This has generally decent performances, good production values, and some really nifty lethal machines. Unfortunately, it's all used in the service of a script that's far more mechanical than the robots, and limps from cliché to cliché, without much regard for sense or suspense. Still, it does move along fairly briskly, if predictably, and there are some signs of imagination and a few good sequences. Nothing more than a time-waster, but you could do worse.

PROGRAMMED TO KILL *(1986)*
wr Robert Short; dir Allan Holzman

Sandahl Bergman plays Samira, a cold-blooded PLO terrorist who is captured by the CIA. She's badly wounded and "dies" on the operating table, but, in an experimental procedure, parts of her body are replaced by robotics and a computer is implanted in her brain. She is then sent back to wipe out her terrorist cell. In the process, she regains some of her memory, and decides to go after the people who transformed her into a relentless, unstoppable killing machine. What we have here is "Robo-Terminatrix," and while Sandahl is not nearly as impressive as those other lethal androids, the parts of the movie involving her are kind of fun. The other parts (and there are too many) comprise dull and rambling stuff about terrorist/CIA infighting. Also, since Sandahl is so much livelier and more interesting than the other characters, we tend to root for her, and the dramatic tension is skewed. The potential existed to do something fairly interesting here, but the script is not up to it.

HANDS OF STEEL *(1986, Italian, partly dubbed)*
wr Martin Dolman, Elisabeth Parker, Jr., Saul Saska, and John Crowther; dir Martin Dolman

After *The Terminator* and *Blade Runner* and before *Robocop*, there was Paco Queruak, a beefcake cyborg who possesses the title appendages as well as a lot of other bionic parts. In the near future, Paco is programmed by an evil industrialist (John Saxon) to kill an important environmentalist, but has a twinge of conscience at the last moment and only injures his target. He then goes on the run from both Saxon's hired assassins and the FBI, ending up at an isolated truckstop in the middle of some impressive Arizona scenery. Although very derivative, lacking much in the way of effects, and not well plotted, this is slightly more interesting than most of the low-budget Italian wasteland epics, which it closely resembles. It's well photographed, has a few good action sequences and fights (including one with a homicidal cyborg bimbo), and Daniel Greene, as the cyborg hunk, is not only good to look at but gives a creditable performance within the limited range required of him. Certainly nothing special but, if you're not feeling very demanding, this is a passable time-waster, consistent with the director's earlier **AFTER THE FALL OF NEW YORK**.

MAKING MR. RIGHT *(1987)*
wr Floyd Byars and Laurie Frank; dir Susan Seidelman

This story about a very human android and the PR consultant (Ann Magnuson) hired to promote him turns out to be much more screwball comedy than science fiction. John Malkovich plays the dual role of a scientist who wants nothing to do with people and his look-alike robot, Ulysses, who is struggling to become as human as possible. From the title, it's clear that one of the main concerns of this movie is the difficulty women have finding Mr. Passable, and how Ulysses seems so much more appealing than the other men in Magnuson's life. The comment on human relationships is not terribly original, nor is the plot especially strong. There are, however, a lot of good performances (especially by Malkovich, who is absolutely wonderful), some nicely observed bits, and enough genuinely comic sequences and situations to make for a very pleasant 90 minutes. By no means great or profound stuff, just a nice little comedy that probably works better on the small screen.

FESTIVAL 26

* * *

UNTAMED WORLDS
Primitive Men, Cave Bimbos, and Jungle Honeys

"We both belong to the tribe of Zot, which lives in the hills
beyond the mountain of fire."
— *Ironmaster*

Connoisseurs of the zestfully silly know that there are few territories more fertile for cinematic nonsense than primitive worlds. Whether featuring a bozo raised by apes or a bimbo battling apemen, jungle adventures and prehistoric epics can usually be relied upon to provide healthy amounts of serious cheapness, vigorous shoddiness, and energetic stupidity.

Clearly fantasies, these adventures in untamed worlds tend to display little-enough common sense, much less any sense of anthropological, geographical, or zoological reality. Instead, we might have backlot jungles, anachronistic dinosaurs, or fake-fur bikinis — in general, worlds that are not so much imaginary as ridiculous ... which is, of course, one of the great appeals of the genre.

The golden age of the jungle movie was the 1930s and '40s when Johnny Weissmuller and Buster Crabbe swung through several dozen Tarzan movies, Frank Buck brought 'em back alive, and the Tiger Woman stalked in *Jungle Gold*. Later, Johnny put on pants to become Jungle Jim for 16 episodes, and Boy grew into Bomba, the Jungle Boy, for eleven very crummy movies.

Tarzan continued into the 1950s with Lex Barker and Gordon Scott, but the decade really belonged to societies of isolated, man-starved Amazon bimbos (into which a few lucky guys just happen to stumble). Titles like *Prehistoric Women* (1950), *Untamed Women* (1952), and *Mesa of Lost Women* (1953) say it all, and are among the proud nominees for the Golden Turkey Award for "The Most Primitive Male Chauvinist Fantasy in Movie History." The Brothers Medved estimate that

> *"Come on — I dared you to cut your leg off."*
> TRUTH OR DARE

some 200 of these things were produced, and a few turn up every once in a while on the "Late Show." I've managed only to sample the riches, but I've never been disappointed, and I never miss an opportunity to add another to my collection.

The third form of primitive fantasy — the caveman movie — was never produced in the same quantities, but nonetheless has built up a respectable body of work over the years. I've been unable to determine its origins, but notable titles include *One Million B.C.* (1940), *When Dinosaurs Ruled the Earth* (1946), and the cave opus that gave Raquel Welch her start, *One Million Years B.C.* (1966).

All three types of untamed adventures continued into the '60s and '70s, but in greatly reduced numbers, and it was clear the genre was on the wane. Sad to say, the decline has continued into the 1980s, despite three of the more successful (and least silly) adventures in primitive worlds — the first half of *Greystoke* (1984), *The Emerald Forest* (1985), and the best-ever prehistoric adventure, *Quest for Fire* (1981).

As you can see from the pathetically small number of entries in this festival — I had to stretch things to get even this many — the genre just isn't what it used to be, either in the quantity or in the quality of its ludicrousness. Once a flourishing field for low-budget exploitation, it has been displaced by other fantasy genres — particularly pecs-and-flex — which are now the chief repositories of cinematic primitivism.

That's not to say, however, that this festival is lacking in rewards for the serious trash collector. Although some of the forays into untamed worlds are too dull or too jokey to be amusing, others contain moments of mindless shoddiness and high silliness that are every bit the equals of what you can find in the earlier classics.

TARZAN, THE APE MAN *(1981)*
wr Tom Rowe and Gary Goodard; dir John Derek

This may be the best-known, most financially successful movie in this book, but it was included because it may not yet have found the audience it deserves. With Bo Derek as Jane and Miles O'Keeffe (who went on to play the lead in the **ATOR** cycle) as Tarzan, it really is a battle between cheesecake and beefcake, and it's a toss-up as to who has the more spectacular chest. We do, however, get to see more of Miles, and those hoping to get a good long look at Bo's dramatic assets will likely be somewhat disappointed; in fact, we're over halfway through the movie before she utters the magic phrase, "I'm going to take a bath." Likewise, those expecting that the movie will be about Tarzan will also be disappointed; the title notwithstanding, this is Jane's story, and the king of the jungle is demoted to bit player. However, those who collect bad acting and appalling dialog will find much here to savor. Jane is supposed to be a virgin, obviously too big stretch for Bo, who had to settle instead for being vacuous. But it hardly matters, since Richard Harris is along as Jane's demented explorer father, and let me tell you, old Richard really lets 'er rip. He acts up a storm, enough for any two or three actors, as though he were trying to fill the thespian void that Bo's presence creates on the screen. Throw in such lines as "There's so many places in this earth still left to be explored and so few men big enough to go after them" and Bo's memorable "Isn't that a rogue elephant?", and we're talking the stuff that classics are made of. Probably not vigorous enough to make the first rank — there's too much scenic padding — its place in the second of tier (Silver Turkeys?) should be pretty secure.

SHEENA *(1984)*
wr David Newman and Lorenzo Semple, Jr.; dir John Guillermin

I trust there's no one out there who thinks a live-action adventure based on the cartoon "Queen of the Jungle" could possibly be a good movie, so I won't even deal with that issue. No, the only question is whether it's dumb enough to achieve classic-turkey status. Sad to say, the dumbness here is mechanical and pedestrian and not at all what it takes to achieve greatness. Not that there aren't inspired fragments — Sheena (Tanya Roberts, quite fetching in a leather halter from Frederick's of Nairobi) sees her first bare-chested white man and exclaims, "Fur! You have fur!" and we are treated to an aerial assault on a helicopter by a flock of pink flamingos. But these highlights are few and far between and are all but squashed by the weight of a ponderously moving plot, enervated performances, and half-witty dialogue. They spent $26 million (!) on this lump of jungle rot and lost a golden (turkey) opportunity beneath the bloat.

> "She was tall, dark and sexy — the ultimate woman."
> DRACULA'S WIDOW

THE CLAN OF THE CAVE BEAR *(1986)*
wr John Sayles; dir Michael Chapman

Based on the best-selling novel by Jean Auel, this is the story of Ayla, a young Cro-Magnon girl who was taken in by a tribe of Neanderthals when her parents were killed in an earthquake 35,000 years ago. She grows up to be Daryl Hannah, and she's not only smarter and blonder than the soon-to-be-extinct Neanderthals, but she's also the world's first feminist, striking a blow for equality with a rock and a sling. Of course, it's not easy to raise the consciousness of a species that doesn't have any, and for her efforts, Daryl is raped, impregnated, banished, then forced to live as a single mother. As an epic adventure, this was a huge flop when it was first released, earning back less than a tenth of its $18 million outlay. But as a monumental turkey, this might be one of the funniest unintentional comedies in your video store. Probably thirty or more times more expensive than, say, *One Million Years B.C.*, it is no less ludicrous, and it's a real challenge to determine which is more ridiculous — its tone of solemn earnestness, its grunted dialog (helpfully translated in subtitles), its heavy-handed feminism, or its utterly absurd anthropology. See Daryl invent counting. See Daryl develop painless dentistry. See Daryl discover eyeshadow. See it to believe it.

WHERE THE RIVER RUNS BLACK *(1986)*
wr Peter Silverman and Neal Jimenez; dir Christopher Cain

When his mother is brutally killed by a prospector, a young boy is left to fend for himself in the Amazon jungle, his only companions being the river dolphins with which he frolics. After he is captured and brought to the city, a kindly priest (Charles Durning) takes an interest in him and places him in an orphanage. There, he sees the man who shot his mother, and starts on a quest for revenge. The premise of a child reared outside of society and civilization is always a strong one, but this does little more than use it as narrative. It touches on some interesting issues — questions of Man and Nature, the relationship with the dolphins, the process of socialization — but never develops any of them. Filmed in Brazil, this is often quite beautiful and interesting to look at, but for the rest of it, the river doesn't so much run as sit in stagnant pools.

An Urban Variant

WILD THING *(1987)*
wr John Sayles; dir Max Reid

Following on from **CLAN OF THE CAVE BEAR**, writer John Sayles returns to primitive themes with a new version of *Tarzan*, only this one's set in an urban jungle. After his parents are killed by a nasty drug dealer, a little boy is raised by a demented but good-hearted baglady in the basements and tunnels of a decaying inner city. Eighteen years later, he's grown into an urban legend known as "Wild Thing" (Rob Knepper) — a phantom creature who makes animal sounds and swings on ropes down the sides of buildings as he patrols the seamy side of town called "The Zone." The Jane equivalent is a social worker (Kathleen Quinlan) who discovers that the legend is real. When Kathleen is taken prisoner by the drug dealer who killed his parents, Wild Thing's quest becomes the classic one of rescue and revenge. The translation of Tarzan to an urban setting has been quite neatly worked out, but it's played very straight, without the sense of irony or fun that the premise seems to require. Maybe there was more of that in Sayles's original script, but the movie itself ends up being not much more than the basic urban action motif of fighting back/getting even. As such, it's not badly done — Knepper, Quinlan, and Robert Davi as the villain give decent performances and there are a few nice moments — but it's also nothing very special. Of interest mainly as a variation on the form.

The Dawn of Dumbness

IRONMASTER *(1982, French/Italian, dubbed)*
wr Alberto Cavallone, Lea Martino, Dardano Sacchetti, and Gabriel Rossini; dir Umberto Lenzi

Cleverly combining the pecs-and-flex genre with your basic Dawn-of-Man epic, this could be called "Quest for Iron." After the eruption of some volcano stock footage, a tribe of Stone Age beefcakes discovers the title element, and before you can say metallurgy, they've figured out how to make broadswords. Using their new technology, they set about slaughtering every living creature in the valley, including numerous villagers and a gang of missing links wearing ape suits. Only Ela, a hunk of beef previously expelled from the tribe, stands between them and total global domination. He rallies a village of pacifist farmers and a bevy of cave bimbos in leather bikinis, with teased hairdos and pastel eyeshadow, then saves the day by inventing the bow and arrow. Not just another cheap sword-and-sandal extravaganza, this is a message picture — a subtle and profound parable of the arms race. And just so we don't miss the point, the spaces between the battles are filled with ludicrously dubbed, solemn philosophical discussions about war, aggression, and the violent nature of Man. Yes, it is as funny as it sounds.

YOR, THE HUNTER FROM THE FUTURE *(1983, Italian, dubbed) wr Robert Bailey; dir A. M. Dawson (Antonio Margheriti)*

Reb Brown plays the title character, cave beefcake in a leather loincloth and fur booties. Not unlike Daryl Hannah in **THE CLAN OF THE CAVE BEAR**, he's a blond in a world of primitive brunettes, and he's on a quest to find his identity and his people. Along the way, he bludgeons to death a dinosaur, battles a pack of blue-faced apemen similar to the brutes in the classic *Untamed Women* (1952), and encounters a gang of fire-worshippers dressed like Egyptian mummies. He also hang-glides from a pterodactyl, watches a Stone Age hula performed by a chorus line of cave bimbos dressed in leather mini-skirts and disco boots, and delivers such quips as "The blood of your enemy makes you stronger." The first half of this is so vigorously inane and astonishingly cheap and shoddy that it's a complete hoot, with technical incompetence combining with utter brainlessness to produce as shabby a spectacle as is ever likely to pass in front of your glazed eyes. The second half is no less dumb, but somehow it loses its zip and turns fairly dull and repetitious (another dinosaur, more apemen). Eventually, Yor and we discover — I hope I'm not spoiling the surprise — that this is in fact a futuristic Stone Age, post-apoc style, complete with android stormtroopers and a villain called "Overlord" who talks through Darth Vader's echo chamber. Still, if not a complete success, it's not for lack of trying, and students of cinema's lower depths will not want to miss this bargain-basement gobbler.

Cave Comedies

CAVEMAN *(1981)*
wr Rudy de Luca and Carl Gottlieb; dir Carl Gottlieb

The opening titles inform us that it is October 9, One Zillion B.C., and that may well be the comic highlight of this one. Ringo Starr is the leader of a group of cave misfits and outcasts that include Dennis Quaid and Shelley Long, and they're always being hassled by the cave bullies headed by John Matuszak, and Barbara Bach in a push-up cave brassiere. Presumably, this is supposed to be a parody of the '50s cave movies, but since it's almost nothing except labored mugging and very primitive schticks, it doesn't come close to being as funny as its targets managed unintentionally. And the fact that everyone speaks in grunts doesn't help matters. There are some quite amusing dinosaurs created by David Allen, but that's about all that can be recommended in this one. Co-writer de Luca went on to make the utterly egregious **TRANSYLVANIA 6-5000**.

CAVEGIRL *(1985)*
wr, prod, dir and photo by David Oliver

Through circumstances scarcely explained, a socially outcast high-school nerd (Daniel Roebuck) is transported back in time 25,000 years. Once there, he meets some cave folk who are missing more than a few links, and spends a good part of the movie trying to get under the animal-skin micro-mini of Eva (Cindy Ann Thompson), a cave bimbo in mascara and a bleached-blonde perm. In essence, then, this is a prehistoric teen comedy, for which it earns a couple of points for recombinant silliness, but nothing for execution. This has all the usual laff favorites — low-brow *double entendres*, a topless locker-room scene, a fart joke, a condom gag — as well as lots of new ones when the cave folk encounter modern technology in the form of a flashlight, a tape recorder, and a can of shaving cream. Besides these "comic" highlights, most of the rest of the movie seems to consist of endless shots of people walking across the rugged countryside. Unfunny, dull, and slow, this is not even vigorous enough in its stupidity to provide much unintentional humor. Another wasted concept.

> *"I've got the feeling the worst is yet to come."*
> GHOSTHOUSE

A Pair of Pointed Parodies

AMAZON WOMEN ON THE MOON *(1987)*
wr Michael Barrie and Jim Mulholland; dir John Landis, Joe Dante, Peter Horton, and Robert K. Weiss

In 1977, John Landis directed *Kentucky Fried Movie*, a series of parodies of television programs that was written by Abrahams, Zucker, and Zucker (*Airplane!*, etc.), and this is essentially another installment of the same. Despite its being released theatrically, this was really made to be seen on the medium it parodies, and must certainly be much improved by the small screen. Like its predecessor, this one is uneven — some bits are funnier than others — but it moves along very quickly and is never tedious. The title refers to the "Late Show" movie being broadcast, a dead-on recreation of 1950s cheap sci-fi male-chauvinist fantasies (most likely modeled on the Zsa Zsa Gabor classic *Queen of Outer Space*). The cast includes dozens of familiar faces and names, from Sybil Danning to Henny Youngman, B.B. King, and Russ Meyer. With a lot of smiles and chuckles and a couple of really spectacular naked women, I don't know what more you want for your rental bucks.

CANNIBAL WOMEN IN THE AVOCADO JUNGLE OF DEATH *(1988)*
wr and dir J.D. Athens

An irresistible title, and the terrific surprise is that there is quite a clever movie behind the outrageous attention grabber. Ethno-historian Margo Hunt (Shannon Tweed), head of Feminist Studies at Spritzer University, goes on an expedition deep into the title greenspace (in the far off and mysterious land of California), accompanied by a chauvinist soldier-of-fortune (Bill Maher) and a bimbous airhead (Karen Mistal) who's studying Home Ec. Hunt's mission is to find what happened to Dr. Kurtz (Adrienne Barbeau), who vanished while on an expedition in search of the mythical Piranha Women, "an ancient commune of feminists . . . so militant that they eat their men." This could easily have been broad and stupid, but it's played perfectly straight, and the script is really quite intelligent as it skewers all sorts of contemporary issues and attitudes — chauvinist, feminist, academic — while serving up nicely done parodies/

recollections/homages of movies like *Romancing the Stone, Apocalypse Now, African Queen, 2001,* and all the '50s Amazonian male chauvinist fantasies. Maher is mostly very funny, and Adrienne shows, after some seriously bad performances in the '80s, that she can do a good job if she has good material. The big surprise is Shannon, usually identified as "ex-Playmate": in several Canadian movies (*The Surrogate,* **OF UNKNOWN ORIGIN**) she showed why she was a Playmate, but not why she thought she could act; here she keeps her clothes on and gives a fine deadpan comic performance. Perhaps most reminiscent of **MORONS FROM OUTER SPACE**, this has the odd clunky bit, but mostly the material and execution are consistently effective, amusing, and well thought-out. Whoever J.D. Athens is, it is a very sharp and talented person. Highly recommended.

A Welcome Throwback

KILMA, QUEEN OF THE AMAZONS *(1975, Spanish, dubbed)* wr Miguel Cusso and Miguel Iglesias; dir M. I. Bonns

Although older than the cutoff date, this one is a must for fans of classic '50s primitive-women flicks. This relatively contemporary Spanish version concerns the discovery by a group of men of an isolated all-female society, the members of which are naturally young, pretty, and dressed in skimpy outfits. Here, it's the eighteenth century (probably because they had some pirate costumes lying around), and the setting is the Island of the Amazons (apparently located somewhere in the neighborhood of Java), where a tribe of warrior-priestesses guards a piece of magic junk known as the "Eternal Light." In practice, this means that they ride around on horseback, brandishing spears and repelling invaders. During the day they wear sporty animal-skin two-piece bathing suits complete with pushup bras, and lots of eyeshadow; at night, they change into filmy rayon negligées for worship at the temple. Besides the absurd costumes (which, by the way, are never removed), other highlights include ludicrous dubbing, wooden acting, a nonsensical plot, and hilariously inept fight sequences. In other words, this is an unqualified triumph — a film in which virtually every aspect is as lame and dumb as it could possibly

> *"All you know is this outhouse of a world. It used to be different. it used to be beautiful."*
>
> OSA

be. It was somehow overlooked in the *Son of Golden Turkey Awards*, but connoisseurs of cheesy, utterly ridiculous filmmaking will not want to miss this heretofore undiscovered treasure.

ESCAPE FROM GALAXY 3
A futuristic primitive throwback; see Festival 24.

PHOENIX THE WARRIOR
Post-apoc Amazonia; see Festival 23.

BONUS FESTIVAL!

* * *

FOOL'S GOLD
Class Projects of the
Edward D. Wood Academy of Cinema Arts

> "There's something sinister over there, Marsha."
> — *Fiend*

I trust that all trash collectors and fans of deviant cinema are familiar with the name Edward D. Wood. Immortalized in the Medved Brothers' original *Golden Turkey Awards*, Ed Wood was given posthumously the Life Achievement Award as the Worst Director of All Time, and his masterpiece, *Plan Nine from Outer Space*, was voted the Worst Film of All Time. While it is doubtful that Ed Wood's place in film history will ever be seriously challenged, the entries in this festival, few though they are, demonstrate that the tradition lives on, and that there are still filmmakers out there who share Ed's belief that a lack of imagination, talent, and money is no reason not to make a movie.

Although Ed died in 1978, while watching a football game, the principles he lived by — and his standards of cinematic excellence — are kept alive at the Edward D. Wood Academy of Cinema Arts ("Low budgets our speciality"). Presented below are some recent class projects at EDWACA that not only suggest the broad range of programs on offer, but demonstrate the advantages of an EDWACA education. Whereas most appallingly cheap and shoddy motion pictures only manage to be dull and unwatchable, filmmakers with EDWACA training know how to add that certain something that makes ineptitude breathtaking, compelling, and fascinating. As to what that magical ingredient is, there is considerable debate and discussion. Some of EDWACA's distinguished faculty maintain that the key is to have the reach far exceed the grasp, while others hold that the secret is to have the grasp fall far short of the reach.

The issue will probably never be satisfactorily resolved, but the entire faculty concurs that each of the following entries is an inspired example of how, in the right hands, an insufficient budget can combine with a paucity

> "It wasn't a shark and it wasn't a barracuda."
> PIRANHA II

of skill and a dearth of creativity to make a cinematic whole (hole?) that is somehow much less than the sum of its already meager parts. In short, each ably demonstrates the proud motto of EDWACA, "Any asshole can make a movie."

* * *

From EDWACA's non-credit program comes this project from the popular course "Make a feature film over a long weekend using the kids' lunch money":

FIEND *(1980)*
wr and dir Don Dohler

As helpfully noted late in the proceedings, a fiend is, in theory, a little-known "supernatural entity, possibly representing the culmination of evil throughout the ages." In practice, it's Don Leifert, a beefy guy with a big black mustache, who has modeled his acting style on Bela Lugosi's late period. We open with an amorphous red optical effect — the fiend in its natural state — entering a grave and animating the inhabitant. Soon Don emerges to strangle a woman sitting on a nearby tombstone, then he's off to buy a suburban house and open a music academy. Boy! Talk about evil incarnate! Periodically, Don the Fiend goes out and strangles various folks in order to suck out their lifeforce, a process that allows the director to recycle the red-optical footage. Astonishingly cheap and amateurish, this one gives new meaning to the critical term "piss-poor," and may provide even the experienced collector of backyard rubbish with something to ponder.

From the EDWACA correspondence course "No mountain too high, no budget too low":

DON'T GO IN THE WOODS *(1981)*
wr Garth Eliassen; dir James Bryan

Those who believe that filmmaking is a complex, sophisticated process conducted by skilled professionals should check out this Utah backyard number. The title advice is ignored and a glut of amateur actors find themselves being hacked and skewered by a demented woodsman whose identity and motivation (other than an understandable intolerance for bad performances) are not disclosed. The production is distinguished by its total ineptitude in all technical and creative aspects and a budget apparently culled from the refunds on bottles found beside the road during filming. Awesomely stupid and shoddy, this is one of those rare movie opportunities for you to actually feel your brain softening. "Avoid any animal approaching you in the woods," we're told and early on, and that's probably good advice here unless you've got an appetite for some wild turkey.

From the EDWACA Honors Seminar "Nightmare: Theme without Variation":

NIGHTMARE WEEKEND *(1985,dubbed, direct to cassette)*
wr Georges Faget-Benard; dir H. Sala

The title notwithstanding, the only nightmare provided by this opus is the one that must have plagued investors after they saw what they got for their money. What a mess! Unbelievably cheap, amateurish in the extreme, ludicrously dumb, and nonsensically incoherent — even the folks at Troma Team who distributed this (and who are not exactly known for the rigor of their standards) must have wondered about letting this one loose. This is one of those movies where they tell you almost all the plot on the box — they have to, because otherwise you'd never be able to figure out what the hell is going on. This patchwork assemblage of bits and pieces of several stupid, cheap kinds of movies seems to have had one goal — fill 90 minutes and call it a day. We've got a mad scientist out to create obedient slaves through computer "techno-voodoo"; we've got a computer so user-friendly it talks through a clown handpuppet; we've got teenage romance; and we've got three co-eds for completely gratuitous sex. This is probably not the most inept movie of the 1980s — the competition is too stiff — but it's a contender for top-of-the-bottom honors and that's no small achievement.

"It feeds on spinal fluid that it sucks out with a needle-like tongue."
SCARED TO DEATH

ZOMBIE NIGHTMARE *(1986, Canadian, direct to cassette)*
wr David Wellington; dir Jack Bravman

It's hard to know where to start with this one. Someone must've figured there was an audience for a voodoo-zombie-revenge movie with a Heavy Metal soundtrack and 10 minutes of Adam (Batman) West smoking a cigar. Assuming there is an audience that's been keenly anticipating this particular combination of elements, it's doubtful that this discriminating group would be satisfied with this effort. The "plot" (and I do not use the term nearly as loosely as the filmmakers do) concerns a nice Heavy Metal bodybuilder (played by Thor, himself a Heavy Metal bodybuilder), who gets killed by five rich brats out joyriding in Daddy's car. A voodoo priestess, with much rolling of her eyes and grimacing, raises Thor from the dead so that he might avenge himself on his killers before moving on to wherever zombies go after they've done their thing. While it's hard to see how this movie could have been any dumber, and while Thor does give a performance that gives new meaning to the term "living dead," the end result falls short of the classic lameness to which it obviously aspired, and settles instead for being laughably bad. Of course, practice does make perfect, and it's hard to keep a Heavy Metal bodybuilder down . . .

ROCK 'N' ROLL NIGHTMARE *(1987, Canadian, direct to cassette)* wr Jon Mikl Thor; dir John Fasano*

Thor is back! And this time, writing and producing in addition to starring. About the best thing that can be said for this effort is that it looks as though it cost more than the reported $75,000 (Can.) that was lavished on it. Lit and generally in focus, but in every other respect it's a strong candidate for anyone's list of all-time gobblers. A band and its groupies goes out to a deserted farmhouse to work on material, but before too long, strange things start to happen. At first it's all fairly predictable stuff, but then we get a surprise twist that is positively awesome in its dumbness. It will not give anything away to reveal that there is a scene in which Thor wrestles Beezlebub that may well be the equal of the famous sequence in Ed Wood's *Bride of the Monster* in which Bela Lugosi has a titanic battle with a rubber octopus.

Honorable Mentions

Although EDWACA's selection committee did not feel the following titles were sufficiently sprightly to be included in this festival, they are nonetheless not without suitable merits.

EVILS OF THE NIGHT
Alien blood drainers; see Festival 1.

EVIL TOWN
Mad-scientist pituitary slurpers; see Festival 4.

GRAY MATTER
Deranged military mind-readers; see Festival 4.

NECROPOLIS
Six-titted witch soul-sucker; see Festival 11.

THE PREY
Human monster backyard backwoods hacker; see Festival 17.

TRUTH OF DARE
Jupiter, Florida, backyard blood-spurter; see Festival 19.

INDEX OF DIRECTORS AND THEIR FILMS

Note: The films for each director are given in chronological order, as far as can be determined in the absence of dates in some instances.

Adamson, Al: *Brain Damage*
Agrama, Frank: *Dawn of the Mummy*
Alston, Emmet: *New Year's Evil* · *Demonwarp*
Amante, James: *The Alchemist*
Anderson, Clyde: *Monster Dog* · *Rats* (co-dir)
Argento, Dario: *Inferno* · *Creepers*
Arslan, Michael: *Lionman II*
Asher, William: *Night Warning*
Athens, J.D.: *Cannibal Women in the Avocado Jungle of Death*
Attias, Daniel: *Stephen King's Silver Bullet*
Avallone, Marcello: *Specters*
Avedis, Howard: *Mortuary*
Azzopardi, Mario: *Deadline*

Baker, Graham: *Impulse*
Baldi, Ferdinando: *The Treasure of the Four Crowns*
Band, Albert: *Ghoulies II*
Band, Charles: *Parasite* · *Metalstorm: The Destruction of Jared-Syn* · *Trancers*
Barker, Clive: *Hellraiser*
Barkett, Steve: *The Aftermath*
Barry, Christopher: *Tripods* (co-dir)
Barwood, Hal: *Warning Sign*
Bava, Lamberto: *Macabre* · *A Blade in the Dark* · *Demons* · *Demons 2*
Belson, Jerry: *Jekyll and Hyde...Together Again*
Benson, Steven: *Endgame*
Bercovici, Luca: *Ghoulies*
Beresford, Al: *Screamtime*
Betuel, Jonathan: *My Science Project*
Bianchi, Andrea: *Burial Ground*
Bido, Anthony: *Watch Me When I kill*
Bigelow, Kathryn: *Near Dark*
Bilson, Danny: *Zone Troopers*
Blake, T.C.: *Nightflyers*
Blanchard, John: *Really Weird Tales* (co-dir)
Bloom, Jeffrey: *Blood Beach*
Bogle, James: *Stones of Death*
Bonns, M.I.: *Kilma, Queen of the Amazons*
Bradley, Al: *The Iron Warrior*

INDEX OF DIRECTORS AND THEIR FILMS

Bravman, Jack: *Zombie Nightmare*
Brock, Deborah: *Slumber Party Massacre II*
Broderick, John: *The Warrior and the Sorceress*
Brown, Edwin Scott: *The Prey*
Bryan, James: *Don't Go in the Woods*
Buechler, John Carl: *Troll*
Burns, Robert A.: *Mongrel*
Burr, Jeff: *The Offspring*

Cain, Christopher: *Where the River Runs Black*
Cameron, James: *Piranha II*
Cammell, Donald: *White of the Eye*
Cardenas, Hernan: *Island Claws*
Cardona, Rene, Jr. *Beaks*
Cardos, John "Bud": *Mutant*
Carpenter, John: *Prince of Darkness*
Carpenter, Stephen: *The Dorm That Dripped Blood* (co-dir) · *The Power* (co-dir) · *The Kindred* (co-dir)
Carroll, Larry: *Ghost Warrior*
Casey, Richard: *Horror House on Highway Five*
Castellari, Enzo G.: *1990: The Bronx Warriors* · *Escape from the Bronx* · *Warriors of the Wasteland*
Castle, Nick: *The Last Starfighter*
Castravelli, Claudio: *Evil Judgement*
Catalanotto, Joseph J.: *Terror in the Swamp*
Chapman, Michael: *The Clan of the Cave Bear*
Cheek, Douglas: *C.H.U.D.*
Christian, Roger: *The Sender* · *Starship*
Christopher, Anthony J.: *Fatal Pulse*
Ciccoritti, Gerard: *Graveyard Shift*
Cimber, Matt: *Yellow Hair and the Fortress of Gold*
Ciupka, Richard: See Jonathan Stryker
Clark, B.D.: *Galaxy of Terror*
Clouse, Robert: *Deadly Eyes*
Coates, Lewis (Luigi Cozzi): *Alien Contamination* · *Hercules*
Coburn, Glen: *Bloodsuckers from Outer Space*
Cohen, Howard R.: *Saturday the 14th* · *Space Raiders*
Cohen, Larry: *Q* · *The Stuff* · *It's Alive III: Island of the Alive* · *A Return to 'Salem's Lot*
Cokliss, Harley: *Warlords of the 21st Century*
Collins, Edward D.: *Evil Town* (co-dir)
Colpaert, Carl: *In the Aftermath*
Connor, Kevin: *Motel Hell*
Cooper, Buddy: *The Mutilator*
Coppola, Christopher: *Dracula's Widow*
Coscarelli, Don: *The Beastmaster*
Cosmatos, George P.: *Of Unknown Origin*

> *"Take me with you, stranger."*
> YOR, THE HUNTER FROM THE FUTURE

Cozzi, Luigi: See Lewis Coates
Craven, Wes: *Deadly Blessing* · *Swamp Thing* · *The Hills Have Eyes — Part II* · *Deadly Friend* · *The Serpent and the Rainbow*
Crichton, Michael: *Runaway*
Crounse, Avery: *Eyes of Fire*
Cunningham, Sean, S.: *A Stranger Is Watching*
Curie, Anthony: *Pink Chiquitas*

Dahlen, Bob: *Monster in the Closet*
Daley, Tom: *The Outing*
D'Amato, Joe: See David Hills
Damiani, Damiano: *Amityville II: The Possession*
Dante, Joe: *Amazon Women on the Moon* (co-dir)
Davenport, Harry Bromley: *Xtro*
Davidson, Boaz: *Hospital Massacre*
Davis, Andrew: *The Final Terror*
Dawn, Vincent (Bruno Mattei): *Night of the Zombies* · *Rats* (co-dir)
Dawson, Anthony M. (Antonio Margheriti: *Invasion of the Flesh Hunters* · *Yor, Hunter from the Future*
Dear, William: *Timerider*
DeCoteau, David: *Sorority Babes in the Slimeball Bowl-o-Rama*
Dehlavi, Jamil: *Born of Fire*
Dekker, Fred: *Night of the Creeps* · *Monster Squad*
DeLuca, Rudy: *Transylvania 6-5000*
Delman, Jeffrey: *Dead Time Stories*
DeMartino, Albert: *Blood Link*
Deodato, Ruggero: *The Barbarians*
Derek, John: *Tarzan, The Ape Man*
DeSimone, Tom: *Hell Night*
Deubel, Robert: *Girls Nite Out*
Dohler, Don: *Fiend*
Dolman, Martin: *After the Fall of New York* · *Hands of Steel*
Donovan, Paul: *Defcon-4*
Doran, Thomas: *Spookies* (co-dir)
Dugan, Michael: *Mausoleum*
Dugdale, George: *Slaughter High* (co-dir)

Eberhardt, Thom: *Sole Survivor* · *Night of the Comet*
Edmonds, Don: *Terror on Tour*
Eggleston, Colin: *Sky Pirates* · *Casasandra*
Egorov, Oleg: *Osa*
Ellison, Joseph: *Don't Go in the House*
Emmerich, Roland: *Making Contact*
Erler, Rainer: *Spare Parts*
Evans, Roger: *Forever Evil*
Ezra, Mark: *Slaughter High* (co-dir)

INDEX OF DIRECTORS AND THEIR FILMS

Farel, Frank M.: *Spookies* (co-dir)
Fasano, John: *Rock 'n' Roll Nightmare*
Faulkner, Brendan: *Spookies* (co-dir)
Fleischer, Richard: *Amityville 3-D* · *Red Sonja*
Fleming, Andrew: *Bad Dreams*
Florea, John: *Invisible Strangler*
Foleg, Peter: *The Unseen*
Fonveille, Lloyd: *Gotham*
Franco, Jesse/Jesus: *Bloody Moon* · *Virgin Among the Living Dead*
Frank, A.M. (Daniel Lesoeur): *Oasis of the Zombies*
Frank, Carol: *Sorority House Massacre*
Franklin, Richard: *Road Games* · *Link*
Freda, Ricardo: *Fear*
Freed, Herb: *Graduation Day*
Freeman, Hal: *Blood Frenzy*
Friedman, Richard: *Doom Asylum*
Froelich, Bill: *Return to Horror High*
Fruet, William: *Funeral Home* · *Killer Party* · *Blue Monkey*
Fulci, Lucio: *Zombie* · *The Gates of Hell* · *Manhattan Baby* · *The House by the Cemetary* · *Conquest* · *The New Gladiators*
Fuller, Tex: *Stranded*
Furie, Sidney J.: *The Entity*

Garris, Mick: *Critters 2*
George, Peter: *Surf Nazis Must Die*
Giannone, Joe: *Madman*
Gilhuis, Mark C.: *Bloody Wednesday*
Goddard, Gary: *Masters of the Universe*
Golding, Paul: *Pulse*
Gordon, Stuart: *Re-animator* · *From Beyond* · *Dolls*
Gornich, Michael: *Creepshow II*
Gottlieb, Carl: *Caveman*
Graver, Gary: *Trick or Treats*
Gray, Mike: *Wavelength*
Green, Martin: *Dark Sanity*
Gremm, Wolf: *Kamikaze '89*
Griffith, Charles B.: *Dr. Heckyl and Mr. Hype*
Guerrini, Mino: *The Mines of Kilimanjaro*
Guillermin, John: *Sheena* · *King Kong Lives*
Gunnlaugsson, Hrafn: *Revenge of the Barbarians*

Haines, Richard W.: *Splatter University* · *Class of Nuke 'Em High* (co-dir)
Hammer, Robert: *Don't Answer the Phone*
Harlin, Renny: *Prison*
Harmon, Robert: *The Hitcher*
Harrison, Jules: *The Exterminators of the Year 3000*

"Lie down — you've got to ditch your body."
SLAUGHTERHOUSE ROCK

Harry, Lee: *Silent Night, Deadly Night — Part 2*
Hasimoto, Koji: *Godzilla 1985* (co-dir)
Hayes, Robert: *Phoenix the Warrior*
Henenlotter, Frank: *Basket Case* · *Brain Damage*
Herek, Stephen: *Critters*
Herrington, Rowdy: *Jack's Back*
Herz, Michael: *The Toxic Avenger* (co-dir)
Hess, David: *To All a Goodnight*
Hickey, Bruce: *Necropolis*
Hillman, David Michael: *The Strangeness*
Hills, David (Joe D'Amato): *Ator — The Fighting Eagle* · *The Blade Master*
Hiltzer, Robert: *Sleepaway Camp*
Hirsch, Bettina: *Munchies*
Hirschman, Ray: *Plutonium Baby*
Hodges, Mike: *Morons from Outer Space*
Hodi, Jeno: *Deadly Obsession*
Hold, John: *Viking Massacre*
Holland, Tom: *Fright Night*
Holzman, Allan: *Forbidden World* · *Programmed to Kill*
Hool, Lance: *Steel Dawn*
Hooper, Tobe: *The Funhouse* · *Lifeforce* · *Invaders from Mars*
Hopkins, John: *Torment*
Horton, Peter: *Amazon Women on the Moon* (co-dir)
Houck, Joy N., Jr.: *Gray Matter*
Hough, John: *Incubus* · *Biggles — Adventures in Time* · *American Gothic* · *Howling IV*
Hughes, Kenneth; *Night School*
Humbert, Humphrey: *Ghosthouse*
Hunt, Ed: *Bloody Birthday*
Huston, Jimmy: *Final Exam* · *My Best Friend Is a Vampire*

Jackson, Donald G.: *Roller Blade* · *Hell Comes to Frogtown* (co-dir)
Jackson, Lewis: *Christmas Evil*
Jackson, Mick: *Threads*
Jaeckin, Just: *The Perils of Gwendoline*
Jamain, Patrick: *Honeymoon*
James, Donald: *Murderlust*
Jeffreys, Arthur: *Demented*
Johnson, Alan: *Solarbabies*
Johnson, Lamont: *Spacehunter*
Jones, Amy: *Slumber Party Masacre*
Jones, Brian Thomas: *The Rejuvenator*
Jones, Don: *The Forest*
Jordan, Neil: *The Company of Wolves*

Kalmanowicz, Max: *The Children*
Katzin, Lee H.: *World Gone Wild*

INDEX OF DIRECTORS AND THEIR FILMS

Kaufman, Charles: *Mother's Day*
Kaufman, Lloyd: See Samuel Weil
Keeter, Worth: *Dogs of Hell*
Keith, David: *The Curse*
Kennedy, Tom: *Time Walker*
Kenner, Elly: *The Black Room* (co-dir)
Kiersch, Fritz: *Gor*
Kimmel, Bruce: *Spaceship*
Kincaid, Tim: *Breeders* · *Robot Holocaust*
King, Stephen: *Maximum Overdrive*
Kirk, Robert: *Destroyer*
Kizer, R.J.: *Godzilla 1985* (co-dir) · *Hell Comes to Frogtown* (co-dir)
Kleven, Max: *The Night Stalker*
Kong, Jackie: *The Being*
Krueger, Michael: *Mind Killer* · *Night Vision*
Kuehn, Andrew J.: *Terror in the Aisles*

Laing, John: *The Lost Tribe*
LaLoggia, Frank: *Fear No Evil* · *Lady in White*
Lamond, John: *Stage Fright*
Landis, John: *Amazon Women on the Moon* (co-dir)
Lane, Andrew: *Jake Speed*
Laser, J.A. (Jean Rollin): *Zombies' Lake*
Laughlin, Michael: *Dead Kids* · *Strange Invaders*
Lawrence, Marc: *Pigs*
Lehman, Lew: *The Pit*
Leitch, Christopher: *Teen Wolf Too*
Lenahan, Jim: *Spacerage*
Lenzi, Umberto: *City of the Walking Dead* · *Ironmaster*
Lesoeur, Daniel: See A.M. Frank
Levy, Shuki: *Perfect Victims*
Lewis, Christopher: *Blood Cult* · *Revenge* · *The Ripper*
Lieberman, Jeff: *Just Before Dawn* · *Remote Control*
Lindsay, Lance: *Star Crystal*
Link, Ron: *Zombie High*
Lipstadt, Aaron: *Android* · *City Limits*
Litten, Peter: *Slaughter High* (co-dir)
Littman, Lynn: *Testament*
LoBianco, Tony: *Too Scared to Scream*
Lofton, Terry: *Nail Gun Massacre*
Logothetis, Dimitri: *Slaughterhouse Rock*
Lomel, Ulli: *Boogey Man* · *Brainwaves* · *The Devonsville Terror*
Lord, Jean Claude: *Visiting Hours*
Loventhal, Charlie: *My Demon Lover*
Luna, Bigas: *Anguish*
Lustig, William: *Maniac*

> *"Whatever happened to the good kids in the world?"*
> SLEEPAWAY CAMP 2: UNHAPPY CAMPERS

Lynch, Paul: *Prom Night* · *Humongous* · *Really Weird Tales* (co-dir)

Maas, Dick: *The Lift*
Makichuk, James: *Ghostkeeper*
Malanowski, Tony: *Night of Horror*
Malone, William: *Scared to Death* · *Creature*
Mancuso, Kevin: *2020 Texas Gladiators*
Mangine, Joseph: *Neon Maniacs*
Mann, Michael: *The Keep*
Mansfield, Scott: *Deadly Games*
Marcel, Terry: *Prisoners of the Lost Universe* · *Jane and the Lost City*
Margheriti, Antonio: See Anthony M. Dawson
Marshak, Philip: *The Nightmare Never Ends* (co-dir)
Martin, Frank (Francesco Martino): *Dr. Butcher, M.D.*
Marvin, Mike: *The Wraith*
Mastorakis, Niko: *The Wind* · *Nightmare at Noon*
Mastroianni, Armand: *He Knows You're Alone* · *The Killing Hour* · *The Supernaturals*
Mattei, Bruno: (see also Vincent Dawn) *Seven Magnificent Gladiators*
Maylam, Tony: *The Burning*
McBrearty, Don: *Really Weird Tales* (co-dir)
McCauley, John: *Deadly Intruder*
McClatchy, Gregory: *Vampire at Midnight*
McCubbin, Peter: *Survival 1990*
McCullough, Jim, Jr.: *Mountaintop Motel Massacre* · *Video Murders*
McGowan, Tom: *The Nightmare Never Ends* (co-dir)
McKeowan, Tom: *The Deadly Spawn*
McTiernan, John: *Nomads*
Meyer, Ken: *Terror at Tenkiller*
Michalakis, John Elias: *I Was a Teenage Zombie*
Mihalka, George: *My Bloody Valentine* · *Eternal Evil*
Milligan, Andy: *Carnage*
Miner, Steve: *House*
Mora, Philippe: *The Beast Within* · *Howling II* · *Howling III*
Mulcahey, Russell: *Razorback* · *Highlander*
Mundhra, Jag: *Open House*
Murakami, Jimmy T.: *Battle Beyond the Stars*
Murphy, Geoffrey: *The Quiet Earth*

Nelson, David: *House of Death*
Nelson, Gary: *Allan Quartermain and the Lost City of Gold*
Nesher, Avi: *She*
Newell, Mike: *The Awakening*
Nicolaou, Ted: *TerrorVision*
Norman, Ben: *Escape from Galaxy 3*
Norton, B.W.L.: *Baby, Secret of the Lost Legend*
Nuchtern, Simon: *Silent Madness*

INDEX OF DIRECTORS AND THEIR FILMS

O'Bannon, Dan: *Return of the Living Dead*
Obrow, Jeffrey: *The Dorm that Dripped Blood* (co-dir) · *The Power* (co-dir) · *The Kindred* (co-dir)
Oliver, David: *Cavegirl*
Olivera, Hector: *Barbarian Queen*
Ouellette, Jean-Paul: *The Unnamable*

Pakula, Alan J.: *Dream Lover*
Patel, Raju: *In the Shadow of Kilimajaro*
Paulsen, David: *Schizoid*
Pavlou, George: *Transmutations* · *Rawhead Rex*
Payton, Leland: *Copperhead*
Peeters, Barbara: *Humanoids from the Deep*
Peña, Nettie: *Home Sweet Home*
Peterson, Kristine: *Deadly Dreams*
Philips, Nick: *Crazy Fat Ethel II*
Pittman, Bruce: *Identity Crisis* · *Hello Mary Lou: Prom Night II*
Plone, Allen: *Night Screams*
Preston, Gaylene: *Dark of the Night*
Prior, David A.: *Killer Workout*
Prosperi, Franco: *Throne of Fire* · *Wild Beasts*
Purdom, Edmund: *Don't Open Till Christmas*
Pyun, Albert: *The Sword and the Sorceror* · *Radioactive Dreams*

Raffill, Stewart: *Ice Pirates* · *The Philadelphia Experiment*
Raimi, Sam: *The Evil Dead* · *Evil Dead II*
Rakoff, Alvin: *Deathship*
Raley, Alice: *Movie House Massacre*
Rawi, Ousama: *The Housekeeper*
Ray, Fred Olen: *Alien Dead* · *Biohazard* · *The Tomb* · *Scalps* · *Deep Space*
Regan, Patrick: *Kiss Daddy Goodbye*
Reid, Max: *Wild Thing*
Reynolds, C.D.H.: *A Day of Judgement*
Richard, Jef: *Berserker*
Richards, Dick: *Deathy Valley*
Richter, Ota: *Skullduggery*
Robbins, Matthew: *Dragonslayer*
Roberson, James W.: *Superstition*
Roddam, Franc: *The Bride*
Rollin, Jean: See J.A. Laser
Rose, Mickey: *Student Bodies*
Rosman, Mark: *House on Sorority Row*
Rowe, Peter: *Splatter: The Architects of Fear*
Ruben, Joseph: *Dreamscape* · *The Stepfather*
Rubens, Percival: *The Demon*
Russell, Chuck: *The Blob*

Russell, Ken: *Gothic*
Rustam, Mardi: *Evils of the Night*

Sachs, William: *Galaxina*
Sala, H.: *Nightmare Weekend*
Santiago, Ciro H.: *Stryker* · *Demon of Paradise*
Sarafian, Deran: *Alien Predator*
Sargent, Joseph: *Nightmares*
Saville, Philip: *Shadey*
Sayles, John: *The Brother from Another Planet*
Scavolini, Romano: *Nightmare*
Schaeffer, Franky: *Wired to Kill*
Schepisi, Fred: *Iceman*
Schmoeller, David: *Crawlspace*
Schultz, Bob: *Robbers of the Sacred Mountain*
Schultz, Carl: *The Seventh Sign*
Scott, Robert: *The Video Dead*
Seidelman, Susan: *Making Mr. Right*
Shackleton, Michael: *Survivor*
Shannon, Frank: *The Invincible Barbarian*
Sherman, Gary A.: *Dead and Buried*
Sholder, Jack: *Alone in the Dark* · *The Hidden*
Silver, R.D.: *She Wolf*
Simpson, Michael A.: *Sleepaway Camp 2: Unhappy Campers*
Simon, J. Piquer: *Pieces*
Sloane, Rick: *Hobgoblins*
Smith, Charles Martin: *Trick or Treat*
Soavi, Michael: *Stage Fright*
Sotos, Jim: *Sweet Sixteen*
Spheeris, Penelope: *The Boys Next Door*
Spiegel, Larry: *Evil Town* (co-dir)
Spottiswoode, Roger: *Terror Train*
Starr, Bruce: *Boogeyman II*
Stewart, Alan: *Ghostriders*
Stewart, Larry: *The Initiation*
Storm, Howard: *Once Bitten*
Stryker, Jonathan (Richard Ciupka): *Curtains*
Stuart, Brian: *Sorceress*

Takacs, Tibor: *The Gate*
Tallos, Greg: *The Nightmare Never Ends* (co-dir)
Taylor, Don: *The Final Countdown*
Teague, Lewis: *Alligator* · *Cat's Eye*
Tenney, Kevin S.: *Witchboard*
Theakston, Graham: *Tripods* (co-dir)
Thomas, R.L.: *Apprentice to Murder*

INDEX OF DIRECTORS AND THEIR FILMS

Thompson, J. Lee: *Happy Birthday to Me* · *King Solomon's Mines* · *Firewalker*
Traynor, Peter S.: *Evil Town* (co-dir)
Trenchard-Smith, Brian: *Escape 2000* · *Dead End Drive In* · *The Quest*
Trikonis, Gus: *Jungle Heat*
Tyler, Stephen: *The Last Slumber Party*

Vane, Norman Thaddeus: *The Black Room* (co-dir) · *Frightmare*
Verhoeven, Paul: *Flesh + Blood*
Vickers, Lindsey C.: *The Appointment*
Vila, Camilo: *The Unholy*
Voskanian, Robert: *Zombie Child*

Walton, Fred: *April Fool's Day*
Warren, Deryn: *Mirror of Death* · *Bloodspell*
Warren, Norman J.: *Alien Prey* · *Horror Planet* · *Bloody New Year*
Wasson, James C.: *Night of the Demon*
Watson, John: *Deathstalker*
Weil, Samuel (Lloyd Kaufman): *The Toxic Avenger* (co-dir) · *Class of Nuke 'Em High* (co-dir)
Weiss, Robert K: *Amazon Women on the Moon* (co-dir)
Wenk, Richard: *Vamp*
Wesley, William: *Scarecrows*
Weston, Armand: *The Nesting*
Weston, Eric: *Evilspeak*
Wiederhorn, Ken: *Eyes of a Stranger* · *Return of the Living Dead II*
Wiener, Charles: *Blue Murder*
Wilder, Glenn: *Masterblaster*
Wiley, Ethan: *House II: The Second Story*
Williams, Tony: *Next of Kin*
Wilson, Yale: *Truth or Dare*
Wincer, Simon: *Dark Forces*
Winer, Harry: *Spacecamp*
Wittman, Peter: *Play Dead*
Worms, Robert A., III: *Terror on Tape*
Worth, David: *Warrior of the Lost World*
Wynorski, Jim: *Chopping Mall* · *Deathstalker II* · *Not of this Earth*

Yates, Peter: *Krull*

Zacharias, Alfred: *Demonoid*
Zimmerman, Vernon: *Fade to Black*
Zito, Joseph: *The Prowler*
Zulawski, Andrezej: *Possession*
Zwicky, Karl: *Contagion*

TITLE INDEX

After the Fall of New York 300
Aftermath, The 313
Alchemist, The 157
Alien Contamination 31
Ailen Dead 99
Alien Predator 32
Alien Prey 32
Allan Quartermain and the Lost City of Gold 289
Alligator 84
Alone in the Dark 232
Amazon Women on the Moon 345
American Gothic 227
Amityville II: The Possession 126
Amityville 3D 137
Android 334
Anguish 242
Appointment, The 185
Apprentice to Murder 160
April Fool's Day 202
Ark of the Sun God, The 295
Ator — The Fighting Eagle 279
Awakening, The 129

Baby, Secret of the Lost Legend 50
Bad Dreams 183
Barbarian Queen 275
Barbarians, The 272
Basket Case 60
Battle Beyond the Stars 317
Beaks 84
Beastmaster, The 270
Beast Within, The 94
Being, The 68
Berserker 157
Biggles — Adventures in Time 291
Biohazard 44
Black Room, The 164
Blade in the Dark, A 233
Blade Master, The 280
Blob, The 58
Blood Beach 54
Blood Cult 156
Blood Frenzy 229

Blood Link 176
Bloodspell 131
Blood Splash — see Nightmare
Bloodsuckers from Outer Space 100
Bloodsucking Nazi Zombies — see Oasis of the Zombies
Bloody Birthday 206
Bloody Moon 214
Bloody New Year 146
Bloody Wednesday 257
Blue Monkey 60
Blue Murder 248
Boogey Man, The 144
Boogey Man II, 145
Born of Fire 113
Boys Next Door, The 257
Brain Damage (1971) 76
Brain Damage (1987) 53
Brainwaves 177
Breeders 38
Bride, The 72
Brother From Another Planet, The 34
Burial Ground 103
Burning, The 224

Cannibal Women in the Avocado Jungle of Death 345
Carnage 140
Cassandra 176
Cat's Eye 189
Cavegirl 344
Caveman 344
Children, The 68
Chopping Mall 246
Christmas Evil 208
C.H.U.D. 59
City Limits 301
City of the Walking Dead 104
Clan of the Cave Bear, The 341
Class of Nuke 'Em High 65
Company of Wolves, The 89
Conquest 277
Contagion 141

TITLE INDEX

Copperhead 85
Crawlspace 73
Crazy Fat Ethel II 250
Creature 30
Creepers 86
Creepshow 2 191
Crittters 34
Critters 2 35
Curse, The 2
Curtains 241

Dark Forces 158
Dark of the Night 148
Dark Sanity 177
Dawn of the Mummy 154
Day of Judgement, A 184
Dead and Buried 153
Dead-End Drive In 308
Dead Kids 71
Deadline 181
Deadly Blessing 123
Deadly Dreams 182
Deadly Eyes 83
Deadly Friend 72
Deadly Games 259
Deadly Intruder 226
Deadly Obsession 220
Deadly Spawn, The 31
Dead Time Stories 189
Death Ship 144
Deathstalker 274
Deathstalker II 274
Death Valley 228
Deep Space 58
Defcon-4 310
Demented 255
Demon, The 247
Demon of Paradise 52
Demonoid 130
Demons 116
Demons 2 116
Demonwarp 33
Destroyer 245
Devonsville Terror, The 151
Doctor Butcher, M.D. 77
Dogs of Hell 81

Dolls 159
Don't Answer the Phone! 247
Don't Go In The House 230
Don't Go in the Woods 349
Don't Open Till Christmas 209
Doom Asylum 240
Dorm That Dripped Blood, The 214
Dracula's Widow 170
Dragonslayer 270
Dream Lover 185
Dreamscape 182
Dr. Heckyl and Mr. Hype 94
Dungeonmaster, The 185

Endgame 307
Entity, The 118
Escape From Galaxy 3 322
Escape From the Bronx 300
Escape 2000 330
Eternal Evil 175
Evil Dead, The 115
Evil Dead II 115
Evil Judgement 248
Evils of the Night 43
Evilspeak 155
Evil Town 75
Exterminators of the Year 3000,
   The 303
Eyes of a Stranger 251
Eyes of Fire 140

Fade to Black 254
Fatal Pulse 218
Fear 231
Fear No Evil 113
Fiend 349
Final Countdown, The 325
Final Exam 214
Final Terror, The 223
Firewalker 289
Flesh + Blood 285
Forbidden World 57
Forest, The 223
Forever Evil 120
Frightmare 153
Fright Night 165

> *"I'm on fire, Lith. I can't wait to fight, to attack, to oppose my law on the valley."*
> IRONMASTER

From Beyond 74
Funeral Home 236
Funhouse, The 244

Galaxina 321
Galaxy of Terror 29
Gate, The 117
Gates of Hell, The 103
Ghosthouse 139
Ghostkeeper 48
Ghostriders 141
Ghost Warrior 328
Ghoulies 121
Ghoulies II 122
Girls Nite Out 216
Godzilla 1985 47
Gor 283
Gotham 149
Gothic 186
Graduation Day 203
Graveyard Shift 166
Gray Matter 77

Hands of Steel 336
Happy Birtday to Me 206
He Knows You're Alone 204
Hell Comes To Frogtown 307
Hell Night 213
Hello Mary Lou: Prom Night II 128
Hellraiser 159
Hercules 281
Hidden, The 35
Highlander 285
Hills Have Eyes — Part II, The 228
Hitcher, The 262
Hobgoblins 122
Home Sweet Home 208
Honeymoon 252
Horror House On Highway Five 233
Horror Planet 29
Hospital Massacre 239
House 138
House II: The Second Story 138
House by the Cemetery, The 136
Housekeeper, The 258
House of Death 231

House on Sorority Row, The 215
Howling II 90
Howling III 91
Howling IV: The Original Nightmare 91
Humanoids from the Deep 68
Humongus 223

Iceman 328
Ice Pirates, The 318
Identity Crisis 233
Impulse 66
Incubus 117
Inferno 135
Initiation, The 217
In The Aftermath 309
In the Shadow of Kilimanjaro 80
Invaders from Mars 40
Invasion of the Flesh Hunters 105
Invincible Barbarian, The 276
Invisible Strangler 174
Ironmaster 342
Iron Warrior, The 280
Island Claws 63
It's Alive III: Island of the Alive 61
I Was a Teenage Zombie 106

Jack's Back 179
Jake Speed 292
Jane and the Lost City 290
Jekyll and Hyde...Together Again 95
Jungle Heat 49
Just Before Dawn 222

Kamikaze '89 330
Keep, The 165
Killer Party 127
Killer Workout 246
Killing Hour, The 178
Kilma, Queen of the Amazons 346
Kindred, The 63
King Kong Lives 48
King Solomon's Mines 288
Kiss Daddy Goodbye 180
Krull 271

Lady in White 148

TITLE INDEX

Last Slumber Party, The 205
Last Starfighter, The 319
Lifeforce 33
Lift, The 145
Lionman II: The Witchqueen 277
Link 80
Lost Tribe, The 176

Macabre 255
Madman 225
Making Contact 180
Making Mr. Right 336
Manhattan Baby 129
Maniac 252
Mark of Cain — see Identity Crisis
Masterblaster 224
Masters of the Universe 284
Mausoleum 127
Maximum Overdrive 146
Metalstorm: The Destruction of
 Jared-Syn 319
Mind Killer 175
Mines of Kilimanjaro, The 295
Mirror of Death 129
Mongrel 93
Monster Dog 93
Monster in the Closet 41
Monster Squad 171
Morons From Outer Space 37
Mortuary 245
Motel Hell 235
Mother's Day 202
Mountaintop Motel Massacre 237
Movie House Massacre 146
Munchies 39
Murderlust 253
Mutant 66
Mutilator, The 226
My Best Friend Is a Vampire 168
My Bloody Valentine 201
My Demon Lover 92
My Science Project 327

Nail Gun Massacre 249
Near Dark 167
Necropolis 152

Neon Maniacs 116
Nesting, The 136
New Gladiators, The 331
New Year's Evil 210
Next of Kin 236
Nightflyers 323
Nightmare 244
Nightmare at Noon 67
Nightmare Never Ends, The 113
Nightmares 188
Nightmare Weekend 350
Night of Horror 140
Night of the Comet 332
Night of the Creeps 101
Night of the Demon 50
Night of the Zombies 104
Night School 212
Night Screams 234
Night Stalker, The 158
Night Vision 179
Night Warning 256
1990: The Bronx Warriors 299
Nomads 166
Not of This Earth 41

Oasis of the Zombies 104
Offspring, The 190
Of Unknown Origin 83
Once Bitten 169
Open House 234
Osa 310
Outing, The 119

Parasite 57
Perfect Victims 261
Perils of Gwendoline, The 291
Philadelphia Experiment, The 326
Phoenix the Warrior 312
Pieces 216
Pigs 82
Pink Chiquitas 44
Piranha II — The Spawning 85
Pit, The 53
Play Dead 152
Plutonium Baby 68
Porn Murders, The — see Blue Murder

> *"On the other hand, I could introduce you to a world of pain. The choice is yours."*
> ROBOT HOLOCAUST

Possession 118
Power, The 130
Prey, The 222
Prince of Darkness 119
Prison 143
Prisoners of the Lost Universe 282
Programmed to Kill 335
Prom Night 203
Prowler, The 213
Pulse 147

Q 49
Quest, The 51
Quiet Earth, The 332

Radioactive Dreams 331
Rats 83
Rawhead Rex 52
Razorback 82
Really Weird Tales 190
Re-Animator 73
Red Sonja 275
Rejuvenator, The 76
Remote Control 42
Return of the Living Dead 100
Return of the Living Dead, Part II 101
Return to Horror High 219
Return to 'Salem's Lot, A 168
Revenge 275
Revenge of the Barbarians 278
Revenge of the Zombie — see Kiss Daddy Goodbye
Ripper, The 132
Road Games 261
Robbers of the Sacred Mountain 294
Robot Holocaust 283
Rock 'n' Roll Nightmare 351
Roller Blade 311
Runaway 335

Saturday the 14th 139
Scalps 131
Scarecrows 142
Scared to Death 57
Schizoid 238
Screamtime 189

Sender, The 182
Serpent and the Rainbow, The 161
Seven Magnificent Gladiators, The 281
Seventh Sign, The 114
Shadey 178
She 311
Sheena 340
She Wolf 93
Silent Madness 217
Silent Night, Deadly Night — Part 2 209
Silver Bullet — see Stephen King's Silver Bullet
Skullduggery 156
Sky Pirates 292
Slaughter High 218
Slaughterhouse Rock 143
Slayer, The 181
Sleepaway Camp 225
Sleepaway Camp 2: Unhappy Campers 226
Slumber Party Massacre 204
Slumber Party Massacre II 205
Solarbabies 308
Sole Survivor 107
Sorceress 272
Sorority Babes in the Slim·ball Bowl-O-Rama 120
Sorority House Massacre 218
Spacecamp 322
Spacehunter — Adventures in the Forbidden Zone 318
Spacerage 320
Space Raiders 317
Spaceship 321
Spare Parts 71
Specters 123
Splatter — The Architects of Fear 312
Splatter University 215
Spookies 154
Stage Fright (1983) 241
Stage Fright (1987) 242
Star Crystal 30
Starship 320
Steel Dawn 306
The Stepfather 254
Stephen King's Silver Bullet 89
Stones of Death 142

TITLE INDEX

Stranded 36
Strange Invaders 40
Strangeness, The 51
Stranger Is Watching, A 259
Stryker 303
Student Bodies 215
Stuff, The 52
Supernaturals, The 141
Superstition 137
Surf Nazis Must Die 305
Survival 1990/Survival Eath 309
Survivor 305
Swamp Thing, The 64
Sweet Sixteen 207
Sword and the Sorceror, The 271

Tarzan, The Ape Man 339
Teen Wolf Too 92
Terror at Tenkiller 227
Terror in the Aisles 191
Terror in the Swamp 64
Terror in Toyland — see Christmas Evil
Terror on Tape 192
Terror on Tour 240
Terror Train 243
TerrorVision 44
Testament 333
Threads 333
Throne of Fire 276
Timerider 326
Time Walker 39
To All A Goodnight 208
Tomb, The 169
Too Scared to Scream 232
Torment 260
Toxic Avenger, The 65
Trancers 327
Transmutations 59
Transylvania 6-5000 171
Treasure of the Four Crowns, The 293
Trick or Treat 154
Trick or Treats 207
Tripods, The 42
Troll 158
Truth or Dare 249
2020 Texas Gladiators 304

Unholy, The 124
Unnamable, The 121
Unseen, The 235

Vamp 170
Vampire at Midnight 167
Video Dead, The 101
Video Murders 255
Viking Massacre 278
Virgin Among the Living Dead 184
Visiting Hours 239

Warlords of the 21st Century 302
Warning Sign 71
Warrior and the Sorceress, The 273
Warrior of the Lost World 304
Warriors of the Wasteland 302
Watch Me When I Kill 248
Wavelength 36
Where the River Runs Black 341
White of the Eye 258
Wild Beasts 81
Wild Thing 342
Wind, The 260
Wired To Kill 301
Witchboard 138
World Gone Wild 306
Wraith, The 147

Xtro 38

Yellow Hair and the Fortress of Gold 294
Yor, Hunter From the Future 343

Zombie 102
Zombie Child 106
Zombie High 75
Zombies' Lake 105
Zombie Nightmare 351
Zone Troopers 37

ABOUT THE AUTHOR

L.A. Morse is an award-winning author of crime novels. His works include such titles as THE FLESH EATERS, THE OLD DICK, THE BIG ENCHILADA and SLEAZE, which may suggest he has some familiarity with the subject of trash.

He is also a life-long devotee of movies, all kinds of movies — good, bad and absolutely awful. As a movie lover he regards the VCR as one of civilization's great achievements because, for the first time, it is now possible to see *everything*. And that is exactly what he has been doing, omnivorously consuming the stock of one of video store after another, seeking out buried treasures and ghastly pleasures. This guide is the result of his unceasing explorations.

Just when you thought it was safe to go back in the video store....

VIDEO TRASH & TREASURES

TWO:

—The Saga Continues—
Further Explorations in the Video Fringe

* * *

Action in the '80s! All the rock 'em! sock 'em! blast 'em! and blow 'em up, real good! favorites from a decade that redefined the term "macho lout."

> Tough cops, assault teams, and violent vigilantes!
> Rescue missions, chases and races against time!
> Standing up! Fighting back! Getting even!
> Wild in the Streets! The Last of the Frontier!

—plus—

> The deadliest arts of the Orient!
> (35 — count 'em, 35 — Ninja Flicks!)

Not Necessarily the Feminist Section. For viewers who know what they like (and what they like is not usually characterized as sensitive, subtle or sophisticated). Yes! A section devoted to fulfilling that fundamental need for sleaze and prurience.

> Women for hire! Bodies for rent!
> And FORTY (40!) sensitive, subtle, sophisticated sagas of
> Bimbos Behind Bars!